560-82

The Economics of
Food Processing

other AVI books

THE ECONOMICS OF FOOD PROCESSING

By W. SMITH GREIG, Ph.D.

Professor of Marketing,
Department of Agricultural Economics,
Washington State University,
Pullman, Washington

in collaboration with specialists

WESTPORT, CONNECTICUT

THE AVI PUBLISHNG COMPANY, INC.

1971

Contributors

WILLIAM A. CROMARTY, Vice President, Connell Company, Westfield, New Jersey

RONALD D. KNUTSON, Department of Agricultural Economics, Purdue University, Lafayette, Indiana

R. E. SCHNEIDAU, Department of Agricultural Economics, Purdue University, Layfayette, Indiana

EDWARD WILLOUGHBY, Director of Civil Engineering, Giffels Associates, Inc., Detroit, Michigan

Preface

The economics of food processing is a vast and complex field. Food processing is still the largest business in the world. Certainly all of the details of the economic aspects of food processing could never be covered. Therefore, the purpose of this book is to provide a general overview of some of the more important economic and business problem areas facing the food processing industry. Many of these problem areas are affected by or caused by changing social, political, and technological conditions.

In a perspective of the economics of food processing systems the boundary line of areas which might be covered was drawn at the national level. That is international trade, international competition, and international regulation were not included. However, a substantial section was devoted to interregional competition. And, in effect, international competition in theory is primarily the same as interregional competition. The methods of approach and methods of analyses of international competition would be quite similar to that presented here on interregional competition.

References to major or particularly relevant studies have been cited to establish authority and to assist the reader who may wish to obtain additional information about a particular subject. Voluminous materials are available on the food processing industry, so obviously all references to the field have not been covered. The literature is widely scattered and few attempts have been made to systematically collect, review, and interpret the published data to provide a meaningful framework for understanding the economics of the system.

Hopefully, this book will provide the businessman and the student with a general understanding of the system as well as provide enough detail and literature citations to form a base or starting point for individual investigations on specialized problems.

W. Smith Greig
Pullman, Washington

June 1970

Contents

CHAPTER 1

W. Smith Greig

Size of the Food Processing Industry in the United States

INTRODUCTION

The enormous size of the food processing industry in the United States is difficult to comprehend. In 1966 the food processing industries employed 1,643,013 people with a value added in manufacturing of $24.8 billion, producing FOB shipments worth $79.6 billion. Further, new investments in plant and equipment were at an annual rate of nearly $1.7 billion per year. These absolute figures are important of course, but what is the relative size of food processing compared to other manufacturing industries, and to farming; and what are the trends?

In 1958 the food processing industry was the largest manufacturing industry in the United States, whether measured by numbers of employees, the value added in manufacturing, in FOB shipments, or in new capital expenditures. In 1958 the food processing industries provided 11% of all factory jobs in the United States. Nearly 1/4 of total disposable income in the United States in 1958 was spent on food or kindred products. (Most, but not all, of this food was factory processed.) However, by 1966, based on numbers of people employed, the food processing industry had been surpassed in size by 3 other industries: transportation equipment (SIC 37)[1], electrical equipment (SIC 36), and machinery (SIC 35), each of these industries employing more than 1.8 million people. In 1966, based on value added, the food processing industries had dropped to a third ranking position, following transportation equipment and nonelectrical machinery. However, the food processing industry in 1966 was still leading in terms of value of products shipped.

Despite steadily rising demand in the United States for processed food products – reflecting rises in population and personal income – the food and kindred products industry is declining in terms of its relative share of total consumption expenditure. For example, the proportion of disposable income spent for food decreased from around 24% in 1958 to about 18% in 1966. With rising incomes, although the absolute expenditure for food increases, the proportion of the total income spent for food tends to decrease. Thus, while total food processing is increasing, it is not increasing at nearly the rate of all other manufacturing; even though gross value of shipments of processed food increased from around $60 billion in 1958 to nearly $80 billion in 1966, other manufacturing industries greatly exceeded this rate of increase. While employment in food processing decreased by nearly 5% between 1958 and 1966, employment in all manufacturing in the United States increased by 29%. Similarly, while value added in food processing in the same period increased 41%, in all

---

[1] SIC is the Standard Industrial Classification used by the Bureau of Census.

manufacturing value added increased 78%. While food processing provided 11% of all factory jobs in 1958, by 1966 this had dropped to only 8%. This decrease in the relative importance of food processing and the decrease of relative importance of total food costs to consumers is a reflection of the standard of living in the United States. The result is that a declining share of the consumer's dollar is spent on food products and an increasing share is spent on goods and services that have lesser demands at lower income levels.

SIZE OF FOOD PROCESSING COMPARED TO
ALL TRANSPORTATION EQUIPMENT INDUSTRIES

If we are to compare the size of the food processing industry to, for example, the transportation equipment industries, we should specify the comparative parts. Table 1.1 lists the 14 segments of the transportation equipment industries, with employment, value added, value of shipments, and capital expenditures given for each. The comparison to be made is the total of these 14 transportation equipment industries to the total for all food processing. We are comparing the totals for trucks, busses, automobiles, planes, ships, locomotives, motorcycles, and bicycles combined to the total for all food processing. In Table 1.2, 1958 and 1966 comparisons are made between the transportation equipment industries and the food processing industry.

In 1958, food processing surpassed the transportation equipment industries in each of the following measurements: employment, value added, value of shipments, and capital expenditures. By 1966 however, the transportation equipment industries led in total employment, value added, and capital expenditures,

TABLE 1.1

EMPLOYMENT, VALUE ADDED, VALUE OF SHIPMENTS,
AND CAPITAL EXPENDITURES FOR THE TRANSPORTATION
EQUIPMENT INDUSTRIES, 1966

	Employees	Value Added ($1000)	Value of Shipments ($1000)	Capital Expenditures ($1000)
Truck and bus bodies	31,624	322,292	718,636	38,460
Truck trailers	28,082	314,409	795,592	25,472
Motor vehicles	798,920	15,499,673	45,630,082	1,113,206
Aircraft	357,218	4,674,598	9,000,074	378,435
Aircraft engines and parts .	188,065	2,764,968	4,572,038	194,910
Aircraft propellers	10,179	133,326	211,082	9,476
Aircraft equipment	189,664	2,458,468	3,781,222	101,450
Ship building	135,309	1,362,030	2,338,931	52,793
Boat building	30,825	247,427	485,121	12,708 (1965)
Locomotives	17,152	318,191	700,719	8,996
Railroad and street cars . . .	43,782	642,229	1,695,704	35,094
Motorcycles, bicycles	11,537	112,571	261,110	5,768
Trailer coaches	38,573	354,890	1,089,306	41,878
Other transportation equip.	9,467	95,107	232,155	3,710 (1963)
Total transportation equip.	1,890,397	29,300,179	71,511,772	2,022,626

Source: Census of Manufacturers, Bur. Census, U.S. Dept. Com.

while food processing still led in value of shipments.

Will the food processing industry continue to decrease in size compared to all other manufacturing in the United States? Undoubtedly so, if gross national product (GNP) and consumers' disposable incomes continue to rise. Will food processing continue to increase in absolute size? Yes, and the increasing size will be proportionately greater than our increase in population if incomes continue to rise. Since most of the food we eat now is in processed form, why will processing increase proportionately greater than population increases? Because we are increasing the services demanded in our processed foods. We are consistently upgrading the quality and the degree of preparedness (or convenience) of our processed foods. In fact, if the same quality and quantity of foods demanded per person were the same as that consumed 25 yr ago, then only approximately 15% of consumer disposable income would have been spent for food in 1966 compared to the 18% actually spent. Much of the food processing industry is a growth industry. For example, the 50 leading food processing industries (out of approximately 94 total industries) increased sales from $18.5 billion in 1958 to $30.5 billion in 1966, or a simple average increase in sales of 8.2% per yr. However, during the same time, value of shipments of TV tubes, semiconductors and computing machines increased over 400%, and many other industrial products increased by over 300%.

SIZE OF FOOD PROCESSING COMPARED TO ALL FARMING OPERATIONS

While the value of farm sales in the United States has increased significantly through time, so have the purchased inputs. If farm purchases, i.e., tractors and equipment, commercial fertilizers, commercial insecticides, weed and disease control chemicals, etc., are subtracted from total sales, the actual value added in farm operations has been decreasing. Ray Goldberg (1968), Harvard University, suggests that the value added in farming has decreased from $16.4 billion in 1947 to around $12.0 billion in 1967.

The purchased inputs by farmers have increased very rapidly — from $12.9 billion in 1947 to an estimated $31.0 billion in 1967.

TABLE 1.2

COMPARISONS OF SIZE OF THE FOOD PROCESSING INDUSTRY
AND THE TRANSPORTATION EQUIPMENT INDUSTRIES, 1958 AND 1966

	Total Employees	Value Added ($1000)	Value of Shipments ($1000)	Capital Expenditures ($1000)
1958 Food processing	1,718,100	17,700,900	59,456,000	1,021,200
1958 Transportation equip.	1,552,566	15,242,250	38,146,424	627,302
1966 Food processing	1,643,013	24,837,811	79,624,917	1,685,078
1966 Transportation equip.	1,890,397	29,300,179	71,511,722	2,022,626

Source: Census of Manufacturers, Bur. Census, U.S. Dept. Com.

As farming becomes more and more efficient, purchased inputs will continue to increase and farm inputs, i.e., the value of land, labor, and management in relation to value of the total output, will probably continue to decrease. Therefore, it is suggested that the value added above that of commercially purchased inputs (other than labor) will probably continue to decrease through time. That is, the value added by the farming operations in the production of food and fiber will continue to decrease.

At the same time the value added in food processing is increasing significantly — from $11.6 billion in 1947 to $26.0 billion in 1967.

It is important to note that we are talking only about the food segment of agriculture when discussing the value added in processing. Cotton, wool, fibers, leather, tobacco, etc., are included in the value added in farming operations, but are not included in the value added in food processing.

While in 1947 the value added in farming was 40% greater than the value added in food processing, by 1967 the value added in food processing was nearly 2.2 times as great as that in farming. During the 20-yr period, 1947-1967, the value added in farming decreased by 27% (Table 1.3).

If the value added in the complete marketing system, processing, wholesaling, and retailing (including restaurants) of food, fiber, and tobacco were combined, then the value added in the marketing system would be 8-10 times the value added in farming alone.

TABLE 1.3

FARM PURCHASES, VALUE ADDED IN FARMING, AND
VALUE ADDED IN FOOD PROCESSING, 1947, 1962, 1967

	1947	1962 (Billion $)	1967
Farm purchases[1]	12.9	21.0	31.0
Value added in all farming[1] (Food, fiber, tobacco, etc.)	16.4	14.9	12.0
Value added in food processing[2] (Food processing only. Does not include fiber, tobacco, leather, etc.)	11.6	20.2	26.0

[1] Goldberg (1968).

[2] 1947 and 1962 data from 1963 Census of Business, Bur. Census, U.S. Dept. Com. 1967 data estimated from Industry Profiles 1958-1966, Business and Defense Serv. Admin., U.S. Dept. Com., Mar. 1968.

BIBLIOGRAPHY

GOLDBERG, R. A. 1968. Agribusiness Coordination: A systems approach to the wheat, soybean, and Florida orange economics. Div. Res., Graduate School Business Admin., Harvard Univ., Cambridge, Mass.

CHAPTER 2

W. Smith Greig | Structure of the
Food Processing Industry

INTRODUCTION

There has been much concern, research. legislation, and legal activity concerning the structure of the food industries in the United States. The basic structure of the food processing industry will be discussed in this chapter; economies of scale and future plant numbers in the following chapter; while the legislative and legal aspects of regulating competition will be discussed in a subsequent chapter.

Two approaches will be used in discussing structure. The first approach will use the normal means of identifying numbers and sizes of firms, amounts and concentration of assets, profitability and concentration of profits, and concentration of sales or market shares. Detailed data will be presented on profitability (and other financial operating ratios) by type and size of firm. The financial data presented not only augments the structural considerations but also provides a yardstick against which an individual firm can measure its operating results. The second approach will review conglomeration, diversification, and technological progressiveness in food processing and suggest that the received economic theories regarding competition and the current laws governing competition among food firms may be becoming irrelevant.

NORMAL STRUCTURAL MEASUREMENTS

Decreasing Numbers of Firms and Establishments

Although the total quantities of food processed in the United States has increased rapidly, the numbers of companies engaged in food processing has decreased substantially since World War II. In 1947 there were 40,174 food processing companies; in 1963, only 32,153 (Table 2.1). Between 1947 and 1963 the average rate of decrease in numbers of firms was 1.25% per yr.

Nearly every segment of the food processing industry has had a declining number of firms. Fluid milk processing decreased from 6250 firms in 1954 to only 4030 in 1963, a decrease of about 35% in 9 yr (Table 2.2). Canned fruits and vegetables decreased from 1461 firms in 1954 to 1135 firms in 1963; bread and related products firms decreased from 5470 in 1954 to 4339 in 1963. Noted exceptions to the declining numbers of firms has been in meat packing firms which increased from 1999 in 1947 to 2833 in 1963; another exception is the frozen fruit and vegetable industry where the number of firms more than doubled between 1954 and 1963 — from 215 to 566.

Not only has there been a declining number of firms, but in most industries there also has been a declining number of processing plants or establishments. The trend has been to larger facilities serving wider geographical areas. Again, there are exceptions to this trend; i.e., the meat packing industry which has been decentralizing and the freezing of fruits and vegetables which has been rapidly increasing in total volume. In nearly all other food processing industries there has been a general decline in number of food processing plants.

Between 1958 and 1967 the number of food processing plants decreased from 41,867 to 32,585, or a 22% decrease in 10 yr. Milk and bread were among the largest losers. Fluid milk plants decreased from 5828 in 1958 to 3488 in 1967 — a 40% drop in 10 yr. Similarly, the bread industry had nearly a 33% drop in numbers of plants — from 6026 in 1958 to only 4049 in 1967.

THE ROLE AND POSITION OF LARGE FIRMS

Some normal measures of concentration in food processing have been the percent of the total assets controlled by the top 25, 50, or 100 firms, the percent of profits (before federal income taxes) by the same firms, the percent of sales in an industry by the leading 4, 8, or 20 firms, and the number of industries in which the top few firms have a large majority of sales. Measures of interindustry processing are also generally used to show the diversification of the larger firms; this will be done later in this chapter.

Relative Size of Food Processing Firms Compared to Other Industrial Corporations

Food processing firms rank among the largest industrial corporations in the world. Based on 1967 sales volume of the 100 largest industrial corporations in the United States, 11 were firms primarily producing food products. Ten industrial firms in the United States had sales over $4 billion — these were all nonfood firms and included General Motors Corp. (over $20 billion in sales), Standard Oil Co. of New Jersey, Ford Motor Co., General Electric Co., Chrysler Corp., Mobil Oil Corp., International Business Machines Corp., Texaco, Inc., Gulf Oil Co., and U.S. Steel Corp. The largest food manufacturing firms were Swift & Co., which ranked 20th of all industrial corporations with sales of $2.8 billion; National Dairy Products (now Kraftco Corp.) ranking 31st with sales of $2.3 billion;

TABLE 2.1

NUMBERS OF FOOD MANUFACTURING COMPANIES
BY CATEGORY OF INDUSTRY, 1947-1963

Industry Category	Number of Companies			
	1947	1954	1958	1963
National and regional industries				
except meat packing	21,045	18,167	17,379	15,785
Meat processing industries	3,329	4,671	5,119	4,948
Local and small regional				
industries	15,805	15,132	13,500	11,420
All food manufacturing	40,179	37,970	35,998	32,153

Source: Anon. (1966B).

Armour & Co., 34th with sales of $2.2 billion; General Foods Corp., 40th with sales of $1.6 billion; and Borden, Inc., 42nd with sales of $1.6 billion. Also included in the top 100 companies were Ralston Purina Co., Consolidated Foods, Corn Products Co., The Coca-Cola Co., Beatrice Foods Co., and the Carnation Company (Anon. 1968).

Similarly, many of the largest industrial corporations outside the United States are food products companies. In 1968, 15 of the 200 largest industrial corporations outside of the United States were food products companies and another 5 produced alcoholic beverages (Anon. 1969). Thus, about 1 in 10 of the largest industrial corporations in the world are primarily engaged in the

TABLE 2.2

FOOD MANUFACTURING INDUSTRIES: NUMBER OF COMPANIES
AND ESTABLISHMENTS, 1947, 1954, 1958, 1963, AND 1967

Industry	No. of Companies				No. of Establishments				
	1963	1958	1954	1947	1967	1963	1958	1954	1947
Meat products									
Meat packing plants	2833	2646	2228	1999	2707	2992	2801	2367	2154
Prepared meats	1273	1430	1254	-	1375	1341	1494	1316	1264
Poultry dressing plants	842	1095	1189	330	839	967	1233	1309	553
Dairy products									
Fluid milk	4030	5157	6250	-	3488	4619	5817	6689	6616
Creamery butter	725	990	1172	1482	546	766	1058	1262	1904
Natural cheese	982	1026	1220	1313	1031	1318	1203	1419	1738
Condensed and evaporated									
milk	167	161	166	182	291	281	313	359	451
Ice cream and frozen desserts	901	1167	1375	1273	851	1081	1382	1587	1690
Canning, preserving and freezing									
Canned fruits and vegetables	1135	1315	1461	-	1228	1430	1607	1758	2265
Dehydrated fruits									
and vegetables	126	130	119	120	179	176	161	148	146
Pickles and sauces	541	566	642	637	527	588	619	717	742
Frozen fruits and vegetables	566	347	215	-	610	650	426	266	291
Canned specialties	154	93	-	-	176	173	107	-	-
Grain mill products									
Flour and meal	510	703	692	1047	541	618	814	803	1243
Cereal preparations	35	23	37	55	46	48	43	46	64
Rice milling	62	61	65	75	68	74	73	80	88
Blended and prepared flour	140	112	123	115	147	165	117	131	123
Wet corn milling	49	53	54	47	45	60	59	58	55
Bakery products									
Bread and related products	4339	5305	5470	5985	4049	5010	5985	6103	6796
Biscuits and crackers	286	280	-	-	350	356	334	311	326
Sugar									
Raw cane sugar	50	45	43	77	83	74	50	49	82
Cane sugar refining	16	16	16	17	34	25	28	23	25
Beet sugar	11	15	15	17	66	65	66	65	74
Fats and oils									
Cotton seed oil mills	115	125	145	172	153	188	214	286	315
Soybean oil mills	68	82	55	105	102	101	117	88	133
Shortening and cooking oils	65	62	-	-	116	112	105	135	127
Miscellaneous industries									
Macaroni and spaghetti	207	205	226	219	205	221	214	233	226

Source: Census of Manufacturers, Bur. Census, U.S. Dept. Com., 1963, 1967.

production of food products or alcoholic beverages.

Food Product Firms with Sales of Over $100 Million

Recently *Canner/Packer* listed 69 food processing firms each of which had over $100 million in sales of food products in 1968 (Table 2.3). The rankings and sales are slightly different from those listed by *Fortune* magazine; however, these differences are minor. The *Canner/Packer* list included only those firms producing consumer foods — it did not, for example, include firms which pro- duced vegetable oils reprocessed or repackaged by another company. Similarly, soft drinks and alcoholic beverage companies are not included in the list. Thus, the total food products industry, as classified by U.S. Census definitions, was not included but the listing does provide much information on some of the U.S. food giants. Many of these large firms will be recognized in subsequent statistical analyses even though they are not listed by company names.

Asset Concentration in the Total Food Industry

The tendency toward largeness in food industries was noted by economists as early as the 1930's (Hoffman, 76th Congress). Since then, the concentration of assets in the food processing industry have been subject to much investigation. Collins and Preston (1961) plotted the trend in asset concentration of the 100 largest food manufacturing firms from 1935 to 1955 and the Federal Trade Commission subsequently brought these data up through 1964 (Anon. 1966B). Essentially, the data from these combined sources show that in 1935 the 100 largest food manufacturers controlled 53.3% of the total assets and in 1964, 59.6% of the total assets in food manufacturing (Table 2.4).

As earlier data did not take into account the noncorporate food processors (the later data did), the trend toward concentration is probably slightly more rapid than shown. From the author's point of view, in view of the theoretical advantages large firms have over smaller firms, it is the relative slowness toward concentration of assets that is surprising, not the rapidity of concentration.

Asset Concentration by Major Industries

In describing the structure and growth in food processing, the U.S. Bureau of Census Standard Industrial Classification system to define specific parts of the food processing industry will be used. For example, the SIC code for all food processing combined is a 2-digit code — SIC 20. The first breakdown is a 3-digit code; for example, the meat products industry is SIC 201, the dairy products industry is SIC 202, the canned and frozen foods industry is SIC 203, etc. The larger the number the more detailed the industry classification. Since SIC classi- fications are used many times throughout the text, the major SIC classes for the food processing industry (SIC 20) are given in Table 2.5.

In describing the concentration of assets in food processing we will first indicate the share of assets and profits by leading firms in each major classifica- tion. The concentration of assets and profits before taxes for the 4 largest and 8 largest firms in major 3-digit SIC classes of the food processing industry for 1962

TABLE 2.3

FOOD PRODUCTS COMPANIES WITH SALES
OF OVER $100 MILLION IN 1968

Food Rank	Company	Principal Food Products	Percent All Food Products Sales	Net Domestic Consumer Food Product Sales ($100,000)			Percent of Prorated Net Food Income 1968
				1960	1965	1968	
1	Swift & Co.[1]	Meat #1	91	2,222.7	2,513.5	2,572.7	(1.3)
2	Kraftco Corp.[2]	Dairy #1	98	1,467.1	1,775.2	2,136.7	3.2
3	Armour & Co.[2]	Meat #2	77	1,336.4	1,589.9	1,625.0	.7
4	General Foods Corp.	Coffee	98	1,004.0	1,261.6	1,349.6	6.3
5	Borden, Inc.[3]	Dairy #2	79	752.4	1,090.4	1,314.8	2.6
6	Ling-Temco-Vought[4]	Meat	37	-	782.6	983.6	1.0
7	Beatrice Foods Co.[5]	Dairy	90	361.6	537.2	778.5	3.5
8	AMK Corp.[6]	Meat	90	-	-	775.7	.6
9	Campbell Soup Co.[7]	Soup #1	100	524.8	655.8	764.4	6.5
10	Carnation Co.	Dairy	100	-	-	716.0	3.8
11	National Biscuit Co.	Crackers	100	370.9	540.5	616.1	5.3
12	Geo. A. Hormel Co.	Meat	100	-	441.6	585.9	1.5
13	Consolidated Foods Corp.[8]	Bakery, fish	44	186.9	385.0	535.3	3.0
14	General Mills, Inc.[9]	Flour #1, cereal	87	400.0	430.0	535.1	4.7
15	Norton Simon, Inc.[9]	Tomato, oil	60	-	-	534.9	-
16	The Procter & Gamble Co	Shortening	20	288.4	411.8	508.5	7.9
17	Del Monte Corp.	Fruits and veg. #1	100	299.6	381.6	508.2	4.5
18	Iowa Beef Packers	Meat	95	-	274.7	507.3	1.0
19	American Sugar Co.[10]	Cane sugar #1	100	399.4	467.5	502.6	2.0
20	CPC International[11]	Corn products	75	331.4	414.6	460.8	4.4

(Continued)

TABLE 2.3 (Continued)

FOOD PRODUCTS COMPANIES WITH SALES
OF OVER $100 MILLION IN 1968

Food Rank	Company	Principal Food Products	Percent of All Food Products Sales	Net Domestic Consumer Food Product Sales ($100,000)			Percent of Prorated Net Food Income 1968
				1960	1965	1968	
21	Ralston Purina Co.[12]	Dry pet food #1	50	204.7	379.2	448.5	2.9
22	The Quaker Oats Co.[13]	Cereals	77	-	355.2	421.3	3.8
23	Oscar Mayer & Co.	Meat	90	220.9	259.7	409.6	2.5
24	The Pillsbury Co.[14]	Flour and mixes	77	256.3	347.7	407.0	2.4
25	Kellogg Co.	Cereals	100	220.3	331.5	401.3	9.0
26	Pet, Inc.	Dairy, snacks	74	-	366.9	400.9	1.5
27	Great Atlantic & Pacific Tea Co., Inc.[15]	Baked goods	12	367.0	358.0	400.0	1.0
28	Nestle Co.[16]	Tea	100	-	-	400.0	-
29	H. J. Heinz Co.[17]	Relishes	100	180.3	280.3	388.6	2.5
30	Kroger Co.[18]	Coffee	15	224.4	306.6	379.3	1.1
31	The Coca-Cola Co.[19]	Citrus #1	35	125.5	257.8	379.1	9.2
32	Foremost-McKesson	Dairy	26	-	287.0	339.0	1.6
33	Standard Brands, Inc.	Margarine #1	50	193.0	269.2	333.7	3.2
34	Land O'Lakes Creameries	Dairy	90	-	-	332.9	2.4
35	American Bakeries Co.	Bakery	100	162.2	254.9	310.5	.9
36	Cudahy Co.[20]	Meat	90	306.8	275.7	300.3	1.2
37	Safeway Stores	Bakery	10	197.5	235.1	294.8	1.5
38	Libby, McNeill & Libby[21]	Fruits and veg.	82	232.3	246.9	282.4	1.6
39	Campbell Taggart Associated Bakeries[22]	Bakery	100	197.6	230.7	280.4	2.9
40	Castle & Cooke, Inc.[23]	Pineapple #1	78	23.9	199.8	273.6	3.0
41	Ogden Corp.[24]	Fruits and veg.	25	105.4	131.2	262.8	2.4
42	Ward Foods	Bakery	80	97.7	137.4	260.0	1.8
43	Hygrade Food Products[25]	Meat	95	291.9	334.2	259.4	(1.6)
44	Stokely-Van Camp, Inc.	Fruits and veg.	100	182.0	220.6	251.4	2.8
45	Squibb Beech-Nut, Inc.[26]	Baby food #2, tea	41	-	202.2	238.5	6.7

	Company	Product	%				
46	The Rath Packing Co.	Meat	100	172.6	-	236.0	.3
47	R. J. Reynolds Industries[27]	Snack foods	12	140.5	203.1	235.5	7.6
48	Interstate Bakeries Corp.	Bread	100		173.2	231.6	1.8
49	Great Western United Corp.	Beet sugar	85		103.6	229.5	6.0
50	Thomas J. Lipton, Inc.	Tea, soup	100			229.2	6.5
51	Fairmont Foods Co.	Dairy	85	98.0	190.7	218.0	2.0
52	Pepsi Co., Inc.[28]	Snack foods	25			212.0	5.5
53	W. R. Grace & Co.[29]	Pickles, snacks	26			200.0	1.9
54	Needham Packing Co.	Meat	90	71.9	127.3	197.6	.7
55	Hershey Foods Corp.	Chocolate #1	90	127.7	158.2	190.0	6.8
56	Gerber Products Co.	Baby food #1	92	118.1	164.9	167.7	9.0
57	General Host	Bakery	80	56.7	55.5	162.2	1.8
58	American Home Products Corp.	Canned foods	14	72.0	114.0	161.7	9.4
59	Dean Foods	Dairy	100		87.3	160.0	1.1
60	Keebler Co.	Crackers	100	130.5	137.8	151.6	.7
61	Green Giant Co.	Vegetables	100	54.5	98.3	151.0	3.3
62	Southland Corp.	Dairy	20		68.5	136.2	1.5
63	American Beef Packers	Meat	90		43.9	132.5	.6
64	Missouri Beef Packers, Inc.	Meat	100			124.5	.7
65	Spencer Packing Co., Inc.	Meat	85	33.4	91.3	122.8	.8
66	California & Hawaiian Sugar Co.[30]	Cane sugar	100			107.0	-
67	California Canners & Growers[31]	Fruits and veg.	100	66.0	96.0	107.0	6.5
68	International Milling Co.	Grain	35	75.9	96.0	101.7	1.5
69	Marhoefer Packing Co.	Meat	95	76.8	84.4	101.3	-
	TOTAL			$15,029.9	$22,470.9	$30,833.6	836.5
	No. of Companies			47	58	69	66

Source: Anon. (1969B)

[1] The $3 million insurance companies of Swift & Co. are not included in their figures.

[2] Armour & Co. gross sales for foods group of divisions (meat products; fresh meat; dairy, poultry, and consumer frozen foods; food oils; and food service) represents 77% of total; profit represents 45% of total; all other figures based on 77% of Armour &

[3] Co. totals; Armour-Dial, Inc., including Armour-Star canned meats, not included. Borden, Inc., Food Division accounts for 33.7% of sales; Dairy and Services Division for 45.0%; 1968 sales figures are actual, other figures are 78.7% of total.

[4] 96% of Wilson & Co. figures are used; approximately 4% of business is in South America, according to total assets for 1968; Wilson sales are approximately 37% of L-T-V.

[5] Beatrice Foods Co. food product sales represent 82% (dairy 45%, grocery and confectionery 37%) of U.S. total; U.S. total represents 100% of 1968, 96% of 1965 and 90% of 1968 grand totals.

[6] AMK Corp. merged with John Morrell & Co. in 1968; Morrell provides 95% of AMK sales and 65% of income; due to Morrell sidelines, 60% used for income and 90% applied to all other AMK figures.

[7] Campbell Soup Co. figures based on U.S. sales of approximately 90% of total in 1968, 92% in 1965, 95% in 1960; all other figures calculated at 90% of total.

[8] Consolidated Foods Corp. figures based on 44% of sales from food products, 40% of earnings from foods; all other figures based on 44% of total.

[9] Norton Simon, Inc. formed in 1968 from Hunt Foods and Industries, McCall Corp., and Canada Dry, had food sales estimated at 60% (Hunt Foods, Wesson Oils, Southern Shellfish, Wakefield Seafoods).

[10] American Sugar Co. figures include operations of Duff-Norton Co., Inc., industrial equipment manufacturer acquired in 1968; Food Service Division, established in 1968, not reported separately.

[11] CPC International figures based on 75% of total U.S. sales in food products (equally divided between consumer and industrial products; U.S. sales are 54% of total); other figures based on 40.5% (75% of 54%) of corporate totals.

[12] Ralston Purina Co. does not include chow plants, hatcheries, soybean plants.

[13] Quaker Oats Co. employee and plant figures are 77% of U.S. figures; sales figures are 77% of total; debt does not include $5 million in obligations of foreign subsidiaries.

[14] The Pillsbury Co. 1968 sales figure includes consumer products and industrial flour; actual figure of 6930 U.S. employees is used.

[15] Great Atlantic & Pacific Tea Co. produces or packs food goods valued at 12% of sales, or about $650 million in 1968; of this amount, an estimated $100 million is fresh produce, and the remainder processed foods, principally bakery items; equivalent wholesale value comparable to sales of other food processors would be about $400 million, or 7% of totals.

[16] Nestle Co., the only non-U.S. company in the list (Nestle Alimentana, Swiss), does not provide any data; figure shown is an estimate; the worldwide company has 200 plants, 86,000 employees.

[17] H. J. Heinz Co. has 53% of sales in U.S.; 43% of net income is U.S.

[18] Kroger Co. food processing accounts for approximately 15% of sales; equivalent wholesale values would reduce the figure to approximately 12%, which has been applied to corporate totals.

[19] The Coca-Cola Foods Division (Minute Maid citrus products, Duncan Foods coffee and tea) and Tenco Division (worldwide private label coffee and tea) sales estimated on basis of premerger soft drink sales and industry growth compared to total company growth; all figures based on 1963 estimate of 32% of corporate total.

[20] Cudahy Co. sales include 30% from processed meats, 52% from fresh and frozen meats, and 18% from all others including dairy and grocery products, leather, pharmaceuticals, etc.; 90% estimate of food operations applied to all other totals.

[21] Libby, McNeill & Libby totals represent 82% (no percentage is given for Dunkley Co., which makes equipment, or for food service division.

[22] Campbell Taggart Associated Bakeries is a bakery holding and service company.

[23] Castle & Cooke, Inc. food sales include foreign operations and fresh banana operations of Standard Fruit & Steamship; sales include foods (72%) and sugar (6% of total); all other figures based on 78% of totals; due to fiscal year change, 1968 represents 11 months.

[24] Ogden Corp. food operations are estimated at 33% of totals, with food service and airline catering accounting for an estimated 8% and food products for 25%.

[25] Hygrade Food Products processed meat products sales are over 1/2 of figures shown, and the remainder fresh meat.

[26] Squibb Beech-Nut merged in 1968; specialty foods and beverages sales in U.S. and Canada account for 24.8% of 1967 sales; confections for 16.5%; food service (not included in totals) for 13.6%; figures given are 1967, based on 41% of total.

[27] R.J. Reynolds Industries sales are 12% from nontobacco products; also includes packaging products; volume per plant based on 28 nontobacco plants, rather than 18 food plants.

[28] 25% figures are used for PepsiCo because transportation and leasing, foreign, and soft drink sales are estimated at 75%.

[29] W. R. Grace & Co. Consumer Products Group accounted for sales of $453 million in 1968, or 26% of total; of this amount, Miller Brewing Co. had $145 million sales; the remaining $308 million is divided between domestic and foreign (including restaurant) operations, including American Freezerships; estimated $200 million domestic sales of food products is 11 1/2% of total: and this percentage was used for other figures.

[30] California & Hawaiian Sugar Co. (C & H) is a cooperative owned by Hawaiian sugar producers, refining 80% of island cane; sales figures is an estimate based on extensions of partial information.

[31] California Canners & Growers is a 1100-member cooperative.

are listed in Table 2.6. The 4 largest firms in the meat products industry in 1962 had 42.6% of the total assets in the industry and 56.0% of the profits before taxes; the 8 largest firms, 51.5% of the assets and 66.2% of the profits. In the canned and frozen foods industry, the 4 largest firms had 43.6% of the assets and 70.4% of the profits before taxes; the 8 largest firms, 50.1% of the assets and 96.2% of the profits before taxes. The concentration in other industries can be obtained from Table 2.6.

While this is a fairly typical method of pointing out the levels of concentration in food processing, several comments should be made concerning the method. First, although concentration of assets is important and does measure the capital involved in the production process, asset ownership is also important. Tentative data for 1965-1966 and 1966-1967 suggest that larger firms have more equity in the business and, therefore, less leverage in profits. The critical test from a manager's point of view is not profits on assets but profits on owners' equity. Second, profits before taxes can also be misleading; it is net profits or profits after taxes that are important and as our present corporate tax laws are semi-progressive, larger firms may pay a higher rate of federal corporate income tax than smaller firms. Another comment that should be made is that the data are for only 1 yr and that the relationships, particularly the percent of total profits, change over time; in fact, 1966-1967 data are substantially different from those for 1962. Detailed data for 1965-1966 and 1966-1967 concerning profitability of large firms will subsequently be presented.

The sources of data for determining levels of concentration both in assets and profits are fairly readily available. Data for financial operations of the large

TABLE 2.4

CONCENTRATION OF TOTAL ASSETS
IN FOOD MANUFACTURING, 1935-1965
(Percent of Total Assets)

Year	By 50 Largest %	By 100 Largest %
1935	-	53.3
1940	-	51.8
1945	-	53.2
1950	41.6	53.7
1955	45.1	55.9
1960	46.9	-
1962	47.6	58.0
1964	49.4	59.6
1965	50.2	-

Source: Anon. (1966B). The original data are from Collins and Preston (1961) and from Federal Trade Commission data obtained from *Moody's Industrial Manual* and the *Quarterly Financial Reports for Manufacturing Corporations* published by the FTC and the Securities Exchange Comm.

TABLE 2.5

BUREAU OF CENSUS STANDARD INDUSTRIAL CLASSIFICATION
FOR THE FOOD AND KINDRED PRODUCTS PROCESSING INDUSTRY (SIC 20)[1]

201   Meat Products
2011   Meat packing plants, including both the slaughter and the meat, canned and frozen as well as fresh, and hides, etc.
2013   Sausage and other prepared meat products
2015   Poultry and small game dressing and packing, wholesale, including processed eggs (frozen, dehydrated, etc.)

202   Dairy Products
2021   Creamery butter
2022   Cheese, natural and processed
2023   Condensed and evaporated milk, including dry milk, lactose, whey
2024   Ice cream and frozen desserts
2026   Fluid milk, including cottage cheese, whipped cream, and route salesmen for dairies

203   Canned and Preserved Fruits Vegetables and Sea Foods
2031   Canned and cured fish and seafoods
2032   Canned specialties (including baby food, ethnic foods, canned bread, etc.)
2033   Canned fruits, vegetables, preserves, jams, and jellies (including juices)
2034   Dried and dehydrated fruits and vegetables (including potato flakes, raisins, soup powders, etc.)
2035   Pickled fruits and vegetables, vegetable sauces and seasonings; salad dressings

2036   Fresh or frozen packaged fish and sea foods
2037   Frozen fruits, fruit juices, vegetables, and specialties (including dinners, pizzas, baked goods, etc.)

204   Grain Mill Products
2041   Flour and other grain mill products (including refrigerated dough and pizza mixes made in grain mills, and some products for brewers' use)
2042   Prepared feeds for animals and fowls (including dry and canned dog food, fish meal, canned horse meats, citrus seed meal, etc.)
2043   Cereal preparations
2044   Rice milling
2045   Blended and prepared flours (including refrigerated doughs and mixes made from purchased flour)
2046   Wet corn milling (including dextrose, oil, edible and industrial starch, etc.)

205   Bakery Products
2051   Bread and other bakery products (except cookies and crackers, not frozen)
2052   Cookies and crackers

206   Sugar
2061   Cane sugar (except refining only)
2062   Cane sugar refining
2063   Beet sugar

207   Confectionery and Related Products
2071   Candy and other confectionery products (including cough drops, salted nuts, etc.)
2072   Chocolate and cocoa products
2073   Chewing gum

208   Beverages
2082   Malt liquors (beer, etc.)
2083   Malt
2084   Wines, brandy, and brandy spirits
2085   Distilled, rectified, and blended liquors
2086   Bottled and canned soft drinks and carbonated waters (including fresh fruit drinks made of fruit juice and water, etc.)
2087   Flavoring extracts and flavoring syrups not elsewhere classified (including crushed fruit for soda fountains, flavors, colors, etc.)

209   Miscellaneous Food Preparations and Kindred Products
2091   Cottonseed mills (oil)
2092   Soybean oil mills
2093   Vegetable oil mills except corn, cottonseed, and soybean
2094   Animal and marine fats and oils
2095   Roasted coffee
2096   Shortening, table oils, margarine and other edible fats and oils not elsewhere classified
2097   Manufactured ice
2098   Macaroni, spaghetti, vermicelli, and noodles
2099   Food preparations not elsewhere classified (including baking powder, instant chocolate, pie fillings, honey, maple syrup, peanut butter, pectin, tea blending, vinegar)

[1] Many of the SIC 5-digit classes are presented in Table 5.6, Chap. 5.

corporations are available from annual reports to stockholders or from *Moody's Industrial Manual*. These data are then compared to total industry data available from the *Quarterly Financial Report for Manufacturing Corporations* published jointly by the Federal Trade Commission and the Securities Exchange Commission or from data published by the Internal Revenue Service, *Source Book of Statistics of Income*.

PROFITABILITY IN FOOD MANUFACTURING

Corporations Versus Unincorporated Food Processing Firms

Because of the difference of availability of data on profitability, a distinction must be made between corporations and individual proprietorships or partnerships. Much data on profitability come from corporations' published annual reports — similar data from unincorporated firms are typically not available. Further, the IRS in its *Source Book of Statistics of Income* makes available much corporate financial data on the food processing industry. These data are from federal corporate income tax returns. Most of the data, by far, that will be presented on profits in food processing are from corporations. However, on a

TABLE 2.6

FOUR- AND EIGHT-FIRM CONCENTRATION OF ASSETS AND PROFITS
IN MAJOR FOOD PROCESSING CATEGORIES, 1962

Industry	Assets % of Total Assets	Profits Before Taxes % of Total Profits
Meat Products (SIC 201)		
4 largest firms	42.6	56.0
8 largest firms	51.5	66.2
Dairy Products (SIC 202)		
4 largest firms	43.6	70.4
8 largest firms	56.9	87.5
Canned and Frozen Foods (SIC 203)		
4 largest firms	40.0	79.5
8 largest firms	50.1	96.2
Grain Mill Products (SIC 204)		
4 largest firms	26.7	35.3
8 largest firms	41.4	59.4
Bakery Products (SIC 205)		
4 largest firms	30.8	65.5
8 largest firms	42.0	75.5
Sugar (SIC 206)		
4 largest firms	42.2	56.0
8 largest firms	61.9	78.6
Confectionery Products (SIC 207)		
4 largest firms	48.3	65.6
8 largest firms	61.1	93.5
Beverages (excluding alcoholic beverages) (SIC 208)		
4 largest firms	39.7	63.0
8 largest firms	43.4	69.9

Source: From FTC data contained in Anon. (1966B). Original data from *Moody's Industrial Manual* and *Quarterly Financial Reports for Manufacturing Corporations,* published by FTC and Securities Exchange Comm.

weighted basis the importance of the corporations is much greater than that of unincorporated firms in food processing. The FTC estimated that in 1964 there were approximately 31,178 food processing firms in the United States. Of these, approximately 1/3 (10,436 firms) were unincorporated businesses and 2/3 were corporations. However, the unincorporated firms had only an estimated 3.6% of the total assets used in food processing and obtained only 6.6% of the total profits after taxes. Thus, while much of the data on profits will come only from corporate sources this does represent a big majority of total food processing.

Profitability in Food Manufacturing Compared to All Manufacturing

In most years, food processing has not been as profitable, on the average, as all manufacturing industries in the United States. Based on profits after taxes as a percent of net worth from a comprehensive sample of all manufacturing firms over the past 20 yr, owners' equity in food processing has returned 9.52% per yr, while all manufacturing has returned 11.22% (Table 2.7). Stated in another way, the average return on net worth in all manufacturing has been 17.85% greater than the return on net worth in food manufacturing. Only in 3 yr of the 20-yr span between 1949 and 1968 did profits on net worth in food manufacturing exceed those in all manufacturing industries.

In viewing these data it should be kept in mind that they represent thousands of firms and that there is a great amount of variability in profits among individual industrial firms, both in food manufacturing and in all manufacturing.

Historically, profitability is difficult to judge because of changes in the value of money; that is, considering amounts of inflation and interest rates. While return on net worth in food processing over the last several years (1964-1968)

TABLE 2.7

PROFITS AFTER INCOME TAXES AS PERCENT OF NET WORTH FOR
ALL MANUFACTURING CORPORATIONS AND FOR
FOOD PROCESSING CORPORATIONS, 1949-1968

Year	All Manufacturing Corporations	Food and Kindred Products[1]	Year	All Manufacturing Corporations	Food and Kindred Products[1]
	% Return on Net Worth			% Return on Net Worth	
1949	11.1	11.8	1959	10.4	9.3
1950	15.4	12.2	1960	9.2	8.7
1951	12.5	8.9	1961	8.8	8.9
1952	10.3	7.6	1962	9.8	8.8
1953	10.5	8.1	1963	10.3	9.0
1954	9.9	8.1	1964	11.6	10.0
1955	12.6	8.9	1965	13.0	10.7
1956	12.3	9.3	1966	13.4	11.1
1957	11.0	8.6	1967	11.7	10.8
1958	8.6	8.8	1968	12.1	10.7
			Simple average:	11.22	9.52

Source: *Quarterly Financial Reports for Manufacturing Corporations*, FTC and Securities Exchange Comm.

[1] Including alcoholic beverages.

TABLE 2.8

SELECTED FINANCIAL DATA ON FOOD MANUFACTURING CORPORATIONS
BY QUARTERS, 1967–1969

| | 1967 | | 1968 | | | | 1969 |
	3rd Quarter	4th Quarter	1st Quarter	2nd Quarter	3rd Quarter	4th Quarter	1st Quarter
All food manufacturing corporations							
Total sales ($1,000,000)	20,663	21,159	20,219	20,829	21,523	22,267	21,391
Profits after taxes as percent of sales (%)	2.8	2.8	2.5	2.5	2.7	2.7	2.4
Profits after taxes as percent of net worth (%)	11.7	11.8	9.9	10.2	11.4	11.4	9.6
Dairy Products							
Profits after taxes as percent of sales (%)	2.5	2.3	2.1	2.4	2.4	2.3	2.1
Profits after taxes as percent of net worth (%)	10.9	9.5	8.6	10.0	10.4	10.1	9.2
Bakery Products							
Profits after taxes as percent of sales (%)	2.5	3.2	2.2	2.7	2.6	2.3	1.8
Profits after taxes as percent of net worth (%)	11.8	14.7	9.6	12.0	12.0	13.3	7.8

Source: *Quarterly Financial Reports for Manufacturing Corporations*, FTC and Securities Exchange Comm.

has averaged over 10%, it should be remembered that interest rates were also high during 1968 and 1969. Some AAA bonds were sold to return higher than 8% interest during this time.

DATA SOURCES ON PROFITABILITY

There are many sources of data on profitability in food processing. Data on individual firms are available in annual reports of the firms or in financial journals such as *Moody's Industrial Manual.* Our concern here, however, is not so much financial reports of individual firms as aggregate statistical data of industries or for total food processing. Three sources of industry statistical data on profitability will be briefly illustrated.

Quarterly Financial Reports of Manufacturing Corporations

Other than reports by individual firms, perhaps the most current data on profitability of major segments of the food processing industry can be obtained from *Quarterly Financial Reports for Manufacturing Corporations.* A condensed sample of some of the data published in this report is given in Table 2.8. Assets, sales, net margins (after taxes), and returns to net worth (after taxes) are listed for all food manufacturing, for the dairy products industry, bakery products industry, and for alcoholic beverages. While these data show overall trends in corporate profitability in food processing, there are no data on many of the major segments in food processing.

Economic News Letter

A profitability series containing several major food manufacturing industries with a restricted but large sample of firms is published annually by the First

TABLE 2.9

RETURN ON NET WORTH BY LEADING CORPORATIONS
IN THE UNITED STATES, 1964—1968

No. of Corpo- rations	Type of Corporation	1964	1965	1966	1967	1968
		Percent Return on Net Worth				
17	Baking companies	11.3	11.2	13.9	15.7	13.7
12	Dairy products	12.2	12.5	12.6	11.8	11.4
26	Meat processors	8.6	5.0	5.2	9.2	8.2
14	Sugar processors	8.1	9.3	9.1	10.2	8.7
81	Other food products manufacturers	11.1	12.2	13.3	12.3	12.5
15	Soft drinks	20.1	20.4	22.0	23.3	23.2
14	Brewing	10.0	10.2	13.4	12.2	13.9
15	Distilling	8.5	9.5	13.9	10.5	9.5
59	Chain food stores	12.5	12.5	12.3	11.1	11.5
3862	Leading corporations	10.3	11.1	11.3	10.6	10.6

Source: Anon. (1964—1968).

National City Bank of New York. A profitability series is maintained on baking companies, dairy products, meat processors, sugar processors, soft drink manufacturers, brewing, distilling, and other food products manufacturers (Table 2.9). These are profits obtained by leading firms. The number of firms in each product category changes somewhat through time. As information on assets owned by the firms on which profits are reported is available in other issues of the *Economic News Letter,* the weight of the sample to the total industries can be estimated. In 1968, the data on food processing were from 172 leading firms. The series probably represents over half the total assets in food processing in the United States.

The differences in profitability by type of food processing is readily apparent in this series. For example, the average return on net worth for 26 meat processing firms for the years 1964-1968 was 7.24% while the return to 15 soft drink manufacturers was 21.8%.

Source Book of Statistics of Income

Perhaps the most complete sample of firms and the most detailed report on profitability of food processing are contained in the *Source Book of Statistics of Income* made available by the Internal Revenue Service. One drawback to this series is the time lag in analysis and publication of results. Often there is a lag of 12-18 months before the data for a specific year's results become available. A minor disadvantage is that the series does not contain the results of nonincorporated businesses. However, the advantages of using this series on profitability is that it contains weighted average results of all firms which file federal corporate income tax returns. Also, the 13 major SIC 3-digit and SIC 4-digit industries in food processing are reported separately and by asset size class of the firms in each industry. In essence, the results of all corporate firms whose principal

TABLE 2.10

PROFITS AFTER TAXES AS PERCENT OF NET WORTH BY
TYPE OF FOOD MANUFACTURER FOR VARIOUS YEARS 1947-1967

Type of Manufacturer	1947	1954	1958	1960	1961	1966	1967
Meat products	10.8[1]	2.6[2]	3.0[2]	3.8[2]	3.7[2]	4.5	6.4
Dairy products	11.9	7.9	7.7	7.5	7.3	8.6	10.2
Canned and frozen foods	10.0	4.9	7.6	7.7	8.5	9.0	10.8
Bakery products	13.5	8.1	9.3	8.1	6.7	7.8	10.1
Grain mill products	16.3	9.3	9.0	8.5	7.5	9.6	9.1
Confectionery manufacturers	23.1	9.8	10.2	11.0	11.4	-	34.8
Nonalcoholic beverages	13.2	7.8	9.3	10.4	10.9	15.0	15.4
Miscellaneous food products	14.3	11.0	12.9	14.1	14.8	14.2	11.4

Source: Source Book of Statistics of Income, IRS, U.S. Treasury Dept.

[1] Estimated: assuming 60% owners' equity on total assets.

[2] Estimated from graph in The Structure of Food Manufacturing, Tech. Study *8*, Natl. Comm. Food Marketing, June 1966.

activity is food processing are included in the reports.

Historical data from this series and profitability of eight major food processing categories are listed in Table 2.10. It should first be noted that there are wide differences in the return on net worth among the major food processing industries. Secondly, within each industry profitability over time changes significantly. Over the last 15 yr the meat products industry has received a low return on owners' equity compared to all other food processing industries — however, the comparative position of the industry appears to be improving over the past 4 or 5 yr. Although the data presented in Tables 2.10 and 2.11 are not directly comparable, notice that both series show considerable improvement in meat processing profits over the past few years. Miscellaneous food products manufacturing has had relatively consistently high returns to net worth. This industry category includes a variety of types of products including roasted coffee, macaroni and spaghetti, ready-to-mix desserts, potato chips, sweetening syrups and molasses, etc.[1]

---

[1] For a complete description of the types of processing in miscellaneous foods see SIC code 209 or SIC codes 2095, 2097, 2098, and 2099.

TABLE 2.11

CONCENTRATION IN PROFITS OR LARGE FOOD MANUFACTURERS, 1957-1967

A. Income Before Taxes of 50 Largest Food Manufacturers as Percent of Income Before Taxes of All Food Processing Firms[1]

Year	Income Before Taxes of 50 Largest Firms %
1957	52.9
1958	55.2
1959	56.6
1960	58.2
1961	58.1
1962	60.2
1963	61.4
1964	61.2

B. Income Before Taxes of 58 Largest Food Manufacturers as Percent of Income Before Taxes of All Corporate Food Manufacturers[2]

	Income Before Taxes of 58 Largest Firms %
1966	55.0
1967	55.0

[1] Companies primarily classified as food manufacturers (excluding alcoholic beverages) ranked by assets each year. Source: *Moody's Industrial Manual*, company annual reports, and *Quarterly Financial Reports for Manufacturing Corporations op cit.* Taken from The Structure of Food Manufacturing *op cit.*

[2] All firms with assets of over $100 million including firms producing alcoholic beverages. Source: *Source Book of Statistics of Income op cit.*

CONCENTRATION OF PROFITS IN ALL FOOD PROCESSING

Table 2.6 indicated the percent of total assets in several food processing industries owned by the top 4 and 8 firms, and also share of profits before taxes obtained by these same firms for 1962. Concentration of profitability will now be discussed in more detail. Some historical data on share of profits before taxes will be presented first; then more recent data on profits after taxes will be discussed. This will be followed by a discussion of return on net worth by size of firm. Notice that 3 different methods of measuring profitability will be discussed: (1) earnings before taxes as a percent of total earnings, (2) earnings after taxes as a percent of total earnings and (3) return, after taxes, on owners' equity. Apparently the FTC has tended to use the first method. This method may, in fact, indicate a greater degree of concentration of profits than do the other two methods. From the managerial point of view, the third measure of profitability is the most relevant. As will be pointed out later in more detail, some firms use more borrowed funds than others and thus have more leverage on profits. From the managerial point of view, financial management is as important as efficiency in management of other aspects of the firm. Thus, returns on assets are not nearly as important a measure of profits as returns on owners' equity. The author takes the point of view that the principal objective of the firm is to increase the long-run value to firm owners and that returns on owners' equity is one of the best measurements of accomplishing these objectives. (The market value of the owners' equity is the ideal measure of the value of the company, but returns on equity strongly influence the market value of the stock.)

The FTC used share of total profits before taxes for the largest 50 food processing firms to suggest increasing concentration of profits (Table 2.11). The sources and methods used by the FTC suggest the 50 largest firms increased their share of total profits from 52.9% in 1957 to 61.2% in 1964. Data sources were from company annual reports, *Moody's Industrial Manual,* and *Quarterly Financial Reports for Manufacturing Corporations.* Data for the tax years 1965-1966 and 1966-1967 indicate the largest 58 firms had only 55% of the profits before taxes. These later data were from the *Source Book of Statistics of Income* and were for the largest 58 firms, including alcoholic beverage manufacturers, each of which had assets of over $100 million. The FTC data on profits of the largest firms are from sources from which each firm probably uses accounting procedures to indicate a maximum income to the firm, i.e., annual reports to the stockholders. Total industry profits are from data filed with governmental agencies where accounting procedures are probably used that would minimize profits (and taxes). (The keeping of two sets of records is perfectly legal — for example, for tax purposes a firm might use a double declining balance method of depreciating a physical asset but use straight line depreciation for reports to stockholders. This would initially increase costs of operations for tax purposes and initially reduce taxes paid.)

In fact, some questions may be raised concerning the accuracy of the FTC

TABLE 2.12

SELECTED FINANCIAL DATA FOR FOOD PROCESSING FIRMS, 1965-1966

	Meat Products (SIC 201)	Dairy Products (SIC 202)	Canned and Frozen Foods (SIC 203)	Grain Mill Products (SIC 204)	Bakery Products (SIC 205)	Sugar (SIC 206)	Confectionery and Related Products (SIC 207)
All firms							
Total number of firms	2,678	3,186	1,963	2,217	2,377	141	836
Firms reporting negative income	935	1,202	660	540	846	80	307
Total assets ($1000)	3,601,164	4,412,163	3,771,281	4,047,459	2,142,077	1,701,312	1,004,600
Total equity ($1000)	2,032,079	2,567,143	2,072,179	2,351,943	1,363,147	1,005,564	717,361
Total business receipts ($1000)	20,520,940	10,506,988	6,367,304	8,585,273	5,265,784	2,120,630	1,749,314
Total profits after taxes ($1000)	91,887	221,333	187,143	224,941	106,106	66,541	84,297
Net operating margin (%)	0.45	2.11	2.94	2.62	2.02	3.14	4.82
Return on assets after taxes (%)[1]	2.55	5.02	4.96	5.56	4.95	3.91	8.39
Return on equity after taxes (%)[1]	4.52	8.62	9.03	9.54	7.78	6.62	11.75
Top Firms[2]	Top 3 Firms	Top 5 Firms	Top 7 Firms	Top 11 Firms	Top 4 Firms	Top 4 Firms	Top 1 Firm
	%	%	%	%	%	%	%
Total assets	38.7	57.5	43.8	55.1	34.4	35.2	17.1
Total equity	40.0	60.2	54.2	56.2	40.1	35.3	21.2
Total profits after taxes	27.1	74.2	55.2	64.5	51.5	50.4	24.7
Return on assets after taxes	1.78	5.69	6.29	6.50	7.40	5.61	11.80
Return on equity after taxes	3.06	10.61	9.20	10.96	9.98	9.46	13.34
All other firms							
Return on assets after taxes	3.04	3.41	3.95	4.40	3.67	2.99	7.45
Return on equity after taxes	5.50	5.60	8.82	7.77	6.31	5.07	10.97

	Malt Liquor and Malt (SIC 2082)	Wines, Brandy, and Brandy Spirits (SIC 2084)	Distilled Liquor (Except Brandy) (SIC 2085)	Bottled Soft Drinks and Flavorings (SIC 2086)	Vegetable and Animal Oils (SIC 2091)	Food Not Otherwise Classified Or Allocable (SIC 2098 and SIC 2099)	Totals: All Food and Kindred Products (SIC 20)
All firms							
Total number of firms	269	180	113	2,777	535	1,843	19,115
Firms reporting negative income	170	56	14	641	124	769	6,344
Total assets ($1000)	2,116,744	307,012	3,052,523	2,416,869	1,492,487	2,865,483	32,931,174
Total equity ($1000)	1,362,551	114,561	1,529,352	1,456,042	812,767	1,788,724	19,137,160
Total business receipts ($1000)	3,863,537	382,803	3,725,617	3,820,546	3,198,712	6,050,366	76,158,014
Total profits after taxes ($1000)	106,595	7,943	96,954	217,828	64,817	209,297	1,685,682
Net operating margin (%)	2.76	2.07	2.60	5.70	2.02	3.46	2.21
Return on assets after taxes (%)[1]	5.04	2.59	3.18	9.01	4.34	7.30	5.12
Return on equity after taxes (%)[1]	7.82	6.93	6.34	14.96	7.98	11.70	8.80
Top Firms[2]	Top 5 Firms	None	Top 6 Firms	Top 2 Firms	Top 3 Firms	Top 5 Firms	Top 58 Firms
	%		%	%	%	%	%
Total assets	41.0		78.8	30.2	51.9	51.6	47.3
Total equity	45.0		78.8	35.1	49.3	55.3	50.0
Total profits after taxes	61.5		62.0	43.1	43.2	60.7	54.6
Return on assets after taxes	7.55		2.50	12.85	3.61	8.59	5.91
Return on equity after taxes	10.69		4.99	18.37	6.99	12.85	9.62
All other firms							
Return on assets after taxes	3.29		5.69	7.35	5.13	5.93	4.41
Return on equity after taxes	5.48		11.32	13.11	8.93	10.28	8.01

Source: Source Book of Statistics of Income, IRS, U.S. Treasury Dept.

[1] Profit after taxes minus the deficits reported by some firms.

[2] All Firms with assets of over $100,000,000.

TABLE 2.13

SELECTED FINANCIAL DATA FOR FOOD PROCESSING FIRMS, 1966-1967

	Meat Products (SIC 201)	Dairy Products (SIC 202)	Canned and Frozen Foods (SIC 203)	Grain Mill Products (SIC 204)	Bakery Products (SIC 205)	Sugar (SIC 206)	Confectionery and Related Products (SIC 207)
All firms							
Total number of firms	2,222	3,545	2,065	2,133	2,717	54	666
Firms reporting negative income	552	1,105	550	644	1,166	10	168
Total assets ($1000)	4,408,878	5,024,265	4,219,467	4,077,049	2,315,507	1,517,955	974,002
Total equity ($1000)	2,234,686	2,832,038	2,191,472	2,439,844	1,362,311	922,375	663,870
Total business receipts ($1000)	23,344,264	12,543,403	7,676,477	9,425,212	5,710,774	1,949,011	3,408,890
Total profits after taxes ($1000)	124,682	242,924	211,999	241,405	115,111	71,832	217,257
Net operating margin (%)	0.53	1.94	2.76	2.56	2.02	3.69	6.37
Return on assets after taxes (%)[1]	2.83	4.83	5.06	5.92	4.97	4.73	22.30
Return on equity after taxes (%)[1]	5.58	8.58	9.71	9.89	8.45	7.79	32.73
Top firms[2]	Top 4 Firms	Top 6 Firms	Top 9 Firms	Top 10 Firms	Top 4 Firms	Top 3 Firms	Top 1 Firm
	%	%	%	%	%	%	%
Total assets	36.7	53.6	48.6	54.6	32.3	32.6	18.2
Total equity	38.9	58.4	58.7	58.8	38.9	30.5	21.2
Total profit after taxes	30.8	80.4	54.9	72.4	50.9	31.0	11.6
Return on assets after taxes (%)	2.38	7.24	5.66	7.86	7.84	4.50	14.25
Return on equity after taxes (%)	4.43	11.81	9.04	12.18	11.06	7.93	17.79
All other firms							
Return on assets after taxes (%)	3.09	2.05	4.41	3.59	3.60	4.84	24.09
Return on equity after taxes (%)	6.31	4.05	10.57	6.56	6.78	7.71	36.72

	Malt Liquor and Malt (SIC 2082)	Wines Brandy, Brandy Spirits (SIC 2084)	Distilled Liquor (Except Brandy) (SIC 2085)	Bottled Soft Drinks and Flavorings (SIC 2086)	Vegetable and Animal Oils (SIC 2091)	Food Not Otherwise Classified Or Allocable (SIC 2098 and SIC 2099)	Totals: All Food and Kindred Products (SIC 20)
All firms							
Total number of firms	145	70	70	2,874	385	1,913	18,859
Firms reporting negative income	64	37	1	756	87	697	5,837
Total assets ($1000)	2,138,929	281,872	3,207,647	2,925,523	1,397,893	3,257,088	35,378,073
Total equity ($1000)	1,484,953	116,334	1,516,847	1,561,685	706,523	1,990,768	19,804,495
Total business receipts ($1000)	4,081,501	339,239	3,755,112	4,632,258	3,095,681	6,309,063	86,270,885
Total profits after taxes ($1000)	117,108	12,124	110,115	222,703	44,553	188,818	1,920,631
Net operating margin (%)	2.87	3.57	2.93	4.81	1.44	2.99	2.23
Return on assets after taxes (%)[1]	5.48	4.30	3.43	7.61	3.19	5.80	5.43
Return on equity after taxes (%)[1]	7.89	10.40	7.26	14.26	6.30	9.48	9.70
Top firms[2]	Top 5 Firms	None	Top 6 Firms	Top 2 Firms	Top 3 Firms	Top 5 Firms	Top 58 Firms
	%		%	%	%	%	%
Total assets	46.0	-	80.9	40.2	57.9	48.9	48.7
Total equity	44.6	-	79.8	43.0	59.7	53.1	51.8
Total profit after taxes	66.8	-	69.3	54.1	55.7	69.8	55.3
Return on assets after taxes (%)	7.95		2.94	10.25	3.06	8.28	6.17
Return on equity after taxes (%)	11.82		6.30	17.95	5.88	12.46	10.36
All other firms							
Return on assets after taxes (%)	3.37		5.52	5.83	3.36	3.43	4.72
Return on equity after taxes (%)	4.72		11.06	11.47	6.94	6.10	8.99

Source: Source Book of Statistics of Income, IRS, U.S. Treasury Dept.

[1] Profit after taxes minus the deficits reported by some firms.

[2] All Firms with assets of over $100,000,000.

data in that records of profits of the 50 largest firms were from public sources where profitability is likely to be enhanced, while the base for the whole industry is from data filed with governmental agencies where profitability is likely to be minimized. This method may tend to show a larger share of total profits by the 50 largest firms than is really the case. Using only the FTC data from 1957 to 1964 shows concentration to be undoubtedly increasing. However, later data, while not suggesting that concentration is not increasing, does suggest that the level of concentration of profits is considerably less than that specified by the FTC. In any case, the top 50 or 58 firms do obtain over half the profits before taxes of the total food processing industry.

CONCENTRATION OF PROFITS BY MAJOR FOOD PROCESSING INDUSTRIES

Financial data, including profits after taxes both on assets and equity, for 13 major food processing industries for 1965-1966 and 1966-1967 are given in Tables 2.12 and 2.13. These data are segregated for firms with over $100 million in assets and for all other corporate firms. The total number of corporate firms in each industry and the number of firms with negative incomes (deficits) for the year are listed. For each industry the total assets, total equity, total sales, and total profit after taxes are given. For example, as shown in Column 1, Table 2.12, the meat products industry in 1965-1966 had 2678 firms, of which 935 reported losses for the tax year. Total assets were $3.6 billion, equity $2.0 billion, sales $20.5 billion, and profits after taxes (with losses of individual firms deducted) were $91.9 million. The net operating margin for the meat products industry was 0.45%, profits as a percent of assets were 2.55% and profits on equity 4.52%. The top 3 firms (based on assets) have 38.7% of the total assets, 40% of total equity, but earned only 27.1% of the total profits. The return to the large firms on assets was 1.78% and the return on equity was 3.06%. However, the smaller firms (all firms with under $100 million in assets) — in this case 2675 firms — averaged 3.04% on assets and 5.50% on equity. Similar data are presented for each of the other 11 food processing industries and for all food processing combined. Notice the wide variability in profitability among the various food processing industries. Returns on assets were only 2.55% in the meat industry, 2.59% in wines and brandy, 3.18% in distilled liquor, and 3.91% in the sugar industry, but were 9.01% in soft drinks. The weighted average return on assets in the tax year 1965-1966 for the total corporate food processing industry was 5.12% and the return on equity 8.80%. In 1965-1966 there were 12 industries where there were firms with over $100 million in assets. In 9 of these 12 industries the large firms had a greater return on equity than did the smaller firms. In the meat products industry, the distilled liquor industry, and in vegetable and animal oils, the small firms averaged a greater return on equity than did the large firms.

Data in identical form are presented for the food processing industry for 1966-1967 in Table 2.13. A surprising development in the 1966-1967 data is that in 5 of the 12 industries in which there were firms with over $100 million in assets, the average smaller firm had a greater return on equity than did the firms with assets of $100 million or more. In the meat products industry, the canned and frozen foods industry, the confectionery industry, the distilled liquor industry, and in vegetable and animal oils, the smaller firms averaged a greater return on equity. In the case of the sugar industry, returns were about the same for both the large and other firms. However, in 6 other industries, where there were firms with over $100 million in assets, the large firms earned substantially more on equity than did the average smaller firm. For the total food processing industry in 1966-1967, the large firms earned 6.17% on assets and 10.36% on equity, while the average smaller firms earned 4.72% on assets and 8.99% on equity. On a weighted average basis the larger firms earned slightly over 15% more on equity than the smaller firms. If only profitable firms were considered, that is, if the losses by some small firms were not deducted from profits of profitable firms, the small firms earned more on equity than the large firms. Or stated in another way, the profitable smaller firm's return on equity was greater than that of a profitable large firm − based on weighted average returns.

These data conform to the results of recent statistical tests of the effect of size (total assets) and market concentration on net profits conducted by Arnould (1969). In a sample of 104 food processing firms he concluded, "The low simple correlation coefficients indicate that there is no reason to believe that a linear relationship exists between either of the power indices (size and concentration) and level of profits." Arnould did find a greater stability of profits in diversified firms; but on the average, no greater profitability in diversified firms over specialized firms. Wittenbert (1970) suggests that profitability of large business firms has been decreasing relative to smaller firms since 1960, and that in many cases the smaller firms have bypassed the large firms.

An interesting phenomenon in our 1966-1967 analysis is that the larger food firms typically have more equity (operate with less borrowed money) and, therefore, have less leverage on profits than do the smaller firms. In fact, the larger returns to net worth of some of the smaller firms in 1966-1967 were partially due to a difference in equity positions between the large firms (over $100 million in assets) and the smaller firms. For example, in the canned and frozen foods industry in 1966-1967 (Table 2.13), the large firms had a greater return on assets but a smaller return on owners' equity than did the average smaller firms. Typically, the larger firms have equity of around 60% while the smaller firms have an equity position of 50-55%.

Certainly the larger firms can obtain capital at the same or lesser costs than the smaller firms. Also, with the U.S. federal corporate income tax system, the cost of interest on loans is a deductible expense. Therefore, if a firm is near the 50% corporate income tax level, the real cost of interest is really only around 1/2 the amount actually paid. Thus, to have an effective leverage position the firm has to make a return on assets only slightly more than 1/2 of the actual cost of borrowed money. Since the larger firms, more typically, are nearer the upper limits of the rate of taxation than the smaller firms, and since they should be able to obtain borrowed funds at the same or lower costs than small firms — why do they maintain a higher equity position which may reflect less return to the owners' interest in the company?

There are at least three possible explanations to this. (1) Management of the larger firms may be more conservative than in the smaller firms. (2) Perhaps the larger firms cannot expand at a rate fast enough to use up retained earnings; that is, the large firms may be unable to explore, screen, analyze, develop prototype systems, and test possible new business ventures at a rate fast enough to use up the undistributed profits. (Although there is a wide range of practices concerning distribution of profits to stockholders, most manufacturing firms seldom distribute over 1/2 the profits to stockholders — the rest are held as retained earnings for business expansion.) There also may be a greater unwieldiness in the management systems of the large firms and they may not be able to react as rapidly to new opportunities as the smaller firms. (3) The FTC rulings on acquisitions and mergers may have prevented expansion of larger firms by this route and the companies have not geared up for internal growth at a rate which would prevent accumulation of undistributed profits.

FINANCIAL OPERATING RATIOS FOR THE
FOOD PROCESSING INDUSTRIES

In the previous sections, financial data were presented on the major industry segments of food processing subdivided into two size classes. However, the total structure of each industry can be better understood with an analysis of several size classes rather than only two. This section will analyze several food processing industries by a detailed analysis of 12 size classes (based on total assets) in each industry.

In one industry — the canning and freezing industry (SIC 203) — I will present aggregate balance sheets and income statements. Then for 12 major industries, I will present some aggregate financial operating ratios (Greig 1968). In each case, 12 asset sizes will be used within each industry.

These data not only provide a more detailed view of the structure of the industry but also provide many operating ratios which can be used as a base to judge the operating characteristics of individual firms. While only 1965-1966 tax year data will be used, they will indicate the depth of financial information that can be developed from publicly available information.

For the federal tax year July 1965-June 1966, 1963 firms classified as "Canners·or Freezers" filed federal income tax returns. These firms had total assets of $3,771,281,000, gross sales or business receipts of $6,367,504,000, and net income after taxes (after deducting losses by those firms having losses) of $187,143,000. Of the 1963 firms, 1303 reported a positive net income while 660 reported losses (Tables 2.14, 2.15, and 2.16).

Of the total net profit after taxes based on total assets, 40% was earned by the 3 largest firms, 55% by the top 7 firms, and 61% by the largest 15 firms. On the average, or in the aggregate, all firms having total assets under $250,000 had net losses. This included 987 firms, or over 1/2 the total number of firms in the

TABLE 2.14

CANNING AND FREEZING INDUSTRY (SIC 2030)
BALANCE SHEETS FOR 1965-1966
ASSET SIZE CLASS ($1000)

	Under 50[1]	50 Under 100	100 Under 250	250 Under 500	500 Under 1000	1000 Under 5000	5000 Under 10,000	10,000 Under 25,000	25,000 Under 50,000	50,000 Under 100,000	100,000 Under 250,000	250,000 and Up	Weighted Average 1963
Total number of firms	346	326	254	288	259	344	43	27	6	2	4	3	660
Firms reporting negative incomes	270	178	51	14	66	36	8	4	1	0	0	0	1963
Average total assets ($1000)	18.4	69.4	174.7	347.7	726.3	2084.3	6928.2	14,099.5	35,071.7	75,610.0	141,668.2	361,914.0	1921.2
Current assets ($1000)	9.0	41.6	100.4	216.0	456.0	1294.8	4292.6	8858.1	21,128.2	47,802.5	81,070.3	203,987.7	1146.3
Current assets (% of total assets)	49.0	60.0	57.5	62.1	62.8	62.1	62.0	62.8	60.2	63.2	57.2	56.3	59.7
Cash (% of total assets)	6.3	6.3	8.9	10.8	4.4	4.9	6.2	3.9	5.7	2.4	2.2	2.5	3.9
Notes and accounts receivable (% of total assets)	21.1	27.2	22.6	15.7	14.5	15.3	16.7	15.2	11.0	13.0	13.9	18.1	15.8
Inventories (% of total assets)	21.4	21.4	22.1	34.2	40.9	38.1	33.6	37.9	40.6	42.2	33.9	33.6	35.8
Investments and govt. obligations (% of total assets)[2]	0.2	5.1	3.9	1.4	2.9	3.8	5.6	5.8	2.8	5.6	7.3	2.2	4.1
Fixed assets ($1000)[2]	9.4	27.8	74.3	131.7	270.3	789.5	2635.6	5241.5	13,943.5	27,807.5	60,598.0	157,899.2	774.8
Fixed assets (% of total assets)	51.0	40.0	42.5	37.9	37.2	37.9	38.0	37.2	39.8	36.8	42.8	43.6	40.3
Land (% of total assets)	2.0	0.8	1.7	4.7	2.4	1.9	2.1	3.0	2.2	0.0	3.6	1.6	2.2
Buildings, equipment and depreciable assets (% of total assets)	34.7	29.8	35.7	25.0	28.1	26.9	29.2	24.7	30.6	25.7	21.8	26.9	26.4
Investments (% of total assets)[3]	0.0	0.4	0.6	3.9	3.6	6.4	4.9	6.4	4.9	9.9	16.1	13.4	9.5
Other assets (% of total assets)	14.3	4.4	4.3	4.1	2.8	2.3	0.7	3.0	2.0	1.1	1.2	1.7	2.0

[1] Not included are 61 firms with zero or negative assets; however these are included in weighted average.
[2] Net fixed assets or fixed assets less depreciation.
[3] Long term investments not included under current assets.

(Continued)

TABLE 2.14 (Continued)

CANNING AND FREEZING INDUSTRY (SIC 2030)
BALANCE SHEETS FOR 1965-1966
ASSET SIZE CLASS ($1000)

	Under 50¹	50 Under 100	100 Under 250	250 Under 500	500 Under 1000	1000 Under 5000	5000 Under 10,000	10,000 Under 25,000	25,000 Under 50,000	50,000 Under 100,000	100,000 Under 250,000	250,000 and Up	Weighted Average
Average total liabilities and net worth ($1000)	18.4	66.3	174.7	347.7	726.3	2084.3	6928.2	14,099.6	35,071.7	75,610.0	141,668.3	361,914.0	1921.2
Average current liabilities ($1000)	6.8	27.8	86.7	104.3	316.6	823.4	2413.5	5083.6	10,923.0	19,493.5	28,971.0	68,542.7	558.2
Average current liabilities (% of total liab.)	36.7	42.0	49.6	30.0	43.6	39.5	34.8	36.1	31.1	25.8	20.4	18.9	29.1
Accounts payable (% of total liabilities)	20.9	28.0	20.4	14.7	10.2	15.7	11.7	13.8	18.7	5.9	8.4	7.6	11.4
Mortgage notes, bonds under 1 yr (% of total liabilities)	13.0	7.6	26.2	11.7	27.9	17.5	16.6	13.9	6.8	15.0	9.4	6.1	12.3
Other current liabilities (% of total liabilities)	2.8	6.4	3.1	3.6	5.4	6.4	6.5	8.4	5.7	4.9	2.7	5.2	5.4
Average long term liabilities ($1000)	11.6	41.5	88.0	243.3	409.0	1260.0	4514.7	9015.0	24,148.7	56,116.5	112,697.3	293,371.3	1362.9
Average long term liabilities (% of total liabilities)	63.3	62.6	50.4	70.0	56.3	60.5	65.2	63.9	68.9	74.2	79.6	81.1	70.9
Loans from stockholders (% of total liabilities)	30.3	13.1	3.3	2.2	1.1	2.6	1.4	0.0	0.0	0.0	0.0	0.0	0.9
Mortgage notes, bonds over 1 yr (% of total liabilities)	14.0	23.6	13.4	8.4	19.0	10.8	7.4	17.4	28.7	25.3	10.6	10.7	13.2
Other liabilities (% of total liabilities)	1.0	0.2	1.1	1.2	1.5	2.1	1.7	1.5	0.9	6.9	3.1	1.2	1.9
Stockholders equity (% of total liabilities)	17.9	25.7	32.6	58.2	34.8	45.0	54.7	45.1	39.2	42.0	65.8	69.1	54.9
Capital stock (% of total liabilities)	95.6	62.0	36.8	23.2	17.7	13.2	14.9	11.5	8.7	8.5	21.1	19.2	16.8
Capital surplus (% of total liabilities)	0.4	2.9	7.6	1.4	2.5	4.2	5.5	7.3	7.2	0.9	13.4	4.1	5.9
Surplus reserves or earned surplus (% of total liabilities)	-78.1	-39.2	-11.8	33.6	14.6	27.6	34.4	26.2	23.3	32.6	31.2	45.8	32.2

TABLE 2.15

CANNING AND FREEZING INDUSTRY (SIC 2030)
INCOME STATEMENTS FOR 1965-1966
ASSET SIZE CLASS ($1000)

	Under 50[1]	50 Under 100	100 Under 250	250 Under 500	500 Under 1000	1000 Under 5000	5000 Under 10,000	10,000 Under 25,000	25,000 Under 50,000	50,000 Under 100,000	100,000 Under 250,000	250,000 and Up	Weighted Average 1963
Total number of firms	346	326	254	288	259	344	43	27	6	2	4	3	660
Firms reporting negative incomes	270	178	51	14	66	36	8	4	6	2	0	0	
Average sales ($1000)	35.4	285.0	465.5	742.9	1402.2	4395.5	11,015.5	27,057.9	57,887.8	114,173.5	197,931.5	480,117.3	3243.8
Average total cost ($1000)	38.0	298.1	466.2	723.1	1308.9	4219.2	10,342.0	25,962.7	55,654.2	109,449.5	185,495.0	434,726.0	3073.6
Cost as % of total costs													
Direct cost of operations and sales	67.8	80.6	77.0	79.1	76.7	81.3	76.6	81.0	78.4	71.8	73.8	70.5	76.7
Compensation of offices	6.4	2.2	4.0	3.0	3.1	1.5	1.2	0.6	0.5	0.2	0.3	0.3	1.1
Repairs	0.4	0.8	0.9	0.3	0.8	0.6	1.2	0.8	1.1	1.6	0.4	1.7	0.9
Bad debts	0.3	0.0	0.1	0.0	0.1	0.1	0.1	0.1	0.1	0.0	0.2	0.0	0.1
Rent paid on business property	1.9	2.2	1.2	0.7	0.6	0.6	0.4	0.6	0.5	0.1	0.7	0.1	0.5
Taxes paid (state and local)	2.3	1.4	1.5	1.9	2.0	1.5	2.0	1.6	1.9	1.7	2.4	2.0	1.9
Interest paid	0.2	0.5	0.7	0.6	1.5	1.0	1.0	1.1	0.7	1.8	0.9	0.6	0.9
Depreciation	3.3	1.3	2.0	1.7	2.0	1.9	2.4	1.8	2.3	2.8	2.5	2.7	2.2
Advertising	4.4	1.5	0.8	0.6	1.4	1.2	3.0	2.1	2.7	4.5	4.1	5.7	3.0
Pensions and annuity plans	0.0	0.0	0.1	0.0	0.2	0.3	0.6	0.2	0.5	0.7	0.6	0.8	0.5
Other deductions	13.1	9.5	11.7	11.9	11.6	10.0	11.4	10.1	11.3	15.0	14.1	15.5	12.3
Total deductions													
Sales minus costs ($1000)	-2.6	-13.0	-0.6	19.8	21.3	176.4	673.5	1095.2	2233.7	4724.0	12,436.5	45,391.3	170.2
Gross income (including losses ($1000)[2]	-2.6	-13.0	-0.6	19.8	21.3	176.4	673.5	1095.2	2233.7	4724.0	12,549.5	46,607.0	172.3
Income subject to federal tax ($1000)[3]	0.4	4.7	9.8	13.5	38.5	157.6	700.0	932.6	2761.2	4723.5	12,359.8	45,975.0	174.1
Federal taxes ($1000)	0.1	1.4	3.0	4.0	14.5	81.9	329.9	435.8	1316.8	2255.0	5828.5	22,281.0	81.1
Net income (including losses) after federal tax	-2.6	-14.3	-3.3	16.2	8.6	110.5	356.5	693.0	985.8	2626.0	6993.5	25,212.7	95.3

[1] Does not include 61 firms with negative assets; however, these are included in weighted average.
[2] Slightly different from "sales minus costs" because of foreign taxable income or losses.
[3] Some individual firms had taxable income, while the weighted average may have been a negative income for the size class as a whole.

TABLE 2.16

CANNING AND FREEZING INDUSTRY (SIC 2030)
FINANCIAL OPERATING RATIOS FOR 1965-1966
ASSET SIZE CLASS ($1000)

	Under 50	50 Under 100	100 Under 250	250 Under 500	500 Under 1000	1000 Under 5000	5000 Under 10,000	10,000 Under 25,000	25,000 Under 50,000	50,000 Under 100,000	100,000 Under 250,000	250,000 and Up	Weighted Average
Total number of firms	346	326	254	288	259	344	43	27	6	2	4	3	1963
Firms reporting negative incomes	270	178	51	14	66	36	8	4	1	0	0	0	660
Average total assets ($1000)	18.4	69.4	174.7	347.7	726.3	2084.3	6928.2	14,099.6	35,071.2	75,610.0	141,668.2	301,914.0	1921
Average stockholders' equity (% of total assets)	17.9	25.7	32.6	58.2	34.8	45.0	54.7	45.1	39.2	42.0	65.8	69.1	54.9
Average net income after tax ($1000)	-2.7	-14.3	-3.3	16.2	8.6	110.4	356.5	693.0	985.8	2626.0	6993.5	25,212.7	95.3
Profits as percent of total assets (%)	-14.4	-20.6	-1.9	4.7	1.2	5.3	5.1	4.9	2.8	3.5	4.9	7.0	5.0
Profits as percent of equity (%)	-80.4	-83.8	-5.8	8.0	3.4	11.8	9.4	10.9	7.2	8.3	7.5	10.1	9.0
Liquidity													
Current assets/ current liabilities	1.3	1.5	1.2	2.1	1.4	1.6	1.8	1.8	1.9	2.5	2.8	3.0	2.1
Leverage													
Total debt/total assets (%)	82.1	75.4	67.4	41.8	65.2	55.0	45.3	54.9	60.8	58.0	34.2	30.9	45.1
Current liabilities/net worth (%)	205.1	163.4	152.3	51.6	125.4	87.7	63.7	80.0	79.5	61.3	31.1	27.4	52.9
Fixed assets/net worth (%)	284.4	142.4	127.7	50.0	95.8	69.1	58.6	68.0	89.0	63.9	40.6	43.6	55.7
Cash velocity (receipts)/ (cash) (govt. security)	30.6	65.3	29.9	18.8	43.5	34.8	18.8	27.5	26.4	63.9	64.7	37.9	33.9
Inventory turnover (sales)/ (inventory)	9.0	19.2	12.0	6.2	4.7	5.5	4.7	5.1	4.1	3.6	4.1	4.0	4.7
Fixed asset turnover (sales)/ (fixed assets)	3.8	10.3	6.3	5.6	5.2	5.6	4.2	5.2	4.2	4.1	3.3	3.0	4.2
Average collection period (days)	39.7	23.8	30.8	26.9	27.3	26.5	38.0	29.0	24.4	31.0	36.1	49.2	34.0
Gross operating margin[1]	-7.3	-4.6	-0.1	2.6	1.5	4.0	6.1	4.0	3.9	4.1	6.3	9.5	5.2
Net operating margin[2]	-7.5	-5.0	-0.7	2.2	0.6	2.5	3.2	2.6	1.7	2.3	3.5	5.3	2.9

[1] Margin above or below direct operating costs.
[2] Margin above or below total costs.

industry. The profits of individual firms in the asset size class "Under $250,000" were outweighed by the losses sustained by other firms in this same size class.

Detailed data on the balance sheets of the 1963 firms in the canning and freezing industry by asset size classes are given in Table 2.14. Included in the Table also is the weighted average balance sheet for all firms in the industry. Assets are subdivided into 4 categories of current assets and 4 categories of fixed or long-run assets. Liabilities are subdivided into 3 categories of current liabilities and 7 categories of long-term liabilities. Each component of assets or liabilities is given as a percent of total assets or total liabilities for ease of comparison between asset size classes and between industry groups.

The income statements, by asset size classes, of the firms in the canning and freezing industry are listed in Table 2.15. Average sales (actually average receipts, as some income other than from sales is included) and the average cost of sales are listed. The cost of operations and sales are subdivided into 12 components. These are given as a percent of total cost of sales. Gross income, income subject to federal income taxes, and net income after taxes (after deducting operating losses of firms with negative income) are all listed by asset size classes. Each column in the Table is the weighted average for all firms in that particular asset size class.

Summaries of financial aspects of these firms may be analyzed by absolute data and also by financial operating ratios. Thirteen financial operating ratios for each size class of firms in the canning and freezing industry are given in Table 2.16. These ratios are as follows. (1) Average stockholders' equity listed as a percentage of total liabilities. (2) Profits as a percentage return, after federal taxes, on total assets. (3) Profits, as a percentage return, after federal taxes, on stockholders' equity. (4) Liquidity — current assets divided by current liabilities. (5) Leverage — total debt divided by total assets. (6) Leverage — current liabilities divided by net worth. (7) Leverage — fixed assets divided by net worth. (8) Cash velocity — annual receipts divided by cash on hand and near cash (government securities). (9) Inventory turnover — annual sales divided by inventory on hand. (10) Fixed asset turnover — annual sales divided by total fixed assets. (11) Average collection period — accounts receivable divided by average daily sales. Daily sales determined by dividing annual sales by 360. (12) Gross operating margin — receipts minus direct operating costs divided by receipts. (13) Net operating margin — receipts minus all costs of sales including indirect costs divided by receipts.

The use of these financial operating ratios will be explained briefly by their use in the canning and freezing industry (Table 2.16). Equity as percent of total assets averaged 54.97% for all the firms, but ranged from 17.92 to 69.14%. In general, equity as a percent of total assets increased as the total asset class size increased.

Profits as a percentage return on total assets and on owners' equity also tended to increase as the size of the firm increased, but there was considerable variation among size classes. The highest return on assets was by the largest size class, i.e., "more than $250,000,000" in assets. But the largest return on equity was in the size class "$1,000,000 to $5,000,000." The size class "$1,000,000 to $5,000,000" in assets will be used to illustrate uses of the financial ratios at a later point.

Liquidity — the ability to pay current liabilities — increased as the size of the firm increased. Current assets were only 1.3 times current liabilities in the smallest firms but averaged 3 times current liabilities in the larger firms.

Leverage — total debts to total assets — decreased as the size of the firm (total assets) increased. For the smallest sized firms, debts were equivalent to 82.1% of total assets, while in the largest sized firms (based on total assets) debts were equivalent to only 30.9% of total assets.

Current liabilities divided by net worth is another leverage measurement. This measures the amount of funds supplied by owners against the amount supplied by current debt. Current liabilities were 205.1% of net worth in the smallest firms but only 27.4% in the largest firms.

Fixed assets to net worth show the extent to which ownership funds are sunk in assets with relatively low turnover. Again, the smallest firms had the highest ratio; this ratio decreased rapidly to the largest firms. Fixed assets were 284.4% of net worth in the smallest sized firms but only 43.6% in the largest sized firms.

A high cash velocity suggests that the cash is being used effectively. However, if the liquidity ratios are weak, a high cash velocity may simply be another indication of the liquidity problem. The high cash velocity of 65.3 for asset size class "$50,000 under $100,000" may be a sign of weakness, while at the same time the cash velocity of 64.7 for size class "$100,000,000 under $250,000,000" may indicate good operating procedures. The cash velocities shown are quite mixed, with little trend by size classes.

Inventory turnover generally decreased as the size of the firm increased. Inventory turnover in the larger firms ranged from 3.6 times per year to 5.5 times a year in the smaller firms. The high inventory turnover in the smaller firms suggests a weak financial position, in that they may be financially unable to maintain a normal stock of raw materials or of finished products.

The fixed asset turnover indicates the above analysis on inventory turnover and cash velocity was probably correct for the smallest sized firms. It should be noted that the small and medium sized firms had a substantially greater fixed asset turnover than did the largest sized firms.

The average collection period tended to be high for small firms, decreased for medium sized firms, and increased again for the largest firms. The average collection period was 34 days for the industry as a whole.

Both gross and net operating margins tended to increase as the size of the firms increased. In both cases, the largest firms had a significant advantage. They had a gross operating margin of 9.45% and a net margin of 5.3% compared to an industry average of 5.25% and 2.94% respectively. It is interesting to note that the net operating margin for the industry as a whole was 2.9% on sales or 2.9¢ per $1.00 of all sales. In all cases, the margins were determined after federal income taxes were considered.

Firms in the asset size class "$1,000,000 to $5,000,000" had the greatest average net return on equity (11.76% after taxes). The financial operating ratios of this size category of firms will be compared briefly to industry averages. First, the liquid assets of the firms were kept working; current assets were 1.6 times current liabilities compared to 2.1 times for the industry as a whole. Second, a substantial amount of total assets were borrowed assets; 55% compared to 45% for the industry as a whole. Thus, leverage was substantial. Third, inventories were kept low. The inventories turned over 5.5 times a year compared to 4.7 times for the industry. Fourth, one of the major keys to profitability was fixed asset turnover. This was 4.1 times compared to an industry average of 3.2 times. Fixed assets were used nearer to capacity than for the average of the industry. Fifth, the average collection period was 26.5 days compared to 34 days for the industry. This showed good collection and accounts receivable management. Finally, although both gross operating margins and net operating margins were less than for the industry as a whole (and substantially less than the largest sized firms) this deficiency was apparently more than made up in the volume of business (measured in asset and inventory turnover) and in management of finances (cash velocity, leverage, and a short collection period). The returns to owners' equity in this size class were 11.8%.

The financial operating ratios presented for the other food processing industries are given in an identical format to that of the canning and freezing industry. These data are presented in Tables 2.17 through 2.28 with no written description.

From these data the managers of almost any food processing business can compare their operations to the industry average of operations of the same asset size class and to different asset size classes. They can also compare operations with other segments of the food processing industry.

It should be noted that when the data on industries are divided into 12 size classes, the largest size class is not usually the most profitable size class. Twelve industries were reported by size classes (Tables 2.16 through 2.28) where there were firms with over $100 million in assets. In 9 of these 12 industries the largest size class was not the most profitable size class based on return on owners' equity. However, there is a great deal of variability among industries in the profitability of the smaller size classes. Aggregating the data for all the industries into 12 size classes does show the largest size class to be most profitable (Table 2.28). However, the 416 firms with assets between $5 million and $25 million were more profitable than the 34 firms with assets of between $100 million and $250 million.

CONGLOMERATION, TECHNOCRACY, AND PRODUCT COMPETITION

So far in our discussion of the structure of the food processing industry, we have not touched the subject of conglomeration or diversification. It would appear that each firm can be classified fairly easily by its principal product field;

TABLE 2.17

MEAT PRODUCTS INDUSTRY (SIC 2010)
FINANCIAL OPERATING RATIOS FOR 1965-1966
ASSET SIZE CLASS ($1000)

	Under 50	50 Under 100	100 Under 250	250 Under 500	500 Under 1000	1000 Under 5000	5000 Under 10,000	10,000 Under 25,000	25,000 Under 50,000	50,000 Under 100,000	100,000 Under 250,000	250,000 and Over	Weighted Average
Total number of firms	617	422	485	317	383	372	34	14	5	5	1	2	2678
Firms reporting negative incomes	395	200	135	86	25	69	6	0	1	3	0	0	935
Average total assets ($1000)	24.3	72.7	169.1	351.1	753.2	1921.3	6590.3	14,053.2	32,763.4	75,673.8	149,148.0	623,417.5	1344.7
Average stockholders' equity (% of total assets)	-21.4	61.6	56.6	47.8	51.1	52.0	54.6	63.1	55.1	58.7	53.3	61.5	56.4
Average net income after tax ($1000)	-1.8	-3.4	8.5	9.1	47.0	71.8	288.2	795.2	808.4	-1293.0	5730.0	9563.5	34.3
Profits as percent of total assets (%)	-7.4	-4.7	5.0	2.6	6.2	3.7	4.4	5.7	2.5	-1.7	3.8	1.5	2.6
Profits as percent of equity (%)	—	-12.2	8.8	5.4	12.2	7.2	8.0	9.0	4.5	-2.9	7.2	2.5	4.5
Liquidity Current assets/ current liabilities	0.7	1.6	2.2	1.8	1.9	1.8	1.9	2.7	2.1	2.0	1.7	3.3	2.2
Leverage Total debt/total assets (%)	121.4	61.6	43.4	52.2	48.9	48.0	45.4	36.9	44.9	41.3	46.7	38.5	43.6
Current liabilities/ net worth (%)	-436.2	91.4	51.2	86.9	61.5	64.1	57.6	30.0	49.1	51.5	60.7	27.9	46.9
Fixed assets/net worth (%)	-144.8	102.7	55.7	55.9	74.0	63.4	67.2	57.0	65.9	62.0	65.5	58.9	62.3
Cash velocity (receipts)/ (cash) (govt. security)	64.1	58.7	58.2	58.1	133.7	68.2	71.4	54.9	41.1	82.3	64.4	126.7	80.6
Inventory turnover (sales)/ (inventory)	52.0	34.2	41.5	26.2	43.9	33.3	30.1	18.6	26.1	21.8	37.0	16.3	24.6
Fixed asset turnover (sales)/ (fixed assets)	24.1	11.3	16.7	22.9	20.0	16.7	15.3	9.0	11.6	13.8	15.0	10.0	13.5
Average collection period (days)	16.3	19.0	19.2	19.0	13.7	15.8	14.8	15.2	15.8	14.8	11.2	19.9	16.4
Gross operating margin[1]	-0.8	-0.8	1.0	0.8	-1.1	1.1	1.4	2.2	1.0	0.0	0.9	0.6	0.9
Net operating margin[2]	-0.9	-0.9	0.8	0.4	0.7	0.6	0.7	1.3	0.5	-0.3	0.6	0.3	0.4

[1] Margin above or below direct operating costs.
[2] Margin above or below total costs.

TABLE 2.18

GRAIN MILL PRODUCTS INDUSTRY (SIC 2040)
FINANCIAL OPERATING RATIOS FOR 1965-1966

ASSET SIZE CLASS ($1000)

	Under 50	50 Under 100	100 Under 250	250 Under 500	500 Under 1000	1000 Under 5000	5000 Under 10,000	10,000 Under 25,000	25,000 Under 50,000	50,000 Under 100,000	100,000 Under 250,000	250,000 and Over	Weighted Average
Total number of firms	289	296	769	292	238	200	27	15	12	2	8	3	2217
Firms reporting negative incomes	131	116	157	52	14	48	4	1	2	0	2	0	540
Average total assets ($1000)	22.5	74.2	148.3	359.4	731.7	2056.6	7734.1	15,056.1	35,157.4	63,589.5	154,895.5	330,528.7	1825.6
Average stockholders' equity (% of total assets)	12.7	50.6	47.9	50.9	53.0	55.8	68.1	63.8	54.8	54.5	59.3	59.3	58.1
Average net income after tax ($1000)	1.7	3.7	7.4	8.2	57.9	47.9	379.8	705.9	1477.8	2425.0	8525.8	25,598.0	101.5
Profits as percent of total assets (%)	7.7	4.9	5.0	2.3	7.9	2.3	4.9	4.7	4.2	3.8	5.5	7.7	5.5
Profits as percent of equity (%)	60.9	9.8	10.4	4.5	14.9	4.2	7.2	7.3	7.7	7.0	9.3	13.1	9.6
Liquidity Current assets/ current liabilities	2.9	3.0	1.6	2.1	2.0	2.1	2.6	2.4	1.9	1.1	1.8	2.1	1.9
Leverage Total debt/total assets (%)	87.3	49.4	52.1	49.1	47.0	44.2	31.9	36.2	45.2	45.5	40.7	40.7	41.9
Current liabilities/ net worth (%)	157.4	47.6	68.0	57.4	56.4	54.5	32.8	40.1	56.4	71.3	48.4	32.0	45.9
Fixed assets/net worth (%)	268.0	58.4	91.5	65.1	70.3	58.9	42.4	52.5	54.4	42.4	56.7	75.0	61.3
Cash velocity (receipts)/ (cash) (govt. security)	38.8	29.4	39.9	31.4	31.8	42.9	30.2	29.5	17.0	142.7	14.2	37.8	25.0
Inventory turnover (sales)/ (inventory)	28.9	13.3	18.0	26.7	15.4	14.3	12.1	9.0	8.4	10.4	9.1	10.9	11.2
Fixed asset turnover (sales)/ (fixed assets)	16.1	9.1	6.6	8.6	7.2	7.4	6.6	5.5	4.2	3.5	3.4	2.9	4.3
Average collection period (days)	9.5	50.6	27.7	32.4	33.3	41.3	29.7	41.3	44.6	28.3	43.5	27.7	36.2
Gross operating margin[1]	1.3	2.4	2.0	0.9	3.1	1.7	3.3	3.8	4.4	3.3	5.7	18.3	4.4
Net operating margin[2]	1.2	1.8	1.5	0.6	2.6	0.8	1.7	2.1	2.3	1.8	3.3	4.3	2.6

[1] Margin above or below direct operating costs.
[2] Margin above or below total costs.

TABLE 2.19

DAIRY PRODUCTS INDUSTRY (SIC 2020)
FINANCIAL OPERATING RATIOS FOR 1965-1966
ASSET SIZE CLASS ($1000)

	Under 50	50 Under 100	100 Under 250	250 Under 500	500 Under 1000	1000 Under 5000	5000 Under 10,000	10,000 Under 25,000	25,000 Under 50,000	50,000 Under 100,000	100,000 Under 250,000	250,000 and Over	Weighted Average
Total number of firms	583	574	707	477	314	343	38	9	4	2	5	2	3185
Firms reporting negative incomes	253	315	211	187	54	74	4	0	1	0	0	0	1202
Average total assets ($1000)	28.5	77.6	153.2	341.9	648.1	2049.8	6557.6	14,918.9	28,585.8	69,935.0	203,023.4	760,117.0	1384.9
Average stockholders' equity (% of total assets)	34.1	48.5	53.6	51.4	42.7	57.3	55.9	49.3	59.4	62.9	56.1	59.0	58.2
Average net income after tax ($1000)	-0.03	-1.3	0.5	3.6	12.6	73.3	267.7	447.4	1633.0	3338.5	11,632.6	53,008.5	69.5
Profits as percent of total assets (%)	-0.1	-1.7	0.4	1.1	1.9	3.6	4.1	3.0	5.7	4.8	5.7	7.0	5.0
Profits as percent of equity (%)	-0.3	-3.5	0.7	2.1	4.6	6.2	7.3	6.1	9.6	7.6	10.2	11.8	8.6
Liquidity Current assets/ current liabilities	1.1	1.2	1.6	1.6	1.5	1.7	1.7	2.1	2.2	1.5	2.5	2.7	2.1
Leverage Total debt/total assets (%)	65.9	51.5	46.4	37.6	57.3	42.7	44.1	50.7	40.6	37.1	43.9	35.7	41.8
Current liabilities/ Net worth (%)	116.8	68.1	56.2	60.1	74.2	52.8	53.8	41.1	40.7	43.6	38.6	29.5	40.3
Fixed assets/net worth (%)	153.4	121.7	83.5	82.8	105.4	68.7	76.2	89.0	66.4	70.6	50.3	66.4	65.3
Cash velocity (receipts)/ (cash) (govt. security)	24.3	37.6	29.5	27.6	39.5	27.9	30.1	31.6	28.3	32.1	27.6	19.4	25.7
Inventory turnover (sales)/ (inventory)	87.0	39.3	38.2	35.1	28.1	29.1	24.7	25.4	26.2	23.3	10.4	9.2	14.7
Fixed asset turnover (sales)/ (fixed assets)	7.8	5.7	7.5	6.3	5.8	5.7	5.0	3.6	4.4	4.0	4.5	3.6	4.6
Average collection period (days)	15.8	21.9	20.9	31.3	30.1	36.0	40.3	45.4	56.6	31.1	37.0	28.7	33.2
Gross operating margin[1]	0.1	-0.3	0.3	0.6	0.9	2.1	2.8	2.4	4.2	3.4	4.6	6.3	3.7
Net operating margin[2]	-0.02	-0.5	0.1	0.3	0.6	1.3	1.6	1.4	2.7	2.0	2.6	3.6	2.1

[1] Margin above or below direct operating costs.
[2] Margin above or below total costs.

TABLE 2.20

BAKERY PRODUCTS INDUSTRY (SIC 2050)
FINANCIAL OPERATING RATIOS 1965-1966
ASSET SIZE CLASS ($1000)

	Under 50	50 Under 100	100 Under 250	250 Under 500	500 Under 1000	1000 Under 5000	5000 Under 10,000	10,000 Under 25,000	25,000 Under 50,000	50,000 Under 100,000	100,000 Under 250,000	250,000 and Over	Weighted Average
Total number of firms	888	376	308	309	173	248	9	10	3	4	3	1	2377
Firms reporting negative incomes	366	178	129	51	42	35	2	1	0	1	0	0	846
Average total assets ($1000)	22.0	74.1	162.9	341.0	742.2	2013.9	6884.1	14,134.2	40,408.0	62,331.8	132,380.0	340,330.0	901.2
Average stockholders' equity (% of total assets)	38.6	42.6	58.5	48.6	70.8	63.0	56.3	73.1	57.7	54.6	71.2	67.8	63.6
Average net income after taxes ($1000)	-0.6	-1.9	-1.2	21.6	-5.4	112.4	208.7	956.2	1616.0	817.3	5741.3	37,385.0	44.6
Profits as percent of Total assets (%)	-2.5	-2.6	-0.7	6.3	-0.7	5.6	3.0	6.8	4.0	1.3	4.3	11.0	5.0
Profits as percent of equity (%)	-6.6	-6.0	-1.2	13.0	-1.0	8.9	5.4	9.3	6.9	2.4	6.1	16.2	7.8
Liquidity Current assets/current liabilities	1.1	1.1	1.8	1.4	2.1	1.8	1.8	2.5	0.9	2.2	1.8	3.9	1.9
Leverage Total debt/total assets (%)	61.4	57.4	41.5	51.4	29.2	37.0	43.7	26.9	42.3	45.4	28.8	32.2	36.4
Current liabilities/net worth (%)	106.2	76.2	47.8	64.0	29.5	35.3	38.8	19.1	58.5	34.3	26.3	17.0	32.0
Fixed assets/net worth (%)	133.1	134.5	79.0	100.4	68.1	82.7	78.3	72.6	107.4	104.1	84.7	48.0	73.5
Cash velocity (receipts)/(cash) (govt. security)	42.5	42.0	16.1	38.0	19.1	21.7	21.1	16.0	51.1	21.5	23.9	17.7	22.6
Inventory turnover (sales)/(inventory)	39.4	28.0	23.1	27.8	36.2	27.8	32.2	16.9	19.1	29.8	15.9	8.2	20.2
Fixed asset turnover (sales)/(fixed assets)	9.2	5.4	6.2	5.9	5.2	4.4	3.6	3.0	3.0	4.8	2.3	2.9	4.0
Average collection period (days)	10.7	15.1	13.9	22.0	19.6	21.2	31.1	16.8	23.7	19.5	17.4	14.8	18.9
Gross operating margin[1]	-0.3	-0.5	0.1	2.6	1.4	3.9	2.8	5.8	3.3	1.0	3.2	12.7	3.7
Net operating margin[2]	-0.5	-0.7	-0.2	1.9	-0.2	2.1	1.4	3.4	1.9	0.5	2.1	6.8	2.0

[1] Margin above or below direct operating costs.
[2] Margin above or below total costs.

TABLE 2.21

BOTTLED SOFT DRINKS AND FLAVORINGS INDUSTRY (SIC 2086)
FINANCIAL OPERATING RATIOS FOR 1965-1966
ASSET SIZE CLASS ($1000)

	Under 50	50 Under 100	100 Under 250	250 Under 500	500 Under 1000	1000 Under 5000	5000 Under 10,000	10,000 Under 25,000	25,000 Under 50,000	50,000 Under 100,000	100,000 Under 250,000	250,000 and Over	Weighted Average
Total number of firms	494	307	790	574	302	232	33	12	3	2		2	2777
Firms reporting negative incomes	251	137	125	55	26	0	0	0	0	0		0	641
Average total assets ($1000)	25.1	67.6	171.4	341.3	715.2	1963.6	6904.9	13,924.7	27,591.0	86,323.0		365,226.5	870.3
Average stockholders' equity (% of total assets)	44.0	65.3	48.4	55.0	47.2	57.1	72.4	56.4	57.7	48.6		70.0	60.2
Average net income after tax ($1000)	2.1	0.3	11.5	25.5	34.2	114.2	587.5	1134.9	3380.3	9100.0		46,939.0	78.4
Profits as percent of total assets (%)	8.2	0.4	6.7	7.5	4.8	5.8	8.5	8.2	12.3	10.5		12.9	9.0
Profits as percent of equity (%)	18.6	0.6	13.9	13.6	10.1	10.2	11.8	14.4	21.2	21.7		18.4	15.0
Liquidity Current assets/ current liabilities	2.0	2.4	1.5	1.7	1.7	1.9	2.1	2.5	1.9	1.4		2.8	2.0
Leverage Total debt/total assets (%)	56.0	34.7	51.6	45.0	52.8	42.9	27.6	43.6	42.3	51.4		30.0	39.8
Current liabilities/net worth (%)	81.6	32.5	54.5	42.7	55.9	38.7	19.3	29.6	43.5	89.7		23.1	35.8
Fixed assets/net worth (%)	64.1	71.1	118.6	103.3	102.6	93.2	89.0	82.6	75.3	67.9		43.8	74.9
Cash velocity (receipts)/ (cash) (govt. security)	11.8	11.3	23.3	24.7	21.7	16.3	17.8	12.7	6.5	11.1		13.9	15.3
Inventory turnover (sales)/ (inventory)	21.6	12.4	15.0	13.1	9.5	13.0	17.9	16.0	14.3	9.1		8.9	11.6
Fixed asset turnover (sales)/ (fixed assets)	11.7	4.4	3.3	3.0	3.4	2.7	2.0	2.6	3.0	4.0		2.5	2.8
Average collection period (days)	27.7	22.2	28.2	33.6	31.9	39.1	21.1	38.7	22.6	41.1		48.8	37.0
Gross operating margin[1]	3.1	0.6	4.2	5.1	4.0	6.3	10.3	9.5	13.8	12.9		14.8	9.2
Net operating margin[2]	2.5	0.2	3.4	4.1	2.6	3.7	6.0	5.3	7.7	6.9		9.5	5.7

[1] Margin above or below direct operating costs.
[2] Margin above or below total costs.

TABLE 2.22

THE VEGETABLE AND ANIMAL OILS INDUSTRY (SIC 2091)
FINANCIAL OPERATING RATIOS FOR 1965-1966

ASSET SIZE CLASS ($1000)

	Under 50	50 Under 100	100 Under 250	250 Under 500	500 Under 1000	1000 Under 5000	5000 Under 10,000	10,000 Under 25,000	25,000 Under 50,000	50,000 Under 100,000	100,000 Under 250,000	250,000 and Over	Weighted Average
Number of firms	51	72	75	115	75	115	18	7	3	1	2	1	535
Firms reporting negative incomes	26	25	37	0	0	27	7	1	1	0	0	0	124
Average total assets ($1000)	36.3	62.8	171.7	373.3	671.2	2050.1	6476.0	14,553.9	32,070.3	5446.0	157,497.5	460,084.0	2789.7
Average stockholders' equity (% of total assets)	16.4	48.8	60.8	66.9	74.1	62.5	54.8	60.8	43.7	37.4	54.8	49.6	54.5
Average net income after tax ($1000)	−1.0	10.1	14.4	45.0	71.4	113.3	272.4	786.1	−48.3	1221.0	4247.5	19,529.0	121.2
Profits as percent of total assets (%)	−2.7	16.0	8.4	12.1	10.6	5.5	4.2	5.4	−0.2	2.2	2.7	4.2	4.3
Profits as percent of equity (%)	−16.4	32.8	13.8	18.0	14.3	8.8	7.7	8.9	−0.3	6.0	4.9	8.6	8.0
Liquidity													
Current assets/current liabilities	0.9	1.2	1.9	2.9	2.4	2.3	2.4	1.8	1.8	1.7	2.3	6.3	2.8
Leverage													
Total debt/total assets (%)	83.6	51.2	39.2	33.1	25.9	37.5	45.2	39.2	56.3	62.6	45.2	50.4	45.5
Current liabilities/net worth (%)	509.2	71.5	48.8	23.8	32.9	34.5	43.9	50.9	83.2	95.0	49.2	23.6	40.5
Fixed assets/net worth (%)	75.3	111.4	45.9	63.7	44.3	70.1	58.4	60.1	69.3	72.0	54.3	40.3	55.2
Cash velocity (receipts)/(cash) (govt. security)	131.3	26.1	15.4	11.0	12.6	17.3	50.1	20.2	31.9	12.0	74.2	13.0	23.2
Inventory turnover (sales)/(inventory)	25.3	16.1	25.4	14.6	185.3	12.9	11.7	12.9	8.2	9.9	9.6	4.1	8.9
Fixed asset turnover (sales)/(fixed assets)	36.5	6.5	6.5	3.6	8.0	4.7	5.8	5.2	5.9	1.2	8.3	3.9	5.5
Average collection period (days)	12.6	2.6	25.6	28.3	23.7	25.5	46.0	37.5	36.9	324.5	24.7	45.2	34.5
Gross operating margin[1]	−0.1	4.3	4.1	9.4	5.1	3.9	3.2	3.9	0.5	7.3	1.4	5.8	3.4
Net operating margin[2]	−0.3	4.2	2.8	6.3	3.1	2.4	1.7	2.3	−0.1	4.2	0.8	3.7	2.0

[1] Margin above or below direct operating costs.
[2] Margin above or below total costs.

TABLE 2.23

SUGAR PROCESSING INDUSTRY (SIC 2060)
FINANCIAL OPERATING RATIOS FOR 1965-1966
ASSET SIZE CLASS ($1000)

	Under 50	50 Under 100	100 Under 250	250 Under 500	500 Under 1000	1000 Under 5000	5000 Under 10,000	10,000 Under 25,000	25,000 Under 50,000	50,000 Under 100,000	100,000 Under 250,000	250,000 and Over	Weighted Average
Total number of firms	39			13	23	27	9	13	7	6	3	1	141
Firms reporting negative incomes	39			13	13	8	2	2	1				80
Average total assets ($1000)				467.6	770.8	2337.	8846.7	17,072.8	36,698.3	76,286.3	109,129.3	270,659.0	1266.0
Average stockholders' equity (% of total assets)				11.2	37.3	59.8	57.6	60.1	54.4	54.8	68.7	48.0	57.0
Average net income after tax ($1000)				−54.1	33.5	53.8	291.4	843.3	817.6	2061.2	7045.7	12,404.0	471.9
Profits as percent of total assets (%)				−11.6	4.3	2.3	3.3	4.9	2.2	2.7	6.5	4.6	3.9
Profits as percent of equity (%)				−103.7	11.7	3.8	5.7	8.2	4.1	4.9	9.4	9.6	6.9
Liquidity Current assets/current liabilities				0.7	1.5	1.7	1.8	1.8	2.1	1.4	2.5	2.1	1.8
Leverage Total debt/total assets (%)				88.8	62.7	40.2	42.4	39.9	45.6	45.2	31.3	52.0	43.0
Current liabilities/ net worth (%)				589.1	99.2	45.7	44.5	31.4	38.7	51.6	23.3	32.4	37.9
Fixed assets/net worth (%)				481.6	60.0	84.6	85.6	90.8	86.7	95.8	50.2	126.2	86.4
Cash velocity (receipts)/ (cash) (govt. security)				77.3	10.5	19.9	14.1	31.3	12.9	29.8	34.3	43.6	24.6
Inventory turnover (sales)/ (inventory)				16.5	6.2	10.8	3.9	9.8	8.2	3.4	3.9	9.8	6.0
Fixed asset turnover (sales)/ (fixed assets)				6.5	4.0	3.3	1.6	2.2	2.6	1.5	1.4	2.6	2.0
Average collection period (days)				21.6	12.4	37.8	42.9	32.0	27.4	35.6	39.1	22.1	30.5
Gross operating margin[1]				−3.3	4.4	2.1	7.8	5.4	3.8	5.5	11.5	4.6	5.5
Net operating margin[2]				−3.3	2.4	1.3	3.7	3.4	1.5	3.0	7.6	2.6	3.1

[1] Margin above or below direct operating costs.
[2] Margin above or below total costs.

TABLE 2.24

MALT LIQUORS AND MALT INDUSTRY (SIC 2082)
FINANCIAL OPERATING RATIOS FOR 1965-1966
ASSET SIZE CLASS ($1000)

	Under 50	50 Under 100	100 Under 250	250 Under 500	500 Under 1000	1000 Under 5000	5000 Under 10,000	10,000 Under 25,000	25,000 Under 50,000	50,000 Under 100,000	100,000 Under 250,000	250,000 and Over	Weighted Average
Total number of firms	25	25	38	25	50	32	5	21	9	7	4	1	269
Firms reporting negative incomes	25	25	25	25	25	13	0	2	1	3	0	0	170
Average total assets ($1000)	46.7	76.0	120.7	370.8	680.3	2215.2	6240.6	15,160.9	33,893.3	67,542.0	141,689.5	301,236.0	7868.9
Average stockholders' equity (% of total assets)	-19.6	25.6	24.9	83.6	78.8	59.0	75.6	71.6	61.3	49.4	73.3	65.6	64.4
Average net income after tax ($1000)	-1.0	-44.5	-10.2	-18.6	-4.5	49.9	354.6	747.9	1259.2	1498.9	10,823.0	22,262.0	396.3
Profits as percent of total assets (%)	-2.1	-58.6	-8.5	-5.0	-0.7	2.3	5.7	4.9	3.7	2.2	7.6	7.4	5.0
Profits as percent of equity (%)	-10.9	-228.6	-34.1	-6.0	-0.8	3.8	7.5	6.9	6.1	4.5	10.4	11.3	7.8
Liquidity Current assets/ current liabilities	0.9	0.2	1.6	2.6	2.3	2.2	2.4	3.3	1.9	1.7	2.5	2.2	2.2
Leverage Total debt/total assets (%)	119.6	74.4	75.1	16.4	21.2	41.0	24.4	28.4	38.7	50.6	26.7	34.4	35.6
Current liabilities/ net worth (%)	-188.6	290.7	131.5	16.2	23.5	40.2	22.3	19.7	38.2	39.2	19.7	21.7	26.8
Fixed assets/net worth (%)	-343.2	325.9	190.3	72.6	75.4	71.5	64.9	62.2	79.7	120.4	82.2	87.6	82.2
Cash velocity (receipts)/ (cash) (govt. security)	35.3	3.8	11.4	20.2	12.1	17.8	12.1	5.9	9.6	26.2	20.5	15.2	13.6
Inventory turnover (sales)/ (inventory)	12.9	12.9	110.0	26.0	21.0	10.9	14.0	13.2	23.5	19.3	13.6	14.9	16.2
Fixed asset turnover (sales)/ (fixed assets)	4.6	0.8	10.3	2.2	3.4	4.9	3.2	3.0	3.2	2.7	2.9	2.7	2.9
Average collection period (days)	0.0	0.0	3.7	24.3	22.9	20.2	18.7	11.8	27.2	24.9	32.6	14.3	22.8
Gross operating margin[1]	-0.7	-84.4	-0.7	-3.5	-0.2	8.1	5.5	5.8	4.4	2.9	8.1	7.4	5.4
Net operating margin[2]	-0.7	-91.8	-1.7	-3.5	-0.3	1.0	3.0	3.0	2.0	1.2	4.6	4.0	2.8

[1] Margin above or below direct operating costs.
[2] Margin above or below total costs.

TABLE 2.25

DISTILLED, RECTIFIED AND BLENDED LIQUORS, EXCEPT BRANDY (SIC 2085)
FINANCIAL OPERATING RATIOS FOR 1965-1966
ASSET SIZE CLASS ($1000)

	Under 50	50 Under 100	100 Under 250	250 Under 500	500 Under 1000	1000 Under 5000	5000 Under 10,000	10,000 Under 25,000	25,000 Under 50,000	50,000 Under 100,000	100,000 Under 250,000	250,000 and Over	Weighted Average
Total number of firms					50	31	13	6	2	4	3	3	113
Firms reporting negative incomes					12	0	0	1	0	0	1	0	14
Average total assets ($1000)					691.6	2769.0	7391.7	14,698.7	38,318.5	66,455.8	169,006.0	632,781.7	27,013.5
Average stockholders' equity (% of total assets)					30.4	38.7	53.1	35.2	70.6	54.8	53.5	49.1	50.1
Average net income after tax ($1000)					35.1	129.4	286.5	744.0	3637.5	3907.5	3927.0	16,099.3	858.0
Profits as percent of total assets (%)					5.1	4.7	3.9	5.1	9.5	5.9	2.3	2.5	3.2
Profits as percent of equity (%)					16.7	12.1	7.3	14.4	13.4	10.7	4.3	5.2	6.3
Liquidity													
Current assets/current liabilities					1.9	1.8	2.9	1.8	4.9	4.0	2.8	2.2	2.4
Leverage													
Total debt/total assets (%)					69.6	61.3	46.9	64.6	29.4	45.2	46.5	50.9	49.9
Current liabilities/net worth (%)					119.5	128.6	53.3	134.7	23.3	38.0	28.7	58.8	53.5
Fixed assets/net worth (%)					106.3	27.9	32.9	36.6	26.1	21.7	36.6	42.4	38.5
Cash velocity (receipts)/(cash) (govt. security)					206.2	41.8	14.7	70.6	26.4	19.7	49.3	25.5	29.7
Inventory turnover (sales)/(inventory)					7.1	5.3	2.4	5.6	4.0	2.6	6.6	3.1	3.7
Fixed asset turnover (sales)/(fixed assets)					9.5	20.1	6.9	18.0	9.2	7.8	2.9	2.4	3.3
Average collection period (days)					25.3	45.8	47.1	42.1	46.0	59.2	34.0	114.0	75.2
Gross operating margin[1]					1.8	3.2	5.1	3.6	9.6	8.1	3.0	4.9	4.7
Net operating margin[2]					1.7	1.8	3.0	2.0	5.0	4.3	1.4	2.8	2.6

[1] Margin above or below direct operating costs.
[2] Margin above or below total costs.

TABLE 2.26

WINES, BRANDY AND BRANDY SPIRITS (SIC 2084)
FINANCIAL OPERATING RATIOS FOR 1965-1966
ASSET SIZE CLASS ($1000)

	Under 50	50 Under 100	100 Under 250	250 Under 500	500 Under 1000	1000 Under 5000	5000 Under 10,000	10,000 Under 25,000	25,000 Under 50,000	50,000 Under 100,000	100,000 Under 250,000	250,000 and Over	Weighted Average
Total number of firms	25	25	38		23	61	2	4	1	1		1	180
Firms reporting negative incomes	25	0	0		0	30	0	0	0	1			56
Average total assets ($1000)	30.6	78.2	18.2		557.4	1593.3	5613.5	19,903.5	35,186.0	61,336.0			1705.6
Average stockholders' equity (% of total assets)	19.6	45.4	31.0		46.1	34.1	46.5	61.7	51.2	0.0			37.3
Average net income after tax ($1000)	-2.1	5.1	4.3		28.1	12.6	201.5	1521.8	1339.0	0.0			44.1
Profits as percent of total assets (%)	-6.9	6.5	23.6		5.0	-0.8	3.6	7.6	3.8	0.0			2.6
Profits as percent of equity (%)	-35.3	14.3	7.6		10.9	-2.3	7.7	12.4	7.4	7.4			6.9
Liquidity													
Current assets/current liabilities	1.6	2.1	1.3		1.7	1.3	1.6	2.4	2.8	2.6			1.8
Leverage													
Total debt/total assets (%)	81.0	54.6	689.9		53.9	69.9	53.5	38.3	48.8	100.0			62.7
Current liabilities/net worth (%)	297.3	80.0	143.3		76.2	132.3	107.8	34.3	49.0	49.0			83.6
Fixed assets/net worth (%)	45.3	54.8	133.4		81.0	87.3	44.2	63.5	54.9	54.9			97.1
Cash velocity (receipts)/ (cash) (govt. security)	63.0	45.8	49.6		61.2	23.7	109.8	15.5	28.8	89.7			28.8
Inventory turnover (sales)/ (inventory)	1.3	4.6	2.2		4.1	3.5	4.4	3.1	4.4	4.9			3.8
Fixed asset turnover (sales)/ (fixed assets)	12.0	11.9	1.5		5.1	3.0	8.9	1.9	4.8	2.7			2.9
Average collection period (days)	22.4	4.7	55.2		14.4	58.6	64.0	44.2	79.7	47.1			52.3
Gross operating margin[1]	-6.5	2.6	3.6		3.0	0.7	2.8	14.3	4.5	0.0			4.0
Net operating margin[2]	-6.5	2.2	2.9		2.5	-0.7	1.9	8.1	2.6	0.0			2.1

[1] Margin above or below direct operating costs,
[2] Margin above or below total costs.

TABLE 2.27

FOOD AND KINDRED PRODUCTS NOT OTHERWISE ALLOCABLE (SIC 2099)
FINANCIAL OPERATING RATIOS FOR 1965-1966
ASSET SIZE CLASS ($1000)

	Under 50	50 Under 100	100 Under 250	250 Under 500	500 Under 1000	1000 Under 5000	5000 Under 10,000	10,000 Under 25,000	25,000 Under 50,000	50,000 Under 100,000	100,000 Under 250,000	250,000 and Over	Weighted Average
Total number of firms	33	1	13				2			1	1	1	52
Firms reporting negative incomes	0	1	0				0			0	0	0	1
Average total assets ($1000)	21.3	183.0	311.1				5994.0			79,688.0	181,003.0	725,379.0	19,288.2
Average stockholders' equity	41.6	2.5	95.0				56.7			71.0	49.2	75.1	69.9
Average net income after tax (% of total assets)	2.8	-8.0	16.4				1154.0			4984.0	1910.0	90,252.0	1918.3
Profits as percent of total assets (%)	13.1	-4.4	5.3				19.3			6.3	1.1	12.4	9.9
Profits as percent of equity (%)	31.5	-200.0	5.5				34.0			8.8	2.1	16.6	14.2
Liquidity Current assets/current liabilities	3.1	1.2	5.1				1.6			2.7	3.0	2.9	2.9
Leverage Total debt/total asset (%)	59.1	97.8	5.0				43.3			29.0	50.8	24.9	30.1
Current liabilities/net worth (%)	68.5	1600.0	3.3				72.4			19.6	37.0	27.7	28.6
Fixed assets/net worth (%)	31.8	2000.0	88.9				57.2			34.3	70.9	45.3	48.0
Cash velocity (receipts)/(cash) (govt. security)	34.6	133.5	3.6				23.0			17.3	60.2	25.6	27.8
Inventory turnover (sales)/(inventory)	13.5	13.7	34.4				83.2			10.5	9.6	6.2	7.0
Fixed asset turnover (sales)/(fixed assets)	27.2	5.0	0.5				12.9			2.0	4.5	4.7	4.4
Average collection period (days)	49.8	22.2	13.2				35.9			33.6	47.1	36.2	38.2
Gross operating margin[1]	3.6	-1.5	13.1				8.3			9.0	0.8	12.1	9.6
Net operating margin[2]	3.6	-1.5	12.4				4.5			4.9	0.5	6.6	5.3

[1] Margin above or below direct operating costs.
[2] Margin above or below total costs.

TABLE 2.28

ALL FOOD PROCESSING
FINANCIAL OPERATING RATIOS FOR 1965-1966
ASSET SIZE CLASS ($1000)

	Under 50	50 Under 100	100 Under 250	250 Under 500	500 Under 1000	1000 Under 5000	5000 Under 10,000	10,000 Under 25,000	25,000 Under 50,000	50,000 Under 100,000	100,000 Under 250,000	250,000 and Over	Weighted Average
Total number of firms	3389	2423	3465	2423	1890	2005	233	183	55	37	34	20	16,488
Firms reporting negative incomes	1781	1174	871	483	277	366	33	12	8	8	3	0	5269
Average total assets ($1000)	23.9	73.0	159.5	347.9	713.3	2021.9	6937.8	14,898.5	34,254.1	70,552.2	154,835.4	478,544.2	1823.4
Average stockholders' equity (% of total assets)	22.1	45.0	50.0	53.2	49.8	54.1	59.6	58.7	54.7	52.5	61.0	60.4	57.7
Average net income after tax ($1000)	-0.3	-2.7	5.5	15.4	29.4	86.3	354.3	799.7	1358.8	2066.9	77,621.0	30,079.2	90.5
Profits as percent of total assets (%)	-1.3	-3.8	3.4	4.4	4.1	4.3	5.1	5.4	4.0	2.9	5.0	6.3	5.0
Profits as percent of equity (%)	-6.0	-8.4	6.8	8.3	8.3	7.9	8.6	9.1	7.3	5.6	8.2	10.4	8.6
Liquidity Current assets/current liabilities	1.1	1.6	1.6	1.8	1.8	1.8	2.0	2.2	1.9	1.9	2.3	2.7	2.1
Leverage Total debt/total assets(%)	77.9	55.3	50.5	44.6	50.1	45.9	40.4	41.3	45.3	47.5	39.0	38.8	42.3
Current liabilities/net worth (%)	219.1	72.1	62.1	55.4	61.8	56.6	44.9	40.1	49.7	49.8	35.6	32.3	42.1
Fixed assets/net worth (%)	187.3	104.9	90.3	80.5	82.1	71.8	65.7	67.7	71.6	79.3	2.0	55.8	63.9
Cash velocity (receipts)/(cash) (govt. security)	33.0	35.8	30.8	30.5	42.5	33.7	30.7	19.3	18.3	33.4	27.4	30.2	29.4
Inventory turnover (sales)/(inventory)	33.9	23.0	23.2	19.3	18.8	15.5	12.1	9.6	10.2	9.8	9.2	7.6	10.7
Fixed asset turnover (sales)/(fixed assets)	11.4	7.1	6.9	6.5	8.1	6.7	5.5	4.2	4.3	4.3	9.7	3.9	4.8
Average collection period (days)	15.9	22.5	22.8	26.6	21.2	26.2	28.5	28.1	31.2	27.0	32.7	36.8	29.7
Gross operating margin[1]	-0.1	-0.8	1.4	1.9	1.7	2.5	3.6	4.4	3.8	2.8	4.4	6.8	3.7
Net operating margin[2]	-0.3	-1.1	1.0	1.4	1.1	1.4	2.0	2.6	1.9	1.3	2.6	3.4	2.1

[1] Margin above or below direct operating costs.
[2] Margin above or below total costs.

however, as conglomeration or diversification is normal for most large firms, classifying them by their principal activities may produce decidedly biased results. Also, the normal economic theory regarding competition is based, not only on definable products, but also on products in a static sense. For many firms the real competition is in their technological progressiveness in developing new products. And, the present economic theories of competition among standard products and the current legal means of insuring competition in a standard product sense may be becoming obsolete.

CONGLOMERATION AND DIVERSIFICATION

The line of demarcation between conglomeration and diversification is quite nebulous. There is no sharp distinction. The differences are not clear. Conglomeration can be defined in several ways: (1) The usual dictionary definition is "a mixture gathered from various sources" or, "to form into a mass or coherent whole" or, "to roll together, to wind into a ball." (2) The definition most frequently used relates to mergers (the original and most prevalent context of the term "conglomerate"). In antitrust language, a conglomerate merger is any merger in which the parties are neither competitors nor vertically related. The FTC has classified; conglomerate mergers according to whether they are "pure" or "product related" mergers. (3) Some authors for statistical compilations define a conglomerate food processor as one who operates in 2 or more of the 9 3-digit SIC classifications (Narver 1969), (that is, in 2 or more of the major industry classifications: SIC 201 — meat products, SIC 202 — dairy products, SIC 203 — canned and frozen foods, etc.). Others may classify a food processor as a conglomerate if he operates in 2 or more of the more numerous 4-digit food processing categories (Blair 1969).

I will use these latter methods as a means of showing interindustry processing by food processors, but prefer to consider this a measure of diversification rather than of conglomeration. Most any kind of food processing is related to other types of food processing. The term conglomeration will be reserved for use in its purest sense of combinations of nearly completely unrelated business enterprises or, more specifically, non-vertical combinations of nonfood and food processing enterprises.[2]

Diversification by the 200 Largest Food Manufacturers

In Three-digit SIC Categories. — It is typical for the largest food manufacturers to process food in several types of food processing industries (both 3-digit and 4-digit SIC classifications) as well as to manufacture products in several nonfood manufacturing industries. One measure of the increase in diversification is to show the increasing numbers of large firms engaged in processing in each of the 9 major 3-digit SIC food processing industries. The number of the 50 largest food manufacturers engaged in each of the major food processing industries

---

[2] Ronald Knutson and R. E. Schneidau, in their discussion of "The Regulation of Competition" (Chap. 4), use a less restrictive definition of conglomeration.

increased in 8 of the 9 industries between 1954 and 1963 (Table 2.29). For example, of the 50 largest firms only 16 were engaged in SIC 203 (the canning and freezing industry) in 1954; however, by 1963, 32 of the top 50 firms were engaged in this activity. Similarly in 1954, only 6 of the top 50 firms processed beverages (SIC 208); but by 1963, 11 of the top 50 firms processed beverages.

Of the firms ranking in size from 51st to 200th largest, again there were significant increases in the number of firms engaged in 7 of 9 of the food processing categories. Only 22 of these firms were engaged in meat packing in 1954, while 30 were engaged in meat processing in 1963 (Table 2.29). The 2 parts of the Table can be combined to show significant increases in participation of the top 200 firms in each of the industry categories, except dairy processing (SIC 202), between 1954 and 1963.

In 1963 the top 50 firms operated in 3.5 of the 9 industry categories, the 51st to 200th largest firms operated in an average of 1.6 industries, and the top 200 firms operated in an average of 2.1 industries.

In Four-digit SIC Categories. – A further refinement of the extent and increase in diversification is available based on four-digit SIC categories. There are around 44 4-digit categories of food processing compared to only 9 3-digit categories.

In 1954, on the average, the 200 leading food manufacturers produced food products in 2.2 industries (4-digit SIC classes); by 1963 this had increased to 3.3 industries (Table 2.30). Interindustry processing is both normal and increasing – a 50% increase between 1954 and 1963. In general, the larger the firm (based on total value added) the more likely it would be to process food in several industry classifications. In 1963, the 20 largest firms processed food in an average of 8.9 industry classes.

The 200 largest food manufacturers typically, also, engage in several nonfood

TABLE 2.29

NUMBER OF SIC THREE-DIGIT GROUPS IN FOOD MANUFACTURING PARTICIPATED IN BY THE 50 LARGEST AND THE 51–200 LARGEST FOOD MANUFACTURERS, 1954, 1958, AND 1963

Size Class and Year	3-Digit Groups								
	201	202	203	204	205	206	207	208	209
50 Largest									
1954	15	18	16	20	14	1	9	6	NA
1958	17	18	25	23	15	2	11	7	30
1963	19	18	32	26	18	4	15	11	32
51–200 Largest									
1954	22	31	22	30	31	12	15	8	NA
1958	19	27	33	33	26	12	12	9	39
1963	30	23	38	37	27	15	18	11	44

Source: Adapted from Anon. (1966B) and cited by Narver (1969).
NA - not available.

manufacturing industries. In 1954, on the average, the 200 largest food processors engaged in 2.1 nonfood manufacturing industries (Table 2.31); by 1963 this had increased to 3.1 industries, a gain of 47%. Again, the larger the firm the greater the propensity to manufacture nonfood products.

Thus, in 1963 the 200 largest food manufacturers were in an average of 2.1 major food processing industries (3-digit SIC codes), 3.3 product categories (4-digit SIC codes), and 3.1 nonfood manufacturing industries (4-digit SIC codes).

Ownership and Industry Specialization Ratios

John Narver (1969) developed both ownership and industry specialization ratios as indices of diversification in the food processing industry using 1958 and 1963 data. In developing the ratios he used 17 categories of food processing.[3] The "specialization ratio" was defined as "the relationship between establishments classified in a category as their owning companies and all establishments classified in the food processing category." His data showed increasing outside ownership, i.e., conglomeration or diversification. However the "outside" ownership in food processing was typically less than for all manufacturing in the United States.

"The 'industry specialization ratio' is the relationship between the primary establishment activities of companies in an industry (food processing) category and the activities of all their operating establishments. This ratio is a useful summary measure of the extent to which companies classified in a given industry

[3] For the 17 subdivisions see Table 2.32.

TABLE 2.30

AVERAGE NUMBER OF SIC FOUR-DIGIT CLASSES
IN FOOD MANUFACTURING PARTICIPATED IN BY THE
200 LARGEST FOOD MANUFACTURERS, 1954, 1958, AND 1963

	Average Number of Food Industries Participated in by Food Manufacturers Ranked[1] Among the Largest				
Date	200 Largest	20 Largest	21-50 Largest	51-100 Largest	101-200 Largest
1954	2.2	5.4	3.2	1.8	1.6
1958	2.5	7.1	3.5	2.1	1.5
1963	3.3	8.9	5.4	2.5	2.0
	Absolute Change of Diversification				
1954-1963	1.1	3.5	2.2	0.7	0.4
	Percent Change of Diversification				
1954-1963	50	65	69	39	25

Source: Anon. (1966B). Original data from special tabulation by Bur. Census, U.S. Dept. Comm.

[1] Food manufacturers ranked by value added in food and kindred products industries, except alcoholic beverages.

category mix their industrial activities." That is, the specialization ratio is another measure of diversification. His data (Narver 1969) showed increasing diversification in 16 of his 17 food processing categories. In 8 of the 17 industries the rate of increase in diversification was greater than for all manufacturing industries in the United States. However, the absolute amount of diversification was greater than the average for all manufacturing industries in only 7 of the 17 food processing categories.

Another aspect of diversification, conglomeration, and integration, suggested by Narver, was that multiindustry food firms are more specialized in manufacturing than nonfood manufacturers. There is less integration into wholesaling and retailing by food manufacturers than by nonfood manufacturers.

Multiindustry Employment

Another method of showing diversification is by employment figures of multiindustry firms in the different categories of food processing. I will again use Narver's classifications of the 17 subdivisions in the food processing industry. The majority of economic activity by multiindustry food processing firms is in the food field, but often a substantial amount of activity is not in the field in which the firm is primarily classified. For example, in 1963 there were 166,052 employees in multiindustry companies classified primarily as fluid milk firms (Table 2.32). However, only 47% of the employees were in fluid milk activities, an additional 24% of the employees were in other food processing activities, and another 24% were in activities outside the food processing field. "Although

TABLE 2.31

AVERAGE NUMBER OF NONFOOD MANUFACTURING INDUSTRIES (FOUR-DIGIT SIC CLASSES) PARTICIPATED IN BY 200 LARGEST FOOD MANUFACTURERS, 1954, 1958, AND 1963

Date	Average Number of Nonfood Manufacturing Industries Participated in by Food Manufacturers Ranked[1] Among the Largest			
	200 Largest	50 Largest	51-100 Largest	101-200 Largest
1954	2.1	2.8	1.5	1.5
1958	2.7	3.3	1.9	2.3
1963	3.1	3.5	3.3	2.4
	Absolute Change in Average			
1954-1963	1.0	0.7	1.8	1.0
	Percent Change in Average			
1954-1963	47	24	117	68

Source: Anon. (1966B). Original data from special tabulation by Bur. Census, U.S. Dept. Comm.
[1] Food manufacturers ranked by value added in food and kindred products industries, except alcoholic beverages.

multiindustry firms in 6 of the 17 categories had less than 1/2 their total employment in the primary category, multiindustry firms in all 17 food industry categories had over 50% of their total employment in the food industries" (Narver 1969).

Blair (1969), in a slightly different analysis using 31 food processing industries, arrived at about the same conclusion as Narver: "In 9 of the group's 31 industries, companies primarily engaged in some other field produced at least 30% of the industry's output."

A difficulty in each of the above studies is that firms processing food but not classified as primarily engaged in food processing were not included or were not handled separately. Thus, we do not know whether the "companies primarily engaged in some other field" were food processors or primarily nonfood processors.

"Pure" Conglomeration

I have restricted this concept of conglomeration (in reference to food processing) to be that of nonvertical combinations among food and nonfood enterprises. The total quantities of food processed by "pure" conglomerate firms, or by firms whose principal activity is some nonfood processing activity are difficult to determine. Blair (1969) gives one measure of the number of firms whose principal activity is nonfood manufacturing, but still own food processing plants: Of the 200 largest manufacturing corporations in the United States, 29 were primarily engaged in food or kindred products, i.e., their shipments in this group were greater than their shipments in any other group. But of the 200 largest firms, 48 had plants in the food processing industry. Thus, 19 of the 200 largest manufacturing firms in the United States owned plants producing food and kindred products, but were primarily engaged in some other industry.

Although we cannot quantify conglomerate food processing, we can illustrate the trend by illustrating some conglomerate type mergers that have occurred in the food field over the past several years. First, nonfood firms who have merged with or acquired food processing plants: Ling-Temco-Vought's acquisition of Wilson & Co.; the General Host Corp. acquisition of Armour & Co.; The American Tobacco Company's acquisition of Sunshine Biscuits, Inc., Duffy Mott Co. (fruit products), and Jim Beam Distilling Co.; Reynolds Tobacco Co. and their acquisition of Chung King, Brer Rabbit Molasses, and Pacific Hawaiian Punch. The Glidden Company has purchased several food products companies; and Montgomery Ward & Co. has merged with Container Corporation of America (a major supplier to the food industry) to become Marcor. Radio Corporation of America has acquired F. M. Stamper Company (Banquet Brand) who processes T.V. dinners and other food products; and Miles Laboratories Inc., has acquired Worthington Foods, a manufacturer of meat analogs. International Telephone and Telegraph Corporation owns Continental Baking Company and has agreed to acquire Gwaltney, Inc., a Smithfield, Virginia food processing company whose products include Genuine Smithfield Hams. H. L. Hunt (Texas

TABLE 2.32

PERCENT OF EMPLOYMENT OF MULTIINDUSTRY COMPANIES IN EACH ENTERPRISE INDUSTRY CATEGORY IN THE FOOD INDUSTRIES, DISTRIBUTED BY THE INDUSTRY CATEGORY CLASSIFICATION OF THE ESTABLISHMENTS, 1963

Industry Category of Companies	Total Employment of Multiindustry Companies	Industry Category of Establishment																	Approximate Percent of SIC 20 Multiindustry Company Employment Engaged in SIC 20 Categories[1]
		20A	20B	20C	20D	20E	20F	20G	20H	20I	20J	20K	20L	20M	20N	20P	20Q	20R	
20A Meat Packing	165,592	60	10		2.0													2.0		75
20B Prepared meats and dressed poultry	16,171	2.0	77				1.0	1.0										1.0	1.0	82
20C Fluid milk	166,052			47	13	2.0	3.0	1.0		2.0								1.0	1.0	71
20D Other dairy products	28,956	1.0		13	35	6.0	1.0	1.0				6.0							3.0	66
20E Canned fruits and vegetables	69,284		1.0			52	9.0				1.0							1.0		68
20F Other canned and frozen foods	89,256		5.0	2.0		10	49				2.0								1.0	70
20G Prepared feeds for animals and fowls	39,290	1.0	15				4.0	35	1.0									2.0		58
20H Other grain mill products	67,300		1.0				2.0	4.0	53	1.0	2.0	1.0						2.0	2.0	68
20I Bread and related bakery products	111,130						2.0			80									1.0	84
20J Biscuits, crackers and cookies	42,165						1.0	1.0	4.0	4.0	49	2.0							6.0	68
20K Sugar	29,054					6.0	1.0	1.0				61								70
20L Confectionery and related products	30,771						2.0					1.0	62					3.0		69
20M Malt liquors	30,804													79	2.0				1.0	84
20N Other alcoholic beverages	39,611														52					53
20P Bottled soft drinks and flavorings	20,604	1.0					4.0								1.0	68			3.0	78
20Q Fats and oils	22,759	8.0	1.0				4.0	3.0	3.0									52	1.0	66
20R Other food products	70,507		1.0				1.0	1.0	9.0	5.0		7.0					1.0	1.0	40	69

Source: Narver (1969). Adapted from Enterprise Statistics, 1963, Part I, U.S. Govt. Printing Office, 1968.
[1] Sums of the items shown in rows may differ from totals due to fractional employment not shown.

oil) has a subsidiary, HLH Foods, with several food processing plants. Second, food processors who have become conglomerates through acquisitions of non-food enterprises: Hunt-Wesson Foods (a subsidiary of Norton Simon Inc.) acquired W. P. Fuller Co. (paints and brushes), a steel company, and a women's magazine. Beatrice Foods Co., acquired a company producing hospital equipment and sporting goods. General Mills Corp., makes toys. Lever Brothers Co., bought a computer service company. Many of the major food processors now have operations in the fast food service industry (the restaurant field). Most of these latter enterprises are probably nearer pure conglomeration rather than being a form of vertical integration.

Reasons for Diversification and Conglomeration

Since diversification and conglomeration in food processing are both substantial and rapidly increasing, we should explore the reasons for this development. Also, concerning conglomeration, there has been a fear that this recently developing phenomenon may even threaten the free enterprise business system. Therefore, we will also discuss the needs for controlling conglomeration and possible methods of its control.

Among the reasons typically given for the increase in diversification and conglomeration are: (1) to spread risks, (2) to gain economies of scale, (3) relative rates of growth of industries change, (4) because of legal restrictions on horizontal mergers or horizontal expansion, (5) to gain economic (and political) power, and (6) growth through tax breaks and/or financial legerdemain.

To Spread Risks. – This is the "Don't put all your eggs in one basket" argument. With several enterprises, profit variation in one enterprise may be compensated for by another enterprise. Arnould (1969) has statistically tested profit variation among firms engaged in food processing with different degrees of diversification. He concluded that "diversified firms, although no more profitable than less diversified firms, do display on the average more profit stability than nondiversified firms." Diversification to spread risks is prevalent in many segments of business. In stock portfolio analysis, diversification is a common method of reducing risk, leading to the development of the large mutual funds so common in the United States.

To Gain Economies of Scale. – While diversification and conglomeration may not lead to economies of scale of physical production facilities in plants and equipment, it may lead to several managerial economies of scale. The reduced risk in profit variation may result in it being easier and less costly to raise funds in the capital market. Similarly there may be economies of scale in advertising and promotion, in procurement, in distribution, and in research and development. By acquisitions or mergers the firm may gain new managerial skills. One serendipitous effect of the merger and conglomerating wave of activity is that it may force more progressive management among firms who do not wish to be acquired by others.

Relative Rates of Growth. – Relative rates of growth and relative profitability of product lines and industries change through time, thus the firm may have to diversify or conglomerate to maintain a "satisfactory" rate of growth. Gort (1962) analyzed in detail the product line additions of 111 manufacturing corporations during 1929-1954. He found that the addition of manufactured products by these companies were heavily concentrated in industries characterized by rapid growth, high labor productivity, and a high ratio of technical employment (engineers and scientists) to total employment. These firms did not tend to choose areas of high cyclical stability as such, but rather chose areas requiring large investments of capital.

Legal Restrictions on Horizontal Mergers. – Many of our rules to maintain competition in the American free enterprise system have been aimed at preventing undue industry concentration.

Diversification and conglomeration, typically, are not aimed at market control or market concentration as such. Apparently, governmental policy on mergers has been "hardest on horizontal merger, easier on vertical, and least severe on conglomerates" (Turner 1965). Thus, while a firm wishing to expand may be legally prevented from making horizontal mergers, it may still diversify or conglomerize.

To Gain Economic Power. – While market concentration and, thus, market power (in terms of monopolizing) may not be gained by diversification or conglomeration, pure economic power may be obtained. With economic power goes both political and social power. When vast enterprises have tremendous economic resources, the potential for influencing governmental agencies, including legislative bodies, becomes real. This is related both to Galbraith's concept of technocracy and to Eisenhower's concern over the "military-industrial complex" (Arnould 1969).

Tax Breaks and Financial Legerdemain. – It is often suggested that some of the wheeler-dealer types of diversification or conglomeration are made possible only by the use of "funny money," "chinese money," or "chain letter" type financing. In many cases, debt securities of the parent company are used to purchase assets of another company. The interest on the debt is tax deductible. While legal, this may result in tremendous leverage ratios for the parent company.

Another aspect includes accounting systems which make initial profitability after purchase of another company appear fantastically good. The financial accounting methods used by Gulf & Western Industries, Inc., in its acquisition of Paramount Pictures Corp., National General Corporation's acquisition of Grosset & Dunlap, and the Ling-Temco-Vought acquisition of Wilson & Co., are examples of this phenomenon (Briloff 1969).

The "chain letter" effect of mergers on stock prices is illustrated by Burck (1969). "Assume company A has a million shares earning $1 each; they are selling at $30 a share because the market judges A's growth favorably. Now assume Company B also has a million shares earning $1 each; they are selling at only $10 a share because B shows no internal growth at all. So A generously offers B's stockholders $15 a share, either in cash, which it can easily raise, or preferably in A's own stock, which has the advantage of exempting B's stock-holders from an immediate capital-gains tax. In other words, A trades 500,000 of its own shares for all of B's million shares. So the new company is capitalized at 1,500,000 shares earning $2 million. This works out not to $1 a share, as before the merger, but to $1.33. Although nothing really has changed in the companies and the economy is certainly no richer, earnings per share are 1/3 higher. On the strength of this showing, the market bids the new stock to an even higher multiple."

CONTROLS OF CONGLOMERATION AND DIVERSIFICATION

The need for control of conglomeration which results in great concentrations of economic power being under the control of a few large firms is the concern of many individuals. Some economists have asserted that the recent wave of merg-ers and conglomeration even poses a threat to our free enterprise system. With-out increased control of conglomeration in the future, our economy could consist of several major business firms dominating our whole economic system. Political and social power would accompany the economic power of these large firms and, in effect, our whole way of life would be changed. Even the basic concept of individual dignity and the opportunity for an individual to have some control over his own personal destiny could be challenged (Reid 1969).

Conglomeration and mergers may be a substantial threat to the quality of life in small and medium sized cities. With merger or conglomeration, corporate headquarters are shifted to major financial centers. The transfer of management and top technostructure personnel from the smaller cities to the large urban areas not only threatens the quality of life in the smaller city but compounds the problems of overcrowding the large urban areas.

First, even if our free enterprise system is not being threatened or the quality of life is not being reduced by large conglomerates, there are still other reasons for more control. One argument against conglomerizing is that it does not really aid in accomplishing a national objective of economic growth — mergers or acquisitions merely shift ownership; they do not create new plants and equip-ment which would add to economic growth or capacity (Reid 1969). Second, the heavy debt ratios accompanying some mergers or acquisitions could easily result in bankruptcy in a recession (Weiss 1969). Third, with large multiindustry firms there is always the threat of reciprocity — you do business with me and I'll do business with you — to the unfair exclusion of smaller firms (Blair 1969; Weiss 1969). Direct frontal attacks or even collusion by large firms to "kill the rival" will probably seldom be used — not only because it is illegal but also because the large firms have more subtle methods of dealing with competition.

Methods suggested for controlling conglomerizing have ranged from changing tax laws to complete prohibition of mergers and acquisitions by all firms above a certain size or ranking in any given industry. Certainly, tax laws and accounting procedures have had an influence on the current merger movement. Possible tax changes could include: (1) an immediate capital-gains tax when assets are sold for stock in another company, (2) nonexemption of intercorporate dividends from federal income tax, and (3) changing the deductibility of interest (as a business expense) on debt securities issued in the acquisition of stock in another firm. From the accounting standpoint, the Securities Exchange Comm. announced proposed amendments to the Commission's reporting requirements which could prevent some financial "sleight of hand." The changes would require companies to report sales and net income by lines of business whenever any such lines comprise at least 10% of the corporation's revenues or income (Briloff 1969).

Some economists fear that the dangers of conglomerizing are so severe that a moratorium should be given on all mergers of large firms until policy recommendations might be suggested through study by a high-level committee. (Reid 1969). Another foremost authority on bigness in the food industries suggests legislation to prohibit mergers and acquisitions by all firms above a certain size or ranking in any given industry (Hoffman 1969).

COMPETITION IN TECHNOCRACY AND PRODUCT DEVELOPMENT

Commodities Versus Packaged Foods

In general, there appear to be two layers of food processing developing in the United States. One layer is nearly a direct extension of farm production — this type of processing results in the production of fairly standard commodities. Much of the meat industry, a substantial part of the canning and freezing industry, the vegetable oil processors, and the sugar industry produce fairly standard commodities. Although there may be brand identification, in most cases there may be few distinguishing characteristics between commodities manufactured by different companies. Typically, the cost of entry into these fields is not high. These firms tend to compete on efficiency of operations and efficiency of distribution of relatively low margin products.

The second layer is the convenience food field, or the "packaged" food industry. "In the packaged food industry the word 'commodity' means a food product that is relatively easy to produce and pack . . . a not very distinctive product with a low profit margin. In fact, in my business, *commodity* is sort of a bad word" (Clausi 1969). In the packaged food industry, or convenience food industry, each firm aims at distinctly different, readily identifiable food products. These may be convenience foods such as breakfast cereals or simply bottled soft drinks. In the packaged foods industry the cost of market entry (in terms of research and development and advertising and promotion) is high and profit margins (on a successful product) are relatively high. The competition here is in advertising and promotion and in the ever-present threat that a superior new product by another firm will capture a large share of a market currently held

Examples of the two layers of processing could be shown in many different examples — for instance, there are many commodity processors in which freezing cherries in 30-lb cans is a principle activity. These frozen cherries are then sold to other firms who reprocess them into pies, tarts, jellies, jams, etc. The jellies or jams may then be further processed into "instant breakfast foods" such as "Toastems" or "Pop Tarts." These latter items are truly packaged food, or convenience food, items. Both the nature of processing and types of competition faced by the packaged food processor, e.g., Kellogg Co., General Foods Corp., and others, are vastly different from the commodity processors of frozen cherries.

Competition in Ability to Produce New Foods

Because more and more of our foods are bought as packaged or convenience foods, greater competition results not only in product development per se but also in advertising and promotion. This tendency toward greater and greater numbers of new products results in substantially different forms of competition and, in effect, our current rules (laws) concerning competition may be becoming obsolete. The real competition among firms will not be competition among standard products, but will be in the ability of the firm to develop new products. With this in mind, let us now look at competition in technocracy and new product development in the rapidly growing packaged or convenience food fields.

An organization can be defined as a group of people working through some type of coordination toward a common objective. A business firm is a form of organization whose objective is to increase the long-run value of the firm to its owners. The nature of the organization and the coordination within large business firms change through time. Some authors suggest that the top executive in large business firms no longer directs his subordinates in an authoritarian manner, but rather makes decisions based on the recommendations of a specialized subordinate staff. Hence to a large degree, particularly in firms involving a large degree of technology, the real power in the firm probably lies in the competence of the staff as compared to the chief executive officer. Galbraith (1968) labels this power structure of the firm the "technocracy." In a large technologically proficient food processing firm, i.e., a firm specializing in internal development of new products, there must be a wide range of staff competencies. This can range from engineers to statisticians, chemists, biochemists, economists, marketing specialists, lawyers, computer programmers, operation researchers, home economists, social psychologists, food technologists, and scientists in agricultural production. Each staff member can have an effective role in new product development. For a firm to be able to effectively utilize these different specialities it must be of substantial size.

The alternative to internal development of new products is the acquisition of other firms who themselves have developed new products. An active acquisition or merger program to obtain new products and to adapt them to the firm's advertising, promotion, and market development program also calls for its own specialized form of technocracy.

Statistical data indicate that perhaps 3/4 of the growth of large food firms comes from internal expansion and only about 1/4 from mergers. However, the merger route is a major method of expanding into new food processing (new four-digit SIC classification). With a large firm's acquisition of a new product, advertising expenditures are generally greatly increased over that of its previous owners. Typically with acquisitions into a new industry, a whole range of new products may be developed. "An example of this is the C.A. Swanson and Sons acquisition by Campbell Soup Co. Swanson produced 12 different products in 1956, the year it was acquired. One year after acquisition, Swanson produced 21 frozen products, and in 1967 it produced 39 frozen products" (Handy and Padburg 1969).

In essence, we are typically dealing with a large firm, probably with substantial undistributed profits or excess reserves, with an active desire for growth, and with a technical staff who can develop new products internally or adapt the acquisition of other firms' new products into their own marketing and developmental procedures. This means, in effect, that the options for new products can arise in nearly any food processing activity - i.e., from the whole range of all SIC food industry classifications as well as synthetics and, of course, nonfoods. Thus, the large companies, particularly in packaged or convenience foods, can no longer be thought of as a pickle processor, or a meat processor, or a vegetable processor. In fact, more and more large firms are not even "food processors" — they are "business firms." These business firms consist of a bundle of resources including capital and a technocracy. The technical competencies of the staff are functional and, thus, the firm can shift and choose among many forms of investments. If the firm chooses new or additional investments in food processing, its options are nearly the complete range of the food processing industry. The effective competition among large business firms may reside in the differences in the ability and foresight of their respective technocracies.

The increased power of the technocracies in business firms, together with improved communications and improved control (particularly the use of the computer) have greatly enlarged the scope of business enterprises which can come under the direction of one central management system. Thus, a broader range of enterprises is now possible for individual business firms than before.

ECONOMIC AND LEGAL CONCEPTS OF COMPETITION BECOMING OBSOLETE

The real competition among these firms is not on standard products and not even on new products, but on their abilities to develop new food products. The products from these firms are of a transient and continuously evolving nature. With the increasing role of new products, how are products and how are markets defined or classified? Do "Pop Tarts"[4] and "Toastems"[4] compete with bread, or with ham and eggs, or with breakfast cereal? Can you have a monopoly in

---

[4]Trade mark of Kellogg Co. and General Foods Corp. respectively, for instant toaster-heated, fruit-filled pastry-type products.

toaster-heated, fruit-filled pastry-type products? Will the meat-like soybean protein analogs compete with meat or only with other protein analogs? The issues of concentration, oligolopy and monopoly are based on definable products and usually products in a static sense. Thus, both the economic theory and the law concerning competition may be irrelevant for handling the real competition in the packaged or convenience food industry.

Handy and Padburg (1969) suggest that policy issues in communication, i.e., truth in advertising, truth in packaging, and unit retail pricing are more important than legal restrictions on diversification or conglomeration in dealing with the "new products competition-conglomerate firm" syndrome. "In other words, we prefer policy to improve the ability of consumers to choose. Policy to arbitrarily restrict certain structures and product alternatives becomes secondary to this task" (Handy and Padburg 1969).

PERFORMANCE OF THE FOOD PROCESSING INDUSTRIES

While we have made some references to performance of the food processing industries, perhaps we should explore this explicitly as performance is the most important aspect of market structure. For example, Bressler (1966) has stated "Market structure refers in a descriptive way to the physical dimensions involved — the approximate definitions of industries and markets, the number of firms and plants in the market, the distribution of firms or plants by various measures of size and concentration, descriptions of products and product differentiation, conditions of entry — all of these descriptions, to be sure, are geared in some way to our concepts and value judgments of elements affecting market competition. Market conduct refers to the behavior of firms under different market structures, and especially to the type of decisions that managers can make under these varying market structures. Finally, market performance is defined as the real impact of structure and conduct as measured in terms of such variables as prices, costs, and volume of output. Performance is the significant element in this taxonomy; descriptive studies of structure are of value only insofar as they explain performance."

Performance is a term used to explain how well the marketing system serves the social aims of the economy. Some notion of social performance on the part of a marketing system or of the entire economic system is contained in any concept of marketing results. According to Sosnick (1962), " . . . what is really intended by the term 'market performance' . . . are the attributes of production and exchange in a segment of the economy that directly influences the welfare of the participants and the society." Sosnick further states " . . . evaluation of the attributes of a market that directly influences welfare involves consideration of at least the following twelve issues: (1) production efficiency, (2) technological progressiveness, (3) product suitability, (4) profit rates, (5) level of output, (6) exchange efficiency, (7) cost of sales promotion, (8) unethical practices, (9) participant rationality, (10) conservation, (11) external effects, and (12) labor relations."

The central question is: What kind of structure of the food processing industries would result in the best performance of the food processing industries? Unfortunately, there does not appear to be an answer to this question based on empirical economic analyses. There have been no recent economic studies connecting structural differences or structural changes to poor performance in the food processing industries. Indeed, the connection of structural differences to performance differences is a very difficult analytical task.

If, in recent periods of time, there has been no research directly relating structure to poor performance, what rules or laws concerning market structure should we have? Should we accept the status quo or should we have new and different laws permitting or restricting structural changes? Both the Natl. Comm. on Food Marketing and the FTC have made recommendations for substantial changes in laws relating to market structure without real evidence to support their contentions that present laws permit market structure to develop which results in poor performance. Some of the recommendations from the Natl. Comm. on Food Marketing (Anon. 1966A) were as follows:

"But if competition is to be an effective regulator of the food economy, high concentration must be prevented even in instances where specific, immediate restraint of trade cannot be identified.

"It is our conclusion that acquisitions or mergers by the largest firms in any concentrated branch of the food industries, which results in a significant increase in their market shares or the geographic extension of their markets, probably will result in a substantial lessening of competition in violation of the Clayton Act.

"A horizontal merger or acquisition by a large firm in an already concentrated field tends to break down conditions necessary for effective competition — perhaps in purchasing as well as in selling — even when specific restraint of trade cannot be demonstrated. An effective policy to limit concentration requires acceptance of the view that such general impairment of competition is a sufficient reason for vigorous antimerger action."

It is my contention that the Natl. Comm. on Food Marketing not only did not submit any analysis to support their recommendations but that from their recommendations one can be guilty even in the absence of proof.

It is also my contention that the food processing industries have performed well. There is a high and increasing production efficiency; they are technologically progressive; they produce a wide range of acceptable products; and their profit rates have been relatively low. The Natl. Comm. on Food Marketing and the FTC have been unduly concerned with concentration or market shares and apparently have nearly equated this one structural characteristic to market performance.

As will be subsequently shown, there are substantial economies of scale available to large scale food processing and, further, there are substantial numbers of firms with plants below a minimum efficient size. However, the regulations suggested by the Natl. Comm. on Food Marketing and recent actions by the FTC try to ensure smallness while the economies of the system dictate a continuing tendency toward largeness. Further, within limits, we have no empirical evidence to support that fewer and larger firms would decrease the performance of the marketing system. On the contrary, there is evidence to support the contention that fewer and larger firms would actually increase the performance of the system (Padburg and Clarke 1965).

It is not my intention to suggest that no regulations are needed to prevent concentrations of market power or to regulate market behavior.

If one takes the polar extremes of "no regulations" on one hand to "complete governmental control" on the other, my optimum position would tend to be nearer "no regulations" than to "complete governmental control." It is suggested that some of the regulations proposed by the Natl. Comm. on Food Marketing and recent rulings by the FTC would not increase performance but, in fact, would have a harmful effect.

SUMMARY

Although total food processing is substantially increasing, both the number of firms and number of food processing establishments are decreasing significantly. The result, of course, is larger plants serving wider geographical areas. While food processing is not nearly as concentrated as some other industries (for example, the automobile industry, the electronic industry, or electrical equipment industry), the top 58 firms in food processing obtain around 55% of the profits after taxes. Each of these 58 top food processing firms had over $100 million in assets in 1966 and 1967. Concentration in food processing has been slowly increasing. In fact, with large theoretical economies of scale, it is the relative slowness of the rate of concentration of assets that is surprising, not its rapidity.

Food processing firms are among the largest industrial firms in the world. About 1 out of 10 of the world's largest industrial corporations are primarily engaged in the production of food or alcoholic beverages.

The typical large food processing firm is engaged in the production of food in several industry classifications as well as being engaged in several nonfood manufacturing industries. Thus, diversification and/or conglomeration are fairly standard operating procedures. The food processing industry, apparently, has less vertical integration into wholesaling and retailing than all manufacturing industries in the United States.

Studies of size and market concentration have not shown a direct correlation between either of these factors and profitability. Similarly, diversification is not related to the degree of profitability, but to the stability of profits. Recent data suggest that the profitability of smaller firms is improving relative to the large firms. This, in fact, may be more related to a different form of competition than to size itself. The smaller firm primarily may produce commodities and compete on efficiency and reductions in cost while the large firms compete on packaged or convenience goods, on new product development, and in advertising and promotion.

Both diversification and conglomeration are increasing rapidly in the food processing industry. The reasons for diversification and conglomeration, possible needs for its control, and possible methods of controlling this phenomenon were analyzed. Business firms should probably be free to allocate resources to any legitimate activity in which it foresees a profitable opportunity. Perhaps however, financing, accounting, and tax privileges should be reviewed. The market itself may be a more effective control of "wheeler-dealer" conglomerization than possible legal restraints. One has only to review market prices of the stock of many conglomerizing firms to suggest that the rate of increase in pure conglomerizing will probably decrease.

In the increasing packaged or convenience food processing field, the real competition is in the ability of the firm to produce or acquire new products. As the concepts of concentration, oligopoly and monopoly, have been based on standard definable products and products in a static sense, both economic theory and legal rules concerning competition may no longer really apply to the real competitive issues.

Some authors fear that our present free enterprise system is being threatened by conglomerate enterprises and suggest immediate moratoriums and/or new legislation to limit conglomerate mergers by firms above a certain size. Others suggest that structural considerations are not as important as policy issues to ensure consumers the opportunity for better choice. The policy issues here would be related to truth in advertising, truth in packaging, unit pricing for better comparability, etc.

Since food processing is less concentrated than many other business enterprises, and since there are no definitive studies to suggest abnormal profits related to either size, structure or concentration, the need for legislation to prohibit diversification, conglomeration, or absolute size appears questionable at this time. Perhaps the greater need is to control methods of diversifying or conglomerizing. This could be through legislation, or control of financing and accounting methods, and perhaps changes in some current federal tax exemptions

The food processing industries have apparently performed well. They have a high production efficiency, they are technologically progressive, they have produced a vast array of goods and services acceptable to consumers, and profit rates have not been high.

BIBLIOGRAPHY

ANON. 1964-1968. Monthly Economic News Letter. First Natl. City Bank of New York.
ANON. 1966A. Food from farmer to consumer. Natl. Comm. Food Marketing, June, 94, 102, 106. U.S. Govt. Printing Office, Washington, D.C.
ANON. 1966B. The structure of food manufacturing. Natl. Comm. Food Marketing, Technical Study 8, June. U.S. Govt. Printing Office, Washington, D.C.
ANON. 1968. Fortune Directory. July 15. Time, Inc., Chicago.
ANON. 1969A. The 200 largest industrial firms outside the U.S. Fortune Magazine LXXX, No. 3, 104-116.

ANON. 1969B. "Complex 20" analysis of the food Industry. Canner/Packer Yearbook, Sept. 25.

ARNOULD, R. J. 1969. Conglomerate growth and profitability. *In* Economics of Conglomerate Growth, L. Garoian (Editor). Res. Found., Oregon State Univ., Corvallis, Ore.

BLAIR, J. M. 1969. An overview of conglomerate concentration. *In* Economics of Conglomerate Growth, L. Garoian (Editor). Agr. Res. Found., Oregon State Univ., Corvallis, Ore.

BRESSLER, R. G. 1966. Market structure and performance—the conceptual framework, *In* Proceedings of Market Structure Workshop, Camp Kett, Michigan, November, W. S. Farris (Editor). Purdue Univ., Lafayette, Ind.

BRILOFF, A. J. 1969. Financial motives for conglomerate growth. *In* Economics of Conglomerate Growth, L. Garoian (Editor). Agr. Res. Found., Oregon State Univ., Corvallis, Ore.

BURCK, G. 1969. The merger movement rides high. Fortune Magazine *LXXIX*, No. 2, 79-82, 158-161.

CLAUSI, A. S. 1969. Our changing social patterns and their impact on food products. Proceedings 15th Agr. Marketing Clinic, Michigan State Univ., East Lansing, Mich., Mar. 11.

COLLINS, N., and PRESTON, L. 1961. The structure of the food processing industries 1935-55. J. Ind. Econ. *9*, 265-279.

GALBRAITH, J. K. 1968. The New Industrial State. New American Library, New York.

GORT, M. 1962. Diversification and Integration in American Industry. Princeton Univ. Press, Princeton, N.J.

GREIG, W. S. 1968. Balance Sheets, Income Statements and Financial Operating Ratios for the Food Processing Industry, 1965-66. Michigan State Univ., Agr. Econ. Rept. *117*, Nov.

HANDY, C. R., and PADBURG, D. I. 1969. Conglomerate growth: policy implications for agriculture and agribusiness. *In* Economics of Conglomerate Growth, L. Garoian (Editor). Agr. Res. Found., Oregon State Univ., Corvallis, Ore.

HIROSHI, M., and GORMAN, W. D. 1966. An empirical investigation into the relationship between market structure and performance as measured by prices. J. Farm Econ. *48*, No. 3, Part II, 170-171.

HOFFMAN, A. C. 1969. The economic rationale for conglomerate growth from a management perspective. *In* Economics of Conglomerate Growth, L. Garoian (Editor). Agr. Res. Found., Oregon State Univ., Corvallis, Ore.

HOFFMAN, A. C. 76th Congress. Large-scale organization in the food industries. TNEC Monogram *35*, 76th Congress, 3rd Session.

NARVER, J. 1969. Conglomeration in the food industries, *In* Economics of Conglomerate Growth, L. Garoian (Editor). Agr. Res. Found., Oregon State Univ., Corvallis, Ore.

PADBURG, D. I., and CLARKE, D. A., JR. 1965. Structural changes in the California fluid milk industry: their effects on competition and market performance. Calif. Agr. Expt. Sta. Bull. *802*, 45-50.

REID, S. R. 1969. The economic rationale for conglomerate growth. *In* Economics of Conglomerate Growth, L. Garoian (Editor). Agr. Res. Found., Oregon State Univ., Corvallis, Ore.

SOSNICK, S. H. 1962. Operational criteria for evaluating market performance. Paper presented at Purdue University on June 12, Mimeograph, 6.

TURNER, D. F. 1965. Conglomerate mergers and Section 7 of the Clayton Act. Harvard Law Review *78*, No. 7, 1322.

WEISS, L. W. 1969. Conglomerate Mergers and Public Policy. *In* Economics of Conglomerate Growth, L. Garoian (Editor). Agr. Res. Found., Oregon State Univ., Corvallis, Ore.

WITTENBERG, F. R. 1970. Bigness versus profitability. Harvard Business Review Jan.-Feb., 158-160.

CHAPTER 3

W. Smith Greig | # Economics of Scale and Future Plant Numbers

In Chap. 2, some of the aspects of structure were covered. In this chapter, the economies of size in food processing will be considerably expanded. Then in Chap. 4, Ronald Knutson and R. E. Schneidau will cover the legal aspects of regulating competition. While this order of presentation may, at first glance, seem peculiar, it was chosen deliberately. Economies of scale are discussed before legal controls of size. The economies of the system apparently dictate largeness while many legal controls are apparently aimed at enforcing smallness.

The tendency toward larger and larger firms in the food processing industries was noticed by economists over 30 yr ago (Hoffman, 76th Congress). Census data support the thesis that, through time, there are both fewer food processing plants in the United States and fewer food processing firms. This chapter will explore briefly why a large firm or a large physical plant theoretically has substantial economic advantages over smaller firms or plants, and will also discuss some direct effects that economies of size are having on U.S. food processing. The expression that economists normally use to explain the cost advantages or economic efficiencies a large firm (or large physical plant) has over a small firm (or small physical plant) is "economies of scale."

ECONOMIES OF SCALE IN RESEARCH AND DEVELOPMENT[1]

Most all the commercially conducted research and development in food processing in the United States is done by a few large firms. Much new product development is a costly and risky business. Buzzell and Nourse (1966) in a study of 72 "distinctive new products" that underwent at least a year of full distribution from 19 large firms between 1954 and 1964, indicated that the net *negative* contribution to the firm after 1 yr of sales was an average of $1,256,000. Quite obviously, many smaller firms cannot manage a negative contribution to the firm of over a million dollars in an attempt to place a new product on the market.

In a sense, even our tax laws affecting new product development are geared to the larger firms. Most research and development expenditures are classified as current expenses from a tax standpoint. Thus, a large well-established firm, typically near the federal corporate income tax rate of 50%, pays an effective rate of only $0.50 for each dollar expended on research and development. The lower the tax rate, the higher the real cost for research and development. A firm that loses money or breaks even has effectively invested one dollar for every dollar spent on research and development. New legislation in taxation and perhaps even a subsidization of research and development for firms under a certain federal corporate tax rate level could encourage more research and development

---

[1]Refer to the Sections "Research and Development in Food Processing" and "Time and Costs in Commercialization of New Products" in Chap. 7.

by smaller firms.

The risk is high in new product development. Although the food processing industry has had its share of success it has also had failures. For example, in 1965 the Post Division of General Foods Corp. had an estimated 1/2 of the total freeze drying capacity in the United States at its Battle Creek, Michigan plant to freeze-dry peaches, strawberries, and blueberries for incorporation into breakfast cereals. After a relatively short time these new breakfast cereals were withdrawn from the market. This single venture into a new food product area could have easily bankrupted lesser firms.

While the large firms can gear up for their own research and development staffs, smaller firms undoubtedly must go to commercial research firms for much research and development, thus increasing their costs per unit of research over that of large firms.

It has been suggested that many small-to-medium sized firms compete on efficiency of plant operations while larger firms compete on new product development and advertising and promotion.

ECONOMIES OF SCALE IN ADVERTISING

Edward Gelsthorpe (1965), when he was General Manager of Ocean Spray, gave a very simple example of economies of scale in advertising. "People frequently ask 'What does a full page ad in *Life* magazine cost you'? Well, a full page, 4-color ad in *Life* for 1 issue costs approximately $55,000. That is, $55,000 each for a 13-issue contract. If you buy 48 issues, the price comes down to around $42,000 per issue. But that is still an enormous amount of money and people say 'My goodness! How can anyone afford to do that'? Well, the economics of advertising are really pretty simple. Let's say that instead of spending all the money on a full-color ad in *Life*, we're going to send out postcards to 13 million people; because one full-color ad in *Life* reaches about 13 million people. If we were going to send a postcard to 13 million people, in the first place our postage, mailing, printing, and buying the list of people we would send it to would cost around 7¢ a card; further, the message would only be as big as the postcard in contrast to the size of a full page in *Life*. If 13 million postcards were sent out it would cost about $90,000 compared to a full page in *Life* at $55,000. In the easiest possible terms, I think this explains the great economy in using national media for advertising."

Most of the national advertising by food firms is concentrated among the largest firms. In 1964, the 20 largest companies primarily classified as food manufacturers spent $610 million in advertising, roughly 44% of the total outlay of food manufacturers. The 50 largest are estimated to have accounted for an excess of 80% (Anon. 1966).

Just as there are substantial discounts in magazines for large scale users, there are also substantial discounts in using television. Professor Harlan Blake, coauthor of "Network Television Discounts," *74 Yale Law Journal 1339* (July 1965) testified before the Senate Antitrust and Monopoly Subcommittee that discounts to the largest advertisers went to an extreme of 75% on rate cards. Gerald Arthur, former advertising executive and owner of radio and TV properties, testified that the largest advertisers, such as General Foods Corp., would get their TV advertising at a cost of $2.50 per thousand households (audience estimated by Nielsen ratings), whereas a smaller advertiser would have to pay $3.50-$4.00 for the same audience. This means that the smaller advertiser would have to pay 40-60% more for the same coverage (Anon. 1966).

Newspapers also may give substantial discounts to volume users — in individual newspapers this may amount to 30-40%.

The nature of advertising discounts may be quite complex. For example, in television network time the costs may depend on viewing time, ratings of the particular program being sponsored, total expenditures for advertising for all products by the particular company during the year, and many other factors.

The FTC has recognized the significance of advertising and promotion as factors contributing to the restraint of trade. For example, this is a key point in the argument by the hearing examiner who ruled that the acquisition of the Clorox Chemical Company by Proctor & Gamble was illegal. Some of the following factors entered into the decision.

"Clorox's dominant market position was increased as a result of the acquisition and the various advertising campaigns, sales promotion programs, and devices subsequently employed by Proctor & Gamble;

"Proctor & Gamble's financial and economic strength and advertising and promotional experience as compared with its competitors in the liquid bleach industry;

"Clorox's ability, through aggressive Proctor & Gamble-inspired advertising and promotional methods to prevent the entry of additional competitors into the industry, and to prevent existing competitors from expanding by normal methods of competition (Anon. 1964)."

ECONOMIES OF SCALE IN MANAGEMENT COSTS

As the size of the firm increases, total management costs increase, but management costs as a percent of total costs typically decrease. From IRS data Greig (1968) calculated the costs of compensation of officers as a percent of total costs for 12 asset sizes of firms (Fig. 3.1). Compensation of officers ranged from an average of 5.3% (in 1965-1966) for firms with assets under $50,000 to only 0.2% of total costs for firms with assets above $100,000,000. Three aspects of the chart are important. First, the decrease in total management costs are substantial; second, while the curve leveled off at 0.2% for the last 2 size classes — the curve did not turn up; and third, the curve was a smooth curve — costs of compensation to officers consistently decreased with each increase in size class.

ECONOMIES OF SCALE IN PHYSICAL EFFICIENCY

Processing

More economic analyses of the economies of scale in physical efficiency in

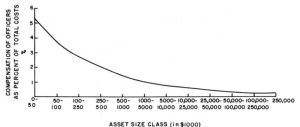

Source: U.S. Dept. of Commerce

FIG. 3.1. COMPENSATION OF OFFICERS AS PERCENTAGE
OF TOTAL COSTS FOR 12 ASSET SIZE CLASSES
OF FOOD PROCESSING FIRMS, 1965-1966

processing have been conducted than studies of economies of scale in most other areas. Much of the early leadership in these studies was by Bressler (1945) at the University of California. One of the best early theoretical and methodological studies was by French et al. (1956).

Typically, three different approaches have been used in studies of economies of scale in processing. One approach is a detailed economic study of different sized plants under actual operating conditions. The second method is an economic-engineering approach to studies of stages in the operation of plants and the building of economic models of combinations of the most economic size of different stages to obtain model plants of different sizes. The third approach is an engineering projection of different sizes of plants. Each method has its advantages and disadvantages, but nearly all the studies conducted suggest optimum plant sizes in most types of food processing to be much larger than typical plants in the industry. For example, the average value of shipments by plants for 18 industries compared to economic-engineering estimates of the minimum optimum size for efficiency are listed in Table 3.1. In most cases the optimum minimum size of plant is several times the average size of plants in the industry.

Most of the food processing plants in the United States are relatively small when compared to other manufacturing industries. In 1963, approximately 63% of the total number of plants had under 20 employees. However, these plants had only 8% of the value added in all food processing (Table 3.2). There were 27% of the plants that had between 20 and 100 employees, and these plants produced 27.1% of the value added; while 1% of the plants had over 500 employees and these produced 21.8% of the total value added in food processing.

Between 1954 and 1963, the plants with under 20 employees declined from 28,902 plants to only 23,185 plants — a decline of nearly 20%. Perhaps a preview of the future numbers of food processing plants in the United States can be glimpsed in a recent study on beef slaughtering by Huie (1969). In 1967 there were 169 beef slaughtering operations in Michigan; Huie's estimate indicated that the optimum number of plants would be 4 plants. This study took into account procurement costs, costs in processing, and shipment of the products to market.

TABLE 3.1

NUMBERS OF PLANTS, AVERAGE VALUE OF SHIPMENTS,
AND VALUE OF SHIPMENTS OF MINIMUM SIZE
EFFICIENT PLANT, BY INDUSTRIES, 1963

Industry Classification	No. of Plants[1]	Avg. Value of Shipments[1] (Million $)	Economic-engineering Studies of Value of Shipments of Minimum Efficient Size Plant[2] (Million $)
2011 Meat slaughtering	2992	4.3	54.0
2013 Meat processing	1341	1.6	52.6-42.0
2015 Poultry dressing plants	967	2.3	63.0
2021 Creamery butter	766	1.2	1.2
2022 Natural and process cheese	1138	1.0	.6
2023 Condensed and evaporated milk	281	3.3	10.0
2024 Ice cream and frozen desserts	1081	1.0	.5
2026 Fluid milk	4619	1.5	8.8
2033 Canned fruits and vegetables	1430	1.9	13.7-6.9
2037 Frozen fruits and vegetables	650	2.4	32.0-4.8
2041 Flour mills	618	3.5	15.4
2042 Prepared animal feeds	2590	1.5	7.4
2044 Rice milling	74	5.7	12.0
2051 Bread and related products	5010	.9	8.0
2063 Beet sugar	65	8.7	10.0
2091 Cotton seed oil mills	188	3.0	6.3
2092 Soybean oil mills	102	14.4	30.0
2095 Roasted coffee	324	5.8	16.0

[1] 1963 Census of Manufacturers, Bur. Census, U.S. Dept. Com.

[2] Source: Adjustments by Natl. Comm. Food Marketing of following studies:

Logan, S. H., and King, G. A. 1962. Economies of scale in beef slaughter plants. Univ. California. Giannini Found. Res. Rept. *260.*

Rogers, G. B., and Bardwell, E. T. 1959. Economies of scale in chicken processing. U.S. Dept. Agr., Agr. Marketing Serv. *331.*

Rowe, G. A. 1952. Economies of cheese manufacturing in Tillamook County, Oregon. Oregon State Coll. Agr. Expt. Sta. Bull. *529.*

Knudtson, A. C., and Koller, E. F. 1960. Processing costs of whole milk creameries. Univ. Minnesota Agr. Expt. Sta. Tech. Bull. *236.*

Babb, E. M., and Taylor, J. C. 1962. Economic-engineering techniques in planning ice cream operations. Purdue Univ. Coop. Ext. Serv. Mimeo *EC-240.*

Boles, J. N. 1958. Economies of scale for evaporated milk plants in California. Hilgardia, Univ. California. Oct. 694.

Cobia, D. W., and Babb, E. M. 1964. Determining the optimum size fluid milk processing plant and sales area. Purdue Univ. Agr. Expt. Sta. Res. Bull. *778.*

Reed, R. H., and Sammet, L. L. 1963. Multi-product processing of California frozen vegetables. Univ. California Giannini Found. Res. Rept. *264.*

Walsh, R. G., and Evans, B. M. 1963. Economics of change in market structure, conduct and performance: The baking industry 1947-58. Univ. Nebraska Studies *28.*

Bain, J. S. 1956. Barriers to New Competition. Harvard University Press, Cambridge, Mass.

Haskell, J. E. 1965. Economics of plant size and utilization in the flour milling industry. MS. Thesis, Dept. Agr. Econ., Univ. Nebraska.

Young, R. A. 1963. An economic study of the Eastern beet sugar industry. Michigan State Univ. Agr. Expt. Sta. Res. Bull. *9.*

Thuroczy, N. M., and Schlegel, W. A. 1959. Costs of operating Southern rice mills. U.S. Dept. Agr., Agr. Marketing Res. Rept. *330.*

Brewster, J. M. 1954. Comparative economics of different types of cottonseed oil mills and their effects on oil supplies, prices, and returns to growers. U.S. Dept. Agr., Agr. Marketing Res. Rept. *54.*

Burbee, C. R., Bardwell, E. T., and Henry, W. F. 1965. Marketing New England poultry — Effects of firm size and production density of spatial costs for an integrated broiler marketing firm. Univ. New Hampshire Agr. Expt. Sta. Bull. *485* as summarized in Farm Index June, 1965.

Federal Trade Comm. 1954. Economic report of the investigation of coffee prices. U.S. Govt. Printing Office, Washington, D.C.

Brewster, J. M., Mitchell, Julia A., and Clark, S. P. 1956. Size of soybean oil mills and returns to growers. U.S. Dept. Agr., Agr. Marketing Res. Rept. *121*.

TABLE 3.2

SIZE OF FOOD PROCESSING PLANTS BY NUMBER
OF EMPLOYEES, VALUE ADDED, AVERAGE VALUE OF SHIPMENTS,
AND NUMBERS OF PLANTS FOR 1954 AND 1963

No. of Employees (1963)	Value Added in Processing (1963) (% of Total)	Avg. Value of Shipments [1] (1963) (Million $)	No. of Plants (1954)	No. of Plants (1963)	Change in No. of Plants 1954-1963
1-19	8.0	.2	28,902	23,185	−5717
20-99	27.1	1.9	10,370	10,027	−343
100-499	43.0	8.1	3,005	3,393	+388
Over 500	21.8	41.5	313	323	+10
	100.0	1.6	42,590	36,928	−5662

Source: Census of Manufacturers, Bur. Census, U.S. Dept. Com.
[1] Weighted average.

TABLE 3.3

IQF FREEZING: PROJECTED FREEZING COSTS FOR
VARIOUS CAPACITIES AND LENGTHS OF USE PER YEAR, 1969

No. of 8-Hr Shifts	Total No. of Hour Use	Freezing Costs (Cents per Pound) by Plant Capacity (Pounds per Hour)					
		2000	5000	10,000	15,000	20,000	30,000
20	160	5.66	4.36	3.74	3.45	3.17	2.85
40	320	3.07	2.34	2.01	1.86	1.71	1.54
60	480	2.21	1.67	1.44	1.33	1.22	1.10
80	640	1.77	1.33	1.16	1.06	.98	.88
100	800	1.52	1.11	.98	.90	.83	.75
150	1200	1.17	.86	.76	.69	.64	.58
200	1600	1.00	.73	.64	.58	.54	.49
250	2000	.89	.64	.57	.52	.48	.42

Source: Greig (1969).

Perhaps in a simplified manner, the economies of scale in physical efficiency can be demonstrated with results .of a recent study on the cost of freezing vegetables (Greig 1969). The costs are for the freezing stage only and are economic-engineering estimates. The costs of freezing with a Lewis Belt type freezing installation ranged from 5.66¢ per lb with a capacity of 2000 lb per hr and 160 hr of use per year to a low of 0.42¢ per lb with a capacity of 30,000 lb per hr and an annual usage of 2000 hr per yr (Table 3.3). Included in these costs are expenses for buildings, equipment, operation, and overhead, including taxes and interest on investment. Preparation for freezing, packaging, and the storage operation are not included. Economies of scale studies at the University of

California have shown about the same relative scale efficiencies in the preparation of vegetables for freezing — that is, in the receiving, grading, washing, trimming, sorting, packaging, and transporting to storage of vegetables to be frozen (Reed and Sammet 1963). The two studies combined show substantial economies of scale in vegetable freezing. The economies of scale in physical efficiency in the processing of vegetables are not unlike the economies shown in other studies (see the footnotes to Table 3.1).

Economies of Scale in Warehousing or Storage

Although many studies have been conducted on efficiency of operations of warehousing or storage of food and other products, only one study will be cited here. The purpose is not so much to review the literature as to generally show that there are physical efficiencies in scale of storage just as there are in processing.

Cost of freezer storage (-10°F) operations for frozen fruits and vegetables for capacities of from 500,000 to 30,000,000 lb (2800-120,000 sq ft) were conducted in 1969 (Greig 1969). Included were costs of land, building, equipment, pallets, racks, lift trucks, supervisory and labor costs, taxes, interest on investment, repairs, and electrical and fuel costs; not included were interest on investment in inventories, or state and local property taxes on inventories. The cost per month for storage of frozen 30-lb cans of fruit were as follows:

Storage Capacity (sq ft)	2800	4400	13,000	21,000	40,000	80,000	120,000
Cost per 30-lb can per mo. (¢)	8.65	8.21	5.05	4.87	4.19	3.58	3.33

Although scale economies may be greater in refrigerated or frozen storage operations than in common storage, economies of scale most certainly exist.

Economies of Scale in Transportation

Transportation costs and rate structures are complex. For brevity, the economies of scale in transportation will be discussed in the simplest terms. The rate structures for most processed food products with most common carriers, (truck, rail, or barge) are set by the Interstate Commerce Commission. Many rate structures are based on minimum loading requirements, with lesser rates the greater the minimum load (within limits).

For LCL (less than car lot) shipments by rail or truck the cost per 100 lb shipped may be 3 to 5 times the rate per 100 lb for a full car lot. Further, as the weight of the loading of a full rail car goes up, the rate per 100 lb goes down. For example, on frozen fruits and vegetables the rate per 100 lb from Seattle, Washington to New York City is $2.19 for a 46,000-lb minimum loading but only $1.87 with a 100,000-lb minimum loading (nearly 15% less).

In addition, some railroads have instigated a 1,000,000-lb rate. Typically, 6 to 10 or more full carload lots must be loaded in 1 day, transported on the same train, unloaded in 1 day at destination, and, in some cases, a minimum charge for further transportation by common carrier must be included. Then the shipper qualifies for a 1,000,000-lb rate which is substantially below normal rates. Going even farther, some railroads have train load rates and others are actually leasing trains to big shippers (grain) by the year. Under the rent-a-train program initiated by the Illinois Central Railroad, Cargill, Inc. has rented a train at an annual rental agreement of $800,000 a year plus a ton-mile charge for the train (Anon. 1968). There has been much speculation that unit train rates and rent-a-train agreements could spread to other commodities (Anon. 1969A).

The railroad rate structures are not as difficult to change as one might imagine. Often a processor in a particular location may obtain a favorable rate to certain destinations in bargaining sessions with the railroads. The author was recently told by a research staff member of a railroad company that the railroad had researched truck transportation costs of grain in one area then set rail rates just below the operating costs for trucks (no fixed costs were used — just operating costs). I cite this example to show that rail rates are changeable and probably negotiable when a large processing plant is concerned.

Needless to say, many small processors cannot take advantage of the rate structures involving large volumes. Even though data were presented only for rail shipments, there are substantial economies of scale of shipments by most methods of transportation.

ECONOMIES OF SCALE IN STATE AND LOCAL PROPERTY TAXES

Because there are economies of scale in physical facilities, there are also economies in state and local property taxes. In most states, state and local property taxes are based on a taxed-based "true" or "real" market value. For example, in Michigan in 1967, the average state and local property tax for fruit and vegetable processing plants was around $22.50 per yr per $1000 market value. Referring to our example on economies of scale in freezing, a freezing line to process 2000 lb per hr of frozen vegetables costs around $97,350 and a line to process 30,000 lb per hr, $799,910. Thus, property taxes would be $2190 for the 2000-lb per hr plant and $17,947 for the 30,000-lb plant. While the larger plant has a capacity 15 times that of the smaller, the state and local property taxes would be only 8.2 times greater than for the smaller plant.

Although undocumented, recent evidence suggests that in some states newer facilities are paying lesser rates in local property taxes than older facilities. This suggests that bargaining with local tax assessment agencies is not uncommon both as to the rate and as to the "true" market value. The implication is that the larger facilities may have greater leverage in bargaining with local tax assessment authorities in some locations.

ECONOMIES OF SCALE IN FINANCING

In an industry as large as food processing, every conceivable type of financing is used; therefore, only a few general types of financing as related to scale will be used here.

First, for example, let us take a small firm in financial difficulties which is being financed largely by trade credit. This is not a difficult situation to imagine since 32% of the food processing firm reported negative incomes for tax purposes in 1965-1966 (Greig 1968). Other studies have shown that trade credit approaches 20% of total assets in firms with less than $1,000,000 in assets (Anon. 1961). Let us further assume that trade credit is being given by suppliers on the basis of "2/10, n/30." This means that there is a 2% discount if the bill is paid in 10 days, and that the net bill must be paid in 30 days. Let's also assume that the processor cannot pay the bill in 10 days but can pay it in 30 days — the effective rate of interest for this type of financing is 36% per yr.[2]

The next step up in financing might be on an unsecured note at a bank. This might cost 10-12% on today's market (1969). Larger firms might obtain secured notes based on inventories at 9-10%. We can follow this trend on to the very largest firms, financially very sound, who can obtain funds at the prime rate (around 7% in early 1969).

Besides differences in cost based on size and a firm's financial soundness there are differences in availability even though the rate may be nearly the same. That is, a small firm equally as financially sound as a large firm may have difficulties in obtaining funds a large firm would not have.

There are also economies to scale in new stock issues and other types of financing.

OTHER ECONOMIES TO SCALE

There are certainly other economies to scale in food processing, economies in procurement of supplies — raw materials, containers, packaging materials — and other inputs to the firm. At some size levels the processor may manufacture his own containers and packaging materials.

There are also economies in by-product utilization. For example, a small applesauce or apple slice manufacturer may sell off-grade apples, peels, and cores to another processor who makes vinegar or apple juice. A larger sized processor may process pasteurized apple juice himself; and with a still larger size, it may be feasible to process concentrated apple juice.

Economies of multiple product processing are very important in seasonal products to enable a larger total processing season throughout the year. Even in nonseasonal products there certainly are economies in selling a multiple-product line compared to a single-product line. Economies also exist in mixed lot shipping to take advantage of full car lot freight rates.

DISECONOMIES TO SCALE

If data on profitability in food processing are greatly summarized or greatly aggregated to a point that most variability is removed, there appears to be a

---

[2] For using the money an additional 20 days, the user loses 2%: 360÷20 = 18 (twenty-day periods a year) times 2% = 36%, the effective annual interest rate.

relationship between the size of the firm and profitability, with, of course, the largest firms being the most profitable (Table 3.4). However, if the data are disaggregated, often the variability by size classes are so great there is not a significant correlation between size and profitability. In recent statistical tests, Arnould (1969) did not find a significant correlation between size and profitability, or between market concentration and profitability in food processing. His results would be partially supported by the variability of profits by size class in food processing in 1965-1966 as shown in Table 3.5. In the 1965-1966 data, profit levels (returns on equity) were not significantly different for firms ranging from over $250,000 in assets to over $100,000,000 but less than $250,000,000 in assets. In fact, for most of the industries listed in Table 3.5, the largest asset size class was not the most profitable. For example, in the canning and freezing industry the most profitable asset size class was from $1,000,000 to $5,000,000, in meat products it was from $500,000 to $1,000,000, and in grain mill products it was also from $500,000 to $1,000,000, etc.

Perhaps the size versus profitability needs further explanation. In 1965-1966 and 1966-1967 there were over 5000 food processing firms with total assets under $100,000. On the average these plants tended to be unprofitable. However, once an asset size of $250,000 or more was reached there were no significant increases in profitability as the size of the firm further increased. While large firms are profitable and the very small firms are unprofitable, after a certain minimum size is reached the data are not consistently clear to show a correlation between size and profitability.

The point to be made is this: despite the large economies of scale theoretically available to larger food processors, either they are unable to use them effectively or apparently they are counterbalanced by other diseconomies to scale. If this is an overstatement perhaps we can ameliorate it and at least suggest that the actual differences in profitability in different size classes of food processing

TABLE 3.4

PROFITS AFTER INCOME TAXES AS A PERCENT OF NET
WORTH FOR FOOD AND KINDRED PRODUCTS MANUFACTURERS,
BY ASSET SIZE CLASS; 1947, 1954, and 1958-1961[1]

| | Asset Size Class ($1000) | | | | | |
Year	Under $100	$100-$1000	$1000-$50,000	$50,000-$100,000	Over $100,000	Total
1947	5.8	12.0	15.3	16.6	12.4	14.2
1954	−4.4	5.0	6.8	7.7	7.8	6.8
1958	−1.3	5.1	7.3	8.7	8.4	7.6
1959	−5.6	6.2	7.5	9.3	9.1	7.9
1960	−5.6	5.6	6.1	7.3	9.6	7.3
1961	−2.7	5.9	6.2	8.1	9.3	7.5

Source: Source Book of Statistics of Income, IRS, U.S. Treasury Dept.

TABLE 3.5

PROFITS AFTER INCOME TAXES AS A PERCENT OF OWNERS' EQUITY
FOR FOOD AND KINDRED PRODUCTS MANUFACTURERS, BY PRODUCT CLASSES
BY ASSET SIZE CLASS, 1965-1966 TAX YEAR

Food Manufacturing Classification	Asset Size Class ($1000)												Weighted Average
	Under 50	50 Under 100	100 Under 250	250 Under 500	500 Under 1000	1000 Under 5000	5000 Under 10,000	10,000 Under 25,000	25,000 Under 50,000	50,000 Under 100,000	100,000 Under 250,000	Over 250,000	
Canning and freezing (SIC 2030)	-80.4	-83.8	-5.8	8.0	3.4	11.8	9.4	10.9	7.2	8.3	7.5	10.1	9.0
Meat products (SIC 2010)	—	-12.2	8.8	5.4	12.2	7.2	8.0	9.0	4.5	-2.9	7.2	2.5	4.5
Grain mill products (SIC 2040)	—	9.8	10.4	4.5	14.9	4.2	7.2	7.3	7.7	7.0	9.3	13.1	9.6
Dairy products (SIC 2020)	-.3	-3.5	.7	2.1	4.6	6.2	7.3	6.1	9.6	7.6	10.2	11.8	8.6
Bakery products (SIC 2050)	-6.6	-6.0	-1.2	13.0	-1.0	8.9	5.4	9.3	6.9	2.4	6.1	16.2	7.8
Bottled soft drinks and flavorings (SIC 2086)	-18.6	0.6	13.9	13.6	10.1	10.2	11.8	14.4	21.2	21.7	—	18.4	15.0
Vegetable and animal oils (SIC 2091)	-16.4	32.8	13.8	18.0	14.3	8.8	7.7	8.9	-0.3	6.0	4.9	8.6	8.0
Sugar processing (SIC 2060)	—	—	—	-103.7	11.7	3.8	5.7	8.2	4.1	4.9	9.4	9.6	6.9
Malt liquors and malts (SIC 2082)	-10.9	-228.6	-34.1	-6.0	-0.8	3.8	7.5	6.9	6.1	4.5	10.4	11.3	7.8
Distilled, rectified and blended liquors except brandy (SIC 2086)	—	—	—	—	16.7	12.1	7.3	14.4	13.4	10.7	4.3	5.2	6.3
Wines, brandy, and brandy spirits (SIC 2084)	-35.3	14.3	7.6	—	10.9	-2.3	7.7	12.4	7.4	7.4	—	—	6.9
Food not otherwise classified (SIC 2099)	31.5	-200.0	—	5.5	—	—	34.0	—	—	8.8	2.1	16.6	14.2
All food processing	-6.0	-8.4	6.8	8.3	8.3	7.9	8.6	9.1	7.3	5.6	8.2	10.4	8.6

Source: Greig (1968).

firms are much less than would be expected based on the theoretical economies of scale.

The author feels that many of the economies to scale are real, but the resulting lack of consistent profitability increases as the firm size increases leaves me in a dilemma. It is this dilemma that I wish to further explore.

First, there are many processing plants below a minimum efficient size (Table 3.1). However, for a minimum efficient size in many processing categories the capital investment is relatively modest. Perhaps many of the physical economies to scale can be obtained by relatively small sized firms. While the total cost curve may continue to decrease with increased plant size, it decreases at a decreasing rate. Perhaps most of the economies to scale in storage, transportation, finance, and even management may be obtained by relatively small sized firms. For example, most of the economies to scale in management (Fig. 3.1) occur by the time an asset size of $10,000,000 is attained. Although management costs tend to continue to decrease they decrease at a decreasing rate.

Second, bigness and economies to scale are not synonymous. While bigness may be a necessary condition for some economies to scale, bigness in itself does not guarantee economies to scale. Big firms can be inefficient, using few of the available economies of scale. Or, diseconomies can outweigh possible economies to scale. Bigness may come about by the aggregation of many product lines, none of which are operating under particularly great economies to scale.

Third, possibly the greatest economies to scale are in research and development and in advertising and promotion. Admittedly, only a substantially sized firm would be able to capture all the economies of scale available to it. However, as has been previously suggested, the large firms may compete in product development and advertising and promotion, while the smaller firms compete on the efficient production of commodities. Perhaps there is as much real competition among the large firms in new product development and advertising and promotion as there is among other firms who rival each other in efficiency of production of commodities.

Fourth, the larger firms appear to maintain a more conservative financial management, i.e., leverage, and operate with less borrowed funds reflecting less return to owners' equity.

There are probably many diseconomies to scale in large business firms. Although we cannot quantify or weight them as to importance, we can at least list some of them. There are probably disadvantages of large scale organizations in administration, decision making, in unwieldiness due to size, perhaps in asset fixity, in finding new ventures for investing profits, and probably in motivation of salaried personnel compared to motivation of key personnel in smaller firms where they may also be owners of the firm.

Nevertheless, there are many plants and firms in food processing operating substantially below the level at which they might capture some economies to scale. Secondly, the desire for bigness would probably be strong even if substantial economies did not accompany it.

RESULTS OF ECONOMIES OF SCALE IN FOOD PROCESSING

The initial direct result of economies of scale in food processing has been the rapid and continuous reduction in the number of food processing plants necessary in the United States. Although the total physical volume and dollar value of processed food continuously increases, the numbers of plants decrease.

Between 1958 and 1967, the number of food manufacturing plants declined from 41,867 to 32,585, a decline of 22.1%. A large decrease was in fluid milk processing where the number of plants fell from 5828 in 1958 to 3488 in 1967, a 40.1% decline. Another large drop was in the bread industry where numbers of plants declined from 6026 to 4049, a decline of 32.8%. Meat packing plants increased from 2810 plants in 1954 to 2992 in 1963, but then dropped to 2707 plants in 1967, so the 10-yr 1958-1967 decline was only 3.7%. This relatively small decline is probably due to the closing of some large terminal facilities and the building of several smaller, more modern plants in livestock production areas. These data on slaughtering plants are not nearly what one woudl expect from the results of economies of scale studies by Logan and King (1962) and by Huie (1969). The long-run tendency will be for significantly fewer and larger slaughtering plants.

Other external effects of economies of scale in processing have been its effect of specialization of production areas, nationalization of markets, and the development of a systems approach in marketing rather than a perfectly competitive market at the farm level. These aspects will be covered later in some detail.

While there has been a great decrease in numbers of plants, there also have been a decrease in the numbers of firms involved in food processing. An example of an industry with a rapidly decreasing number of firms is the cherry processing industry. In a survey of cherry processing firms in the Great Lakes Region in 1966, nearly 50% had merged with or acquired other firms in the past 5 yrs (Ricks et al. 1966). This tendency toward merger would probably be even greater if it were not for the FTC scrutiny of most mergers. In fact, while the economic tendency is toward largeness, the FTC, through prohibition of many horizontal mergers because of "undue competition" and "restraint of trade," continually tries to enforce smallness through merger restriction. The FTC regulations may be hurting the ones they are trying to protect. Performance tests indicate no undue profits by either food processors or food retailers. Since the economic tendency is toward largeness, it would not appear that the consumer "is being protected" by the FTC. Much evidence points in the opposite direction – that is, that food would be cheaper with more larger firms. Also, the smaller processors who are in financial difficulties or who need capital for expansion are not being protected by the FTC. In fact, it is these firms who may be harmed the most as the market for their firms may be quite limited. Many of the smaller firms, if merged into a larger organization, might be very viable with the infusion of new capital, new management, and multiplant economies. But because the FTC regulations prevent the absorption of these firms by larger firms, the result is slow strangulation and eventual bankruptcy.

FUTURE NUMBERS OF PROCESSING PLANTS

We have discussed economies to scale, presented data on average size of food processing plants compared to "minimum efficient size" and have discussed statistical census data showing declining numbers of processing plants. However, before generalizing from these data, one more dimension should be added. Three case examples of studies which suggest possible optimum numbers of plants for a specific industry, either for a region or for the United States as a whole, will follow; one on soybean crushing, one on beef slaughtering plants, and one on the green pea freezing industry.

SOYBEAN CRUSHING

Leunis (1968), in his excellent study, centered his analysis on location of production and processing. While he did not specifically determine the minimum number and sizes of plants for an optimum solution, he did use differences in sizes of plants amoung areas in determining processing costs. From his data on economies of scale and from subsequent data from Arkansas soybean crushing plants (Stuart and Morrison 1969), one could estimate the numbers of crushing plants that might be required.

Essentially, in developing his analysis of location of soybean processing, Leunis used the following inputs: (1) The supply of soybeans produced in each region (a region was a state or group of states). (2) He assumed that the process of converting soybeans into meal and oil was similar among regions — but that costs differ based on plant size and various other inputs including labor wage rates. (3) He assumed that the processing capacity was given (or fixed) for each region at its present level (1967-1968). (4) He developed costs of transfer for soybeans, meal, and oil from industry transportation cost data. (5) He developed regional and international demands for meal and oil. These were represented by price-dependent demand functions.

In his linear programming solution of a minimum cost production, processing, and distribution system, he also developed the cost advantages among regions. This was done using 1967-1968 production data.

In an analysis of future locations, Leunis projected 1975-1976 production and, using similar procedures as for the 1967-1968 model, resolved the problem. In this second analysis he relaxed the assumption that processing capacity was fixed in any area. As in the first model, the analysis determined the optimal regional quantities of soybeans crushed; the optimum resulting flow pattern of soybeans, meal and oil; and the set of price differentials consistent with the optimum flow pattern.

The optimum crush of soybeans for the 1967-1968 season, compared to 1967-1968 soybean crushing capacity, is given in Table 3.6. Notice that for an optimum solution some areas should utilize only about 1/2 their present crushing capacity.

The optimum pattern for 1975-1976 soybean crush is also listed in Table 3.6.

[3] See Table 3.6 for the definitions of the regions.

TABLE 3.6

OPTIMUM CRUSH OF SOYBEANS, BY REGIONS, WITH EXCESS CAPACITY
AND PERCENTAGE OF CAPACITY UTILIZED, 1967-1968 AND 1975-76

Region	1967-1968 Optimum Crush (Metric Tons)	1967-1968 Excess Capacity (Metric Tons)	1967-1968 Capacity Utilized %	(1975-1976) Optimum Crush (Million Tons)
1. New York, Vermont, New Hampshire, Maine, Massachusetts, Connecticut, Rhode Island, Pennsylvania, New Jersey	0	0	—	29,787
2. Delaware, Maryland, Virginia, West Virginia	457,327	145,483	76	365,466
3. North Carolina, South Carolina	739,200	—	100	1,362,330
4. Alabama, Georgia, Florida	851,100	—	100	2,367,745
5. Kentucky and Tennessee	971,864	610,236	61	474,699
6. Ohio and Michigan	1,031,100	—	100	1,914,948
7. Indiana	1,336,600	—	100	2,099,891
8. Illinois	2,298,142	1,987,158	54	1,752,036
9. Louisiana and Mississippi	491,645	711,255	41	718,370
10. Arkansas	1,010,129	604,671	63	1,399,420
11. Missouri	561,796	185,604	75	699,671
12. Iowa	2,660,686	255,314	91	3,009,862
13. Minnesota and Wisconsin	1,418,631	149,869	90	1,491,089
14. North Dakota and South Dakota	—	—	—	519,885
15. Nebraska and Kansas	809,002	77,498	91	1,597,136
16. Texas and Oklahoma	65,500	—	100	493,716
17. Arizona and New Mexico	—	—	—	—
18. Montana, Indiana, Wyoming, and Colorado	—	—	—	—
19. California and Nevada	—	49,100	0	—
TOTAL	14,702,722			20,296,051

Source: Leunis (1968).

Some regions are projected to decrease their crush in spite of the greatly increased total U.S. crush projected for 1975-1976. The regions that would decrease crush are Region 2 (Delaware, Maryland, Virginia, and West Virginia), Region 5 (Kentucky and Tennessee), and Region 8 (Illinois). Many of the other areas will substantially increase their crush. However, even with the big increase in total crush projected for 1975-1976, only Regions 1, 3, 4, 6, 7, 14, and 16 will have to increase their processing capacity.[3] The other regions with projected increases in crushing would already have the processing capacity to handle the projected increases.

Apparently, there are considerable economies of scale in soybean crushing. Leunis (1968) suggested that "the processing cost per bushel of soybeans decreases from a high of 17.00¢ for a processing mill with annual capacity of 3,300,000 bu to a low of 12.25¢ for a processing mill with annual capacity 22,000,000 bu." Stuart and Morrison (1969), in a more detailed study including procurement costs, suggested that economies of scale existed in a range of plant sizes from 5,500,000 bu per yr to at least 19,800,000 bu per yr. In their study of model plants they suggested, "as indicated by the decreasing costs per bushel, the internal economics of size in transforming soybeans into products were not offset by the external diseconomies of distance [in procurement] over the range of densities and plant sizes studied."

This would suggest the optimum size of plant, for which data are available from past studies, would be in the range of 20-22 million bushels per year. Dividing this capacity into total crush would give around 28-30 plants needed for the 1967-1968 crush and around 38-40 plants for the 1975-1976 crush.

Actually, the soybean industry is probably operating nearer to estimates of optimality than most other food processing enterprises. In 1967 there were an estimated 102 plants in the United States and this number has been decreasing. Thus, the number of plants is only around three times that of estimated economic optimums. (How far economies of scale may exceed the 19.8-22 million bushel capacity and when procurement costs exceed additional economics in physical processing has not yet been specified in research work to date.) Changes in production densities, freight costs of soybeans, meal, and oil, processing costs, location of demand and in-demand relationships between oil and meal will, of course, affect locations and numbers of plants.

BEEF SLAUGHTERING PLANTS

Huie (1969) analyzed the optimum number, size, and location (by counties) of beef slaughtering plants in Michigan for 1980. While in 1967 there were 169 commercial beef slaughtering plants in Michigan, his analysis for 1980 indicated that 4 plants would be the optimum number.

Input data for his model included: (1) Cattle marketings by county (with two exceptions) were projected to 1980. (2) Beef consumption by areas (multi-county areas) were projected to 1980. (3) An estimate of the average transportation rate charged for hauling live cattle by for-hire truckers. (4) An estimate of the average cost of transporting carcass beef was made. (5) Fifteen potential plant sites were selected to represent various areas of the state. (6) An estimate of the relationship between cost of beef slaughtering and size of plants was made which drew heavily from original data on economies of scale in beef slaughtering as determined by Logan and King (1962).

Huie used a trade-off between economies of scale in plants compared to raw product procurement costs (Stollsteimer 1963) and then a transshipment model to include distribution costs of the carcass beef. Under his assumptions four slaughtering plants would be the optimum number in 1980 (Table 3.7). Using the computer, the total costs from the optimum location of 1 plant, 2 plants, 3 plants — on up to the total costs for the locations of 15 slaughter plants were calculated. Total costs of procurement and processing started to increase at the level of four plants. Adding the transshipment model of distribution of carcass beef to Michigan's markets did not change the numbers of plants.

Plant location was not as critical as the numbers of plants. The 4 plants for Michigan could have been located in 35 different combinations of the 15 original sites chosen with less than a 5% increase in total costs.

TABLE 3.7

ESTIMATED LIVESTOCK ASSEMBLY AND PROCESSING COSTS
FOR BEEF SLAUGHTERING BY NUMBER OF PLANTS WITH
SPECIFIED LOCATIONS IN MICHIGAN, 1969

No. of Plants and Least-cost Locations	Livestock Assembly Cost Total Cost	Decrease in Cost[1]	No. of Head Processed	Annual Processing Cost[2]	Increased Processing Cost	Change in Total Cost
1 Plant						
Jackson	$3,519,666	—	1,226,155	$10,328,774	—	—
2 Plants						
Alma	2,880,682	$638,984	502,996	4,327,856	$153,895	$−485,089
Adrian	—	—	723,159	6,154,813	—	—
3 Plants						
Saginaw	2,522,795	357,887	424,422	3,675,833	153,895	−203,992
Adrian	—	—	449,735	3,885,886	—	—
Sturgis	—	—	351,998	3,074,845	—	—
4 Plants						
Alma	2,307,217	215,578	295,613	2,606,951	153,895	−61,683
Sandusky	—	—	169,932	1,564,025	—	—
Adrian	—	—	449,735	3,885,885	—	—
Sturgis	—	—	310,875	2,733,598	—	—
5 Plants						
Alma	2,223,655	83,562	167,272	1,541,952	153,895	+ 70,333
Sandusky	—	—	169,932	1,564,025	—	—
Iona	—	—	242,352	2,164,980	—	—
Adrian	—	—	455,726	3,935,600	—	—
South Bend	—	—	190,873	1,737,997	—	—

[1] Source: Huie (1969). Decrease in assembly cost compared to the previous number of plants.

[2] Based on total processing cost function of $y = \$153,895 + \$8.2982\ X$, where y = total annual processing cost and X = number of head slaughtered annually.

THE GREEN PEA FREEZING INDUSTRY

Heifner and Greig (1970) used a Stollsteimer model in each area of commercial production and then a minimum cost transshipment model from production areas to markets in the 48 mainland states to determine numbers, sizes, and locations of green pea freezing plants. In a sense, they used procedures similar to that used by Huie, but combined studies of each production area into a national model.

Among the inputs in the model were procurement costs compared to economies of scale in processing. A different cost function was developed for processing in each state based on length of the processing season; hours of processing per day; differences in fuel and electrical costs; differences in labor wage rates; differences in state, local and federal taxes; and complementarity of product mix (based on industry averages from industry surveys). The market for frozen peas was the U.S. market, based on weighted per capita consumption by states. Raw product prices by states were obtained from the U.S. Dept. of Agr. Crop Reporting Service.

The analysis showed that major shifts in location of green pea freezing should occur. Green pea freezing would take place only in Wisconsin, the Washington-Oregon-Idaho area, and the Delaware-Maryland area. There would be 3 plants in Wisconsin, 2 plants in Washington (Washington-Oregon-Idaho complex) and 2 plants in Delaware (Delaware-Eastern Shore of Maryland), totaling 7 plants serving the U.S. market.

However, within an area, the numbers and locations of plants could change materially without greatly affecting total costs. Shifting 3 or 4 plants among several locations within a state changed total costs less than 5%. Similarly, in many cases changes in plant numbers from 2 to 4 or 5 did not greatly increase costs. The big difference in costs in the green pea freezing analysis was cost differences among states. Changing a location within a state might not be significant, but changing from one state to another substantially affected costs.

After a point is reached near an optimum number of plants, the costs do rise continuously with additional plants. The further from the optimum number the greater the total industry costs. Thus, while there may be many institutional factors to preclude there being only seven green pea freezing plants in the United States, the nearer the industry comes to this the less the total costs of procurement, processing, and distribution. Although a good count of the actual number of green pea freezing plants in the United States is not available, it probably is 2 to 4 times the optimum suggested by Heifner and Greig (1970), and most likely a large proportion of these are in the "wrong" locations.

AN OVERVIEW AND SUMMARY

While the author has stated the economic analyses done by Leunis, Huie, and Heifner and Greig in a positive clear-cut manner, in reality this is probably not the case in any of the three studies. In performing an analysis, many assumptions must be made. How near the assumptions approach reality are not known in many cases. The analysis may reflect industry averages, while perhaps it should be of "best" plants rather than state averages. Hopefully, the models are better than a mere computational exercise; none of those described are better than the inputs used in the models. A careful review of the details and assumptions made in the analysis of each of the models should be made before accepting the results at face value.

Hoover and Vernon (1962) expressed this quite succinctly: "When all is said, the calculus of location is still something to be done firm by firm, plant by plant. Any synthesis which fails to take into account the myriad different cost structures of the different plants could easily mislead. Accordingly, any effort at synthesis would be foiled at the outset if it were not for the fact that most of the forces move so clearly in the same direction."

In any case, the three models presented (and many others have been conducted along similar lines) show substantial potential industry savings by reductions in the numbers of food processing plants. The reduction in numbers of plants range from around a 50% reduction in soybean crushing, to a 50-75% reduction in frozen green pea processing, to a nearly phenomenal reduction in beef slaughtering plants.

Perhaps a major part of the efficiencies in larger plants is that machinery and equipment are replacing manual labor in much of food processing, and there is apparently much economies to scale in many types of equipment. The equipment can work 24 hr a day, 7 days a week, whereas it may be difficult and costly to get labor to work on this sort of schedule. Thus, the size of a food processing plant is becoming less dependent on restrictions as to a local labor supply. The cost per unit of output from a machine decreases continuously with increased length of use per season — while it is entirely possible that with increased use of labor (considering overtime) the cost per unit of output might actually increase. Therefore, a highly mechanized operation would tend to work longer hours per year than one using large quantities of manual labor, again decreasing the total numbers of plants needed.

If we follow this trend to its ultimate end we can visualize a food processing plant that works continuously the year around and the only labor involved is that of an engineer monitoring computer-controlled engineering systems. Because of the variability and seasonality of raw agricultural products, this type of operation may, at first glance, appear to be some time away. In fact, this variability and seasonality of many raw agricultural products is a major factor contributing to costly operations. The same factors yield incentives to overcome both variability and the resulting high cost in processing — leading to rapid mechanization of many processes that were once largely manual operations. This is one of the large incentives in the production of analogs, substitutes, and synthetics. There need not be either variability of inputs or seasonality of production, and much of the operations become complete mechanized. Speaking of meat analogs, one food technologist says, "In 10 years, I'll have a plant that will turn out mile-long 'beefsteaks.' Machines will stamp them out, wrap them, and freeze them" (Anon. 1969B).

Although census data do show a rather continuous decrease in both numbers of plants and firms in food processing, the author's thesis is that the trend will accelerate. Even at current stages of knowledge of technologies of processes and equipment, the optimum numbers of processing plants from an efficiency standpoint should probably be from 50-75% less than current numbers.

BIBLIOGRAPHY

ANON. 1961. Quarterly report for manufacturing corporations (Third Quarter 1961). Federal Trade Comm. and Securities Exchange Comm. 28-33.

ANON. 1964. Commerce Clearing House, Pat. No. 15,773, Nov. 1962, Trade Regulation Reports, Procter & Gamble Co. Second Mutual Order to Cease and Desist, as quoted by James Shaffer. Agricultural Market Analysis, Bur. Business Econ. Res. Graduate School of Business Admin., Michigan State University, East Lansing, Mich.

ANON. 1966. The structure of food manufacturing. Natl. Comm. Food Marketing, Tech. Study 8.

ANON. 1968. Wall Street J., Oct. 31.

ANON. 1969A. Rent-a-train controversy continues to rage in grain industry – will concept spread to other commodities. Weekly Dig. 75, No. 32, 5, Feb. 15.

ANON. 1969B. Meatless meats – several firms develop soybean-based copies of beef, pork, and chicken. Wall Street J. Oct. 2.

ARNOULD, R. J. 1969. Conglomerate growth and profitability. In Economics of Conglomerate Growth, L. Garoian (Editor). Agr. Res. Found., Oregon State Univ., Corvallis.

BRESSLER. R. G. 1945. Research determination of economies of scale. J. Farm Econ. 27, 526-539.

BUZZELL, R. D., and NOURSE, R. E. M. 1966. Product innovation, the product life cycle and competitive behavior in selected food processing industries, 1947-64. Report to the Natl. Comm. Food Marketing, Arthur D. Little, Acorn Park, Mass., Feb.

FRENCH, B. C., SAMMET, L. L., and BRESSLER, R. G., 1956. Economic efficiency in plant operation with special reference to the marketing of California pears. Hilgardia 24, No. 19, July.

GELSTHORPE, E. 1965. New product merchandising. Talk at 11th Ann. Agr. Marketing Clinic, Michigan State Univ. East Lansing, Mich., Mar. 1965.

GREIG, W. S. 1968. Balance sheets, income statements and financial operating ratios for the food processing industry, 1965-66. Michigan State Univ., Agr. Econ. Rept. 117, Nov.

GREIG, W. S. 1969. Economies of Scale in Freezing Operations. Michigan State Univ., Dept. Agr. Econ. Mimeo 1969.

HEIFNER, R. G., and GREIG, W. S. 1970. Locating green pea freezing plants to serve the U.S. market Dept. Agr. Econ., Michigan State Univ. (in press).

HOFFMAN, A. C. 76th Congress. Large scale organization in the food industries. TNEC Monogram 35, 76th Congress, 3rd Session.

HOOVER, E. M., and VERNON, R. 1962. Anatomy of a Metropolis. Anchor Books, Garden City, N.Y.

HUIE, J. M. 1969. Number, size, and location of beef slaughtering plants in Michigan. Ph.D. Thesis, Dept. Agr. Econ., Michigan State Univ., East Lansing, Mich.

LEUNIS, J. V. 1968. A spatial analysis of the United States soybean industry. Ph.D. Thesis, Univ. Illinois, Urbana, Ill.

LOGAN, S. H., and KING, G. A. 1962. Economies of scale in beef slaughter plants. Univ. California Agr. Expt. Sta. Giannini Found. Res. Rept. 260.

REED, R. H., and SAMMET, L. L. 1963. Multiple-product processing of California frozen vegetables. California Agr. Expt. Sta. Giannini Found. Res. Rept. 264.

RICKS, D. et al. 1966. Great Lakes tart cherry industry processor survey. Michigan State Univ., Agr. Econ. Rept. 58.

STOLLSTEIMER, J. F. 1963. A working model for plant numbers and locations. J. Farm Econ. 45, Aug.

STUART, C., JR., and MORRISON, W. R. 1969. Economies of size in soybean processing plants. Arkansas Agr. Expt. Sta. Bull. 743, May.

CHAPTER 4

Ronald D. Knutson[1]
R. E. Schneidau[1]

Regulation of Competition in Food Marketing

Our economy is a capitalistic free enterprise system. In such a system profits are the primary motivating force. Consumers' desires, through changes in the price signal, direct the production of the most extensive array of products in the history of the world. There is no doubt that our consumers are among the most pampered and best fed in the world. . .and are accomplishing this on less than 18% of their disposable incomes.

Yet there exist, at times, business practices which tend to lessen competition, drive out competitors, raise prices, and concentrate economic power to the detriment of other business firms and consumers alike. Such practices have precipitated many of the regulations which exist in both food and nonfood industries.

Because the extent of regulation is so closely tied to the competitive conditions and practices existing in an industry, it follows that any specific regulation may have far-reaching implications to individual firms. A basic understanding of the functioning of the competitive system can better provide a foundation for understanding and interpreting the reasons for any likely effects of regulation.

THE NATURE OF A COMPETITIVE MARKET ECONOMY

The focus of a competitive market economy is on the free interaction of buyers and sellers in determining price. The competitive market relies upon conditions existing such that firms are motivated to reduce costs through increases in efficiency. Price reductions in line with cost reductions occur because of the ever-present danger of the inefficient firm being driven from the market by new or existing competitors producing similar products.

Consumers in such a system are free to spend their incomes in such a way so as to guide business firms as to what and how much to produce. Since business firms make decisions of what and how much to produce on the basis of price-cost relationships, the higher price is over costs the more the industry will produce. If too little is produced, price will rise above costs and production will increase in response to profits. If too much is produced, price will fall below costs and productive resources (land, labor, capital) will shift to more highly valued alternatives. This process will continue until, in the long run, all products are priced at their long-run average cost including a normal level of profits.

In summary, a competitive market economy exists in a situation where many firms are selling similar products in a single market, and where no one firm is

[1]Ronald D. Knutson and R. E. Schneidau are in the Department of Agricultural Economics, Purdue Univ., Lafayette, Ind.

large enough to wrest a significant share of the market so as to influence market price. Individual firms react to market conditions independently and in their own interest without concern over the actions of other firms in the market. The competitive market results in a distribution of returns to productive resources (land, labor, capital) equal to their productive contribution. It results in production of products desired by consumers at their lowest possible cost. It results in a maximum amount of goods available for sale consistent with economic efficiency.

Government direction and control of competitive factors is largely unnecessary under such a competitive free enterprise system, since market power is diffused or decentralized rather than concentrated or centralized in the hands of a few firms.

IMPERFECTLY COMPETITIVE MARKET ECONOMY

Many of the characteristics of the competitive market economy exist across all forms of business organization. Yet it is departure from competitive markets which gives rise to much of the regulation in our economy. The essence of the imperfectly competitive market lies in the varying degrees of concentration or centralization of economic power possessed by the firms in different markets. There are several basic reasons as to why this concentration of economic power comes about:

Desire to Gain Increased Technical Efficiency and Reduced Costs

Most productive processes can be done more efficiently through specialization of labor and substitution of capital, in the form of machines, for labor. Both of these factors result in larger production units. In some industries (automobiles, as an example) it may well be that just a few firms are necessary to produce all the output demanded. To reduce their size may significantly raise their production costs and prices to final consumers.

Desire For Market Power

A second force which may result in the concentration of economic power is the desire for market power. If firms can use their market power to influence prices and output, they can isolate themselves from normal competitive pressures and increase profits. Firms in a dominant market position generally have substantial market power.

Desire for Social And Political Power

With size or centralization of economic power often comes political power and social standing. Firms and their executives are frequently evaluated on the basis of sustained firm growth. Thus, firms may grow for the sake of growth alone. Interest in the political power of business has recently been renewed by a growing alliance between business and government.

These forces acting to concentrate economic power, result in a market organization where the individual buyer or seller finds that an increase or decrease in his output affects the market price for the commodity it produces. In this situation there are so few buyers or sellers that the action of one is no longer independent of the actions of others.

Such interdependence among firms is characteristic of imperfect competition. The actions of one firm are felt by all others in the market. In some situations any attempts to reduce price are swiftly met by retaliatory actions on the part of other firms. Because of interdependence of prices, firms may soon realize that price competition is not in their general profit-making interest. Firms operating in such an environment may find it to their advantage to attempt to influence consumers' buying decisions through advertising and promotion. If successful, a disproportionate flow of income may be generated for the firm or industry doing the advertising. This income comes at the expense of firms or industries not involved in extensive advertising. Large firms in highly concentrated industries are most able to advertise.

Because the individual firm may find that an increase in its output may decrease the market price for the commodity, the firm may find it to its advantage to restrict output. . .which also means restricting his demand for the inputs of land, labor and capital. This releases an "excess supply" of these factors for use in another sector of the economy, lowering their value and therefore their income.

In a dynamic market economy, a new demand for these resources may be generated thereby maintaining full levels of resource employment. Even so, the restriction of their use in some industries still results in a reallocation or redistribution of income to these factors. If the resource is relatively abundant, the restriction in its use will lower the returns to all units of that resource provided a new use for that resource is slow in developing.

Such is the world of imperfect competition — a centralized economic system resulting in lowered levels of production (output), higher and more stable prices, and redistribution of returns to the factors of production (land, labor, and capital).

POLICY TOWARDS COMPETITION

Even if we desired to follow a policy of fostering a system approaching the competitive market, it is obvious that we would find several forces prohibiting movement in this direction, among them the benefits of economies of size. Obviously each industry in each market must be analyzed separately in terms of its effects on consumers and other business firms. The fact that centralization of economic power may result in a restriction of output, manipulation of prices, redistribution of returns to the factors of production, and restrictive practices towards other business firms, suggests industries so organized need to be regulated. The effects of concentrated or centralized economic power on other business firms and consumers bears careful analysis by all parties involved.

CLASSIFICATION OF REGULATIONS

The extensiveness of regulation in the food industry makes it difficult for one to adequately summarize, interpret, and analyze each specific regulation. Instead, it is possible by a classification scheme to group regulations into various categories and then to discuss the economic and legal aspects of regulations falling into each category.

Such a classification scheme is possible because certain regulations are designed primarily to regulate the structure of food industry markets. Other regulations place emphasis upon regulating the behavior or strategies which sellers and buyers utilize with respect to one another in the market. A third group of market regulations directly regulates the performance of firms in a market by regulating prices and other terms of sale.

The basis for such a classification scheme lies in economic theory. Economic theory indicates that the structure of a market, or how it is organized in terms of number and size of firms, degree of product differentiation, and extent of barriers to the entry of new firms into the market, affects how firms behave in the market and in turn how the market performs. It is, for example, apparent that in more highly concentrated markets where only a few firms compete there is a tendency for firms to avoid competition — particularly price competition. At the extreme of monopoly there is virtually no competition. Normally, the results of a lack of competition are higher prices, lower levels of output, and a lack of progressiveness and innovation. To restore such a market to a state of viable competition one can regulate the market in any one of three ways. First, the structure of the market could be decentralized by breaking up firms into a larger number of smaller firms where more competition is likely to exist. Second, forms of firm behavior such as price fixing, tying, or basing point pricing, which are particularly inimical to competition, could be prohibited. Third, direct regulation or performance by price and quality regulation could be instituted.

Conceptually, the most appropriate regulatory tool involves the weighing of the need for large firms and high levels of concentration as determined by the extent of economies of scale against costs in terms of higher prices associated with market imperfections and free enterprise economy values favoring the least amount of regulation necessary to maintain a competitive economy. If, for example, high levels of concentration in a market are not necessary to achieve economies of scale, competition may be most easily preserved by restricting mergers among firms in the market. If, on the other hand, economies of scale are substantial, large firms may be allowed to develop and exist, but the competitive behavior of firms may be regulated. At the extreme of necessary monopoly to achieve economies of scale, prices and quality of production may be regulated.

REGULATIONS OF STRUCTURE

There are four laws which directly regulate the structure of food industry markets. They are the monopolization prohibitions of the Sherman Act Section 2, merger and acquisition prohibition of the Clayton Act Section 7, interlocking directorate prohibitions of the Clayton Act Section 8, and the Packers and Stockyards Act.

Monopolization

Section 2 of the Sherman Act declares acts of monopolizing, attempting to monopolize, or conspiring to monopolize illegal. It is primarily concerned with a situation where a single firm or corporation achieves or seeks to achieve a position of such size or power that it is capable of exercising monopoly powers to restrain competition.

The basis for prohibitive monopoly is clear. From an economic standpoint monopoly results in a misallocation of resources with higher prices and lower levels of output than one would expect if competition prevailed. History during the late 1800's demonstrates that trusts and holding companies in such products as petroleum, whiskey, sugar, lead, cottonseed oil, and railroads were able to effect substantial monopoly power and thereby control markets and prices. This involves not only maintaining higher than competitive prices but also cutting prices were necessary to eliminate competition.

A single firm can be found to have violated the monopolizing and attempt to monopolize provisions of Section 2 of the Sherman Act if, in addition to possessing monopoly power, it engages in conduct or practices indicative of an intent to monopolize. Thus in *U.S. vs Grinnell*, the Supreme Court states, "The offense of monopoly under Section 2 of the Sherman Act has two elements: (1) the possession of monopoly power in the relevant market, and (2) the willful acquisition or maintenance of that power as distinguished from growth or development as a consequence of a superior product, business acumen, or historic accident."[2]

The proportion of the market that a firm must control to be considered to have monopoly power is reasonably clear-cut. In *U.S. vs Alcoa*, the Court stated that a firm's control of over 90% of the market is enough to constitute monopoly. At the same time it stated ". . .it is doubtful whether 60–64% would be enough; and certainly 33% is not." [3] In the Alcoa case, the combination of over 90% control of the relevant market with evidence that Alcoa had diligently sought to accomplish and maintain such control, through means such as the maintenance of substantial excess capacity and similar exclusionary practices, led the Court to conclude that Alcoa had monopolized the market in violation of Section 2 of the Sherman Act. Cases such as Alcoa would indicate that if a corporation dominates about 75% of a market and, in addition, has the power to fix prices or exclude competitors, it is in a very vulnerable position for a Section 2 violation.

In the food industries, there have been relatively few cases where a firm has been convicted for violating Section 2 on a monopolization or attempt to monopolize

---

[2] *U.S. vs Grinnell Corp.*, 384 U.S. 563,570, (1966).
[3] *U.S. vs Alcoa*, 148 R. 2nd 416, 424, (1nd Cir. 1945).

charge. An exception is the *Maryland-Virginia Milk Producers* case where a cooperative controlling 86% of the Washington, D.C., milk supply purchased the largest independent dairy in the market and excluded its producers from shipping milk into Washington, D.C. The Court held that 86% control combined with the acquisition and subsequent effort to exclude milk was sufficient to violate Section 2.

The absence of monopoly in the food industries can probably be best explained by the fact that in most food processing areas, economies of scale are not so large as to require high levels of market concentration.[4] In addition, technological changes in processing and distribution techniques as well as new product developments in the food industries have almost continously been taking place. These changes have resulted in major reorganizations of food industries which might otherwise have become subject to Section 2 prosecution. An example is provided by the rise of the big four meat packers and subsequent decentralization of the meat industry. Also, improved transportation techniques have expanded many food industry markets to regional or even national scope. Finally, in certain food industries a trend toward monopoly structures has been substantially averted by the prohibition of mergers in several product areas.

Mergers

A food concern contemplating the acquisition of all or part of the stock of another company needs to carefully consider the possible application of Section 7 of the Clayton Act to the acquisition or merger. While the antitrust laws do not prohibit all mergers, food industry firms have been subject to substantial Section 7 litigation.

Section 7 of the Clayton Act provides that an acquisition by a corporation engaged in interstate commerce of all or part of the stock or assets of another corporation engaged in interstate commerce is illegal "where in any line of commerce in any section of the country, the effect of such an acquisition may be to substantially lessen competition or create a monopoly."[5] Either the U.S. Dept. of Justice or the FTC can proceed against mergers under Section 7.

The structure or organization of a market can be substantially changed by extensive merger activity. Mergers among the largest firms in a market, for example, can swiftly convert a market from a relatively low level of concentration to markets where the 4 or 8 largest firms control 50% or more of the market sales. Section 7 was designed to prevent such high levels of market concentration from being achieved via the merger route. In a word, it was designed to stem the anticompetitive effects of mergers in their incipiency.

An implicit assumption of Section 7 is that firm growth by internal means has greater economic benefit than growth by merger. A firm which grows internally, it

---

[4]National Commission on Food Marketing, *Food From Farmer to Consumer*, Washington, D.C., June 1966, pp. 93-94.

[5]*Clayton Act*, 15 U.S.C. Sec. 15, (1964).

is said, has met the market test. That is, it has shown that through superior efficiency, service to customers, or innovation it has gained the favor of the consuming public. On the other hand, growth by merger is said to be born from a desire for market power with few efficiency, service, or innovation motives.

Such broad generalizations are, however, dangerous. First, internal growth may be motivated by a desire for market power as much as growth by merger. Alcoa's rise to dominance in the aluminum industry through primarily internal means provides an illustration. Second, mergers may be motivated by a desire to achieve sufficient size so that certain economies of processing or distribution may be realized. Third, mergers among smaller firms in a market may actually enhance, rather than stifle, competition in a market because the resulting larger firm may be in a better position in terms of cost and size to wage effective competition.

Mergers may be classified into three categories—horizontal, vertical, and conglomerate. Horizontal mergers are those where the merging companies produce one or more closely related products in the same geographic market. Examples, are 2 flour mills merging or 2 fluid milk distributors in New York City combining. A vertical merger is one where a seller or potential seller merges with a buyer or potential buyer. An example is a grocery chain acquiring a meat packer or vegetable processor. All other mergers are conglomerate.

Conglomerate mergers may be subclassified into three types—geographic market extension mergers, product extension mergers, and pure conglomerate mergers. Geographic market extension conglomerate mergers exist when firms producing the same product but located in different geographic markets combine. An example would be the combination of a California regional grocery chain and a Chicago regional grocery chain. Product extension conglomerate mergers are those where the acquired and acquiring firms are functionally related in production or distribution but the products do not directly compete with each other. A merger between a fruit and a vegetable processor would be an illustration. Sometimes product extension mergers become difficult to distinguish from vertical mergers. For example, a merger between an onion dehydrator and a food processor-retailer may be classified as a product extension merger in that the onion dehydration process is functionally related to other food processing and retailing activities. On the other hand, dehydrated onions may be an input for the processing of the acquiring firm's products such as in the case of ketchup.

The law with respect to mergers becomes increasingly uncertain as one moves from horizontal to vertical and conglomerate mergers. If it is determined by the Court that a particular merger may lessen competition in the relevant product and geographic market, the merger violates Section 7.

In the case of a horizontal merger relatively small and insignificant mergers may be held to violate Section 7. This is particularly true where market concentration is high, the acquiring firm is a leader in the market, and there has been a trend toward increasing concentration. All of these factors were combined in the dairy merger cases in the early 1960's when the 4 largest dairy companies were ordered to divest of certain acquired milk plants and desist from further merger activity for a 10-yr period without prior FTC approval. The dairy merger guidelines set forth in the *Beatrice* decision state that "...any acquisition of a not insubstantial dairy company by one of the industry's giants (roughly, a company having annual sales of more than $200 million) is highly suspect."[6]

Section 7 is not just applicable to horizontal mergers by the "industry giants." In the case *U.S. vs Von's Grocery*, a merger between a 27- and 34- store grocery chain with combined sales of less than $200 million and only 7.2% of the total groceries sold in the Los Angeles market was held to violate Section 7 and divestiture was ordered.[7] FTC merger guidelines in food distribution indicate horizontal mergers which result in combined sales of over $100 million are of sufficient size to warrant investigation for Section 7 violation.[8] Premerger notification is required for such mergers.

U.S. Dept. of Justice horizontal merger guidelines indicate that a merger where the acquired and acquiring firms each controlled over 5% of the market would ordinarily be challenged. If the acquiring firm controlled 25% of the market or more, mergers where the acquired firm has as little as 1% of the market would be challenged. An exception to such guidelines exists where the acquired firm was a failing concern in that there was no reasonable prospect of it remaining viable, and no other smaller purchaser could be found.

Experience would indicate that vertical mergers are somewhat less vulnerable to Section 7 prosecution than horizontal mergers. In the case where the company is acquiring a supplier—backward integration—the critical question is whether the merger will deprive the acquiring company's competitors of a source of supply necessary for their effective competition with the acquiring company. Such vertical mergers between significant firms are said to create barriers to the entry of new firms into the market because to effectively compete, the entering firm must control both production facilities and a source of resource supply. U.S. Dept. of Justice guidelines would indicate that a vertical merger would be challenged where the acquiring company has more than 6% of its product's market and the acquired supplier has 10% or more of sales in its market. A similar standard is used with respect to forward integration or the case where a company acquired a customer. Here the concern is whether competitors of the acquired concern have been deprived of a substantial customer which is necessary for their effective competition.

Relatively few vertical acquisitions have been challenged in the food industries. While such acquisitions have not been particularly common, there have been some sizeable acquisition of milk processors by chain stores which have gone unchallenged in particular market areas.

At the same time, it should be realized that in many cases food processors and retailers have found it advantageous to vertically integrate by internal growth.

[6]*CCH Trade Regulation Reporter, FTC Complaints and Orders, 1965-1967*, para 17, 244, pp. 22,337.

[7]*U.S. vs Von's Grocery Co.*, 384 U.S. 270, (1966).

[8]*1 CCH Trade Regulation Reporter*, para. 4510, pp. 6801, (1969).

Chain construction of fluid milk and meat processing facilities as well as food processor financing and/or construction and operation of poultry and cattle feeding operations are illustrations of such internal vertical integration efforts.

It would appear that unless the integrating firm reaches monopoly proportions in a particular market there are few antitrust dangers in internal vertical growth. This point is illustrated by the case *Hiland Dairy Inc. vs Kroger* where Kroger constructed a fluid milk plant with sufficient capacity to serve 20% of the St. Louis market needs. Kroger sold 8% of the groceries in St. Louis. Hiland contended that Kroger was attempting to monopolize the market by constructing the facility. The Court of Appeals concluded that Kroger would not have the power to raise or lower prices and with such a small market share was not, without further evidence, a threat to monopolize.[9]

The law with respect to conglomerate mergers is unsettled. Yet food industries are becoming increasingly conglomerated as nonfood corporations expand into the food industries and as food corporations expand into nonfood areas. It has, for example, been found that in 16 of 17 enterprise food categories, multi-industry companies were conglomerated both into other food categories and into other sectors of manufacturing at large.[10] It has also been suggested that by 1973 15–25% of total food processing will be controlled by nonfood companies.[11]

Market extension conglomerate mergers have been particularly significant in the food industries as national or regional food processors and retailers have extended their sphere of influence to additional markets by acquiring independent concerns in the same product line. Contested mergers in baking, dairy, and food retailing have had important market extension aspects. The *National Tea* case provides an interesting illustration.[12] From 1951 to 1958 National Tea acquired 26 companies owning a total of 485 stores in 188 cities of 16 states. Most of these acquisitions were of the market extension variety rather than horizontal. In addition to a trend toward concentration in food retailing on a national basis and a finding that local chain competition was an important competitive force in food retailing, the most damaging evidence against National Tea was a finding that it was making substantially higher gross margins in some markets than in others. The FTC interpreted this evidence as indicating that National Tea was using its market power to charger higher prices to consumers in some markets to support below-cost operations in other markets — a conclusion which may or may not have been justified.

Product extension conglomerate mergers have also come under close scrutiny in the food industries. The focus of attention in the *Consolidated Foods* case was the

---

[9]*Hiland Dairy, Inc. vs Kroger Co.*, 402 F 2nd 968 (1968) cert. denied 395 U.S. 961 (1969)

[10]John Narver, "Conglomeration in the Food Industries", *Economics of Conglomerate Growth*, Oregon State University, Corvallis, November 1969, pp. 40.

[11]E.B. Weiss, "Food Becomes Glamorous," *Advertising Age*, July 8, 1968, pp. 78.

[12]*In the Matter of National Tea Co.*, CCH Trade Regulation Reporter, para. 17, 463, FTC DKT .7453, (1966).

acquisition of Gentry, Inc., a dehydrator of onions and garlic, by Consolidated, a food processing and retailing concern.[13] The Court found that the acquisition would foreclose competition from a substantial share of the markets for dehydrated onions and garlic. This finding was based not only on the fact that Consolidated was a substantial purchaser of onions and garlic for its processing, wholesaling, and retailing operations, but also because Consolidated could use their food purchasing power to "force" other food processors to buy dehydrated onions and garlic from Gentry.

Such reciprocal buying arrangements are increasingly becoming subject to antitrust prosecution. If, in addition to reciprocity considerations the acquiring firm is a potential internal growth entrant into the acquired firm's product area, a product extension merger will likely be highly suspect. FTC guidelines for grocery product manufacturing product extension conglomerate mergers indicate legal questions may be expected to arise when the combined assets of the acquired and acquiring concerns are over $250 million, where the acquiring company is 1 of the 4 largest producers of a number of food products, and where the acquired company has more than a 5% share of its market.[14]

The law still remains to be established for the pure conglomerate merger. Indications are that such mergers are likely to be challenged if the acquiring firm is a potential entrant into the acquired firm's market or if reciprocal dealing arrangements are likely to result from the merger. In addition, the U.S. Dept. of Justice has indicated that it will oppose any merger among the 200 largest manufacturing firms or any merger between 1 of the 200 largest and a leading producer in any concentrated industry.[15]

Meat Packing Consent Decree and the Packers and Stockyard Act

Several antitrust investigations into the structure and practices in the meat packing industry have singled this industry out for special structural regulation. In 1910, a FTC study concluded that the five largest meat packers were manipulating livestock markets, controlling prices of dressed meat, extending other control to fish, poultry, eggs, and butter as well as fruits, vegetables, and staple groceries. As a result of this FTC investigation, the U.S. Dept. of Justice brought antitrust action against Swift, Armour, Wilson, and Cudahy for violating the Sherman Act. In 1920 these 4 packers signed a consent decree which prohibited them from: (1) owning public stockyard companies, public cold storage plants, or stockyard terminal railroads; (2) handling or letting others use their facilities to handle 114 nonmeat products including fish, vegetables, fruits, canned goods, and cereals; (3) handling fresh cream or milk except for sale in processed form; (4) operate retail meat markets in the United States. Although attempts have been made to nullify the

---

[13]*FTC vs Consolidated Foods Corp.*, 380 U.S. 592, (1965).

[14]*1 CCH Trade Regulation Reporter*, para. 4530, (1968).

[15]*5 CCH Trade Regulation Reporter*, para. 50, 247, (1969).

consent decree, none have been successful, and it thus remains in effect today. This is true even though conditions in the meat industry have changed dramatically with the decline of the central market as well as the market share of the big four packers. One can, in fact, question whether the consent decree provisions are necessary considering the considerably more diffused structure of the meat industry and the enhanced power position of food chains.

What effect the consent decree has had and is having upon the structure of the food industry is, of course, largely speculative. The big four meat packers were among the largest food industry concerns in the early to mid 1900's. The consent decree has restricted their activities largely to meat and other products entirely outside the food industry. The meat packers, over time, would have been potential entrants into grocery processing and retailing were it not for the consent decree. While only four meat packers are subject to the consent decree, administrative enforcement activities by the Packers and Stockyard Division appear to have made the decree's provisions applicable to the meat packing industry as a whole.

REGULATIONS OF CONDUCT

Regulations of conduct are those laws designed primarily to regulate the behavior or policies of firms with respect to one another in the marketplace. In many American industries, market organization is typified by a structural situation where a few firms control a relatively large share of the market. For both political and economic reasons these concentrations of economic power have not been broken up by regulation of market structures. While Section 2 of the Sherman Act and Section 7 of the Clayton Act will continue to be used to prevent further increases in concentration by merger, an important focus of regulation of food industries is upon the price and nonprice policies which firms use in competition and negotiation with one another.

Regulations of market conduct may be subdivided into two groups: (1) those designed to prevent collusive and restrictive forms of conduct, and (2) those designed to prevent unfair trade practices.

Regulation of Collusive or Restrictive Conduct

The main antitrust statutes which regulate the conduct of food firms include the Sherman Act, Section 1; Clayton Act, Section 3; and the Federal Trade Commission Act, Section 5. Section 1 of the Sherman Act prohibits contracts, combinations, or conspiracies in restraint of trade. The term, restraint of trade, covers a host of forms of market conduct including price fixing, market sharing, territorial allocation, boycotts, and reciprocal dealing. The terms, contracts, combinations, or conspiracies, refer to concerted actions among firms. Thus a single firm, acting alone, cannot generally violate Section 1. Section 5 of the Federal Trade Commission Act prohibits "Unfair methods of competition in commerce, and unfair or deceptive acts or practices in commerce..."[16] The

---

[16] Federal Trade Commission Act, 15 U.S.C. sec. 41, (1964).

terminology, unfair methods of competition, has been interpreted to cover all the practices prohibited by the Sherman Act, Section 1. This interpretation has had the effect of giving the FTC the power to issue cease and desist orders against firms engaging in practices which would otherwise violate the Sherman Act.

The most common violations of Section 1 of the Sherman Act and Section 5 of the Federal Trade Commission Act by food industry firms involve conspiracies to fix prices.[17] In a market with a number of competitors, it is often difficult to understand why firms find it necessary or even desirable to get involved in price fixing conspiracies. The answer appears to lie, in part, in the fact that food products, like many primary industry products, are reasonably homogeneous. As a result, any change in price or nonprice strategy on the part of one firm almost immediately affects other firms in a market. The result is a tendency for the firm to shy away from price competition. These factors may result in efforts to coordinate pricing activities among firms in food markets. Yet there is always a potential reward for the firm that cuts prices slightly and increases its volume of sales. This potential reward makes attempts to fix prices in food industries quite unstable.

Explicit price fixing agreements provable by documentary evidence are per se illegal under Section 1 of the Sherman Act. Per se illegal means that there is no way the accused parties can justify to the Court their rationale for engaging in the arrangement.

Illegal price fixing arrangements cover a wide range of interfirm attempts to influence the level of price in a market. The most obvious illegal price fixing arrangement is the case where competitors sit down together and agree upon the level of price to be charged in a market area. Yet the Sherman Act goes beyond such explicit price fixing practices to cover any "combination formed for the purpose and with the effect of raising, depressing, fixing, pegging, or stabilizing the price of a commodity. . ."[18] Thus, any agreement among firms on price or variables influencing the level of price can be held to violate Section 1. In the *Socony-Vacuum* case an effort to stabilize prices by purchasing quantities of gasoline which would otherwise have depressed the market price of gasoline was held to be an illegal price fixing conspiracy.[19] Of course, combinations of processors to allocate distribution territories or to allocate "competitive bids" would also violate Section 1.

Trade associations are particularly important in the food industries. Many of the activities which trade associations perform such as cooperative research, management and sales workshops, cooperative printing, collective bargaining, insurance, trade publication, and legislative and administrative influence may actually enhance competition and thus have few antitrust implications.

Three activities of trade associations have important antitrust

---

[17]National Commission on Food Marketing, *Special Studies in Food Marketing,* Technical Study No. 10, Washington, D.C., June 1966, pp. 151, 175.

[18]*U.S. vs Socony-Vacuum Oil Co.,* 310 U.S. 150, 223, (1940).

[19]*Ibid.*

implications—pricing, statistical reporting, and costing. In terms of pricing, when competitors congregate in a trade association there may be a tendency for discussions to gravitate toward price. Such discussions should be avoided because of their serious legal implications. Statistical reporting activities on production, inventories, sales, and so forth are generally no problem if they are available to both buyers and sellers. However, efforts by the association to interpret, predict, and suggest production or pricing policies for the future have been held to be illegal.[20] In addition, where cost reporting is combined with explicit or implicit markup suggestions, an illegal price fixing conspiracy could be found to exist.

Price leadership refers to a situation where prices undergo simultaneous or nearly simultaneous changes by all firms in a market. Even cursory study of price movements in the American economy leads one to conclude that price leadership is a fairly common market phenomenon. In homogeneous commodities, price uniformity among competitors is a virtual necessity. Without uniformity buyers would switch en masse to the lower price seller. In addition, where costs and cost changes are nearly identical among firms, prices would be expected to move in a reasonably simultaneous fashion. This was the essence of the ruling of the Court of Appeals in the case *Pevely Dairy Co. vs U.S.* where the Court stated that even though there was evidence of price uniformity and uniformity of price movement, economic factors prompting the price changes were the same for all firms.[21] However, in another case, the 3 leading cigarette manufacturers were convicted on the basis of extensive parallel conduct among the 3 firms combined with efforts to forestall entry by new firms into the tobacco industry.[22] It would appear from the American Tobacco, Pevely, and other cases that evidence of leadership itself is not enough to violate the Sherman Act, but it may be considered illegal when accompanied by other anticompetitive forms of behavior.

Several collusive or restrictive practices other than price fixing may be held to violate the Sherman or Federal Trade Commission Acts if the effect of the practice is to injure the competitive position of another firm in the market. For example, while a firm generally has the right to chose to sell to whomever he desires, if such a policy is pursued for the purpose of injuring another firm, with the effect of fixing prices, or for the purpose of maintaining a dominant market position, it may be held illegal.

Section 3 of the Clayton Act is designed primarily to keep the channels of competition and negotiation open by prohibiting firms from selling goods on the condition that the buyer not deal in the goods of competitors. Such exclusive dealing arrangements have the economic effect of foreclosing markets to

---

[20]*American Column and Lumber Co. vs U.S.*, 257 U.S. 553, (1936).

[21]*Pevely Dairy Co. vs U.S.*, 178 F 2nd. 363, (8th Cir. 1949), cert. denied 339 U.S. 942, (1950).

[22]*American Tobacco Co. vs U.S.*, 328 U.S. 781, (1964). For a truly outstanding discussion of this interesting case see W.J. Nicholls, *Price Policies in the Cigarette Industry*. Nashville, Vanderbilt Univ. Press, 1951.

competitors. They are illegal whenever a substantial amount of commerce is affected.

Closely related to the exclusive dealing arrangement is the case where a seller requires that if a buyer wants to purchase one product, he must purchase another product. Those in the canning industry will recall that American Can Company and Continental Can Company in leasing their can-closing machines required that the buyer also purchase cans from them.[23] Such tying arrangements were held to be illegal.

This discussion with respect to exclusive dealing and tying should not be interpreted as prohibiting legitimate output contracts where the seller agrees to supply a buyer with a certain proportion of his output, or requirement contract where the buyer agrees to purchase a portion of the seller's output. Such contracts are becoming increasingly important as the need for market coordination in terms of source of supply or market outlet increases. They appear to have legal implications only where they cover an unduly long time period or have no economic justification.[24]

Regulation of Unfair Trade Practices

The laws which have been discussed up to this point all have as a basic premise the idea that it is necessary to stimulate competition among firms by either developing a more competitive structure or by preventing firms from engaging in anticompetitive forms of market behavior. Another group of regulations presumes that there are situations where competition among firms may become too intense. These regulations are designed to suppress rather than stimulate competition—at least in the short run. The latter group of laws may be referred to as unfair trade practice regulations. These regulations include state and federal price discrimination, sales below cost, and fair trade laws. While most economists recognize the need for and desirability of laws designed to stimulate competition, unfair trade practice regulations are receiving increasing criticism from economic, business, and consumer circles.

The food industry has been subject to more unfair trade practice regulation than any other industry. It has played a central role in the establishment, evaluation, and interpretation of the Robinson-Patman Act. An FTC investigation of the food industry which found discriminatory concessions being given by food processors to chains contributed materially to the passage of the Robinson-Patman Act in 1936. Through time, discriminatory practices of food processors and the exacting power position of chains have continued to play a central role in the interpretation and enforcement of the Robinson-Patman Act. Between June 1950 and June 1964 the FTC filed 53 complaints against food marketing concerns charging illegal discrimination.

---

[23] *U.S. vs American Can Co.,* 87 F. supp. 18, (1949).

[24] *Tampa Electric Co. vs Nashville Coal Co.,* etal, 365 U.S. 320, (1961).

Unfair trade practice regulation in the food industry is not limited to the Robinson-Patman Act. There are 29 states with general price discrimination laws. There are 48 states with special interest price discrimination laws which apply specifically to such products as milk, liquor, and cigarettes. There are 28 states with laws which state that sellers cannot sell products at less than cost—frequently cost is stated at the seller's invoice price plus a certain fixed percentage margin. There are 29 states with special interest sales-below-cost laws applying to products such as milk and cigarettes. In addition, 38 states have fair trade laws which allow manufacturers to fix the price at which a particular product will be resold—a practice which, if systematically pursued, would otherwise be prohibited by Section 1 of the Sherman Act.

Many cases can be sighted where the effect of unfair trade practice regulation has been to hamstring the pricing policies of business firms. This is true because the efficient and progressive firm is encouraged by the Sherman Act to compete for new business. On the other hand, he is, in effect, told by unfair trade practice laws that he cannot obtain new business by giving a price concession.

So far as the food industries are concerned, the most important of the unfair trade practice laws are those which regulate price discrimination. While many of these laws exist at the state level, most state laws follow the interpretation of the Robinson-Patman Act—our federal price discrimination law.

The Robinson-Patman Act is concerned only with price differentials not based on costs. This provides that a seller shall not charge buyers different prices unless the price difference can be justified on the basis of a difference in the average cost of serving different buyers. The law does have three major exceptions in addition to cost justification: (1) The product must be of like grade and quality. (2) It must be determined that the discrimination may injure competition, or tend to create a monopoly, or injure, destroy or prevent competition with any person who grants or knowingly receives the benefits of the discrimination, or with customers of either of them. (3) Discrimination may be practiced when it is done to meet competition.

The like grade and quality requirement has some interesting food industry aspects. Can a vegetable processor, for example, sell identical peas packaged in a private label package at a different price than an otherwise identical packer brand? While a marketing sophisticate would argue that the products are not of like grade and quality in the eyes of the consumer, they are of like grade and quality in the eyes of the law.[25] Price differences would likely be allowed between such products only to the extent of differences in production and marketing costs.

In order for a discrimination to be illegal, it must also meet the requirement of competitive injury. This requirement has been interpreted broadly by both the FTC and the courts. In fact, recent cases would tend to indicate that if another firm is injured by a discrimination to the extent of simply reducing his

---

[25] *FTC vs Borden Co.,* 382 U.S. 807, (1966).

profits, rather than driving him out of the market, the discrimination can be held to have violated the Robinson-Patman Act. The case in point is a food industry case where three pie bakers were convicted of geographic price discrimination when they attempted to enter the Salt Lake City frozen pie market by discriminatory pricing.[26] In the case, the Supreme Court found the requisite competitive injury even though the independent pie company bringing suit continued to increase sales during the period of discrimination and also made a profit.

Probably the strongest defense for a price discrimination charge is that the discrimination was undertaken for the purpose of meeting competition. The meeting competition defense means that a processor can meet but not beat the price of a competitor. Recent decisions indicate that the meeting competition defense applies to efforts to obtain new customers as well as efforts to retail old customers.

The cost justification defense has a strong economic basis. It allows sellers to discriminate among buyers in terms of price when there are demonstrable differences in the average cost of serving different customers. It is important to note that cost justification from a legal standpoint is an average concept rather than a marginal concept. A processor cannot, for example, justify a discriminatory price on a new customer because the added volume will substantially lower his unit processing cost. From a cost standpoint, he can justify a price difference only if there are uniquenesses about the new customer's account which require fewer services, less packaging costs, or a less expensive product. Price differences based on functional differences in volume of delivery, point of delivery, services on delivery, or packaging differences are considerably easier to justify than price differences based on such criteria as chain or independent grocery customers. The later criteria for price differences are inherently suspect of violating the Robinson-Patman Act.

Food processors should be aware that the Robinson-Patman Act is even more stringently applicable to brokerage payments, merchandising allowances, and services. Section 2(c) of the Robinson-Patman Act states that it is illegal for a seller to pay a buyer's broker a sales commission. Section 2(c) is aimed at "under the table" price concessions to buyers through brokers. Section 2(c) is absolute and does not allow meeting competition, cost justification, or competitive injury defenses.

Sections 2(d) and 2(e) of the Robinson-Patman Act require that all merchandising and services be available on a proportionately equal basis to all competing buyers. Thus Tri-Valley Packing Company was held to have violated Section 2(d) of the Robinson-Patman Act when it gave an advertising allowance of $150 per year to 1 Boston retailer and not to 2 competing retailers. Sections 2(d) and 2(e) do not allow either the cost justification or competitive injury defense but do allow the meeting competition defense.

---

[26] *Utah Pie Co. vs Continental Baking Co.*, 386 U.S. 685, (1967).

It should be recognized that buyers may be prosecuted under Section 2(f) of the Robinson-Patman Act and under Section 5 of the Federal Trade Commission Act for either inducing or knowingly receiving the benefits of price discrimination. The difficulty of proving inducement and knowledge has resulted in few cases in this area. However, recently the FTC found that a large chain had violated Section 2(f) when it induced a discrimination by giving a seller false information about the size of competitive bids on its fluid milk account.

Sales below cost are prohibited at the federal level by Section 3 of the Clayton Act and by many general and state specialty laws. At the federal level, Section 3 has been applied in relatively few cases. It appears to be inapplicable unless the sales below cost were made with predatory intent.[27]

Other Conduct Regulations

The contemporary consumer movement and its associated legislative enactments as well as several conduct-oriented laws with respect to specific food areas make a complete discussion of conduct regulations virtually impossible within the limited confines of this chapter. It should, however, be realized that general laws such as the Federal Trade Commission Act also proscribe unfair or deceptive practices which injure consumers. This provision has been used to reach practices such as payments by processors to employees of buyers in return for delivering the buyer's business; procuring trade secrets of competitors by espionage or bribing their employees; false statements about competitors; passing off goods as products of competitors; lottery and "rigged" games of chance; improper filling of orders, as well as false or misleading advertising. Truth-in-packaging legislation has been enacted to standardize weights, measures, and labeling of products. A closely related truth-in-lending law has standardized the lending practices of firms offering credit with the sale of goods.

Some U.S. Dept. of Agr. legislation is mainly concerned with providing consumers a basis for differentiating among different quality food products. The U.S. Dept. of Agr. establishes grades and standards for fresh meats, fruits, and vegetables. Such regulations have many desirable aspects from the standpoint of improving the basis for decisions. On the other hand, grades may not reflect consumer desires.

The Food and Drug Administration establishes standards of identity, quality, and fill on many processed food products. These regulations set minimum standards which products must meet before they can be marketed. They are economic regulations in the sense that the standards established are frequently considerably above or different from those required for minimum health considerations. These regulations may also, if not properly administered, hamper the introduction of otherwise safe and desirable food products.

---

[27]*U.S. vs National Dairy Products Corp.,* 372 U.S. 29, (1963).

An Economic Perspective on Conduct Regulation

It is obvious that conduct regulation covers a wide range of the market activity engaged in by firms in the food industry. These regulations fall into three main areas—those which regulate collusive or restrictive conduct, those which regulate unfair trade practices, and those which are designed to improve consumer decisions in the market place. While all of these regulations merit consideration individually, they also merit evaluation in terms of their total impact upon markets. It was noted previously that while the laws regulating both structure and collusive market practices are designed to stimulate competition, unfair trade practice regulations may be closing many legitimate avenues of competition to the firm. The motives for price discrimination or sales below cost vary from market penetration to monopoly.[28] While price discrimination for the purpose of obtaining monopoly is clearly undesirable, it is not clear that it is desirable for the legal system to discourage firms from seeking new and profitable market opportunities. Yet this may well be the effect of price discrimination and sales below cost legislation at both state and federal levels. In similar terms, while a system which promotes rational consumer decision-making may act to stimulate competition among firms, regulations which restrict the flow of new healthful products onto the market may have quite the opposite effect. The inconsistencies in conduct regulations—particularly in the food industries—need to be carefully analyzed by all segments of the industry—including consumers.

REGULATIONS OF PERFORMANCE

Thus far two broad policies toward regulation of competition in food industries have been discussed—structure and conduct regulations. Both of these policies are designed to maintain a market environment where buyers and sellers through competition and negotiation bring about acceptable levels of prices, output, and firm efficiency. A third policy involves direct regulation of market results by administrative establishment of prices and other terms of sales in the market.

Performance regulation is based upon the presumption that free competition and negotiation cannot be relied upon to establish terms of sale which are in the public interest. A survey of performance or price regulation in the American economy reveals two quite different cases where it has been established. The first is the public case where the so-called "natural monopoly" is necessary in order to have efficient production of services such as transportation, telephone, electricity, gas, and sometimes water or sewer. Our reconomic system allows these services to be supplied by private corporations but regulates their prices and services in a manner consistent with the public interest. The premise upon which this regulation is based is that without regulation production would not

---

[28] R.E. Schneidau and Ronald D. Knutson, "Price Discrimination in the Food Industry," *American Journal of Agricultural Economics*, Dec. 1969, pp. 1143.

only be more inefficient but exploitation of the consuming public would result.

The second case for performance regulation is one where the primary fear is not monopoly but the contention that without regulation competition will become so chaotic and price fluctuation so erratic that the supply of the product involved might either be jeopardized or the producers of the product might be injured to an extent which is not in the public interest. Market performance regulation in food industries is generally based on this second case. Most of this regulation is at the producer level. Being at the producer level, this regulation affects food processors only to the extent that it affects the prices paid by processors for farm products. In the case of most products, it sets a floor on the level of price such as a support price, rather than fix the exact level of price. An important exception exists in the case of Federal Milk Marketing Orders where direct administrative decisions are made with respect to the exact price to be paid by milk processors. As is typical of rate regulation procedures, prices are determined by regulatory officials—in this case the Dept. of Agr.—after hearings in which interested parties are allowed to present evidence as to the proper level of price from their point of view.

Direct regulation of wholesale or retail prices in food industries is relatively uncommon. For most industries, competitive interaction is the primary price determining force. About the only exception, again, exists in the case of fluid milk where approximately 15 states currently establish either wholesale or retail milk prices. A limited number of other cases can be cited where commission rates paid in the marketing system are established by either state or federal authority. Packers and stockyards regulation of central livestock marketing charges provide an illustration.

Perhaps the area of performance regulation which has had the greatest general impact upon food industries is regulation of transportation. The Interstate Commerce Commission is the oldest federal independent regulatory agency. Its establishment, in large part, grew out of the discriminatory pricing and monopoly conditions in the railroad industry, especially as it relates to the shipment of agricultural products. The main responsibility of the ICC is to regulate the rates of all common and contract carriers so that they are just, reasonable, and nondiscriminatory. While ICC authority to regulate is broad, it specifically exempts from economic regulation motor vehicles carrying agricultural, horticultural, and fish commodities. This partial treatment of agricultural industries had been the subject of considerable criticism.

FUTURE OF FOOD INDUSTRY REGULATION

It is difficult to predict what the nature of food industry regulation will be by the end of the decade. There are, however, certain areas of regulation which are likely to receive close attention with considerable clarification of the law. For example, conglomeration of the food industries is one of the important structural changes which is presently occuring. Additional guides are likely to be established with respect to the extent to which food industry firms can conglomerate via product extension mergers. These guides will likely substantially restrict conglomerate growth by merger within the food industry. In addition, large nonfood firms will likely not be allowed to continue to acquire leading firms in the food industry. Similarly, leading food industry firms will likely be restricted in acquisition of leading nonfood firms.

Over time, it is likely that ultimate power in food marketing will lie in the hands of the retail segment as opposed to processing or agricultural production. It is here where the decisions are made as to what brands will be displayed, how much shelf space will be allocated and, in many cases, what the final price of the product will be. Such potential power in the hands of a segment of the food marketing sector which is rapidly becoming increasingly vertically and horizontally integrated could result in harmful business practices to processors, farmers, and consumers. It is likely that increasing concern will be focused on this segment of our food marketing system.

Food industries have, in many cases, promoted the establishment of general and special interest in unfair trade practice regulation. Today, question can be raised as to whether many of these laws are in the interest of either the food industry or consumers. There is evidence to indicate that undue regulation of the marketing practices of food processors may be encouraging chain store integration into processing activities. The industry, thus, may need to reevaluate their regulatory status in light of the changing economic forces in the industry.

While the great majority of business firms dealing with the public have and will continue to perform efficiently and in the best interests of consumers, those firms that engaged in discriminatory or misleading business practices have stimulated a backlash of consumerism which is likely to have continued far-reaching effects on retail merchandising practices. Because of the lack of consumer organization, government has and will likely continue to fill the role of consumer representative through more strict enforcement of current legislation and passage of new, more restrictive, merchandising regulation. We must make sure, however, that such government involvement does not stifle the creativeness and efficiency of the food industry.

CHAPTER 5

W. Smith Greig | # Measures of Growth in Food Processing

INTRODUCTION

The description and analysis of the structure and financial operating ratios of the food processing industry (Chap. 2) were primarily based on 13 subcategories of food processing. The statistical data used were from the IRS, *Source Book of Statistics of Income.* Statistical series on the growth of food processing industries are available on an annual basis from the U.S. Dept. of Com. (1968, 1970). Annual changes in employment, value added, value of shipments, and capital expenditures for the food processing industry divided into 44 major processing segments are available (44 4-digit SIC codes). Further, annual data on value of shipments are available from the same sources for over 90 subclassifications of the food processing industry (5-digit SIC codes). This latter series is the most detailed breakdown on which annual data are available from governmental sources. Individual product data (7-digit SIC codes) are available only on census years (Census of Manufacturers), i.e., 1958, 1963, 1967, etc.

To again briefly explain the Standard Industrial Classification (SIC) system: the system of classification goes from a 2-digit code (SIC 20) for all food processing combined, to a 7-digit code which is a very specific product class. There are 9 product classifications in 3-digit codes, 44 product classifications in 4-digit codes, over 90 product classifications in 5-digit codes and probably several hundred product classifications in 7-digit codes in the complete food processing industry. To show how the codes become more specific with increasing numbers of digits, we list the following example:

SIC 20	Food Processing Industry
SIC 203	Canning and Freezing Industry
SIC 2037	Frozen Fruit and Vegetable Industry
SIC 20372	Frozen Vegetables
SIC 20372-11	Frozen Asparagus

In the following materials on growth in food processing we will use the 4-digit codes and the 5-digit codes; the 7-digit codes are too numerous to list. (For these details the Census of Manufacturers, Bureau of the Census, U.S. Dept. of Com., is a good reference).

An explanation of the differences in IRS data and Dept. of Com. data should be given, as the data are not directly comparable. For example, the IRS value of sales for the tax year July 1965—June 1966, was $70.2 billion for the food processing industry; while the Dept. of Com. estimate was $74.3 billion in 1965 and $79.6 billion in 1966. The differences are at least partially due to the fact that the IRS data is only for business corporations, and the Dept. of Com. data are from a sample of all food processing firms. The data from the two governmental agencies are obtained in different manners and used for different purposes, and it is not possible to say which is the most accurate. However, in

TABLE 5.1

CHANGES IN TOTAL EMPLOYMENT IN MAJOR FOOD PROCESSING CATEGORIES, 1958-1967

SIC Code and Industry Category	Total Employment (1000)										Ratio 1967/ 1958	Rank of Increase
	1958	1959	1960	1961	1962	1963	1964	1965	1966	1967		
SIC 2011 Meat packing plants	201	197	194	189	186	181	183	180	174	171	.86	34
SIC 2013 Meat processing plants	49	49	48	46	47	49	51	49	48	54	1.10	17
SIC 2015 Poultry dressing plants	62	66	68	71	67	70	71	72	75	83	1.34	3
SIC 2021 Creamery butter	17	17	17	16	16	12	11	10	9	9	.53	43
SIC 2022 Natural and process cheese	17	17	18	18	18	18	18	13	19	20	1.18	9
SIC 2023 Condensed and evaporated milk	13	13	14	13	12	12	13	13	12	13	1.00	19
SIC 2024 Ice cream and frozen desserts	35	34	35	34	33	29	28	27	28	25	.71	41
SIC 2026 Fluid milk	212	207	204	199	196	185	183	178	169	166	.78	39
SIC 2031 Canned and cured seafoods	17	15	17	17	16	17	16	16	17	16	.94	29
SIC 2032 Canned specialties	24	24	25	25	25	25	26	27	29	27	1.13	15
SIC 2033 Canned fruits and vegetables	108	107	104	NA	NA	102	102	101	101	101	.94	30
SIC 2034 Dehydrated food products	8	8	9	9	NA	9	9	10	10	11	1.37	2
SIC 2035 Pickles, sauces, salad dressings	20	19	22	22	21	19	19	20	21	20	1.00	20
SIC 2036 Fresh and frozen packaged fish	18	18	19	17	16	20	21	19	19	22	1.22	7
SIC 2037 Frozen fruits and vegetables	40	42	44	45	45	52	54	59	62	66	1.65	1
SIC 2041 Flour mills	28	29	27	27	26	22	22	21	20	20	.71	42
SIC 2042 Prepared animal feeds	57	57	56	56	56	55	53	51	51	53	.93	32
SIC 2043 Cereal preparations	11	11	11	12	12	11	12	12	12	13	1.18	10
SIC 2044 Rice milling	4	4	4	4	4	4	4	4	4	4	1.00	21[1]
SIC 2045 Blended and prepared flour	NA	NA	NA	NA	NA	7	8	7	7	7	1.00[1]	22[1]
SIC 2046 Wet corn milling	14	13	14	14	14	13	12	13	14	14	1.00	23
SIC 2051 Bread and related products	258	261	260	256	254	237	234	236	232	222	.86	35
SIC 2052 Biscuits, crackers, and cookies	44	44	43	43	42	43	42	42	43	43	.98	28
SIC 2061 Raw cane sugar	7	7	7	7	7	8	9	8	8	8	1.14	14
SIC 2062 Cane sugar refining	15	15	15	14	13	12	12	11	11	12	.80	38
SIC 2063 Beet sugar	10	11	10	11	11	11	12	12	12	12	1.20	8
SIC 2071 Confectionery products	67	65	65	65	66	64	66	65	67	68	1.01	18
SIC 2072 Chocolate and cocoa products	8	8	9	9	9	9	9	8	8	8	1.00	24
SIC 2073 Chewing gum	6	6	6	6	6	6	6	6	7	7	1.17	11

											Ratio[1]	
SIC 2082 Malt liquors	72	71	70	68	66	63	62	60	61	61	.85	36
SIC 2083 Malt	2	2	3	3	2	2	2	2	2	2	1.00	25
SIC 2084 Wines and brandy	6	5	NA	5	NA	6	6	6	7	7	1.17	12
SIC 2085 Distilled liquor except brandy	21	20	20	19	19	18	18	19	19	19	.90	33
SIC 2086 Bottled and canned soft drinks	97	100	103	104	105	107	111	114	118	123	1.27	4
SIC 2087 Flavorings	9	9	NA	NA	NA	9	9	9	11	10	1.11	16
SIC 2091 Cottonseed oil mills	8	9	9	8	8	8	8	8	7	6	.75	40
SIC 2092 Soybean oil mills	8	8	8	8	7	6	6	7	7	8	1.00	26
SIC 2093 Vegetable oil mills (not elsewhere classified)	2	2	2	2	2	2	2	NA	2	2	1.00	27
SIC 2094 Animal and marine fats and oils	15	14	14	13	13	14	14	14	NA	14	.93	31
SIC 2095 Roasted coffee	19	NA	NA	NA	NA	17	17	16	16	16	.84	37
SIC 2096 Shortening and cooking oils	12	12	12	13	NA	14	12	13	14	15	1.25	5
SIC 2097 Manufactured ice	15	13	14	13	13	11	11	10	10	8	.53	44
SIC 2098 Macaroni and spaghetti	7	7	7	7	7	7	7	8	7	8	1.14	13
SIC 2099 Food preparations (not elsewhere classified)	49	NA	NA	NA	NA	54	58	56	59	61	1.24	6
Total all categories	1,712	1,704	1,709	1,689	1,655	1,640	1,649	1,640	1,643	1,654	.97	—

Source: Census of Manufacturers, *Bur. Census U.S. Dept. Com.*

[1] Ratio 1967/1963

NA - not available

this section we will use Dept. of Com. data.

CHANGES IN GROWTH BY 44 MAJOR SUBDIVISIONS IN
FOOD PROCESSING (4-DIGIT SIC CODES)

In this section we will discuss changes in employment, value added, value of shipments, and capital expenditures for the total food processing industry and the 44 major subdivisions which make up the total industry. Essentially, employment has decreased for several years but appears to be leveling off for the industry as a whole; while value added, value of shipments, and capital expenditures have shown consistent increases. However, there has been wide variability in these trends among the 44 major subdivisions.

TOTAL EMPLOYMENT

Based on composite data of the 44 industry classifications in food processing, total employment decreased from 1,712,000 people in 1958 to 1,654,000 in 1967. However, total employment has varied little since 1962. (In all the statistical data presented here it should be pointed out that the data on census years, 1958, 1963 and 1967 are more reliable than data for noncensus years. In noncensus years the data are obtained from a substantially smaller sample.)

Individual industries have varied widely in trends in employment levels. For example, the number of employees in SIC 2037 (frozen fruits and vegetables) increased 65% between 1958 and 1967; while there was a 33% decrease during the same time in employees in SIC 2097 (manufactured ice). Changes in employment for each of the 44 subdivisions and for the industry as a whole are listed in Table 5.1. Some industries showing the greatest increases in employment are (1) frozen fruits and vegetables, (2) dehydrated food products, (3) poultry dressing plants, (4) bottled and canned soft drinks, and (5) shortening and cooking oils. Industries showing the greatest decreases are (1) manufactured ice, (2) creamery butter, (3) flour mills, (4) condensed and evaporated milk, and (5) cottonseed oil mills.

Value added, value of shipments, and capital expenditures are increasing while total labor requirements have decreased. This indicates a substitution of capital for labor and at the same time undoubtedly suggests an increase in labor productivity.

VALUE ADDED IN FOOD PROCESSING

Value added is a commonly-used measure of economic activity. In food processing, value added is derived by subtracting the cost of raw materials, supplies, containers, fuel, and purchased electricity from the FOB value of shipments. The value added should be a measure of the economic activity added by the processing function itself. Thus, the value of the containers is used to obtain the value added in the container industry not in the food processing industry. Theoretically, there would be no double counting in a national accounting system of value added.

Value added in food processing increased from $17.58 billion in 1958 to $26.35 billion in 1967. This was a 50% increase in 9 yrs. or a simple average increase of over 5% per yr. It should be noted again that the total value added in farming has decreased significantly through time, while the value added in food processing is still increasing significantly each year.

Several food processing categories have had very large increases in value added between 1958 and 1967. Value added in flavorings increased 2.7 times, dehydrated food products 2.36 times, frozen fruits and vegetables 2.34 times, fresh and frozen packaged fish 2.06 times, and raw cane sugar 1.99 times. Only a few industries had absolute decreases in value added between 1958 and 1967—these were cottonseed oil mills, creamery butter, vegetable oil mills (not elsewhere classified), and manufactured ice. The changes in value added for each of the 44 categories of food processing for the years 1958–1967 are listed in Table 5.2. A note of caution should be mentioned: these are absolute data, the effect of price inflation has not been taken into account. Thus, the real growth in value added is substantially below that listed. The same note applies to the following sections on value of shipments and capital expenditures.

VALUE OF SHIPMENTS

The value of shipments of all food processing increased from $59.5 billion in 1958 to $81.7 billion in 1967. This was a 37% increase in 9 yrs. or a simple average increase of around 4% per yr. The increase in value of shipments has been consistent over the time period; that is, each year has shown an increase in value of shipments.

The food processing industry is characterized by widely different growth rates among its various segments. For example, between 1958 and 1967 value of shipments of flavorings increased 2.4 times, while the value of shipments of manufactured ice decreased 21%.

The 44 food processing industries and their changes in value of shipments between 1958 and 1967 are listed in Table 5.3. In the last column the industries are ranked from (1), the greatest increase in value, to (44), the greatest decrease in value of shipments. The greatest increases in value of shipments have been in (1) flavorings, (2) soybean oil mills, (3) bottled and canned soft drinks, (4) natural and process cheese, and (5) raw cane sugar. Absolute decreases in value of shipments have occurred only in SIC 2093 (vegetable oil mills, not elsewhere classified) and SIC 2097 (manufactured ice).

In Chap. 2 it was indicated that in 1954 only 16 of the 50 largest food processing firms were engaged in SIC 203 (canning and freezing industry) but by 1963, 32 of the 50 largest food processing firms were engaged in this activity. This is not by accident but by design. Industries under SIC 203 have been among the most rapidly expanding industries. For example, between 1958 and 1967 SIC 2032 (canned specialties) increased 76%, SIC 2037 (frozen fruits and vegetables) increased 70%, SIC 2036 (fresh and frozen packaged fish) increased 65%, and SIC 2035 (pickles, sauces and salad dressings) increased 64%.

To answer the question, "Is food processing a growth industry?" depends upon which specific sections are discussed. Of the 44 4-digit industries, the value of shipments of the top 5 nearly doubled between 1958 and 1967.

TABLE 5.2

CHANGES IN VALUE ADDED IN MAJOR FOOD PROCESSING CATEGORIES, 1958-1967

SIC Code And Industry Category	Value Added (Million $)										Ratio 1967/ 1958	Rank In Increase
	1958	1959	1960	1961	1962	1963	1964	1965	1966	1967		
SIC 2011 Meat packing plants	1749	1834	1912	1890	1987	1908	2128	2060	2025	2191	1.25	36
SIC 2013 Meat processing plants	442	461	461	458	493	563	597	607	625	683	1.55	26
SIC 2015 Poultry dressing plants	311	331	369	367	374	411	422	466	559	540	1.74	17
SIC 2021 Creamery butter	147	152	154	158	161	133	161	117	126	136	.93	41
SIC 2022 Natural and process cheese	133	138	161	170	175	180	191	208	246	236	1.77	15
SIC 2023 Condensed and evaporated milk	203	218	285	265	249	236	298	285	310	326	1.61	24
SIC 2024 Ice cream and frozen desserts	395	409	428	427	432	433	443	433	431	461	1.17	38
SIC 2026 Fluid milk	1998	2125	2165	2190	2266	2203	2272	2259	2232	2358	1.18	37
SIC 2031 Canned and cured seafoods	131	119	143	147	151	175	166	191	204	193	1.47	28
SIC 2032 Canned specialties	341	347	429	470	473	541	565	613	645	650	1.91	8
SIC 2033 Canned fruits and vegetables	850	889	988	988	988	1029	1113	1179	1286	1391	1.64	19
SIC 2034 Dehydrated food products	76	79	98	104	104	116	128	131	162	179	2.36	2
SIC 2035 Pickles, sauces, salad dressings	165	181	221	238	243	249	255	280	273	301	1.82	12
SIC 2036 Fresh and frozen packaged fish	84	90	100	104	101	118	128	138	152	173	2.06	4
SIC 2037 Frozen fruits and vegetables	324	346	402	403	429	550	561	627	679	758	2.34	3
SIC 2041 Flour mills	393	411	444	447	441	373	400	406	434	460	1.17	39
SIC 2042 Prepared animal feeds	799	804	808	861	881	984	978	972	1032	1089	1.36	33
SIC 2043 Cereal preparations	243	255	266	284	326	365	391	416	443	467	1.92	7
SIC 2044 Rice milling	53	52	60	63	66	81	70	85	86	104	1.96[1]	6[1]
SIC 2045 Blended and prepared flour	NA	NA	NA	NA	NA	178	215	205	206	235	1.32	34
SIC 2046 Wet corn milling	249	262	278	282	277	291	292	303	347	349	1.40	30
SIC 2051 Bread and related products	2119	2236	2266	2285	2334	2404	2492	2513	2658	2745	1.30	35
SIC 2052 Biscuits, crackers, cookies	523	542	577	592	618	627	656	673	713	730	1.40	31
SIC 2061 Raw cane sugar	68	79	82	74	77	136	106	108	121	135	1.99	5
SIC 2062 Cane sugar refining	185	189	225	211	234	254	205	268	263	299	1.62	22
SIC 2063 Beet sugar	130	132	152	144	167	201	191	198	220	212	1.63	21
SIC 2071 Confectionery products	513	531	566	591	600	635	692	721	756	799	1.56	25
SIC 2072 Chocolate and cocoa products	135	144	158	168	174	185	168	166	180	196	1.45	29
SIC 2073 Chewing gum	105	111	118	122	130	136	146	158	177	189	1.80	13
SIC 2082 Malt liquors	1117	1200	1248	1247	1271	1286	1366	1360	1412	1539	1.38	32

											Ratio[1]	
SIC 2083 Malt	55	51	40	32	49	44	58	51	48	56	1.02	40
SIC 2084 Wines and brandy	114	107	107	121	121	137	159	167	193	209	1.83	11
SIC 2085 Distilled liquor except brandy	458	488	463	464	465	624	660	713	723	741	1.62	23
SIC 2086 Bottled and canned soft drinks	862	954	1006	1061	1128	1234	1388	1373	1471	1630	1.89	9
SIC 2087 Flavorings	249	285	285	285	285	400	448	487	555	673	270	1
SIC 2091 Cottonseed oil mills	64	66	78	89	77	101	72	103	104	61	.95	42
SIC 2092 Soy bean oil mills	140	147	132	166	148	152	170	157	209	233	1.66	18
SIC 2093 Vegetable oil mills (not elsewhere classified)												
SIC 2094 Animal and marine fats and oils	42	46	34	42	34	43	44	44	38	38	.90	43
SIC 2095 Roasted coffee	152	140	129	164	168	193	211	248	248	271	1.78	14
SIC 2096 Shortening and cooking oils	461	461	461	461	461	608	677	628	668	692	1.50	27
SIC 2097 Manufactured ice	222	229	227	222	222	265	272	295	350	362	1.63	20
SIC 2098 Macaroni and spaghetti	108	106	100	101	103	90	89	94	98	96	.89	44
SIC 2099 Food preparations (not elsewhere classified)	67	74	76	80	83	96	105	110	106	123	1.84	10
	605	605	605	605	605	843	905	940	1023	1061	1.75	16
Total all categories	17,580	18,426	19,411	19,643	20,177	21,811	23,054	23,556	24,837	26,352	1.50	—

Source: Census of Manufacturers, *Bur. Census, U.S. Dept. Com.*
[1] Ratio 1967/1963

TABLE 5.3

CHANGES IN VALUE OF SHIPMENTS IN MAJOR FOOD PROCESSING CATEGORIES, 1958-1967

SIC Code And Industry Category	Value of Shipments (Million $)										Ratio 1967/ 1958	Rank Of Increase
	1958	1959	1960	1961	1962	1963	1964	1965	1966	1967		
SIC 2011 Meat Packing plants	11,972	11,810	11,828	11,939	12,491	12,435	12,973	13,931	15,069	15,335	1.28	31
SIC 2013 Meat processing plants	2,066	2,005	2,008	2,048	2,134	2,130	2,297	2,323	2,502	2,633	1.27	32
SIC 2015 Poultry dressing plants	1,888	1,898	2,054	2,084	2,078	2,241	2,330	2,490	2,754	2,788	1.48	19
SIC 2021 Creamery butter	1,023	1,063	1,108	1,219	1,294	989	1,080	943	976	1,042	1.02	41
SIC 2022 Natural and process cheese	874	893	994	1,110	1,107	1,171	1,226	1,325	1,552	1,715	1.96	4
SIC 2023 Condensed and evaporated milk	821	851	936	1,037	963	938	1,021	1,050	1,100	1,167	1.42	25
SIC 2024 Ice cream and frozen desserts	951	1,006	1,048	1,086	1,093	1,076	1,090	1,085	1,142	1,194	1.26	33
SIC 2026 Fluid milk	6,412	6,649	6,763	6,835	6,889	7,026	7,299	7,185	7,435	7,742	1.21	36
SIC 2031 Canned and cured seafoods	389	352	401	402	429	452	445	492	548	523	1.34	28
SIC 2032 Canned specialties	847	861	989	1,058	1,086	1,169	1,231	1,368	1,457	1,491	1.76	6
SIC 2033 Canned fruits and vegetables	2,334	2,335	2,516	2,516	2,516	2,743	2,966	2,982	3,315	3,414	1.46	20
SIC 2034 Dehydrated food products	273	264	289	304	304	319	321	364	395	413	1.51	16
SIC 2035 Pickles, sauces and salad dressings	525	564	630	694	696	677	726	784	818	859	1.64	13
SIC 2036 Fresh and frozen packaged fish	310	317	328	331	345	391	428	464	493	511	1.65	11
SIC 2037 Frozen fruits and vegetables	1,206	1,112	1,207	1,275	1,324	1,549	1,652	1,816	1,885	2,047	1.70	8
SIC 2041 Flour mills	2,087	2,166	2,240	2,231	2,369	2,177	2,193	2,146	2,345	2,383	1.14	39
SIC 2042 Prepared animal feeds	3,238	3,265	3,262	3,478	3,652	3,880	3,870	3,987	4,438	4,640	1.43	24
SIC 2043 Cereal preparations	444	460	483	503	577	625	671	707	743	783	1.76	7
SIC 2044 Rice milling	312	294	316	329	399	423	443	457	458	521	1.67	10[1]
SIC 2045 Blended and prepared flour	NA	NA	NA	NA	NA	434	509	489	503	533	1.23[1]	35
SIC 2046 Wet corn milling	529	558	566	584	602	622	629	680	755	744	1.41	26
SIC 2051 Bread and related products	4,099	4,267	4,333	4,365	4,446	4,506	4,618	4,725	5,007	5,125	1.25	34
SIC 2052 Biscuits, crackers and cookies	983	998	1,051	1,074	1,134	1,150	1,198	1,236	1,327	1,383	1.41	27
SIC 2061 Raw cane sugar	178	198	200	229	233	379	325	294	313	349	1.96	5
SIC 2062 Cane sugar refining	997	1,025	1,068	1,076	1,140	1,271	1,185	1,182	1,220	1,327	1.33	29
SIC 2063 Beet sugar	392	384	410	418	456	564	546	531	579	563	1.44	23
SIC 2071 Confectionery products	1,229	1,268	1,318	1,362	1,395	1,455	1,553	1,583	1,681	1,799	1.46	21
SIC 2072 Chocolate and coca products	447	446	451	446	462	479	477	452	471	526	1.18	37
SIC 2073 Chewing gum	185	192	200	204	212	225	242	260	282	305	1.65	12
SIC 2082 Malt liquors	1,983	2,095	2,179	2,200	2,282	2,315	2,470	2,497	2,670	2,949	1.49	17
SIC 2083 Malt	195	203	205	207	191	184	216	204	206	228	1.17	38
SIC 2084 Wines and brandy	264	282	282	305	305	368	385	396	401	433	1.64	14
SIC 2085 Distilled liquor except brandy	941	959	927	938	946	1,090	1,134	1,288	1,332	1,371	1.46	22
SIC 2086 Bottled and canned soft drinks	1,558	1,714	1,806	1,911	2,031	2,211	2,409	2,505	2,735	3,066	1.97	3
SIC 2087 Flavorings	477	535	535	535	535	730	833	837	974	1,148	2.41	1
SIC 2091 Cottonseed oil mills	421	429	443	478	512	555	527	555	561	449	1.07	40

											Ratio[1]	2
SIC 2092 Soybean oil mills	1,081	1,147	1,133	1,284	1,346	1,473	1,538	1,732	2,010	2,151	1.99	2
SIC 2093 Vegetable oil mills (not elsewhere identified)	315	358	332	328	309	324	252	252	266	258	1.82	43
SIC 2094 Animal and marine fats and oils	389	353	318	376	401	474	550	669	669	660	1.70	9
SIC 2095 Roasted coffee	2,039	2,039	2,039	2,039	2,039	1,846	2,113	2,090	2,083	2,064	1.01	42
SIC 2096 Shortening and cooking oils	1,239	1,190	1,052	1,285	1,285	1,324	1,326	1,489	1,688	1,629	1.31	30
SIC 2097 Manufactured ice	150	145	138	139	137	123	116	126	124	118	.79	44
SIC 2098 Macaroni and spaghetti	180	192	195	200	201	223	235	238	238	267	1.48	18
SIC 2099 Food preparations (not elsewhere classified)	1,393	1,393	1,393	1,393	1,393	1,786	1,900	2,062	2,206	2,285	1.64	15
Total all categories	59,456	60,535	61,974	63,855	65,739	68,522	71,598	74,271	79,626	81,705	1.37	—

Source: Census of Manufacturers, *Bur. Census, U.S. Dept. Com.*
[1] Ratio 1967/1963

However, the bottom 5 showed practically no growth during this period.

CAPITAL EXPENDITURES

Capital expenditures for plants and equipment have increased at a faster rate in food processing than either value added or value of shipments. Between 1958 and 1967 annual capital expenditures increased from $1.01 billion to $1.73 billion or an increase of 72%. This is a simple average increase of around 8% per yr., while value added has increased at a little over 5% per yr., and value of shipments at a rate just over 4% per yr.

The increasing capital expenditures indicate a continuous modernization, adoption of new technologies, and a substitution of capital for labor. United States food processing industries have historically suffered from excess capacity and the high rate of capital expenditures would suggest that this will continue to be the case.

Changes in capital expenditures are listed in Table 5.4. The capital expenditures for an individual industry are much more variable than for value added or value of shipments. For example, the capital expenditures in SIC 2072 (chocolate and cocoa products) increased from $4.1 million in 1958 to $21.7 million in 1966 and then dropped to only $9.3 million in 1967. While annual capital expenditures in SIC 2026 (fluid milk) are quite variable, the trend is toward decreasing expenditures. The patterns of capital expenditures in many industries are quite variable with no real consistent trends.

The industries with the greatest increases in capital expenditures have been (1) SIC 2044 (rice milling) with 1967 expenditures 7 times that of 1958; (2) SIC 2063 (beet sugar) expenditures in 1967 were at a level 4.4 times that of 1958 (but annual expenditures have been quite variable); (3) SIC 2073 (chewing gum) capital expenditures in 1967 were 3.9 times that of 1958; (4) SIC 2037 (frozen fruits and vegetables) expenditures increased 3.7 times in 9 yrs; and (5) SIC 2087 (flavorings) expenditures increased 3.2 times in the 9 yr., 1958–1967.

Those showing decreasing trends in capital expenditures are SIC 2093 (vegetable oil mills), SIC 2062 (cane sugar refining), SIC 2026 (fluid milk), SIC 2091 (cottonseed oil mills), SIC 2097 (manufactured ice), and SIC 2021 (creamery butter).

The Principal Four-Digit Industry Classes

Six of the 44 subdivisions account for much of the total economic activity. In 1967, meat packing, fluid milk, canned fruits and vegetables, bread and related products, confectionery products, and bottled and canned soft drinks accounted for over 50% of the total employees and around 40% of the value added, value of shipments, and capital expenditures. Specifically, these 6 4-digit food processing industries accounted for 51.53% of the total employees, 40.12% of the value added, 41.98% of the value of shipments, and 39.26% of the total capital expenditures in 1967.

The percentages of 1967 totals for each of the 44 industries are listed in

Table 5.5 under the headings of Employment, Value Added, Value of Shipments, and Capital Expenditures.

GROWTH RATES OF 94 SUBDIVISIONS IN FOOD PROCESSING
(5-DIGIT SIC CLASSIFICATION)

Each of the 44 4-digit SIC food processing industries we have discussed may consist of several 5-digit SIC classes and each of the 5-digit SIC classes may consist of several "product classes" or 7-digit SIC codes. This section is primarily in tabular form, with little discussion. The purpose is to list the relative rate of growth in value of shipments of 94 subdivisions in food processing for the period 1958–1967 (Table 5.6).

As each 4-digit SIC classification may consist of several 5-digit SIC codes, the rate of growth of the more specific 5-digit SIC codes may be substantially different from the master 4-digit code. For example, the value of shipments of SIC 2037 (frozen fruits and vegetables) increased 70% between 1958 and 1967; however, its subparts increased as follows: SIC 20371 (frozen fruits, juices and ades) increased only 17%. SIC 20372 (frozen vegetables) increased 174%. SIC 20373 (frozen prepared foods) increased 177%.

Again, the rate of growth in food processing varies among different segments. The value of shipments of the 10 most rapidly increasing 5-digit codes increased from $2790 million in 1958 to $6861 million in 1967, a 140% increase, or a simple average increase of around 15% per yr. The 10 5-digit industries with the least growth increases, or those that decreased in growth, had shipments valued at $3393 million in 1958 and only $3039 million in 1967, a decrease of 10%.

The five-digit code industries increasing most rapidly have been processed poultry (except soups), processed cheese and related products, frozen prepared foods and soups, frozen vegetables, flavorings, other soybean mill products (other than oil), dog and cat food, sugar cane mill products, chips (potato, corn, etc.), and catsup and other tomato products. While the specific product classes included in these five-digit food processing categories will not be listed, they can be found in *The Census of Manufacturers, 1967*. The 94 food processing categories (5-digit codes) are listed in Table 5.6 by their rate of growth in value of shipments.

Industry classes with absolute decreases in value of shipments from 1958 to 1967 include evaporated milk shipped in bulk, baking powder and yeast, animal and marine oil mill products, concentrated coffee, linseed oil, veal (fresh and frozen), manufactured ice, and lard.

SUMMARY

Total employment in food processing has decreased over the past 15 yr but appears to have nearly leveled off during the last 4–5 yr (1963–1967). Value added, value of shipments, and capital expenditures have increased significantly.

The rate of increase in capital expenditures for new plants and equipment has exceeded the rate of growth in both value added and value of shipments. This indicates a substantial substitution of capital for labor and may indicate a

TABLE 5.4

CHANGES IN CAPITAL EXPENDITURES IN MAJOR
FOOD PROCESSING CATEGORIES, 1958-1967

SIC Code And Industry Category	Capital Expenditures (Million $)										Ratio 1967/1958	Rank of Increase
	1958	1959	1960	1961	1962	1963	1964	1965	1966	1967		
SIC 2011 Meat packing plants	65.9	67.5	77.2	75.5	90.9	80.2	94.7	101.1	104.3	110.4	1.68	25
SIC 2013 Meat processing plants	17.2	14.0	20.1	17.3	19.3	21.4	29.8	51.6	33.3	30.3	1.76	22
SIC 2015 Poultry dressing plants	28.1	24.5	23.0	19.2	19.3	34.3	21.3	31.9	43.6	57.5	2.05	20
SIC 2021 Creamery butter	17.1	16.1	12.5	19.6	19.6	9.9	16.1	9.9	10.2	10.3	.60	44
SIC 2022 Natural and process cheese	13.7	17.0	10.2	11.0	12.1	15.9	11.8	13.9	13.4	17.3	1.26	32
SIC 2023 Condensed and evaporated milk	12.7	13.6	14.1	14.3	13.4	12.1	17.4	21.2	13.6	21.0	1.65	26
SIC 2024 Ice cream and frozen desserts	26.2	23.8	24.8	20.2	26.4	31.9	30.6	32.7	26.7	26.8	1.02	37
SIC 2026 Fluid milk	135.5	147.9	120.9	117.6	116.7	126.1	139.8	114.6	105.2	120.0	.88	41
SIC 2031 Canned and cured seafoods	3.5	7.7	6.8	7.8	9.0	6.3	6.0	6.3	6.6	9.4	2.69	8
SIC 2032 Canned specialties	16.5	17.3	14.2	20.1	23.8	25.6	24.0	30.7	40.8	28.1	1.70	24
SIC 2033 Canned fruits and vegetables	43.7	43.5	46.3	46.3	46.3	66.6	78.3	74.5	84.8	102.2	2.34	13
SIC 2034 Dehydrated food products	6.7	7.8	8.0	7.1	7.2	16.2	10.4	11.0	14.1	14.8	2.20	17
SIC 2035 Pickles, sauces and salad dressings	11.2	13.1	13.7	12.6	13.3	11.0	16.9	11.0	14.4	14.6	1.30	31
SIC 2036 Fresh and frozen packaged fish	3.7	6.9	4.0	3.4	10.0	6.1	5.4	6.2	9.4	8.7	2.35	12
SIC 2037 Frozen fruits and vegetables	21.0	23.1	28.7	28.4	40.1	44.6	50.0	62.9	81.9	77.6	3.70	4
SIC 2041 Flour mills	22.1	31.1	28.5	24.1	25.7	23.5	21.1	21.9	36.0	26.2	1.19	35
SIC 2042 Prepared animal feeds	55.0	56.3	49.6	44.7	56.7	53.4	50.4	66.3	62.1	75.8	1.38	30
SIC 2043 Cereal preparations	17.7	21.5	14.4	17.5	20.9	15.3	21.2	16.2	19.2	19.1	1.08	36
SIC 2044 Rice milling	1.4	1.2	3.0	3.7	5.0	3.3	4.5	5.0	7.2	9.8	7.00[1]	1
SIC 2045 Blended and prepared flours	NA	NA	NA	NA	NA	6.1	8.7	9.8	8.9	9.4	1.54	28
SIC 2046 Wet corn milling	18.1	25.0	27.0	33.9	28.1	26.1	47.9	47.7	43.7	40.5	2.24	16
SIC 2051 Bread and related products	104.1	127.2	101.9	96.4	92.6	95.3	115.0	142.0	148.6	126.4	1.21	34
SIC 2052 Biscuits, crackers and cookies	15.5	14.5	12.7	14.2	38.0	26.4	15.3	30.9	33.2	24.3	1.57	27
SIC 2061 Raw cane sugar	8.0	8.4	7.8	10.5	20.8	19.3	24.4	17.6	24.6	21.4	2.68	9
SIC 2062 Cane sugar refining	26.8	19.4	23.3	14.7	11.4	16.2	22.8	18.6	25.6	24.1	.90	40

											Ratio[1]	
SIC 2063 Beet sugar	8.0	10.6	13.1	17.0	22.3	38.1	54.9	22.0	17.5	35.7	4.46	2
SIC 2071 Confectionery products	24.8	22.7	22.6	22.2	29.3	28.1	35.7	41.2	48.1	53.0	2.13	19
SIC 2072 Chocolate and cocoa products	4.1	5.7	4.4	5.2	6.7	8.3	9.6	11.9	21.7	9.3	2.27	15
SIC 2073 Chewing Gum	3.4	2.6	3.1	3.2	4.4	2.9	6.7	6.4	12.9	13.3	3.91	3
SIC 2082 Malt liquors	72.9	64.4	75.9	89.9	84.6	86.2	105.4	115.4	168.8	140.6	1.93	21
SIC 2083 Malt	3.1	7.7	5.6	4.3	1.7	3.0	3.0	4.4	4.1	7.1	2.29	14
SIC 2084 Wines and brandy	7.9	4.8	4.8	4.8	4.8	7.3	7.3	11.3	11.8	9.6	1.22	33
SIC 2085 Distilled liquor except brandy	9.9	11.6	15.9	14.5	19.8	15.5	13.5	23.4	32.1	26.9	2.72	7
SIC 2086 Bottled and canned soft drinks	64.1	66.0	76.4	69.4	81.4	100.8	110.8	111.0	151.1	168.2	2.62	10
SIC 2087 Flavorings	5.4	6.6	6.6	6.6	6.6	12.3	12.2	14.8	23.6	17.5	3.24	5
SIC 2091 Cotton seed oil mills	6.6	5.0	5.0	6.0	26.0	12.5	12.5	6.4	6.4	5.0	.76	42
SIC 2092 Soybean oil mills	14.7	26.6	13.8	14.8	14.1	10.2	10.8	17.7	13.7	21.2	1.44	29
SIC 2093 Vegetable oil mills (not elsewhere classified)	2.0	1.7	1.1	0.5	1.2	1.6	1.4	1.4	2.5	1.9	.95	39
SIC 2094 Animal and marine fats and oils	12.7	19.2	13.9	15.3	20.6	13.7	14.7	12.7	12.7	21.7	1.71	23
SIC 2095 Roasted coffee	23.1	23.1	23.1	23.1	23.1	23.3	21.4	25.0	25.5	49.9	2.16	18
SIC 2096 Shortening and cooking oils	12.4	12.5	17.6	20.3	20.3	19.5	22.7	20.3	17.3	29.3	2.36	11
SIC 2097 Manufactured ice	6.4	3.3	2.4	3.2	3.6	5.7	3.9	3.9	3.9	4.8	.72	43
SIC 2098 Macaroni and spaghetti	5.3	4.7	5.1	4.5	10.0	4.8	4.8	7.0	8.4	5.2	.98	38
SIC 2099 Food preparations (not elsewhere classified)	31.1	31.1	31.1	31.1	31.1	39.9	70.0	61.2	91.4	86.6	2.79	6
Totals all categories	1009.6	1078.3	1034.3	1036.3	1178.1	1226.8	1405.0	1472.8	1685.1	1733.0	1.72	—

Source: Census of Manufacturers, *Bur. Census, U.S. Dept. Commerce.*
[1] Ratio 1967/1963

TABLE 5.5

TOTAL EMPLOYMENT, VALUE ADDED, VALUE OF SHIPMENTS
AND CAPITAL EXPENDITURES BY MAJOR FOOD PROCESSING CATEGORIES, 1967

SIC Code And Industry Category	Total Employment		Value Added		Value of Shipments		Capital Expenditures	
	Number (1000)	Percent of Total	Value (Million $)	Percent of Total	Value (Million $)	Percent of Total	Amount (Million $)	Percent of Total
SIC 2011 Meat packing plants	172.1	10.41	2,191	8.31	15,355	18.52	110.4	6.37
SIC 2013 Meat processing plants	54.4	3.29	683	2.59	2,633	3.18	30.3	1.75
SIC 2015 Poultry dressing plants	83.4	5.04	540	2.05	2,788	3.36	57.7	3.33
SIC 2021 Creamery butter	9.0	.54	136	.52	1,042	1.26	10.3	.59
SIC 2022 Natural and process cheese	20.1	1.22	236	.89	1,715	2.07	17.3	1.00
SIC 2023 Condensed and evaporated milk	12.8	.77	326	1.24	1,167	1.41	21.0	1.21
SIC 2024 Ice cream and frozen desserts	24.7	1.49	461	1.75	1,194	1.44	26.8	1.55
SIC 2026 Fluid milk	166.1	10.04	2,358	8.94	7,742	9.34	120.0	6.93
SIC 2031 Canned and cured seafood	15.6	.94	193	.73	523	.63	9.4	.54
SIC 2032 Canned specialties	27.3	1.65	650	2.46	1,491	1.80	28.1	1.62
SIC 2033 Canned fruits and vegetables	101.0	6.11	1,391	5.28	3,414	4.12	102.2	5.90
SIC 2034 Dehydrated food products	11.2	.68	179	.69	413	.50	14.8	.86
SIC 2035 Pickles, sauces and salad dressings	19.5	1.18	301	1.14	859	1.04	14.6	.84
SIC 2036 Fresh and frozen packaged fish	21.5	1.30	173	.66	511	.62	8.7	.50
SIC 2037 Frozen fruits and vegetables	65.6	3.97	758	2.87	2,047	2.47	77.6	4.48
SIC 2041 Flour mills	20.3	1.23	460	1.74	2,383	2.87	26.2	1.51
SIC 2042 Prepared animal feeds	53.2	3.21	1,089	4.13	4,640	5.60	75.8	4.37
SIC 2043 Cereal preparations	12.7	.77	467	1.77	783	.94	19.1	1.10
SIC 2044 Rice milling	4.2	.25	104	.39	521	.63	9.8	.57
SIC 2045 Blended and prepared flour	7.1	.43	235	.89	533	.64	9.4	.54
SIC 2046 Wet corn milling	14.1	.85	349	1.32	744	.90	40.5	2.34
SIC 2051 Bread and related products	221.6	13.40	2,745	10.41	5,083	6.13	126.4	7.29
SIC 2052 Biscuits, crackers and cookies	43.1	2.60	730	2.77	1,383	1.67	24.3	1.40
SIC 2061 Raw cane sugar	7.9	.48	135	.51	349	.42	21.4	1.23
SIC 2062 Cane sugar refining	11.5	.70	299	1.13	1,327	1.60	24.1	1.39
SIC 2063 Beet sugar	11.5	.70	212	.80	563	.68	35.7	2.06
SIC 2071 Confectionery products	68.0	4.11	799	3.03	1,799	2.17	53.0	3.06
SIC 2072 Chocolate and cocoa products	8.0	.48	196	.74	526	.63	9.3	.54

SIC 2073 Chewing gum	6.8	.41	189	.72	305	.37	13.3	.77
SIC 2082 Malt liquors	60.5	3.65	1,539	5.83	2,949	3.56	140.6	8.11
SIC 2083 Malt	2.0	.12	56	.21	228	.28	7.1	.41
SIC 2084 Wines and brandy	6.6	.40	209	.79	433	.52	9.6	.55
SIC 2085 Distilled liquor except brandy	19.4	1.17	741	2.81	1,371	1.65	26.9	1.55
SIC 2086 Bottled and canned soft drinks	123.4	7.46	1,630	6.18	3,066	3.70	168.2	9.71
SIC 2087 Flavorings	10.1	.61	673	2.55	1,148	1.38	17.5	1.01
SIC 2091 Cottonseed oil mills	5.6	.34	61	.23	449	.54	5.0	.29
SIC 2092 Soybean oil mills	8.0	.48	233	.88	2,151	2.59	21.2	1.22
SIC 2093 Vegetable oil mills (not elsewhere calssified)	1.7	.10	38	.14	258	.31	1.9	.11
SIC 2094 Animal marine fats and oils	13.8	.83	271	1.03	660	.80	21.7	1.25
SIC 2095 Roasted coffee	16.1	.97	692	2.62	2,064	2.49	49.9	2.88
SIC 2096 Shortening and cooking oil	15.1	.91	362	1.40	1,629	1.96	29.3	.28
SIC 2097 Manufactured ice	8.0	.48	96	.36	118	.14	4.8	.28
SIC 2098 Macaroni and spaghetti	7.5	.45	123	.47	267	.32	5.2	.30
SIC 2099 Food preparations (not elsewhere classified)	61.4	3.71	1,061	4.02	2,285	2.75	86.6	5.00
Total all categories	1653.5	100.00	26,370	100.00	82,909	100.00	1733.00	100.00

Source: Census of Manufacturers, *Bur. Census, U.S. Dept. Commerce.*

TABLE 5.6

RATE OF GROWTH OF 94 PRODUCT CLASSES
(5-DIGIT SIC CODES) IN FOOD PROCESSING, 1958-1967
(RANKED FROM GREATEST TO LEAST INCREASE IN VALUE OF SHIPMENTS)

SIC Code	Class of Product	Value of Shipments (Million $)										Ratio 1967/1958	Rank of Increase
		1958	1959	1960	1961	1962	1963	1964	1965	1966	1967		
20154	Processed poultry, except soups	26	34	34	35	36	39	44	44	60	142	5.46	1
20222	Process cheese and related products	246	NA	NA	NA	NA	389	416	406	476	739	3.00	2
20373	Frozen prepared foods and soups	319	340	434	474	539	608	646	765	838	883	2.77	3
20372	Frozen vegetables	231	234	271	289	291	396	439	512	565	584	2.74	4
2087—	Flavorings	477	535	535	535	535	730	833	837	974	1148	2.40	5
20922	Other soybean mill products (other than oil)	487	566	551	572	660	831	826	854	1036	1135	2.33	6
20423	Dog and cat food	305	313	343	354	366	442	492	508	568	706	2.31	7
20610	Sugar cane mill products and by-products	159	180	192	217	226	373	321	291	310	364	2.29	8
20992	Chips (potato, corn, etc.)	294	340	381	424	472	466	501	538	581	648	2.20	9
20336	Catsup and other tomato products	246	234	280	293	325	298	342	391	450	512	2.08	10
2086—	Bottled and canned soft drinks	1558	1714	1806	1911	2031	2211	2409	2505	2735	3066	1.97	11
20153	Turkeys	258	270	296	306	313	372	398	451	503	505	1.96	12
20440	Milled rice and by-products	281	268	281	295	374	407	438	448	450	547	1.95	13
20361	Frozen packaged fish and other seafood (including soups)	203	211	224	228	239	267	288	327	333	384	1.89	14
2045V	Prepared flour and flour mixes	356	346	410	429	409	526	605	518	562	646	1.81	15
20422	Livestock feeds	959	1051	1049	1140	1225	1388	1349	1409	1638	1700	1.77	16
20521	Biscuits, crackers and pretzels	350	382	397	409	415	450	462	461	464	618	1.76	17
20234	Ice cream mix and ice milk mix	118	148	134	156	165	158	148	155	163	203	1.72	18
20324	Soup mixes	NA	NA	NA	NA	NA	45	50	51	64	76	1.69	19
20430	Cereal Breakfast foods	432	442	452	484	517	561	608	652	691	714	1.65	20
2073—	Chewing gum	185	192	200	204	212	225	242	260	282	305	1.65	21
2084—	Wines and brandy	264	282	282	305	305	368	385	396	401	433	1.64	22
20221	Natural cheese, except cottage cheese	516	NA	NA	NA	NA	681	707	766	920	829	1.61	23
20991	Desserts (ready-to-mix)	139	148	150	142	156	182	179	215	225	218	1.57	24
20942	Feed and fertilizer by-products	174	170	145	171	193	247	253	275	291	274	1.57	25
20999	Other food preparations (not elsewhere classified)	684	755	859	891	927	883	922	991	1080	1078	1.56	26
20962	Margarine	296	269	276	336	334	323	346	372	431	457	1.54	27
20354	Salad dressings, mayonnaise and sandwich spreads	241	237	231	258	271	279	305	348	387	372	1.54	28

Industry												Ratio	No.
20352 Pickles and other pickle products	170	191	202	212	219	220	233	238	261	260		1.53	29
20231 Dry milk products	421	433	505	600	590	504	564	548	573	634		1.51	30
20151 Hens (or fowl) and other chickens	1178	1172	1320	1319	1341	1480	1526	1640	1800	1784		1.51	31
20232 Canned vegetables, except hominy and mushrooms	639	623	652	697	692	768	762	827	883	966		1.51	32
20980 Macaroni and noodle products	165	179	178	178	190	216	233	222	225	248		1.50	33
20333 Canned hominy and mushrooms	35	38	36	40	41	39	44	42	44	52		1.49	34
2082- Malt Liquors	1983	2095	2179	2200	2282	2315	2470	2497	2670	2949		1.49	35
20111 Beef fresh and frozen	5019	5355	5396	5337	5717	5708	6018	6429	6899	7492		1.49	36
2032A Canned and frozen soups excluding seafoods	475	489	533	552	567	515	548	613	673	703		1.48	37
20323 Canned dry beans	167	180	186	203	203	200	216	246	256	246		1.47	38
2071- Confectionery products	1229	1268	1318	1362	1395	1445	1553	1583	1681	1799		1.46	39
2085- Distilled liquor	941	959	927	938	946	1090	1134	1288	1332	1371		1.46	40
20119 Hides, skins and pelts	196	366	340	356	368	223	218	275	389	285		1.45	41
2013- Meat processing plant products	2066	2005	2007	2048	2133	2130	2297	2323	2502	3001		1.45	42
20993 Sweetening syrups and molasses	96	114	116	122	130	137	150	137	141	138		1.44	43
20353 Meat sauces (except tomatoes) and unfinished pickles	68	75	80	82	89	102	101	107	111	98		1.44	44
20630 Beet sugar refining	392	383	410	418	456	564	545	531	580	561		1.43	45
20334 Canned fruit juices	294	284	311	306	301	381	417	397	444	414		1.41	46
20961 Shortening and cooking oils	895	780	715	864	930	907	955	1103	1210	1242		1.39	47
20921 Soybean oil	426	420	402	408	422	459	469	581	642	593		1.39	48
20264 Buttermilk, chocolate milk and other flavored milk drinks	213	230	234	251	259	253	271	267	281	288		1.35	49
20460 Wet corn milling	483	488	494	534	553	547	547	618	655	647		1.34	50
20512 Sweet yeast goods	295	327	346	346	355	330	357	369	384	394		1.34	51
20932 Vegetable oils (other than cottonseed, soybean and linseed)	83	125	121	120	110	105	115	110	113	111		1.33	52
20996 Vinegar and cider	44	48	57	65	69	54	57	52	53	58		1.32	53
20114 Pork, fresh and frozen	2124	2056	2074	2177	2240	2203	2346	2505	2800	2786		1.31	54
20517 Doughnuts (cake type)	125	128	134	132	140	141	149	158	168	164		1.31	55
20321 Canned baby foods, except meat	185	189	190	203	215	231	232	246	238	243		1.31	56
20331 Canned fruits	640	659	679	726	741	722	823	768	824	823		1.29	57
20941 Grease and inedible tallow	247	227	219	252	230	264	338	388	418	303		1.27	58
20511 Bread and bread type rolls	2221	2325	2410	2457	2456	2497	2552	2586	2774	2798		1.26	59
20514 Pies	201	214	219	208	219	206	215	228	232	252		1.25	60

(Continued)

TABLE 5.6 (Cont'd)

RATE OF GROWTH OF 94 PRODUCT CLASSES
(5-DIGIT SIC CODES) IN FOOD PROCESSING, 1958-1967
(RANKED FROM GREATEST TO LEAST INCREASE IN VALUE OF SHIPMENTS)

SIC Code	Class of Product	Value of Shipments (Million $)										Ratio 1967/1958	Rank of Increase
		1958	1959	1960	1961	1962	1963	1964	1965	1966	1967		
20338	Jams, jellies and preserves	198	231	239	253	NA	250	227	237	251	247	1.25	61
20412	Wheat bran and middlings	168	178	181	180	189	200	201	192	207	205	1.22	62
20341	Dried and dehydrated fruits and vegetables (except soups)	NA	NA	NA	NA	NA	285	282	328	366	345	1.21	63
20263	Cottage cheese	185	190	209	209	213	189	192	194	206	220	1.19	64
20232	Canned milk	352	339	343	311	286	363	387	395	420	417	1.18	65
2072—	Chocolate and cocoa products	447	446	451	446	462	479	477	452	471	526	1.18	66
2083—	Malt	195	203	205	207	191	184	216	204	206	228	1.17	67
20424	Other prepared animal feeds	236	279	289	310	321	280	288	289	300	275	1.17	68
20371	Frozen fruits, juices and ades	358	416	415	433	421	436	449	414	421	419	1.17	69
20310	Canned and cured seafoods	367	336	377	384	398	384	379	419	470	421	1.15	70
20522	Other dry bakery products including machine made cookies and ice cream cones	619	597	622	629	683	680	707	743	822	698	1.13	71
20515	Pastries and cookies	40	26	37	25	22	51	51	74	97	45	1.13	72
20513	Soft cakes	413	430	423	411	417	438	450	472	491	461	1.12	73
20261	Fluid milk and cream	817	899	921	952	967	950	1013	962	1102	925	1.12	74
20240	Ice cream and ices	1138	1193	1231	1243	1237	1210	1271	1264	1330	1275	1.12	75
20335	Canned vegetable juices	93	88	90	95	97	91	100	98	95	104	1.12	76
20411	Wheat flour, except blended or prepared	1399	1352	1429	1455	1535	1491	1503	1482	1596	1557	1.11	77
20262	Bottled milk and cream	4110	4242	4356	4362	4414	4285	4358	4433	4599	4473	1.09	78
20421	Poultry feeds	1474	1351	1336	1480	1456	1445	1401	1447	1582	1570	1.07	79
20156	Liquid dried and frozen eggs	151	160	146	156	129	140	156	151	170	164	1.05	80
20620	Refined sugar cane	NA	NA	NA	NA	NA	1255	1172	1150	1191	1337	1.05	81
20210	Creamery butter	802	841	875	914	989	820	866	768	741	852	1.05	82
20155	Other poultry and small game	19	15	15	25	24	14	20	16	18	20	1.05	83
20113	Lamb and mutton, fresh and frozen	305	308	296	287	291	300	298	308	335	312	1.02	84
20951	Roasted coffee, whole bean or ground	1367	NA	NA	NA	NA	1206	1385	1446	1415	1384	1.01	85

										86	87	88		89	90	91	92	93	94
20910 Cottonseed oil mills	421	429	443	478	512	555	527	555	560	409								.97	
20233 Evaporated milk shipped in bulk	84	93	87	94	87	75	74	83	97	81								.96	
20994 Baking powder and yeast	83	86	85	86	87	81	82	80	83	79								.95	
20943 Animal and marine oil mill products, including foots	104	83	82	103	110	111	107	120	124	97								.93	
20952 Concentrated coffee	401	NA	NA	NA	NA	396	448	370	380	366								.91	
20931 Linseed oil	63	68	53	54	60	50	62	51	52	48								.76	
20112 Veal, fresh and frozen	414	374	351	328	344	311	305	327	333	310								.75	
20970 Manufactured ice	115	114	111	111	108	95	90	93	97	85								.74	
20115 Lard	332	281	274	288	257	224	237	255	227	180								.54	

Source: U.S. Dept. of Commerce, (1968,1970).

continued over-capacity, historically a problem in much food processing.

Increasing capital expenditures can occur through needs for absolute increases in capacity, or by adopting new technologies, or by relocations of industries. Since value added and sales are increasing while labor requirements are decreasing, this should indicate at least some degree of technological progressiveness by the industry.

Six of the 44 major food processing industries (4-digit codes), meat packing, canned fruits and vegetables, bread and related products, confectionery products, fluid milk, and canned and bottled soft drinks account for over 50% of the total employees in all food processing and around 40% of the value added, value of sales, and capital expenditures.

The rate of growth in food processing varies greatly depending upon the individual industries. The 10 leading processing categories (5-digit SIC codes) have increased value of shipments at a simple average rate around 15% per yr. However, at the other extreme, the 10 slowest growing industries have had absolute decreases in value of shipments.

The great differences in growth among the food processing industries may account for some of the increasing diversification and conglomeration.

BIBLIOGRAPHY

U.S. Dept. of Com. 1968. Food & Tobacco Manufacturing. BSDA Ind. Trend Ser. *1* U.S. Dept. Com., Washington, D.C., Oct.

U.S. Dept. of Com. 1970. 1967 Census of Manufacturers, Preliminary Reports. Bur. of Census, U.S. Dept. Com., Washington, D.C.

CHAPTER 6

W. Smith Greig | ## The Markets for Foods in the United States

INTRODUCTION

The mores and customs of the American people are changing rapidly. With higher incomes, better education, more leisure, and greater mobility, eating habits are changing as rapidly as many of our social institutions. Instant breakfasts, more snacks, quick-service meals, drive-in restaurants, take-out food services, vending machines, TV dinners, low calorie foods, cosmetic diets, health diets, the emerging individualistic rather than family-centered activities, more younger people, and more older people are all changing the markets for food.

Historically, our food marketing system has been based on the concept of scarcity and economizing. Some economists would suggest that in the United States (to a large extent) we have passed the scarcity stage and are now in a "postindustrial" stage of abundance and affluence. Thus, the basic concepts on which much of our current food systems were built are not in tune with present and future needs.

Some authorities make the point that the chains of retail supermarkets were created by environmental factors, i.e., the automobile, good communication with national brand promotion, etc., not by the genius of a few individual men. They suggest that environments change continuously and that affluence, leisure, and changes in social institutions may outmode the supermarket (Doody and McCammon 1970). But as one institution supersedes another and as one invention supersedes another, the result is generally increased economic activity. Thus if supermarkets decline, nonstore food retailing should result in substantially increased total economic activity in food retailing.

Other economists suggest that the sophisticated consumer, with both leisure and money, is becoming insensitive to the economic aspects of food purchasing, and blase to the social and entertainment aspects of shopping in grocery stores. Consumer sophistication also affects advertising, promotional methods, and consumer acceptance of new products.

Since our food distribution systems are based on economic and social factors, perhaps some long-run projections of these factors should be listed as an aid in understanding possible changes in the food system itself. A principal long-run study of projections of trends and speculation concerning future economic and social conditions is that of Kahn and Wiener (1967). Many of the following projections were adopted from their study.

(1) Even at a moderate rate of population growth, i.e., from 1.1 to 1.2% per yr, the United States would still have around 300 million people by the year 2000.

(2) Gross National Product could range between $2 to $3 trillion compared to less than $1 trillion in 1970.

(3) The workweek could decline to around 30-32 hr per week compared to slightly over 40 hr in 1965.

(4) The mean family income in the year 2000 (in 1965 dollars), before federal taxes, will probably be over $20,000 compared to around $8000 in 1965. Over 50% of the families would have an income over $15,000; and over 25%, a family income of over $25,000.

Other speculations include:

(1) A decline in importance of production-oriented industries, i.e., farming, mining, processing and manufacturing, and an increase in importance of service-oriented industries.

(2) The role of the "market" will decrease relative to the governmental sector.

(3) Major innovations will come from the governmental sector rather than private business.

(4) "Efficiency" will no longer be primary.

(5) Erosion of work-oriented, achievement-oriented, advancement-oriented values.

(6) Effective floor on income and welfare.

(7) Sensate, secular, humanist, perhaps self-indulgent criteria become central.

While we will not make specific long-run projections of the U.S. food markets, future economic and social trends should be considered while reading the following sections on food retailing. This should make the statistics presented on the retail grocery stores and the away-from-home food markets more meaningful, as the statistics are interrelated with and tend to support some of the above social and economic trends.

STATISTICAL FOOD SALE SERIES COMPLEX AND INCOMPLETE

The statistical series for food sales in the United States are complex. On the surface it is difficult to rationalize FOB sales of food processing plants to statistical series of retail sales of grocery stores and to sales of food by hotels, restaurants, and institutional feeding places. Some of the difficulties exist because the processing of alcoholic beverages is counted as food processing at the processing level, but is not included in food sales of retail grocery store sales at the retail level. Also, in the increasingly important food service industry, statistical series of value of sales have been available only on public eating places which account for only a little over 1/2 the value of sales of the total away-from-home food market. A third complicating factor is that the "Retail Grocery Store Sales" series include sales of many nonfood items.

While some of the details from the sources of data will be presented later, let's look at the gross total market for food in the United States after making corrections for the three discrepancies cited.

According to IRS data, total FOB sales by food processing plants in 1965-1966 were $70.2 billion (Greig 1968). However, alcoholic beverage FOB sales by processors were approximately $7.9 billion, leaving processor FOB sales of food at $62.3 billion. Dept. of Com. series on food retailing for 1966 indicated sales to be $71.1 billion. Of this, "Retail Grocery Stores" sales were $65.1 billion and "Bakeries, Meat Markets, etc." were $6.0 billion (U.S. Dept. of Com. 1967). However, retail grocery store sales of $65.1 billion included nonfood sales. Adjusting these data for nonfood sales using *Food Topics* "Annual Survey" (Anon. 1967A) gives retail food sales by grocery stores of $51.7 billion. Thus, the total estimated retail store sales of food in 1966 would be around $57.7 billion (retail grocery stores plus bakeries, meat markets, etc.). Public eating places (SIC 5812) sales of food in 1966 were approximately $17.4 billion. However, comprehensive data from surveys conducted by the U.S. Dept. of Agr. suggest the total food service industry sales in 1966 were approximately $28.0 billion (Van Dress and Freund 1968A). Sales by segments of the food service industry will be specified later.

Thus, the 1966 data show:

	(Billion $)
FOB food sales by processors	62.3
Sales of food by retail grocery stores	51.7
Sales of food by other retail stores	6.0
Sales of food by food service industry	28.0
Total retail sales of food	85.7

In 1966 the estimated total disposable personal income in the united States was approximately $508.8 billion. According to the above estimates the retail sales of food would be approximately 16.8% of the total disposable personal income. This estimate is slightly below the estimate of 18.3% of total disposable income suggested for 1966 by the U.S. Dept. of Agr. (Hiemstra 1968).

The difference is that in 1966, the U.S. Dept. of Agr. estimated all food purchases at $93.0 billion, compared to our figure of $85.7 billion. The U.S. Dept. of Agr. data probably include some family food purchases not covered by the categories on which the Dept. of Com. keeps data. We will not argue which figure is more nearly correct — they were obtained by substantially different methods. Much of the Dept. of Com. data are derived from a sampling of store sales, while the U.S. Dept. of Agr. estimates are partially derived from samplings of family spending.

In the following sections we will develop more detailed data on the two principal retailing segments of the food market — retail grocery stores and the food service industry (the away-from-home food market).

THE RETAIL GROCERY STORE MARKET

The retail grocery store has been the subject of many comprehensive economic studies. In 1959, the FTC (Anon. 1959) published their bulletin, *Economic Inquiry into Food Marketing*; in 1960 Mueller and Garoian (1960) wrote *Changes in the Market Structure of Grocery Retailing*. In 1966, the Natl. Comm. on Food Marketing (Anon. 1966B) published their 568-page bulletin, *Organiza-*

tion and Competition in Food Retailing. In 1969 Daniel Padburg (1969), one of the project leaders of the latter study, published a book, *Economies of Food Retailing.* All of these dealt rather specifically with the retail grocery store segment of food retailing. Since there is so much data available, the purpose of this section is not to present new information, but to briefly summarize some of the facets of food retailing particularly relevant to the food processing industry.

RATE OF GROWTH OF SALES OF RETAIL GROCERY STORES

Sales of retail grocery stores increased from $44.5 billion in 1958 to approximately $66.1 billion in 1967 (Table 6.1). However, much of this 48% increase in sales was due to (1) increasing nonfood sales and (2) inflation. If nonfood sales are subtracted from food sales, and if food sales are deflated to a common price basis, sales of food by grocery stores have increased at a rate not much above population growth.

After subtracting nonfood sales and deflating prices, sales of retail grocery stores between 1958 and 1967 increased at an average rate of around 2.5% per yr. During this same period, population growth in the United States probably increased at a rate from 1.2 to 1.5% per yr.

As most firms undoubtedly strive to increase sales at a rate greater than 2.5% per yr, competition in the retail grocery business has been intense. As will be shown later, one of the reasons for lack of a substantial rate of growth in the retail grocery store sales is the increasing importance of the away-from-home food market.

NUMBERS AND SIZES OF STORES

The number of grocery stores in the United States reached a peak in the early 1940's and has since greatly declined. In the census year 1939, there were 387,337 grocery stores in the United States and over 50% of the total sales of groceries were wtih stores having annual sales of less than $50,000. By 1963 there were only 222,442 grocery stores and over 50% of the total sales were from stores having annual sales of over $1,000,000. The supermarkets to a large extent replaced the corner grocery stores during the 1940's and 1950's. These trends are well known.

A recent development has been the growth of "convenience stores." These stores feature convenience of location, quick service, and long hours; but offer a narrower selection and somewhat higher prices. Between 1960 and 1965 the number of these stores increased from 1500 to an estimated 6000, with estimated total sales in 1965 of around $1 billion. Apparently the trend toward greater numbers of convenience stores is continuing.

ORGANIZATIONAL STRUCTURE

Chain store sales (a chain is defined as a firm having 11 or more units) increased from 34.4% of total grocery store sales in 1948 to 47.0% in 1963.

TABLE 6.1

ESTIMATED RETAIL GROCERY STORE SALES OF *FOOD* IN THE UNITED STATES, 1958 – 1967

	1958	1959	1960	1961	1962	1963	1964	1965	1966	1967
All retail sales by food group[1] (Millions $)	50,263	51,680	54,035	55,421	57,607	59,117	62,191	66,822	71,125	72,137
Retail grocery store total sales[1] (Millions $)	44,546	46,043	48,332	49,910	52,124	53,527	56,273	61,068	65,105	66,109
Retail grocery store food sales[2] (Millions $)	37,820	39,132	40,672	41,495	42,877	43,585	46,430	49,001	51,745	51,796
Deflated grocery store food sales[3] (Millions $)	37,557	38,466	39,449	40,208	40,680	40,846	42,950	44,587	45,752	44,537
Deflated grocery store food sales[4] (% increase over previous year)		2.4	2.6	1.9	1.2	0.5	5.2	3.8	2.6	−2.7

[1] Source: U.S. Dept. Com., Retail Trade Annual Report for various years. Includes sales of retail grocery stores as well as other retail stores such as bakeries, meat markets, etc.

[2] Adjusted for nonfoods and nonedible foods – adjustments derived from *Food Topics* Annual Survey for various years.

[3] Deflated by a consumer price index (1957-1959=100) from Economic Indicators, U.S. Dept. Com. for various years.

[4] The simple average increase in sales per year is around 2.5%.

Much of the recent growth has been by new chains or smaller chains. The share of the market held by the top 20 chains increased from 26.9% in 1948 of total sales to 34.1% in 1958. However, between 1958 and 1963 their share dropped to 34% (Padburg 1969).

To combat their losses to the chains, independent retailers formed cooperative wholesaling units. Independent wholesalers also assembled voluntary groups of independent retailers together into integrated chain-type organizations. These "affiliated" independent retail groups' share of the total retail food market increased from 35% in 1948 to 43.9% in 1963 (Table 6.2). At the same time the unaffiliated retailers' share of the market decreased from 30.2 to 9.1%. In 1963, the last year for which census data were available, chains had 47.0% of the retail grocery store market; affiliated independents, 43.9%; and unaffiliated independents, 9.1%.

As stated previously, the market share of the top few largest grocery store chains has not increased significantly through time. The top 4 chains' share of the market has been around 20% in each of the 4 census years, 1948, 1954, 1958, and 1963 (Table 6.3). Smaller chains have held an increasing share of the market; for example, the 5th to 20th largest chains increased their market share from 6.8% in 1948 to 14% in 1963. After subtracting the top 20 chains, the rest of the chains increased their share of the market from 7.5% in 1948 to 13% in 1963.

An ordered ranking of chains by sales volume changes through time. The top 40 chains in 1968 are listed in Table 6.4 with sales volume and number of retail outlets.

TABLE 6.2

ESTIMATED SHARE OF GROCERY STORE SALES:
BY CHAINS AND BY AFFILIATED AND UNAFFILIATED
INDEPENDENTS, 1948, 1954, 1958, AND 1963

	1948	1954	1958	1963
Total grocery store sales[1] (Millions $)	24,710	34,421	43,696	52,566
Grocery store sales by chains[2] (Millions $)	8,532	13,553	19,213	24,721
Share of grocery store sales by chains (%)	34.4	39.4	44.0	47.0
Grocery store sales by independents[3],[4] Millions $)	16,238	20,868	24,483	27,845
Share of independent grocery store sales by affiliated independents[5] (%)	54.05	56.23	73.02	82.95
Estimated grocery store sales by affiliated independents (millions $)	8,777	11,734	17,877	23,097
Estimated share of grocery store sales by affiliated independents (%)	35.4	34.1	40.9	43.9
Estimated share of grocery store sales by unaffiliated independents (%)	30.2	26.5	15.1	9.1

Source: Anon. (1966B).

[1] From 1963 Census of Business.

[2] Chains are defined as firms of 11 or more units.

[3] Independents are defined as grocery stores with 10 or fewer units.

[4] Line 1 minus Line 2.

[5] From Progressive Grocer April 1965.

PROFITABILITY AND MARGINS OF RETAIL GROCERY STORES

There are several statistical sources that provide profit data on various segments of the retail grocery store business. Perhaps the most comprehensive data are those compiled by the Internal Revenue Service (1969) in its *Source Book of Statistics of Income, Corporate Income Tax Returns*. This is available by years with a 1- to 2-year lag in publication. Financial data from which profitability can be calculated are developed by various asset size classes. The First National City Bank of New York compiles the financial data on 59 food chains. Harvard University and, more recently, Cornell University (Brown and Day 1968-1969) have published a series on *Operating Results of Food Chains*; and the Natl. Comm. on Food Marketing (Anon. 1966B) published net profit after taxes for 45 individual chains for the years 1948-1965. Profits after taxes for various classifications of retail grocery store operations are listed in Table 6.5.

All of the series on profits of retail grocery stores generally show declining profits after 1956-1957. The IRS data — obtained from federal income tax reports for all retail food corporations — showed the lowest rate of return as a percent of net worth. This ranged from a high of 10.2% in 1959 to a low of 7.1% in 1961. The First National City Bank of New York, in their series on 59 chains, reported profits of from 15.8% of net worth in 1957 to only 12.5% for 1965 (Table 6.5).

For the profit data from 1955-1965, some tentative conclusions may be reached. First, the large chains have been more profitable than all grocery retailing corporations. Secondly, profits apparently have been declining. Third, the level of profits has not been unusually high, either on an absolute basis or when compared to other segments of the food industry.

Profits after taxes as a percent of sales is a financial statistic often quoted by the retail grocery store industry. Of course, there are as many sources of this statistic as there are for the statistics on profits after taxes as a percent of net worth or owners' equity. The data from the *Source Book of Statistics of Income* for all retail grocery store corporations indicate that between 1953 and 1962 profits after taxes as a percent of sales were only 1.0% or under for each of the years. For 59 chains, the First National City Bank of New York reported 1.4%

TABLE 6.3

MARKET SHARE OF LEADING GROCERY STORE CHAINS
BY SIZE GROUPS, 1948 — 1963
Percent of Total Grocery Store Sales

	1948	1954	1958	1963
1st to 4th Largest chains	20.1	20.9	20.9	20.0
5th to 8th Largest chains	3.6	4.5	5.8	6.6
9th to 20th Largest chains	3.2	4.5	6.6	7.4
21st Largest chain and up	7.5	9.5	9.9	13.0
1st to 20th Largest chains	26.9	29.9	34.1	34.0

Source: Anon. (1966B).

TABLE 6.4

THE FORTY LEADING GROCERY CHAINS: THEIR SALES, RANK, AND STORES
OPERATED FOR THE YEAR 1968

Company	Dollar Sales[1]	Sales Rank	No. of Stores
Great A & P Tea Co.	5,409,694,100[2]	1	4731
Safeway Stores	3,685,690,368	2	2241
Kroger Co.	3,160,837,821	3	1495
Loblaw Companies, Ltd.	2,449,484,163[2]	4	390
Food Fair Stores	1,510,330,684[2]	5	630
Acme Markets	1,469,716,670[2]	6	894
Jewel Tea Companies	1,332,719,383	7	580
Winn-Dixie Stores	1,210,000,000[2]	8	773
National Tea Co.	1,177,048,660[2]	9	875
Grand Union Co.	1,039,744,646[2]	10	567
Lucky Stores	1,028,000,000	11	334
Allied Supermarkets	861,255,000[2]	12	358
First National Stores	700,927,020[2]	13	426
Stop & Shop	641,121,063[2]	14	193
Southland Corporation	622,000,000	15	2954
Dominion	618,659,810[2]	16	381
Loblaw Groceterias	602,000,000[2]	17	260
Supermkts General Corp.	569,371,354	18	77
Arden-Mayfair	568,000,000	19	224
Colonial Stores	562,321,049	20	439
Steinberg's, Ltd.	480,125,113	21	175
Albertson's, Inc.	412,000,000[2]	22	210
Cook Coffee Co.	407,820,140[2]	23	91
Red Owl Stores	404,213,000[2]	24	219
Borman Food Stores	389,358,228[2]	25	158
Giant Food	377,569,099[2]	26	85
Publix Super Mkts	354,000,000[2]	27	143
Fisher Foods	309,706,500	28	77
Thrifti-mart Corp.	287,798,865[2]	29	159
Loblaw	269,650,095[2]	30	166
Von's Grocery Co.	246,887,515	31	73
Ralph's Grocery Co.	240,000,000[2]	32	52
Waldhaum's	228,939,487[2]	33	82
Pueblo Supermkts	224,745,844[2]	34	90
Shop Rite Foods	213,855,695	35	213
H. C. Bohack Co.	212,407,433[2]	36	175
J. Weingarten	208,450,261	37	81
Penn Fruit	202,200,128	38	71
Fred Meyer Corp.	201,008,486[2]	39	48
Dillon Companies	194,485,660[2]	40	122

Source: *Progressive Grocer* April 1969.

[1] Calendar year wherever possible. In some cases, figures reflect manufacturer-whole-saler-retailer sales and no attempt is made to separate these.

[2] Estimated.

TABLE 6.5

RETAIL GROCERY STORE PROFITS AFTER TAXES AS A PERCENT OF NET WORTH, VARIOUS CLASSIFICATIONS, 1955 – 1965

	1955	1956	1957	1958	1959	1960	1961	1962	1963	1964	1965
Total of 59 chains[1]	13.4	15.5	15.8	15.2	13.9	13.0	12.2	11.5	11.5	12.5	12.5
All retail food corporations[2]	9.4	9.6	9.5	10.2	8.6	8.8	7.7	—	—	—	—
Chains of over $50,000,000 assets[2]	9.9	11.5	11.2	11.9	9.6	11.0	9.9	—	—	—	—
Total of 30 major chains[3]	12.1	13.3	14.1	13.5	12.6	12.2	11.2	10.8	10.8	11.0	—

[1] Source: First National City Bank of New York.
[2] Source: Book of Statistics of Income, IRS
[3] Source: Natl. Comm. on Food Marketing.

or under during the years 1955-1965. The Natl. Comm. on Food Marketing gave profits as a percent of sales for 30 individual chains for 1948-1964; the weighted average of these 30 chains was never over 1.3% between 1954 and 1964.

An interesting aspect is the following recent profitability data by size of retail chain stores. Data from Brown and. Day (1968-1969) at Cornell University suggest the rate of return on assets is greater for large chains while the rate of return on equity is greater for small chains, indicating a greater leverage position of the small chains. This was the same phenomenon that was exhibited among "large" and "small" food processing firms in Chap. 2. For example, Brown and Day's data indicate:

	Small Chains (Sales Under $20 Million) %	Medium Chains (Sales $20-100 Million) %	Large Chains (Sales Above $100 Million) %
Returns on assets (avg 1962-1963 to 1968-1969)	5.35	5.80	6.24
Returns on Net Worth (avg 1962-1963 to 1968-1969)	12.22	11.26	10.81

Although unsubstantiated by data presented here, it is suggested that competition in the retail grocery store business intensified between 1964 and 1969, and that profit levels probably have not increased above those given for previous years.

FOOD PROCESSING OPERATIONS BY RETAIL FOOD CHAINS

An aspect of grocery store chain operations which has long been a concern to food processors is the backward integration of these retailers into food processing. Hoffman (76th Congress), over 30 yr ago, noted that food processing operations by large retail chains were common. At that time the 5 largest chains operated bakeries; 2 owned meat packing plants; 4 had milk plants; and most had coffee roasting plants. In addition, one had a salmon canning plant and mayonnaise, spices, jellies, and beverages were also processed. The FTC study (Anon. 1959), the Mueller and Garoian study (1960), and the recent Natl. Comm. on Food Marketing study (Anon. 1966B) also reported in some detail the food processing operations of retail grocery store chains. Mueller and Garoian suggested in 1958 that food chains manufactured 39% of their bakery requirement and 38% of their coffee requirement. They also processed 5% of their meat products; 8.9% of their dairy products; 6.8% of their canned products; and 1.2% of their processed poultry products. Mueller and Garoian theorized the retail chains would enter those areas of food processing where the industry was most concentrated — that is, the food products processing in which there was the most opportunity for oligopolistic profits. Heflebower (1956) suggested that the failure of large retailers to integrate into a product area "is a *prima facie* evidence that the supplying industry is competitive and efficient . . . unless the product is unimportant or consumers are so strongly welded to established brands that a large volume cannot be sold advantageously under a distributor brand."

In addition to the motive for oligopolistic profits there are several other reasons for increasing backward integration. (1) There may be technological economies that favor joining two or more stages of production and marketing into a combined process. (2) Integration may eliminate uncertainties resulting from imperfect market knowledge. (3) Selling costs may be reduced.

This latter reason may suggest that food chains are the leading potential entrants into many food processing industries because chains can more easily overcome the product differentiation barrier to entry. The high advertising and promotion costs necessary to obtain shelf space and initiate consumer trial use can largely be overcome when chains sell under their own brands. A chain can use shelf space, special displays, and local newspaper food advertising to introduce and promote its own brands. These strategies are not available to other potential entrants into food manufacturing industries.

This in itself may be increasing the cost of entry of a new nonchain firm or the cost of putting a new product on the market by an established nonchain processing firm.

Despite the seemingly apparent theoretical advantages of chain store processing, statistical data do not entirely support the thesis of expanding retail chain store food processing (Table 6.6). For example, while the value of shipments of chain store processing increased 50.9% between 1954 and 1963, the value of all retail sales (of the top 40 chains) increased 78.7%. Data on specific categories of food processing covered by the FTC in 1954, 1958, and 1963 (see the footnote to Table 6.6) showed that food processing by chains decreased from 9.8% of retail sales in 1954 to 8.2% of sales in 1963. On the other hand, if all food processing is considered (including categories not covered in the SIC codes in the FTC surveys) then between 1958 and 1963 there was a slight increase in chain processing relative to total chain sales — from 8.7 to 8.8% (Anon. 1966B).

TABLE 6.6

CHANGE IN VALUE OF SHIPMENTS OF FOOD PROCESSED
BY RETAIL GROCERY STORE CHAINS COMPARED WITH
CHANGES IN THEIR FOOD STORE SALES, 1954 — 1963

| Rank of Chain | Percent Change in Value of Shipments[1] | | | Percent Change in Food Store Sales | | |
	1954-1958	1958-1963	1954-1963	1954-1958	1958-1963	1954-1963
4 Largest	11.0	−5.6	3.9	30.3	10.9	44.5
5 to 8 Largest	42.5	78.6	154.5	60.9	37.3	120.9
9 to 20 Largest	15.2	288.7	347.8	81.3	34.2	143.3
21 to 40 Largest	128.2	−19.6	83.8	76.1	46.6	158.2
40 Largest	24.7	21.0	50.9	45.6	22.7	78.7

[1] Based on categories of food products included in the 1959 FTC survey. These SIC product categories were: meat packing (2011), prepared meats (2013), poultry, dressing (2015), dairy (202), canning, freezing, and preserving (203), bread and related products (2051), confectionery and related products (207), and miscellaneous food preparations (209). Source: FTC.

It is noteworthy that the four largest chains have had a substantial relative decrease in processing compared to total retail sales. The increase in processing by food chains has been from the 5th to the 20th largest chains — here the relative increase in processing compared to total retail sales has been very substantial.

The greatest amount of integration (based on value of shipments) has been in bread products, fluid milk, meat packing, coffee, and canned fruits and vegetables (Table 6.7). (The decrease in coffee processing between 1958 and 1963 is largely a price phenomenon, not one of decreases in physical quantities.) According to the FTC data, food processing of the 40 largest chains, measured in value of shipments, increased from $1.4 billion in 1958 to $1.8 billion in 1963. While this was from 8.2 to 8.8% of total chain retail sales of these chains in 1963, the rate of increase in processing by chains between 1958 and 1963 was substantially greater than the increase in all food processing between 1958 and 1963.

There are still other statistical series to measure the extent of food processing by chains. In 1958, the FOB value of shipments by all food processors (SIC 20) was $59.5 billion and in 1963, $68.5 billion. Therefore, using the data in Table 6.7, chain store food processing was around 2.43% of all food processing in 1958, and around 2.63% in 1963.

Statistical data do not completely support the hypothesis that retail grocery store chains are rapidly integrating into food processing. While apparently chain food processing is increasing more rapidly than nonchain processing, chain processing as a percentage of all retail sales of chains has been increasing only slightly, if at all.

Potential chain processing is, of course, an ever-present threat to the nonchain processors. Although profit levels are difficult to compare, apparently chain store profits have been greater than average profit levels for many of the segments of food processing. Even for the very large food processors, apparently, there are few monopolistic or oligopolistic profits.

Although food processors may be concerned over the rapid increase in food processing by the smaller chains (the 5th to 20th largest) at the same time the decrease in relative processing by the 4 largest chains should also be considered.

Chain store processing certainly is a continuing threat to nonchain store processing. At the same time, extensive private label programs strengthen the chains' competitive position. While much of the chain store food processing is under their name brands, many purchases from nonchain store-owned processors may also be packed under the chain store brand. In the latter case, chain stores can shift suppliers and maintain their own brands with no evidence of the shift carrying on to the consumer. This type of purchasing can significantly strengthen the bargaining power of the chain store buyers. The extent and nature of private label operations in the retail grocery store food market segment is specified by David L. Call (1966) in his study for the Natl. Comm. on Food Marketing.

TABLE 6.7

VALUE OF SHIPMENTS OF FOOD PRODUCTS MANUFACTURED BY
40 LARGEST RETAIL GROCERY STORE CHAINS, 1958 – 1963

Census Industry Code		Nos. of 40 Corporate Chains Reporting Production			Value of Shipments of Top 40 Corporate Chains ($1000)			Percent Change in Total Industry Value of Shipments 1958-1963
		1958	1963	Net Change	1958	1963	Percent of Change	
2011	Meat packing plants	4	4	0	153,600	216,766	41.1	5.0
2013	Meat processing plants	7	9	+2	46,000	46,100	0.2	3.0
2015	Poultry dressing plants	5	6	+1	19,300	22,746	17.9	21.1
2021	Creamery butter	7	6	−1	18,975	10,410	−45.1	1.5
2022	Natural and process cheese	5	8	+3	8,227	8,187	−0.5	39.9
2023	Condensed and evaporated milk	7	9	+2	36,200	48,700	34.5	11.1
2024	Ice cream and frozen desserts	10	18	+8	49,177	90,096	83.2	5.8
2026	Fluid milk	8	14	+6	137,100	258,776	88.7	8.5
2031	Canned and cured seafood	2	2	0	1	1	—	4.9
2032	Canned specialties	4	4	0	23,654	22,745	−3.8	14.0
2033	Canned fruits and vegetables	12	14	+2	91,000	104,977	15.4	16.2
2034	Dehydrated food products	2	3	+1	1	1	—	12.1
2035	Pickles, sauces and salad dressings	10	11	+1	26,483	26,471	0	23.6
2036	Fresh and frozen packaged fish	2	3	+1	2	6,720	—	29.5
2037	Frozen fruits and vegetables	6	10	+4	27,119	56,653	108.9	58.8
2041	Flour mills	2	3	+1	1	8,113	—	—
2044	Rice milling	1	0	−1	3	1	—	44.7
2045	Blended and prepared flour	0	1	+1	—	1	—	—
2046	Wet corn milling	0	1	+1	—	3	—	14.4
2051	Bread and related products	22	31	+9	354,500	426,791	20.4	6.6
2052	Biscuits, crackers and cookies	12	15	+3	39,655	47,436	19.6	18.2
2063	Beet sugar	1	1	0	4	4	—	45.8

TABLE 6.7 (Continued)

FOOD PRODUCTS MANUFACTURED BY 40 LARGEST CHAINS, 1958 AND 1963

Census Industry Code	Number of 40 Corporate Chains Reporting Production			Value of Shipments of Top 40 Chains Reporting Corporate			Recent Change in Total Industry Value of Shipments 1958-1963
	1958	1963	Net Change	1958	1963	Percent Of Change	
2071 Confectionery products	7	9	+2	49,460[1]	50,900[1]	2.9	18.8
2072 Chocolate and cocoa products	1	1	0	—	—	—	13.0
2086 Bottled and canned soft drinks	4	7	+3	2,425	21,939	804.7	51.1
2087 Flavorings	6	6	0	4,125	5,753[2]	39.5	51.1
2091 Cottonseed oil mills	1	1	0	[3]	[2]	—	27.5
2092 Soybean oil mills	1	1	0	[3]	[2]	—	41.9
2095 Roasted coffee	21	21	0	225,900[4]	157,652[4]	-30.2	-9.4
2096 Shortening and cooking oil	2	2	0	[2]	[2]	—	3.2
2098 Macaroni and spaghetti	1	1	0	—	—	—	30.6
2099 Food preparations not elsewhere classified	13	15	+2	67,162	80,988	20.6	33.7
Total				1,447,214	1,800,846	24.4	11.7

Source: FTC (1959).
[1] Sales between $100,000 and $500,000.
[2] Sales between $1 million and $10 million.
[3] Sales below $100,000.
[4] Sales over $10 million.

Padburg (1969) suggests that on the selling end "the economic performance of retail food operations is excellent. A wide variety of food products is offered in clean attractive surroundings in convenient locations and at prices resulting in reasonable profits." However, economic "performance in the procurement of merchandise probably results in lower than optimal prices and returns in the food processing industries. This suggests that consumers are to some extent subsidized by the processing industries and ultimately by the farmer. The thrust of competitive activity within the retail sector creates a downward pressure on prices. The acceptance and success of the largest and strongest retailers are largely based on lower prices to consumers. Vertical integrations and private label programs are important means by which prices and costs are forced down. For the most part, this aspect of competitive policy is appraised as a healthy and positive part of industry behavior, because it gives consumers better values. Depressed prices within many processing and farming industries, however, may be to some extent a consequence of competitive pricing behavior (of the large retail organization). This 'other side of the coin' must also be recognized."

THE FOOD SERVICE INDUSTRY

The Size of the Food Service Industry

The hotel, restaurant, and institutional trade is a major outlet for processed food products. In 1966, sales of this segment accounted for around 33% of the total dollar sales of food to U.S. consumers, and were estimated at $28 billion dollars. Our estimates indicate that by 1975 these sales will be around $44-46 billion, nearly 40% of the retail value of food sold in the United States.

Good historical series of the growth of the food service industry are not available. The U.S. Dept. of Com. does have a series of data on sales from public eating places but sales are estimated to be less than 1/2 of the total food service industry sales. In fact, definite data on the total size of the food service industry has been mostly unavailable until recently, when a survey of the size of this industry was undertaken by the U.S. Dept. of Agr. (VanDress and Freund 1968A). In this survey the military services, elementary and secondary schools, and some food service industries of minor importance were not included. The adjustment of the original survey with estimates for these latter industries was made in a subsequent publication (VanDress and Freund 1968B). These publications are specifically cited because previously there has been numerous estimates of the size of the food service industry, many of which were no more than educated "guesstimates." Perhaps one of the principal reasons why 1966 estimates of the size of the food service industry varied so greatly (from $20 billion to well over $30 billion) is that definitions of what was included in the food service industry were different. The definition and subdefinitions of the food service industry as used here are those listed in Table 6.8. The estimated size of the total industry in 1966 was sales equivalent to approximately $28 billion dollars.

TABLE 6.8

U.S. PUBLIC EATING PLACES AND INSTITUTIONS WITH FOOD SERVICE:
NUMBER OF ESTABLISHMENTS AND RETAIL AND PURCHASE VALUE OF
FOOD AND NONALCOHOLIC BEVERAGES SERVED, 1965–1966[1]

Kind of Business	No. of Establishments[2]	Retail Value (Million $)[3]	Cost of Food Purchased[3] (Million $)
Public eating places			
Separate eating places	201,734	12,733.9	5,585.5
Separate drinking places	51,646	1,034.6	483.2
Drug or proprietary stores	12,013	321.0	141.7
Retail stores	22,820	907.8	389.7
Hotels, motels, or tourist courts	16,558	1,628.0	720.0
Recreation or amusement places	19,411	737.5	328.5
Civic, social or fraternal associations	4,355	193.6	76.1
Factories, plants, or mills	6,784	486.0	284.4
Other public eating places	8,429	499.0	207.4
Total	343,749	18,541.4	8,180.5
Institutional establishments			
Hospitals	5,931	1,450.4	703.8
Sanatoria, convalescent, or rest homes	5,118	233.3	112.4
Homes for children, the aged, the handicapped, or the mentally ill	4,092	294.7	135.8
Colleges, universities, professional, or normal schools	2,766	1,100.2	504.0
Other institutions	9,738	320.5	144.8
Total	27,645	3,399.1	1,600.8
Military, elementary and secondary schools	–	5,400.0	–
Federal hospitals, correction institutions, commercial passenger carriers, and boarding houses	–	600.0	–
Total	–	6,000.0	–
Grand Total	371,394	27,940.5	9,781.3

Source: U.S. Dept Agr.

[1] Data are projected estimates based on a national probability sample of food service outlets.

[2] As of Aug.-Sept. 1966.

[3] For latest accounting year, which for most establishments was calendar year 1965.

TABLE 6.9

ESTIMATED GROWTH RATES FOR PUBLIC EATING PLACES, 1958-1967

	1958	1959	1960	1961	1962	1963	1964	1965	1966	1967	Simple Average Increase per Year 1958-1967 %
Public eating place sales[1] (Millions $)	9,874	10,488	11,007	11,311	12,023	12,609	13,980	15,682	17,437	18,550	
Deflation index (1957–1959=100)[2]	100.7	102.2	103.1	104.2	105.4	106.7	108.1	109.9	113.1	116.3	
Deflated public eating places sales (Millions $)	9,805	10,262	10,676	10,855	11,407	11,817	12,932	14,269	15,417	15,950	
Public eating places growth (percent over previous year deflated basis)	—	4.7	4.0	1.8	5.1	3.6	9.4	10.3	8.0	3.4	5.6
Growth in grocery store[3] sales (percent per year over previous year deflated basis)	—	2.4	2.6	1.9	1.2	0.5	5.2	3.8	2.6	-2.7	2.5

[1] U.S. Dept. Com., Retail Trade Annual Report for various dates.
[2] Consumer price index (1957–1959 = 100) from Economic Indicators, U.S. Dept. Com, for various years.
[3] See Table 7.1.

The Growth of the Food Service Industry

The absolute growth in sales of the food service industry from 1954-1963 has been estimated to have been as much as 5.7% per yr compared to a growth in sales by retail food stores of only 3.1% (Anon. 1967E). However, again definitional problems arise since the exact nature of each was not specified. Data are available for specific comparisons between the rate of growth in sales of separate public eating places (SIC 5812) and grocery store sales (SIC 541) (excluding sales by delicatessens and sales of nonfoods). In 1965 separate public eating place sales accounted for nearly 50% of sales of the total food service industry. Census data show that sales of this segment of the food service industry increased 98% between 1958 and 1967 (Table 6.9). In constant dollars (after subtracting the effects of increased price levels) the increase in sales was 63%. For the same period, sales of retail grocery stores increased about 43% in current dollars and 19% in deflated dollars (1957-1959=100). Thus, the sales of separate public eating places (SIC 5812) on a deflated basis have increased at an annual rate of around 5.6% between 1958 and 1967, compared to sales of retail grocery stores which increased at a rate of approximately 2.5% per yr.

In 1966, while sales in the food service industry were estimated to be around $28 billion, at the same time sales of retail grocery stores were approximately $65.8 billion. However, if nonfood sales of retail stores are subtracted to leave only food sales by retail stores, the total food sales of retail grocery stores and bakeries, meat markets, etc., were approximately $57.7 billion. Thus, sales of food by the food service industry in 1966 were approximately 33% of the combined food sales of grocery stores and the food service industry.

Estimates have varied widely on the projected or forecasted growth of the food service industry. The following are three examples.

In 1966, Dr. K. E. Ogren, of the U.S. Dept. of Agr. estimated that in 1965 the away-from-home food market was $20 billion or more (he was not including the military, or elementary and secondary schools) and that by 1975 this market might be as high as $35 billion (Ogren 1966).

Arno H. Johnson (1966), Staff Economist, J. Walter Thompson Company, again in 1966, suggested that "total consumer expenditures for purchased meals and beverages (from the food service industry) which, at the end of 1965 were at the rate of $20 billion annually, could more than *double* by 1975, a potential market (in 1966 constant dollars) of well over $40 billion."

Another report by a well-known consulting firm estimated in 1965 that total food sales by 1975 would be $155 billion and that food service sales would be 40% of this, that is, $62 billion per year.

The estimate I will use here is that the total food service industry (including military and elementary and secondary schools) with sales equivalent of around $28 billion per year in 1966 will increase at a rate of at least 5% per yr. Thus, sales by the total industry should be around $44 - $46 billion in 1975. This would be equivalent to nearly 40% of the sales of food by the food service industry and retail grocery stores combined. These figures assume a 5% per yr increase in the industry sales and a 3% per yr increase in food sales of retail grocery stores, each starting from the base year 1966. In that year, food service industry sales were $28 billion and retail food sales were around $57.7 billion (excluding nonfood sales but including sales of bakeries and meat markets).

Factors Affecting Growth of the Food Service Industry

The factors most commonly cited as affecting the growth of the food service industry are population growth, rising income, more women in the labor market, increased urbanization, and more leisure time. Of these, rising consumer income is apparently the most important.

Population Growth. — The rate of population growth is based on the number of children born per women of child-bearing age and the death rate. The number of children born has been declining in the United States as has the death rate. Even so, the birth rate is much higher than the death rate with substantial increases in the U.S. population. The U.S. Dept. of Com. publishes four series of population projections based on differing assumptions of the birth rate. Using their moderately high rate of birth, the population of the United States in 1970 was predicted to be 206.3 million; in 1975, 222.8 million; and in 1980, 242.3 million. Thus, the population by 1975 will be around 11% greater than in 1968 and around 21% greater in 1980 than in 1968 (U.S. Dept. of Com. 1968).

Increasing Consumer Incomes. — Perhaps even more important than the expected population growth is the projected increase in income. As incomes increase substantially increasing proportions of the family food dollar are spent for away-from-home eating. For example, in 1960-1961 food expenditures away from home for a family with an income of $4000 was $200, but 4 times as much was spent for away-from-home food with a family income of $20,000.

In recent years, the increase in family incomes has been dramatic. The median income of U.S. families doubled between 1950 and 1964, from $3300 to $6600. Projections of income based on a full-employment economy show that by 1975 incomes will rise by more dollars per person than in the past (Fig. 6.1).

No factor appears to be more important than income to the size of the food service industry. For example, data from the U.S. Dept of Agr. 1965 Household Food Consumption Study, show that families with incomes of $10,000 or more spend $14 per week per family for food away from home. This is about 8 times as much as that spent for food eaten away from home by families with incomes under $3000. The purchased meals and snacks by these high income families represented 27% of their total food dollar. A recent study in Minneapolis-St. Paul, obtained data on expenditures of away-from-home food for families with incomes over $20,000. These families were spending an average of more than $1200 per year for away-from-home food, amounting to 40% of their total food expenditures (Burk 1966).

All the data available on the relationship between income and away-from-home expenditures for food indicate a strong relationship. The higher the income, the greater the amount of money spent on away-from-home food (see

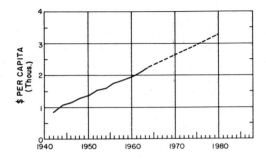

Source: U.S. Dept. of Commerce

**FIG. 6.1. DISPOSABLE U.S. PERSONAL INCOME,
1940-1965, WITH PROJECTIONS TO 1980**

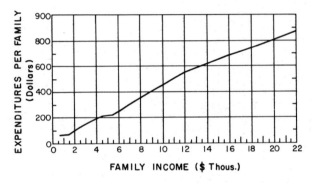

Source: U.S. Bureau of Labor Statistics

**FIG.6.2 AWAY-FROM-HOME FOOD EXPENDITURES BY
FAMILY INCOME, 1960-1961**

Fig. 6.2 for 1960-1961 data) and projections are for increasing levels of family income.

Working Women. – The number of women working acts in two ways to increase the consumption of away-from-home eating: (1) it increases family income and (2) it decreases the time available for preparing foods at home. Since 1947, 25% more women than men have been added to the civilian, non-agricultural employed labor force in the United States (Table 6.10).

Between 1947 and 1968, 12,149,000 women were added to the labor force compared to 9,683,000 men, many of these married working women. In 1940, only 16.7% of the married women held jobs compared to 37.9% in 1967 (Table 6.11). Recent data indicate that the trend toward increasing numbers of married women in the labor market is continuing.

TABLE 6.10

U.S. EMPLOYED CIVILIAN
NONAGRICULTURAL LABOR
FORCE, 1947—1968

Year	Men (1,000)	Women (1,000)
1947	34,351	14,797
1950	35,578	16,182
1955	37,357	18,367
1960	39,431	20,887
1963	40,849	22,227
1964	41,782	23,000
1965	42,792	23,934
1966	43,675	25,240
1967	44,315	26,212
1968 (March)	44,034	26,946

Source: Statistical Abstracts of the U.S., 1968.

TABLE 6.11

FEMALE LABOR FORCE AS PERCENT OF
FEMALE POPULATION 14 YEARS OF AGE
OR OLDER FOR VARIOUS YEARS, 1940—1967

Years	Percent in Labor Force		
	Single	Married	Total
1940	48.1	16.7	27.4
1950	50.5	24.8	31.4
1960	44.1	31.7	34.8
1965	40.5	35.7	36.7
1966	40.8	36.5	37.3
1967	41.3	37.9	38.2

Source: Statistical Abstracts of the U.S., 1968.

Increasing Urbanization. — The differences between urban and nonurban families' eating habits, while still discernible in statistical sources, are becoming less and less distinguishable. In 1960-1961 urban families spent, on the average, double that of farm families on food away from home and about 2/3 more than rural nonfarm families. However, because of rapid urbanization and because farm and rural nonfarm families are becoming more and more similar in their eating habits, the differences found in 1960-1961 are much less important today. For example, farmers more than doubled their meals eaten out between 1955 and 1965, while urban families increased theirs by only 1/4 (U.S. Dept. of Agr. 1965).

Structural Changes in the Food Service Industry

In 1966 there were around 371,000 public eating places or institutions with food service in the United States (U.S. Dept. of Com. 1967). Separate eating and drinking places now rank as the No. 1 retail outlet in the United States. They outnumber grocery stores and service stations. Big as the industry is (3.3 million employees), it is composed mostly of independent entrepreneurs operating single outlets. However, chain operations are increasing very rapidly. In 1966, chain restaurants or institutional feeding establishments were estimated to have 25% of all outlets and 1/3 of all commercial away-from-home food sales (Anon. 1966A). (The military and elementary and secondary schools were apparently not included in these estimates.) This is an increase from less than 10% of the units and around 12% of dollar sales in 1948.

More recent data however, show a nearly spectacular rate of growth of chain feeding establishments. *Institutions Magazine* estimated that sales of the top 400 leading chain restaurants and institutional feeders increased from $8.7 billion in 1965 to $13 billion in 1968, a growth of 48.8% in 3 yr. Further, the top 100 chains increased 58.8% during this same time (Anon. 1968A). (This top 400 does include the military and the U.S. Dept. of Agr. school lunch program.) Comparing *Institutions Magazine* estimates of chain sales to those of the U.S. Dept. of Agr., estimates of total sales in 1966 would give these top 400 chains well over 1/3 of the total food service industry sales.

The sizes of the top 20 chain feeding establishments in the United States are given in Table 6.12, listing both the dollar food sales and the number of units in each chain. The military services and the school lunch program (including the U.S. Dept. of Agr. school programs) were not included in the data although they are at the very top of the list as institutional feeding establishments. These top 20 food service industry firms had 26,991 separate units in 1968 and sales amounting to $4.4 billion. Two things are important here. The absolute size of volume of sales and the rapid growth rate.

In 1969 and 1970, the rate of growth in franchised restaurant chains appeared to have been slowing. Several franchise chains were apparently in serious financial trouble and the expansion plans for many chains were cut back or curtailed. Even Kentucky Fried Chicken, a front runner in the franchise take-out food service industry, reported lower share earnings in 1969 than in 1968. These factors could indicate a slowing in the rate of increase in the consumer desire for purchasing prepared foods — but this is probably not completely the case. The rate of increase in the demand for completely prepared ready-to-serve foods may have lessened but total demand is still increasing. In addition to the general economic slowdown in the United States in 1969 and 1970, there has been a change in the institutions that are meeting the increasing demand for prepared foods. The retail grocery stores are rapidly providing both luncheonettes and take-out prepared food services. In 1969 less than 5% of the supermarkets had luncheonettes and only a handful were offering take-out food services. However, it has been projected that by the mid-1970's over 50% would have luncheonettes

TABLE 6.12

SALES VOLUME AND NUMBER OF UNITS OF THE TOP 20 CHAINS IN THE FOOD SERVICE INDUSTRY (EXCLUDING THE MILITARY SERVICE) 1968

Rank	Organization	Headquarters	Volume (Million $)		Units	
			1968	1967	1968	1967
1	Marriott Corp.	Washington, D.C.	649.1	645.0	4655	3327
2	Kentucky Fried Chicken	Nashville	333.5	288.0	1785	1578
3	Automatic Retailers of America	Philadelphia	317.0	280.0	1200	950
4	Howard Johnson	Wollaston, Mass.	300.0	400.0	843	800
5	International Dairy Queen	Minneapolis	277.5	200.0	3633	3600
6	McDonalds Corp.	Chicago	266.4	218.5	967	862
7	Holiday Inns of America	Memphis	255.8	230.0	960	875
8	Canteen Corp.	Chicago	245.6	281.2[1]	250	130
9	Servamation	New York	181.5	160.4	349	283
10	Army & Air Force Exchange Service	Dallas	176.0	149.0	2500	2500
11	A&W International (United Fruit Subsidiary)	Santa Monica, Calif.	168.2	163.8	2557	2520
12	Sheraton Corp.	Boston	160.8	143.0	482	442
13	New York Dept. of Mental Hygiene	Albany	150.4	—[2]	878	—[2]
14	F.W.Woolworth	New York	150.0	150.0	1964	2000
15	Tastee Freez Industries	Chicago	141.3	115.0	1812	1732
16	Interstate United Corp.	Lincolnwood, Ill.	137.0	137.3	534	534
17	Burger Chef Systems, Inc. (General Foods Subsidiary)	Indianapolis	136.9	109.8	740	610
18	Greyhound Food Management Corp.	Detroit	120.9	115.8	536	510
19	Hilton Hotel Corp.	Chicago	120.0	109.0[3]	180	149
20	Veterans' Administration	Washington, D.C.	115.0	69.0[3]	166	185
	Total of top 20		4402.9	3982.8	26,991	23,587

Source: Anon. (1968A).
[1] Included in 1967 nonfood sales.
[2] Formerly a part of New York State and not reported separately.
[3] Computed values.

and over 85% would offer take-out food services. In an industry that has grown as rapidly as the away-from-home market there are sure to be many readjustments and changes in institutional arrangements.

TECHNOLOGICAL CHANGES IN THE FOOD SERVICE INDUSTRY

There has been and is continuing to be a technological revolution in restaurant kitchens, probably even greater than that in household kitchens. The trend is definitely toward foods that reduce the need for expensive kitchen staffs. Many convenience foods have been accepted at the institutional level much more rapidly than at the household level. For example, dehydrated mashed potatoes represented more than 1/2 the potatoes used in mashed form at the institutional level before a 10% level was reached in households (Greig 1959). Further, well over 1/2 the frozen French fried potatoes are sold through institutional outlets. Similarly, dehydrated onion usage in Detroit institutions represented over 30% of total onion usage – probably before a 4-5% level was reached in households (Marine and Greig 1966). Various issues of *Quick Frozen Foods* magazine indicate that well over 1/2 of many frozen vegetables are packaged in institutional sized packages, which suggests a much higher usage proportionately at the food service industry level than at the household level. Dehydrofrozen products, i.e., apples, are used almost exclusively at the bakery or institutional level. None are distributed to the household market in dehydrofrozen form (Greig and Stuckman 1960).

These examples are cited to show that, historically, most new food products were aimed at the household market with little thought toward institutional sales. Now the principal market for many new products will be the food service industry. While the examples of vegetables and fruit do show the rapid acceptance by institutional users, this does not, by far, represent the total technological revolution in the food service industry. Many establishments are using completely prepared entrees. Further, in some cases a frozen entree may be heated or cooked in seconds with a microwave oven. The trend toward convenience in preprepared foods is amply demonstrated in a few quotations from recent trade publications.

"When the chef scrambles eggs for a breakfast for 2000, who cracks the eggs at the famed Waldorf-Astoria Hotel, New York? Nobody. 'We get the eggs already cracked that make better scrambled eggs than we used to have, and look at the hours we have saved' says Carl Mottek, Vice President for food operations. The hotel staff doesn't chop greens, peel potatoes, or trim the fat off of meat either. These kitchen chores are handled at the purveyor's plant" (Anon. 1967B). This *Wall Street Journal* article continued, "Howard Johnson Company has built its menus around convenience foods that come mostly from its own commissaries. Even charcoal broiled steaks and chops are cut, seared almost black, and frozen in the commissaries before they are sent to restaurants to be cooked to customer order."

"The University of Maryland has cut costs more than 35% with a food service program that involves disposables, prepared foods, outside catering, and only one piece of cooking equipment" (Anon. 1967C). This total systems approach, unique to the institutional industry, will eventually dominate all of the University of Maryland's 7 food service operations (80,000 meals daily on a 28-day cycle menu).

"The Commonwealth of Massachusetts has decided to swing to frozen convenience foods in all 46 of its state institutions. A study showed that only 3 kitchen personnel were needed to prepare dinner for 1600 patients compared with 11 prior to the convenience foods program" (Anon. 1968B).

Future changes in technology will probably be great. Until 1968, most food scientists would have predicted at least a national introduction, or national market testing of irradiated foods, especially meats. However, the Food and Drug Administration questioned data submitted by the Army on the safety of irradiated foods and refused to accept the Army's petition for clearance for canned ham (Anon. 1968C). Later the U.S. FDA rescinded their prior approval for canned ham.

Subsequently, Dr. Edward S. Josephson, Associated Director, Food Irradiation, U. S. Army Natick Laboratories, suggested that retesting and resubmitting petitions to the U.S. FDA would take at least 5 yr (Anon. 1969). Other reputable scientists have suggested a delay of up to 15 yr. While plans for commercial irradiation of foods in the U. S. have been dampened, if not drowned, reportedly at least three commercial scale food irradiation facilities are in operation in Russia. According to Dr. Josephson, irradiated foods are being served on Russian railroad dining cars and in commercial restaurants.

While irradiated foods have not got off the ground in the U. S., significant uses cannot completely be ruled out in the future. Many less profound technological innovations are continually being developed. This rate of development will undoubtedly accelerate in the future.

IMPLICATIONS OF THE CHANGING FOOD SERVICE INDUSTRY TO THE FOOD PROCESSING INDUSTRY

The implications of the changing structure of the food service industry on the operations of food processing firms are many. (1) Not only must increasing amounts of food products be processed for this segment but the products sold to this industry will increasingly have more services attached. (2) As the impact of chains increases, more and more products will be procured directly from food processors. (3) Competition for sales to the food service industry will largely be on product quality and price, not on brand labels, advertising, and promotion. (4) Forward pricing or sales arrangements under long-term contracts will probably be essential. Planning is essential for bigness, and price control is essential for planning. (5) As competition for products sold to the food service industry will be on price and quality, and there are apparently significant economies of scale in food processing, food processors will probably have to be of considerable size to deal with the major food service industry chains. (6) With a high rate of technological advances, the processing firms will probably require larger and larger staffs of trained food scientists to keep abreast of developments and to maintain or expand the market for their products. Obsolescence rates for plant and equipment may greatly increase.

Research activities by colleges, universities, and governmental agencies in the area of the away-from-home food market have, to date, been limited. However, recently the U. S. Dept. of Agr. compiled an annotated bibliography of 242 separate research projects related to this market (Nejelski 1969) which should be quite valuable to those with interests in this specific food market.

BIBLIOGRAPHY

ANON. 1959. Economic inquiry into food marketing – interim report, June 30. Federal Trade Comm., Washington, D.C.

ANON. 1966A. Restaurant market profile – Chains show the growpower. Chain Store Age Restaurant Managers Edition *42*, No. 2, 28-30.

ANON. 1966B. Organization and competition in food retailing. Natl. Comm. Food Marketing Tech. Study 7.

ANON. 1967A. Annual survey. Food Topics, Conover-Nast Publications, New York.

ANON. 1967B. More restaurants turning to convenience foods as labor shortages continue to mount. Wall Street J. May 16.

ANON. 1967C. Systems for service: Case book No. 1 "The total approach to convenience." Institutions Magazine 146-149, Jan.

ANON. 1967D. Commerce Department enthusiastic over bright potential for irradiated meats. Weekly Dig. *73*, No. 34, 2.

ANON. 1967E. New concepts for food industry marketing and planning. Arthur D. Little, Acorn Park, Mass.

ANON. 1968A. Institutions 400. Institutions Magazine 28-32, July.

ANON. 1968B. Frozen Food Age Magazine, May.

ANON. 1968C. Food and Drug chief's criticism clouds irradiated foods future. Wall Street J. May 13.

ANON. 1969. Irradiated ham debut postponed about 5 years. Supermarket News *18*, No. 16, 20, Febr. 10.

BROWN, E., and DAY, R. 1968-1969. Operating results of food chains. Cornell Univ., Ithaca, N.Y.

BURK, MARGUERITE C. 1966. Food expenditures by Minneapolis – St. Paul families: variations and implications. Minnesota Farm Business Notes *480*, Jan.

CALL, D. L. 1966. Private label products in food retailing. Natl. Comm. Food Marketing Technical Study *10*, June.

DOODY, A. F., and McCAMMON, B. C., JR. 1970. Strategies for a maturing industry. Presented at the 36th Ann. Leadership Forum of the Natl. Assoc. Chain Stores as quoted in The Weekly Dig. Jan. 3.

GREIG, W. S. 1959. Unpublished data.

GREIG, W. S. 1968. Balance sheets, income statements, and financial operating ratios for the food processing industry. Michigan State Univ. Agr. Econ. Rept. *117*, Nov.

GREIG, W. S., and STUCKMAN, N. W. 1960. Market potentials for dehydro-frozen and dehydro-canned apple slices. Michigan State Univ. Agr. Econ. Mimeo *801* Sept.

HEFLEBOWER, R. B. 1956. Mass distribution: A phase of bilateral oligalopy or of competition. Papers and proceedings of the Sixty-ninth Annual Meeting of the Am. Econ. Assoc., Cleveland, Dec.

HEIMSTRA, S. J. 1968. Food consumption, prices and expenditures. U.S. Dept. Agr., Agr. Econ. Rept. *138*, ERS, July.

HOAFNAGLE, W. S. 1968. The food service industry in the space age. Talk at 23rd Annual Conf. on Hotel, Restaurant and Institutional Education, Jung Hotel, New Orleans, Dec. 27.

HOFFMAN, A. C. 76th Congress. Large Scale Organization in the Food Industries. TNEC Monogram *35*, 76th Congress, 3rd Session.

INTERNAL REVENUE SERV. 1969. Source Book of Statistics of Income, Corporate Tax Return. Published yearly by Statistical Div., IRS, Washington, D.C.

JOHNSON, A. H. 1966. An economist's view of the food service industry. Presented at the 47th Natl. Restaurant Conv., Chicago, May 25.

KAHN, H., and WIENER, A. J. 1967. The Year 2000. The Macmillan Co., New York.

MARINE, C. L., and GREIG, W. S. 1966. Estimating sales potential for new food products — new onion products. Michigan State Univ. Agr. Exp. Sta. Res. Rept. *55*, Nov.

MUELLER, W. F., and GAROIAN, L. 1960. Changes in the market structure of grocery retailing 1940-58. Res. Rept. *5*, Agr. Exptl. Study, Univ. Wisconsin, Madison, Wis.

NEJELSKI, L. 1969. Selected research abstracts and unpublished reports pertaining to the food service industry. U.S. Dept. Agr. *ARS-52-46*, Dec.

OGREN, K. E. 1966. Marketing Research: A tool for decision making — A look ahead at the food service industry. Talk given at the Soc. Advan. Food Res., Washington, D. C. Apr. 18.

PADBURG, D. I. 1969. Economies of food retailing. Food Distribution Program, Cornell Univ., Ithaca, N. Y.

U.S. DEPT. OF AGR. 1965. Consumer expenditures and income rural farm population, United States, 1961. Consumer Expenditure Survey Rept. *5*, Apr.

U.S. DEPT. OF COMMERCE. 1967. Retail Trade Annual Reports.

U.S. DEPT. of COMMERCE. 1968. Populartion estimate. Febr. 13. Bureau of Census, U.S. Dept. Commerce, Washington, D.C.

VAN DRESS, M., and FREUND, W. H. 1968A. The food service industry: Its structure and characteristics. Statist. Bull. *416*, Febr. U.S. Dept. Agr., Washington, D.C.

VAN DRESS, M. and FREUND, W. H. 1968B. Dimensions of the food service industry. Marketing and Transportation Situation, ERS, May. U.S. Dept. Agr., Washington, D.C.

CHAPTER 7

W. Smith Greig

The Changing Technological Base in Food Processing

The importance of technocracy in the development of the business firm and in the rapidly developing packaged or convenience consumer products field has been previously emphasized in Chap. 2. However, the implications of a changing technological base go deeper than this. Technocracy affects both the production of commodities as well as packaged or convenience foods. Any food product is characterized by the technology that produced it. Because of the importance of the changing technological base in food processing, as well as its complexity, the discussion of this facet of food processing will be subdivided into the following sections.

The Role of New Product Development. — The relationship between new product development and growth of the firms and the theory of the firm as related to product competition.

Why Food is Processed. — Food is often processed for convenience, quality control, and cost reduction — not only for preservation.

Research and Development in Food Processing. — A discussion of both private and public research activities in food processing.

Time and Costs of Commercialization of New Products. — Time horizons in new product development and estimates of costs in various steps of commercialization.

Analogs, Substitutes and Synthetics. — Current achievements, present status, and long-run implications in production of synthetics, substitutes, and food analogs.

A Review of Some Recent Processing Technologies. — Both a technological and economic review of 13 "new" processing technologies with some implications of possible product adaptability.

THE ROLE OF NEW PRODUCT DEVELOPMENT

Most of the U.S. food products sold to consumers have been factory processed. For example, nearly all the grains, milk products, meat products, fats and oils, and around half of the fruits and vegetables are factory processed before they are sold to consumers. However, even if all foods were factory processed, the potential limits of food processing would still not be reached. But, products would be processed with greater quality control into more convenient forms.

Just because all livestock are killed and dressed in commercial packing plants now does not mean that processing will always end there. It is within the realm of possibility that in the future most meats will reach the consumer precooked, or in irradiated convenient forms requiring no refrigeration.

152

But, if no new food products are developed it does suggest that food processing as an industry will only grow as rapidly as population growth, which is currently less than 1.5% per yr. To management's viewpoint this is certainly an unacceptable company growth rate. For the U.S. food processing industry as a whole, the undeflated rate of growth over the past several years has been closer to 5% per yr. From the industry viewpoint and from the individual firm's viewpoint, continued growth to a large degree must be based on the development of new products.

The Firm and Product Competition

In an advanced capitalistic society most firms actively try to differentiate the quality of their product to avoid being "perfectly" competitive. Differences in product quality and new product development are the normal rule rather than the exception. Quality competition among the majority of firms, including food processing firms, may be greater than price competition. With increasing industrialization and product variation, prices do tend to become more sticky or sluggish. This does not mean that competition decreases, only that the area of competition shifts to nonprice areas: advertising and promotion, and quality competition through new product development (Greig 1964).

The thesis of this section is that management decisions on new product development may well predetermine the future of the firm.

The Theory of Firm Behavior

Each firm produces products based on expected consumer wants. The quality of the product (shape, color, form, taste; size, and service attached to its sale) is determined by the firm's estimates of current or expected consumer wants. As the firm does not have perfect knowledge concerning current consumer wants, product quality is constantly subject to change when new knowledge is uncovered. The firm strives to exploit existing demands for its products and to create new demands. It can do the latter in two ways: (1) by altering consumer attitudes and beliefs concerning the product through advertising and promotion, or (2) by altering the product quality to more closely conform to current preferences or prejudices. A principal strategy of many firms in product planning, or determination of what will be produced in the future, is to capitalize on changing consumer wants.

Importance of New Product Competition

It has been suggested that innovations are the truly dynamic elements in the economy, the sources of credit, interest, and profit as well as business fluctuations (Solo 1951). Innovation or new product development and the competition among firms it creates is often intense. This is pointed out by Schumpeter (1947): "But in capitalist reality as distinguished from its textbook picture, (the) ... kind of competition which counts is the competition from the new commodity, the new technology, the new source of supply, the new type of organization . . . it is hardly necessary to point out that competition of the kind we now have in mind counts not only when it is in being, but also when it is merely an ever-present threat — it disciplines before it attacks."

Innovation or product development, while a creator of wealth and competition, is also a destructive force. Any new innovation must supersede the old. Whale oil replaced tallow, kerosene replaced whale oil, and electricity replaced kerosene in lighting homes. Schumpeter used the term "creative destruction" to describe this phenomenon. However, in nearly every case where the new destroys the old, the new has resulted in more total economic activity (Schumpeter 1949).

Product planning for a firm is both strategic and long-run; projections of social, economic, political, and technological factors which may affect the demand for a new or proposed product should be studied and analyzed. Within certain limits, each of these factors may be predictable. Essentially, the success of a firm may depend upon how well it predicts changes and how early it discovers new growth fields and new growth products (Stewart 1959). A growth field is one in which there is substantial evidence that a real potential exists for expansion of sales in a product line. One of the most critical tasks in long-range planning by a firm is the early identification of the basic reasons why growth fields emerge and change. Historical studies have shown that there is a high correlation between the rate of growth of an individual firm and the total market for its primary products (Stewart 1959).

While the development of new products may bring large profits, the risk may also be very great. Since the allocation of the firm's resources among products is a critical managerial decision, most large firms have a set of procedures by which possible new products are sought for and analyzed with a view toward commercial production. The procedures, which may be classified in many ways, are basically these: (1) exploration for possible products; (2) screening possible products to select the most promising ones; (3) business analyses to determine if costs, prices, and profits would be in line with desired company goals; (4) development of pilot lines or commercial production facilities; and (5) testing to determine marketability.

Price Competition Versus Product Competition

In monopolistic markets competitors can react almost immediately to price changes. Where demand is inelastic, price cuts will not expand market sales greatly; since competitors can react quickly price competition will reduce profits to all producers. In new product development, on the other hand, there are two distinct time lags in adjustments by competitors. The first is the time it takes a competitor to determine whether a rival firm's innovation is successful. This may not be easily measurable at early stages of commercialization. The second lag is the time for the competitor to adjust to the innovation. This may take days or years, depending on the nature of the innovation. Further, the innovation in some cases may be protected by patent rights. Several major food processing and food distributing companies within the United States have succeeded largely on the basis of patents which prevented duplication by rivals (Hoffman 76th Congress).

Edith Tilton Penrose (1959) in her book *The Theory of the Growth of the Firm* states that new product development is a necessity for continued growth of a firm. "Even when a firm exploits to the fullest possible extent the opportunities for monopolistic gain available to it (through exclusive patents, by destroying competition), the protection afforded, though often extensive, can neither be complete nor absolutely certain. For many if not most firms, the more effective long-run protection against direct competition as well as against indirect competition of new products will lie in the firm's ability to anticipate, or at least to match threatening innovations in processes, products, and marketing techniques. In a society characterized by a widespread 'spirit of enterprise' and a highly developed technology, the threat of competition from new products, new techniques, new channels of distribution, new ways of influencing demand, is in many ways a more competitive influence on the conduct of existing producers than any other kind of competition. Its primary effect is to force a firm wanting to maintain itself in the market for any given product to learn all it can about the product, its market, and, in particular, the relevant technology, and to endeavor to anticipate the innovations of other firms."

The Role of Scientific Research in New Product Development

The development of new food processing technologies and new food products has changed from the chance discovery by an individual inventor or individual entrepreneur, to that of systematic efforts by scientists in organized research laboratories. There are more scientists living today than have lived in all previous history; likewise, there are more scientists in the food processing industry than ever before.

While in the Schumpeterian context, innovation is an extraordinary event and the result of extraordinary efforts of new men and new business firms, the author's thesis is that innovation and new product development is a planned, organized, and managed normal activity of most large business firms in an industrial society. Innovation or new product development as an integral part of firm activity is a fairly recent phenomenon, having for the most part developed during the 20th century. It has resulted not only from an increased technological base of firm activity but also from changing social institutions. As early as the 1930's, authorities in the field noted that the tendency toward large-scale organization, the outstanding characteristic of modern business, is largely a result of changing technology: better communication and transportation, better preservation of foods, technological developments in manufacturing, and developments in managerial control equipment (Hoffman 76th Congress). The development of the technological base and the development of social institutions, particularly limited liability for owners of firms, have given rise to bigness in business. With bigness, technological development, and limited liability have come the birth of the company research laboratory with planned inventions and innovation.

The increasing activity of business firms in science and technology was noted by Schmookler (1957) after analysis of a large number of patents: "Invention changed (during the first half of the century) from an activity overwhelmingly dominated by independent individuals to one less overwhelmingly dominated by business enterprise." Schmookler then indicated that nearly half the inventions were coming from research and development (R&D) staffs of business firms. (A much larger proportion probably is from business firms now.)

In emphasizing the role of R&D in firm growth, Mees and Leermakers (1950) state: "It is asserted far too often that small business cannot afford to support research. Few businessmen can afford to support research. They carry out their research, as they do the rest of their operations, for profit, i.e., to be supported by it, and if they are successful, they do not remain small, they grow."

It will be shown in a subsequent section that by far the largest amount of scientific R&D in food processing is done by a relatively few large firms.[1] Typically, these larger firms make a higher return on investment than do the smaller firms (Greig et al. 1958). Recent analysis at Cornell University suggests that the larger firms tend to compete among themselves on product development while the smaller firms tend to compete on efficiency of production of more standard products (Handy 1968).

The lack of R&D by many smaller firms was demonstrated in a survey of cherry processors in the North Central Region of the United States in 1966. The total new product development research on cherries by all the 44 primary cherry processors combined, had been less than six man-months a year for the past 2 yr (Ricks et al. 1966).

WHY FOOD IS PROCESSED

At one time food was processed principally for preservation. Grapes were made into wine or were dried, olives were brined, meat was smoked or salted, and milk was made into butter or cheese. More recently, perishable fruits and vegetables were canned; later still, they were frozen. This early food processing was primarily a means of preservation. Agricultural products were preserved, by some form of processing, at the peak of seasonal production for later use throughout the year. While processing for preservation is still paramount, many products are now processed for convenience, quality control, and cost reduction.

Prepared breakfast cereals were probably the forerunner of many instant prepared foods; these were processed with "built-in" convenience and quality control. Instant coffee, instant tea, dried soup mixes, cake mixes, frozen prepared foods, frozen vegetables in different sauces, and much potato, onion, citrus, and apple processing are examples of products processed for convenience, quality control, and cost reduction, as well as for preservation. Each of the

---

[1] See the section on Research and Development Expenditures.

above products are found in simpler processed forms or are readily available the year-round in fresh form at reasonable cost.

While many products are processed for convenience, others for quality control, and still others for cost reduction, let's explore in some detail a product in which all three characteristics are involved. The processing of potatoes is a nearly classic example. Fresh potatoes are available all year in the United States, usually at very reasonable prices. Therefore, there is little reason to process potatoes simply for preservation. Yet potato processing has had a fantastic rate of growth in the United States over the past 10 - 15 yr (Table 7.1). Per capita consumption of processed potato products in the United States more than tripled between 1956 and 1967, from 14.6 to 48.2 lb per person per year (Table 7.2). In 1967 approximately 42% of the potato crop was processed, while 25 yr ago less than 1-2% was processed. Processed potato chips can seldom be duplicated from fresh potatoes either by a housewife or a chef in a typical restaurant. The more recent dehydrated mashed potato products are of consistently high quality and normally offer considerable savings, particularly to the institutional user. While processing often is thought of as an added service to a fresh product, often the processed product can be delivered to the consumer at less cost than its unprocessed counterpart. Studies in 1957, comparing retail costs of 52 relatively unprocessed foods to their highly processed counterparts indicated that a consumer would have to pay less than one % more for equivalent quantities of highly processed foods (Harris and Dwoskin 1958). Another study comparing retail prices in New York City on orange juice from fresh oranges, canned oranges, and frozen orange juice concentrate showed that the retail price was considerably higher on fresh oranges than on the processed products (Clement 1960). Further, in a study of 110 convenience foods, price per serving was

TABLE 7.1

U.S. IRISH POTATO UTILIZATION, 1956 — 1967

	1956	Crop Year 1960 (Million Cwt)	1967
Sold fresh	146.0	149.4	131.7
Sold for food processing	24.7	49.3	94.4
Total sold for food utilization	170.7	198.7	226.1
Percent sold for processing	14.5(%)	24.8(%)	41.8(%)
Processing categories			
Potato chips and slices	14.6	21.3	32.3
Frozen French fries	4.3	13.4	34.6
Dehydration	3.2	10.1	19.1
Frozen (other)	0.3	1.7	5.0
Canned	1.0	1.6	1.9
Hash, soups, stews	1.3	1.2	1.5
Total Processed	24.7	49.3	94.4

Source: Adapted from Irish Potatoes, Utilization of the 1967 Crop with Comparisons, U.S. Dept. Agr., Crop Reporting Board, Sept., 1968.

shown to be one of the most important factors in determining the demand for these convenience products (Harp and Miller 1965).

Let us explore how the price of a highly processed food product may, in fact, cost less than its fresh unprocessed counterpart. We will use dehydrated mashed potatoes supplied to the hotel, restaurant, and institutional trade as an example. (1) In commercial processing lye or steam peeling is used. This results in less waste and in less labor in peeling than if hand peeling or even batch abrasive peeling were used in a large restaurant. (2) Misshapen or small sizes of potatoes may be used in processing that are not economical to ship fresh. (3) The product is reduced to under 14-16 lb per each 100 lb of raw product, thus greatly reducing freight costs. (4) Storage and handling costs are greatly reduced by the reduction in weight and in perishability. (5) In institutional containers, a 10 to 15 cent container may hold the equivalent of 40-50 lb of raw potatoes, so packaging costs may be reduced over that for the fresh product. (6) Potatoes are processed in the relatively low cost fall crop producing areas and these processed potatoes compete in the summer months with other higher cost seasonal potato production areas. (7) Potatoes are contracted for with growers in advance of planting resulting in a reduction of price risk and thus a reduction in cost compared to fresh potatoes which are seldom contracted for in advance. (8) There is a reduction in the chef's cooking time in the restaurant or institution. (9) Mashed potatoes can nearly be prepared to order, reducing the possibilities of waste in leftovers. Thus, particularly to the large scale user, dehydrated mashed potatoes may be significantly less costly than an equivalent quantity of fresh potatoes (Greig and Larzelere 1957).

Even if the added services to food cost more, but convenience and quality control were obtained, there is considerable evidence to suggest that consumers would still demand these added services. Cross sectional data from the U.S. Dept. of Agr., Survey of Consumer Expenditures for Food, showed that with a 10% increase in per capita income consumers would increase their per capita expenditures for food by about 4%, but would increase their expenditures for food away from home by about 8% (Hiemstra 1968). Waldorf (1964) suggested that with a 10% increase in income, consumers would spend 5.7% more for

TABLE 7.2

PER CAPITA CONSUMPTION
OF POTATOES, 1956 — 1967

	1956 (Lb)	1960 (Lb)	1967 (Lb)
Fresh[1]	86.0	82.0	67.2
Processed[1]	14.6	27.0	48.2
Total	100.6	109.0	115.4

[1] Of the commercial crop sold for food uses.

manufactured food products, but would spend 8.6% more for food manufacturers' services. These data indicate that additional food services are more highly desired with increasing incomes than additional foods. Additional services are not only demanded with increases in incomes, but also because more housewives are working and because of increasing educational attainments. A study of purchases of commercially prepared fruit pies by families of three or more persons indicated purchases were twice as high in instances where the housewife was employed (French 1958). Educational levels also have an effect on some types of food services. For example, urban homemakers with higher levels of education used more frozen and canned fruits and vegetables than less educated homemakers in the same types of household (Dept. of Agr. 1960).

These data all indicate an increasing demand for services — increased convenience and quality control attached to the sale of food. Thus, the reasons for processing food have changed from the simple function of preservation to those of preservation plus convenience, quality control, and cost reduction.

Research and Development (R&D) in Food Processing

R&D efforts in food processing by the industrial sector are probably best described by statistical data from the Natl. Science Foundation, while governmental activities are best illustrated with a narrative nonquantified description. The accomplishments of both sectors are amply shown in the wide variety of foods available at reasonable prices on the American market.

In this section we will discuss the R&D expenditures of the industrial (commercial) food processing firms and the nonindustrial (governmental) R&D activities in the food processing sector of the economy.

R&D Expenditures
by the Industrial Sector

R&D expenditures by industrial firms quadrupled between 1953 and 1965 (Anon. 1967B). Expenditures increased from $3.6 billion in 1953 to $14.2 billion in 1965. These expenditures on R&D by industrial firms include federally-financed research. Funds from federal sources to these industrial firms are well over 1/2 the total expenditures on R&D (Table 7.3). R&D expenditures in the food and kindred products industry (SIC 20) doubled between 1957 and 1965 but are a very small part of the total expenditures by all industrial firms (only slightly over 1% of total industrial R&D expenditures.) In the case of food, nearly all financing was by company funds, while in the case of aircraft and missiles over 80% of R&D funds is from federal sources.

In relation to most other industrial sectors, by most terms of measurement, R&D expenditures in the food processing industry have been relatively small. Further, nearly all R&D in food processing is done by a few large firms. Approximately only 5% of the total expenditures for R&D in the food processing industries was done by firms with less than 1000 employees, while 87% was done by industrial firms in food processing which had over 5000 employees.

In fact, an estimated 68% of all R&D expenditures in food processing was conducted by the largest 20 firms (Table 7.4). There are approximately only 7 R&D scientists or engineers per 1000 employees in the food processing sector, while the average for all industry is 30 per 1000 employees. Of those food processing firms doing R&D, only 0.4% of the value of their sales was devoted to that activity, while for all industries, 4.3% of sales value of the industry was devoted to R&D. While total expenditures for R&D in food processing doubled between 1957 and 1965, R&D as a percent of sales increased only slightly, from 0.3% in 1957-1959 to 0.4% from 1960-1965. Arthur D. Little, Inc. reported that 18 large food manufacturing firms increased their R&D expenditures from 0.37% of sales in 1954 to 0.60% in 1964 (these firms represent a little less than 1/3 of national expenditures in this area) (Buzzell and Nourse 1966). However, subsequent data by the Natl. Science Foundation suggest that these data did not represent the national trend since, nationally, R&D in food processing has not increased this rapidly. R&D as a percent of sales, of those firms where applicable, remained at a constant 0.4% of sales between 1960 and 1965. However, if we compare the research expenditures of $150 million against total FOB sales of all food processing firms then R&D expenditures are slightly over 0.2% of sales.

R&D in Food Processing
in the Governmental Sector

Four separate agencies of the U.S. government do substantial amounts of research involving new food products, new food processing methods, and new methods of handling and preserving food products. These agencies are the U.S. Dept. of Agr., U.S. Dept. of Defense, U.S. Dept. of the Interior, and the Atomic Energy Commission (Bird *et al.* 1968). The activities of these governmental agencies will be discussed in a very generalized manner. The R&D program of colleges and universities will only be mentioned.

TABLE 7.3

R&D EXPENDITURES BY U.S. INDUSTRIAL FIRMS, 1957 — 1965

	Company Financed R&D Expenditures (Billion $)	Federally Financed R&D Expenditures (Billion $)	Total Industrial R&D Expenditures (Billion $)	Food and Kindred Products R&D Expenditures (Million $)
1957	3.4	4.3	7.7	74
1958	3.6	4.8	8.4	83
1959	4.0	5.6	9.6	91
1960	4.4	6.1	10.5	104
1961	4.7	6.2	10.9	125
1962	5.1	6.4	11.5	121
1963	5.3	7.3	12.6	130
1964	5.8	7.7	13.5	141
1965	6.4	7.8	14.2	150

Source: Anon. (1967B).

TABLE 7.4

TOTAL R&D FUNDS;
PERCENT OF TOTAL TO TOP 4, 8, AND 20 FIRMS;
NUMBER OF FULL TIME SCIENTISTS AND ENGINEERS;
NUMBER PER 1000 EMPLOYEES; AND R&D FUNDS
AS PERCENT OF SALES VALUE, BY INDUSTRIES, 1965

Industry	Total R&D Funds	Percent of Total R&D Funds			No. of Full-time R&D Engineers and Scientists	No. of Engineers and Scientists per 1000 Employees	Funds for R&D as Percent of Sales
	(Million $)	Top 4 Firms	Top 8 Firms	Top 20 Firms			
Food and kindred products	150	25	42	68	5,800	7	0.4
Textiles and apparel	34	46	62	83	1,300	3	0.4
Lumber, wood and furniture	13	36	50	65	600	5	0.5
Paper and allied products	76	27	46	73	2,700	6	0.7
Chemical and allied products	1,377	39	50	68	41,400	40	4.2
Petroleum refining and extraction	435	53	74	94	10,000	17	1.2
Rubber products	166	71	84	90	6,000	18	1.9
Stone, clay and glass products	119	57	75	87	4,400	12	1.6
Primary metals	216	42	56	77	5,700	5	0.8
Fabricated metal products	145	42	58	71	6,400	15	1.4
Machinery	1,129	50	64	77	34,100	27	4.1
Electrical Equipment and Communications	3,167	53	69	84	91,200	53	9.4
Aircraft and missiles	5,120	52	76	97	100,700	113	28.0
Professional and scientific instruments	387	58	67	81	11,300	36	6.2
Other manufacturing industries	67	28	38	57	2,500	8	0.7
Nonmanufacturing industries	359	35	47	62	10,200	10	0.7
Motor vehicle and transportation equipment	1,238	91	93	98	24,700	20	3.1
Totals	14,197	21	34	55	358,900	30	4.3

Source: Anon. (1967B).

U.S. Dept. of Agr. – While much work is done in various sections of the U.S. Dept. of Agr. on crop production, economics of agriculture, and on marketing, the section most related to the development of new food products and processing methods is the Agricultural Research Service (ARS) with its four regional utilization laboratories. These four laboratories are located in Peoria, Illinois; New Orleans; Albany, California; and Philadelphia. A fifth laboratory has been recently added to the system at Athens, Georgia. A brief description of the research and some of the accomplishments of each of these regional utilization laboratories follows.

The Northern Laboratory. – At Peoria, they conduct utilization research on grains, i.e., corn, wheat, grain sorghum, soybeans, flaxseed and other oil seed crops and/or new crops that may develop commercial uses in the United States. The main emphasis is on finding new and improved industrial uses of agricultural products through chemistry. Recent work has been basic and applied research on high-protein low-cost foods for developing countries.

The Southern Laboratory. – At New Orleans researchers work on cotton, plant fibers, seed proteins, rice, citrus fruits, oilseeds, naval stores, sweet potatoes and other fruits and vegetables indigenous to the South. Some accomplishments have been contributions to the development of wash-and-wear, stretch, durable press, and flame resistant cotton fabrics. Contributions have also been made in citrus concentrates, sweet potato flakes, foam-mat drying of citrus fruits, and defatted peanuts.

The Western Laboratory. – At Albany, there is emphasis on fruits and vegetables, wheat, barley, rice, forage crops, poultry and eggs, tree nuts, dry beans and peas, castor seed, sugar beets, and wool and mohair. Some of its researchers have made significant contributions in food dehydration including dehydrofreezing and canning, foam-mat drying, vacuum drying, freeze drying, microwave dehydration, and osmotic dehydration. Also, much research has been conducted on new human food uses for grain through new processing methods.

The Eastern Laboratory. – At Philadelphia research is done on animal products, fruits and vegetables, tobacco, and maple products. The essence recovery process (fruit juices) originated here. Foam-spray drying, vacuum foam drying (whole milk), explosive puffing of fruits and vegetables, and the dehydration of mashed potatoes on a heated metal drum are all accomplishments of the eastern laboratory. Much of the dehydrated mashed potatoes produced in the world today are made using the eastern laboratory's flake process. Their work in low fat natural cheese and the reverse osmotic concentration of maple syrup shows promise.

U.S. Dept. of Defense. – Their most important department facility in terms of food research is the Natick Laboratory, Natick, Mass. Here research is conducted on new foods, combat rations, space food, etc. Early work on freeze drying was done by Defense Department workers. A major effort over the past several years (since 1950) has been in the development of techniques for the irradiation preservation of foods. The progress of this work was recently set back by at least five years when the Food and Drug Administration refused a petition for clearance to market irradiated canned ham. Another phase of research has been to improve food items already in use by the Armed Forces. Quick-serve meals are constantly made better through research on texture, nutrition, appearance, palatability, and cost. The Department also does work in analyzing and understanding food preferences. This is readily understandable as the U.S. Dept. of Defense has the largest institutional food service in the United States, the Armed Forces. The space food program is only one area of unusual research; research on the development of photosynthetic protein foods derived from plants is another. At the current time, emphasis is on improving yields from algae sources.

U.S. Dept. of the Interior. — The Bureau of Commercial Fisheries in the Dept. of Interior has three main research laboratories, at Gloucester, Mass., Seattle, Washington, and College Park, Maryland. The Gloucester laboratory has a pilot irradiation laboratory and a continuing program on food irradiation research. Work is also conducted on flavor and odor components of fish.

The College Park laboratory has conducted much work on fish protein concentrate. This is part of a continuing departmental program to utilize a greater proportion of the total fish catch. The Seattle laboratory work centers around ways to inhibit oxidation of fish and fish products.

Atomic Energy Commission. — The Atomic Energy Commission at Oak Ridge, Tennessee conducts studies on irradiation of foods. While the Army has studied high dose applications of irradiation primarily for the sterilization of meats, the AEC has conducted low dose irradiation studies on seafoods, meats, and fruits and vegetables (Urbain 1968). The AEC studies have not been aimed at complete sterilization, but at a general reduction in spoilage organisms so as to greatly increase the shelf-life of products under good commercial handling practices.

Colleges and Universities. — Many universities now have substantial research programs in food science, food technology, in engineering work related to the food processing industry, and in other related fields. Many, if not most, of the land grant colleges and universities have some research programs in the field of food processing.

TIME AND COSTS OF COMMERCIALIZATION OF NEW PRODUCTS

A Definition of a New Product

A new food product is difficult to define. Exactly when is a "new product" new? Recently a sales manager suggested, "If you don't have 'NEW' on the package you had better have '7¢ OFF'!" Most advertising and promotion aimed at the general public usually try to portray a minor change in product formulation, or container characteristics as a "Revolutionary New Advance." For example, does the addition of a little more chili pepper to a standard "Chili with Beans" creating a "NEW HOT Chili with Beans" really qualify as a new product?

To draw any generalizations or tentative conclusions regarding either the time necessary or the costs involved in new product development, a definition of a new food product is necessary. The author's definition of a new product is one that comes under one or more of the following classifications: (1) Products produced by substantially different new food processing technologies.[2] (2) Innovative items which are significantly different from others in the field. (3) Distinctly new products which are significantly different from a company's existing products and are of sufficient importance to merit separate treatment by the firm in terms of organizational responsibility, budget, market planning, etc.

Although it is difficult to draw hard and fast lines among types of new products, the following are not considered to be within this definition of a new food product: (1) Product line extensions such as new flavors, colors, package sizes, or other minor variants introduced to supplement existing products. (2) Product improvements such as modifications in the formulation, minor improvements in processing technologies, packaging, etc., of existing products.

Thus, few of the great proliferation of product lines and few of the greatly increasing numbers of products offered to consumers are really new products under the above definition.

The Incidence of New Food Product Development

To indicate the great extent of product proliferation, a survey by *Progressive Grocer* suggested that the average food manufacturer increased the number of products he offered by 10% a year between 1959 and 1965 (Nielson 1960). Further, Magle (1966) quoted the president of a grocery chain: "... buyers for the company are required to consider between 4000 and 5000 new items a year, of which 1000 are accepted. This means the discontinuance of many labels in order to make space for new products." The article went on to state that General Foods had introduced 17 new products the previous year, Heinz 4 new products, General Mills 10, and that Campbell Soup had about 100 items in various stages of testing. At the end of World War II Campbell Soup had a total of 27 products; by 1965 there were 400.

While it is true that the average supermarket may have several thousand more items than 20 yr ago, few of these additions are substantially new products. One report by the Natl. Comm. on Food Marketing (Anon. 1966B) stated: "The results of research and development expenditures (by the food processing industry) can be evaluated in part by looking at the food products of the postwar (WW II) period. Products which could be considered newly developed or which achieved their initial sales growth in the postwar period accounted for between

---

[2] A partial review of some new processing technologies is included as a subsequent part of this chapter.

5-7% of grocery store sales in 1964.[3] Few of these 'new products' are the result of even moderately complex technologies, and essentially all the more complex technologies were developed with public funds." Apparently the Natl. Comm. on Food Marketing closely associated their definition of a new food product with the development of new processing technologies. With the author's definition of a new food product given above, the impact would probably be at least twice that suggested by the Commission.

The Time Horizon in New Product Development

Undoubtedly the most definitive study of time and costs in new food product development was reported by Buzzell and Nourse (1966), two Harvard professors. The following material will draw heavily from this source.

Buzzell and Nourse, in a survey of all large food processing firms, obtained data from 19 firms on 124 "distinct new products" introduced between 1954 and 1964. R&D expenditures of the firms on which data were obtained was around 1/3 of the national total in food processing.

Generally, many months were involved from the evolution of the product concept to the time of limited distribution of the product. The stages in product development which most new products undergo are as follows. (1) R&D – research, design, engineering and technical specifications, manufacture of prototypes, and similar activities involving technical development. (2) Product testing – professional and/or consumer evaluation of the products. This may precede or coincide with test marketing. (3) Test marketing – offering the product for sale in one or more local or regional market areas on a test basis only. (4) Limited area introduction – offering the product for sale in one or more regions or areas, comprising something less than a company's total market area. (5) Full-scale introduction – introduction in substantially all areas in which a company normally distributes its products.

The average number of months from the beginning of technological research and development to the time of full distribution for 124 "distinctly new products" for 19 large food processing firms is given in Table 7.5. On the average, 37 months elapsed between beginning R&D and initial full distribution. Of the products analyzed, new breakfast cereals required the greatest time in total development – an average of 55 months.

Costs in New Product Commercialization

Costs in R&D (as defined by Buzzell and Nourse) are a very small part of the total cost of commercialization of a new food product. Much confusion exists in

---

[3]The Natl. Comm. on Food Marketing largely developed these data from "How Consumers Spend Their Grocery Dollars," *Food Topics*, Sept. 1965, pp. 14-23. The new products analyzed by the Commission were: frozen concentrated juice, prepared mixes, low calorie foods and drinks, canned and frozen prepared foods, baby foods, dry milk products, instant beverages, frozen poultry, and refrigerated biscuits.

TABLE 7.5

AVERAGE[1] NUMBER OF MONTHS SPENT IN EACH STAGE OF
PRODUCT DEVELOPMENT BEFORE PROCEEDING TO THE NEXT STAGE

Product Category	R&D	Product Testing	Test Marketing	Limited Distribution	Total Months from First Activity to Limited Distribution	Total Months from First Activity to Full Distribution
Breakfast cereals (cold)	32	14	6	5	56	55
Cake mixes	15	9	6	11	22	29
Dog food	11	9	14	9	29	40
Frozen dinners and specialties	18	13	12	12	22	41
Margarine	15	9	10	8	23	33
All product categories (including the above)	18	11	10	10	32	37

Source: Buzzell and Nourse (1966).

[1] Averages are based on only those products which actually underwent a stage, and do not include products which "skipped" the stage in question.

the literature on the definition of development. The extremely high costs of the commercialization of new food products normally come from the expenses of test marketing, and from the very high advertising and promotion expenditures during the initial product introduction, rather than from R&D. Redman (1928) correctly distinguished between the costs of "research" and "development." "The rank and file of men in business, and not a few in the halls of learning, appear to have the impression that knowledge gained in research, if of potential value in industry, is ordinarily capable of immediate applications. They have heard it said that research is a gamble, but in this they fail to distinguish between research proper, which is relatively inexpensive, and the industrial exploitation of research, commonly called 'development' which may be a costly procedure. They are surprised when told that it is not unsuccessful research that gives most cause for concern but it is the successful research that is to be exploited (commercially) in terms of a workable process (sellable product)."

In all of the product categories studied by Buzzell and Nourse, the cost of R&D and the cost of marketing research could nearly be called a minor cost when compared to the costs of market testing (Table 7.6). The average cost of R&D and market research for 111 new food products were $68,000 and $26,000 respectively, while the average net negative contribution during test marketing was $248,000. Net negative contribution was defined as "gross profit from test market sales, minus costs for marketing, R&D, and market research incurred during test marketing." The net negative contribution actually understates test marketing costs as some fixed overhead costs are not included.

The marketing costs during the first year of regular distribution tend to be quite high — averaging $1,396,000 (Table 7.6). Because of the high levels of preintroduction costs, and even more because of the high costs of marketing during the early history of a new product, few distinct new products begin to make any contribution to overhead costs and profits within 1 yr, or even 2 yr. Of the new product introductions studied, 30% broke even in the first year following introduction, 44% in 2 yr, 61% in 3 yr, and 73% in 4 yr. However, it should be recognized that not all the products developed by R&D departments reach the point of regular distribution. Of the 124 new products under consideration, 27 were discontinued after test marketing, 10 after limited distribution, and 11 after receiving full distribution. Thus of the 124 products developed by R&D which passed the marketing research stage, 39% were discontinued at some subsequent stage of development.

Perhaps the most expensive step in commercialization is the final step: placing the product in the company's whole marketing area. The initial advertising and promotion costs may be extremely high. For example, 5 companies (General Foods Corp., Borden Co., General Mills, Inc., McCormick & Co., and Pillsbury Co.) had a combined advertising budget in 1 yr (1960) of $8,705,000 for dehydrated mashed potatoes (Anon. 1961A).

If the cumulated costs are subtracted from gross profits after the first year of introduction, the cumulative contribution to sales is obtained (last column,

TABLE 7.6

COSTS OF R&D, MARKETING RESEARCH, TEST MARKETING, AND MARKETING
EXPENDITURES DURING 1st YEAR OF DISTRIBUTION FOR DISTINCTLY NEW FOOD PRODUCTS, 1954 — 1964

Product Category	Cost of Product R&D ($1000)	Cost of Marketing Research ($1000)	Net Negative Contribution During Test Marketing ($1000)	Marketing Expenditures 1st Year Regular Distribution ($1000)	1st Year Regular Distribution Sales Cumulative Contribution as Share of Cumulative Sales ($1000)	%
Breakfast cereals (cold)	122	60	921	3401	4365	−40
Cake mixes	27	13	61	464	942	−29
Dog food	91	37	531	1926	3943	−48
Frozen dinners and specialties	15	8	47	83	416	−26
Margarine	65	17	NA	2003	6684	−84
All product categories (including those above)	68	26	248	1396	3142	−40
Number of new products being considered	(111)	(111)	(72)	(less than 72)	(less than 72)	(less than 72)

Source: Buzzell and Nourse (1966).

Table 7.6). Specifically, "cumulative contribution" is defined as the net difference between the total gross profit earned on a produce since regular introduction and the following costs: (1) Preintroduction R&D and marketing research. (2) Total costs for marketing, R&D, and marketing research incurred since large scale introduction. (3) Net "loss" (gross profit minus costs for marketing, R&D, and marketing research) on test marketing prior to large scale introduction, if any.

For example, the average cumulative contribution as a share of cumulative sales after the first year of regular introduction was —40% or (40% times sales of $3,142,000 = $1,256,800) a loss of $1,256,800 after the first year. This "loss" or cost of introduction over returns is an understatement of the total cost because some overhead costs of operating are not included in the calculations.

Survey results of Buzzell and Nourse clearly support the generalization that product innovation is a costly and risky venture. The "stakes of the game" are indicated in terms of expenses incurred prior to introduction and the typical negative net contribution after 1 yr of large scale marketing.

SOME UNDOCUMENTED GENERALIZATIONS

While no documentary evidence will be cited, it is the author's opinion that the time span in new product development is decreasing. This decreasing time span has resulted from: (1) The more general acceptance on the part of large firms of the necessity of new product development as a requirement for continued growth. (2) Concomitantly, the better integration of R&D staffs into the corporate development function of the larger firms. (3) Generally better communication between governmental research scientists and college and university scientists and the R&D departments of food firms. (4) Generally a larger and broader scientific and technological base from which new products may be developed. Further, more and more new food products are now aimed at the away-from-home food market. Market research, market testing, and initial introductions of new food products to this market segment may require substantially less time than for a consumer product.

The costs of new product commercialization by large food firms to the consumer segment of the market will undoubtedly increase through time. However, all new food product commercialization is certainly not as expensive as that discussed previously in this chapter. Many new food products are now initially aimed at the hotel, restaurant, and institutional market. Methods of obtaining initial trial-use of a new food product by a large proportion of the institutional market is typically much less expensive than obtaining trial-use by a large proportion of individual consumers. Further, in the case of the institutional market, the feedback to the manufacturer is more direct. Although not specifically stated, the case studies reported by Buzzell and Nourse (1966) were undoubtedly new product introduction costs to the consumer market. New food product introductions to the institutional market should cost considerably less.

ANALOGS, SUBSTITUTES, AND SYNTHETICS

Current Limits of Synthetics in Food Science

We should start by dispelling the science-fiction notion that soon the complete nutritional requirement of man will be satisfied by swallowing a pill. Around 2600 calories of energy is the average requirement for an adult of moderate size and moderate activity. "If we take only the essential protein, fat, and carbohydrates to make us run, put them together in a pill, you get this — a pill about the size of a pound of butter" (Hoover, 1967). Similarly, the notion that soon the complete food requirements can economically be produced synthetically should also be dispelled. Hoover (1967) reported that with the present limits of knowledge of food science, the cheapest methods of producing carbohydrates, proteins, and fats is through the conversion of light energy into chemical energy by photosynthesis in living plants. "If the price of farm products derived from crops were doubled, they would still be cheaper than synthetic sources for the production of protein, carbohydrates, and fat." However, these current limits of knowledge are continually being broken; R&D on the production of yeast or bacterial cells as a source of feed or food protein from petroleum is being actively carried on in industry and in universities in this country and abroad (Anon. 1967; Johnson 1967).

Although protein, fats, and carbohydrates cannot yet be produced economically by synthesis from nonagricultural sources, certain of the essential amino acids and most all of the supplemental vitamins can. The synthetic production of these amino acids and vitamins are extremely important in today's world food picture. R. R. Williams (1956), noted authority on nutrition, looked at the problem of providing food to underdeveloped nations chiefly as one of dietary supplementation. He emphasized that most dietary deficiency diseases are caused by a lack of certain amimo acids and vitamins in the diets of people who primarily consume grain, and sometimes by the lack of certain fatty acids in the diet. The problem is not often a lack of carbohydrates, but if sufficient grains were used to produce the required proteins, not enough carbohydrate sources would be left to supply energy requirements or to fill stomachs. The cost of proteinaceous foods is prohibitive relative to income in most of the countries in which large numbers of people suffer from dietary deficiencies. There is a possibility for underdeveloped nations to provide adequate supplies of grains to their growing populations if diets can be upgraded without expensive animal proteins.

In general, vegetable proteins have less of the essential amino acids than do animal proteins. Vegetable proteins are lower in lysine, tryptophan, methionine, and threonine. Sidney Fox (1963), biochemist with the Chemistry Department and Institute of Space Biosciences, Florida State University, presented cost figures in 1962 for large-scale synthetic production of lysine, tryptophan, and methionine. Annual requirements of these 3 essential amino acids for an adult could be produced for around $5.50. Fox also pointed out that in large-scale manufacturing the cost per person for the annual requirements of vitamin A, thiamine, riboflavin, nicotinic acid, ascorbic acid, calcium pantothenate, and pyridoxine would be around $0.55 in 1962. These are the vitamins commonly used in tablets as nutritional supplements. Both Fox and Williams suggest that chemical synthesis is probably the most satisfactory long-run means of satisfying the nutritional needs of people for amino acids and vitamins. Fox (1963) went further, however, in suggesting chemical synthesis of carbohydrates; "In a long-term sense, the control of production of nutritional molecules by manufacturing from other molecules seems almost to be an inexorable development."

CURRENT USAGE OF SYNTHETICS, SUBSTITUTES, AND ANALOGS

As used here, a synthetic food (or fiber) product is one formed by chemical reactions; the origin of the chemicals are normally nonagricultural sources. A substitute is one form of agricultural product used in place of another, i.e., margarine instead of butter. An analog is a term used to describe more complex synthetic and/or substitute food products analogous to some foods in current usage. For example, the meat-like products made from spun protein fibers from soy beans to which various flavor components (usually synthetic) have been added are called analogs.

Many American consumers, on nearly a daily basis, consume both synthetic and substitute food products, and the use of analogs is rapidly becoming widespread. Both vitamins (see above) and low calorie sweeteners are truly synthetic food products. The low calorie sweeteners consist of saccharin and cyclamates both of which are derived from organic chemicals. Margarine is probably the most widespread food substitute where vegetable oils are substituted for butterfat, i.e., palm oil, soybean oil, cottonseed oil, corn oil, etc. In fact, the use of margarine is so prevalent some people no longer consider it a substitute. To date, one of the few analogs which has had any national distribution is General Mills' BacOs, a soybean protein textured and flavored product analogous to fried crumbled bits of bacon. (It is added to dressings for baked potatoes, in salads, chip dips, etc.)

Let's look at some of the food and fiber industries in which synthetics, substitutes, and analogs are having some effects. Corkern and Poats (1968) present a very conservative viewpoint on the impact of synthetics and substitutes. They suggest that in 1967, for 12 quite specific industries, the market loss to traditional agricultural industries has been around $895 million (Table 7.7). However, these are probably extremely conservative estimates.

Impact of Substitutes in the Dairy Industry

McBride (1968) suggests that "an estimated 25% of the market for dairy products is now being supplied by products containing 1 or more substitute ingredients. This represents losses in sales of about $2.75 billion annually in this $11 billion industry." The per capita consumption of butter has dropped from around 17 lb preWorld War II to about 6 lb in 1966. At the same time, margarine consumption in the United States is about 2.2 billion pounds per year. If margarine is considered a substitute for butter and if butter were priced at only $0.50 per lb, the loss of this market alone would be equivalent to $1.1 billion, much more than the total listed by Corkern and Poats in Table 7.7.

Quackenbush (1966) supports the 25% replacement in dairy products. He also suggested (Quackenbush 1967) that substitute dairy whiteners had captured 35% of the coffee cream market and nondairy whipped toppings 60% of the market. "Mellorine has about 5% of the frozen dessert market, but is growing fast. The potential, however, is indicated by the fact that mellorine has about 40% of the frozen dessert market in Texas and 15% in California."

Perhaps the greatest competition to the dairy industry will come from filled milk (skim milk with vegetable fat added) or from nondairy milk substitutes (e.g., defatted soya flour plus vegetable fat). Nondairy milk substitutes are being sold in several states including Oregon, Ohio, California, and Hawaii. Data in one publication (McBride 1968) suggest that nondairy substitute ingredients would cost only 2.9¢ per qt compared to a whole milk price of 8.2¢ per qt (with a Federal Market order base price of $4.00 per 100 lb of 3.5% butterfat milk).

TABLE 7.7

ESTIMATED LOSS OF TRADITIONAL AGRICULTURAL MARKETS TO SYNTHETICS AND AGRICULTURAL SUBSTITUTES AND TOTAL AGRICULTURAL MARKET, 1967

Agricultural Product or Market	Market Loss Quantity	Market Loss Value[1] (Million $)	Estimated Total Market[1] (Million $)
Cotton (million lb)	1780	456	1124
Wool (million lb)	235	176	385
Cane and beet sugar ($1000)	370	76	1954
Oilseed meal ($1000)	358	30	537
Fats and oils for soap[2] (million lb)	460	31	53
Drying oils for paints[3] (million lb)	248	32	64
Glycerine (million lb)	46	7	25
Starch for dextrin for adhesives[4] (million lb)	54	4	43
Soya meal and casein for adhesives[4] (million lb)	76	6	24
Leather for shoe uppers[5] (million sq ft)	51	31	491
Citrus[6] (million gal.)	52	45	334
Fluid milk[7] (million lb)	12	1	3162
Total		895	8196

Source: Corkern and Poats (1968).

[1] Prices used to compute value were: cotton — 25.6¢ per lb; wool — 75.0¢ per lb; sugar — 10.2¢ per lb; oilseed meal — $83.20 per ton; fats and oils — 6.7¢ per lb; drying oils — 12.9¢ per lb; glycerine — 16.1¢ per lb; starch and dextrin — 7.5¢ per lb; soya meal and casein — 7.5¢ per lb; leather — 60.0¢ per sq ft; citrus — 85.7¢ per gal.; fluid milk — $5.43 per cwt.
[2] Fats and oils used in soaps related to total sales of soap and detergents.
[3] Drying oils used in paints related to total paint sales.
[4] Market share relationship existing in 1962 applied to 1967.
[5] Market share relationship existing in 1965 applied to 1967.
[6] The market loss in 1967 is assumed to be equal to synthetic drink sales.
[7] The market loss in 1967 is assumed to be equal to known filled milk sales during Nov.-Dec. 1967. This value is understated since synthetic milk sales and total filled milk sales are not available.

Protein Supplements and Meat Analogs

E. A. Day (1967) suggested that the markets most likely to be aimed at by manufacturers of substitutes or analogs are the meat and milk markets. "The meat industry constitutes approximately a $30 billion market at the retail level. A company that is only moderately successful with meat substitutes could still have a $300 million market if it captured only 1% of the total market . . . Milk products represent an $11 billion retail market and, like meat, represent a lucrative target for a company with resources that can afford the risk to develop substitute products."

On an international basis Hartman (1967) reported that "approximately 4 million tons of amino acids or 10 million tons of high quality proteins a year are needed by 1980 to close the gap between conventional food production and the minimum needs of the hungry 2/3 of the world's population."

Central to the issues of world protein deficiency and also to the potential price competition between protein supplements, meat analogs, and meats is the fact that "an acre of land will produce for human nutrition only 1/4 as many calories when plants are fed to animals as when they (the plants) are consumed directly." ". . . In terms of our protein supply, it is wasteful to feed protein to animals. It is estimated that 23% of the protein fed to a cow is recovered for humans; that 12% of the protein fed to hogs is recovered for humans; and that only 10% of the protein fed to steers is recovered for humans" (Palm 1967).

Protein Supplements. – Much of the following information was adopted from a U.S. Agency for International Development (AID) publication (Tech. Assistance Inform. Clearing House 1968). Tests are being conducted in many underdeveloped countries of the world for economical commercial ways to supplement diets with additional protein. One of the first high protein supplements used after milk powder was Incaparina, a mixture of corn, sorghum, cottonseed flour, yeast, calcium carbonate, and vitamin A. Developed by the Institute of Nutrition of Central America and Panama (INCAP), it was first used in Central America and is now being sold commercially in some other countries. The Pillsbury Company recently completed a production and consumer test in El Salvador for U.S. AID of a high protein mix of wheat germ, sesame, sugar, and flavor. The pioneer and also epitome of commercial success in high protein soft drinks is the Hong Kong-made Vitasoy. As with its followers, it is nutritious, needs no refrigeration, and is sold at the same price as other local soft drinks (about 3 1/2¢ per 7 oz bottle). Monsanto Company has a joint venture with Vitasoy's inventory to adapt it to taste in other parts of the world, initially in Venezuela. Coca Cola Refrescos de Brazil is producing and test marketing a drink called Saci made of Brazilian soybeans, cocoa beans, and sugar with vitamins added. U.S. AID has contracted with several commercial firms to test acceptance of high protein (usually from soybeans) beverages in several countries: the Commercial Research Foundation in India, General Mills in Pakistan, and Krausse Milling Company and Monsanto in Brazil.

Another source of high protein which seems to offer great possibilities for further development is FPC (Fish Protein Concentrate). This is not a fish flour or fish meal but a high protein powder made from the whole fish which, when added to flour or cereals, enhances the protein content considerably. The world fish catch is about 50-60 million tons a year now. Estimates of the tonnage that could be taken yearly without depletion start at 400 million tons and vary up to astronomical figures. The U.S. Food and Drug Administration approved fish protein concentrate made from hake in 1967, but research is now under way to make acceptable many other kinds of fish to derive benefits from these vast resources of the sea. It is said that 200 million tons of fish would provide enough daily protein for 5 billion people for a year.

Single Cell Protein (SCP) also holds promise but apparently is still uneconomical, at least in the United States. For example, a large crop of protein from bacteria or yeast can be grown in petroleum hydrocarbons in 1-4 hr. The protein must then be separated from the solution, inactivated or sterilized, and dried. The result is a tasteless powder with up to 70% protein. British and Japanese petroleum companies are building factories for the manufacture of SCP for animal feed. Pilot plants are producing protein from petroleum hydrocarbons on an experimental basis at the Indian Institute of Petroleum, Dehradrn, and the Regional Research Laboratory, Jorhat. Meanwhile, Standard Oil of New Jersey and Nestle Alimentana of Switzerland are working together on the longer-term project of producing this kind of protein for human consumption.

Meat Analogs. – A challenging development is in the production of meat analogs. Prototypes of sausage, hot dogs, chicken, meat loaf, turkey roasts, ham, luncheon meats, and bacon have been developed. W. E. Hartman (1967), Director of Research, Worthington Foods, describes the process as follows: "For the past 10 yr, Worthington has pioneered in the field of vegetarian protein foods seeking suitable protein isolates for spinning, developing spinning technology, and formulating and adapting these spun protein fibers to end-products acceptable to the consumer. Nearly every meat or meat product has been fairly well simulated in experimental prototype products. A great potential and versatility exist in these soya fiber products because they can be formulated to any protein, fat, or carbohydrate level. Proteins may be blended to accomplish very favorable amino acid ratios. Vitamins, minerals, color, flavor, amino acids, etc., may be added as desired. Actually, the small and narrow field of plant-protein technology has scarcely been touched."

The process of producing the fibers is similar to that of the rayon industry. Soy protein isolate is converted into a "dope" after being solubilized in a base with a pH of 12.0. The "dope" is forced through "spinnerettes" much the same as for rayon. The filaments are extruded into a coagulating bath and collected on reels. The fibers are then rinsed and washed before formulating into products. Color, flavor, and supplements can be added to engineer a product to meet taste, texture, and nutritional requirements.

Sales of protein analogs to date (1969) have been small. In 1966, it was estimated that sales of the largest producing firm (Worthington Foods) was a little over $2 million, and that most of this was to members of the Seventh-Day Adventist Church who do not eat meat (Ives 1966). By 1969 total sales by all firms were estimated at $10 million. Several companies are now producing meat analogs including Worthington Foods, Inc., Worthington, Ohio; Loma Linda Foods, Arlington, Cal.; Brown's Frosted Foods, Philadelphia; General Mills, Inc., Minneapolis; Ralston Purina Co., St. Louis; Swift & Company, Chicago; and Archer-Daniels-Midland, Minneapolis. The latter firm now markets meat analogs in Egypt, Lebanon, the Philippines, Japan, and Taiwan. Worthington Foods and Africa Basic Foods are working together under a U.S. AID contract to explore production possibilities of high protein foods and beverages in Uganda. Worthington will also introduce soybeans in the New Delhi area of India where few are currently cultivated. Plans are to use the first crops for soya milk and later possibly make a high protein soy snack.

Most of the firms producing meat analogs have had only limited distribution for their products. Reputedly, General Mills spent $30 million in R&D on vegetable protein products before building a new facility for commercial production in Iowa (Anon. 1968). General Mills was the first company to try to nationally market a vegetable protein analog. National distribution of BacOs (resembling cooked, crumbled bacon bits) to be used in salads, with eggs, chip dips, etc., was started in 1968. General Mills is also distributing to the institutional trade several meat analogs under their "Bontrae"[4] trademark. Worthington, in the fall of 1967, did a market test on a 2-lb meatless turkey roast, but plans for general market entry did not materialize. Worthington is now market testing "Stripples," a precooked bacon analog, apparently feeling that a market does exist for a protein analog as a main course (breakfast). It is interesting that while governments and nutritionists have placed emphasis on the possible low cost of vegetable protein analogs, both General Mills and Worthington initially aimed at a high price market — bacon. Allegedly, the protein in cooked bacon costs the consumer over $5.00 per lb in the United States.

Synthetics and Substitutes in Fruit Products

While Day (1967) suggested that dairy products and meat will be the principal areas of development for synthetics, substitutes, and analogs, fruit products have long been an area with much synthetic replacement. Corkern and Poats (1968) suggest a loss to the citrus industry of around $45 million in 1967 through synthetics and substitutes. Again, this is probably a conservative estimate. For example, Black and Polopolus (1966) stated that "30% of an almost 1 billion dollar annual national fruit beverage market is now being supplied by products containing 1 or more synthetically-derived ingredients. Synthetics account for 5% , substitutes 25% and juice 70% of the U.S. fruit

---

[4] General Mills' trade name for its protein analogs.

beverage market." They went on to explain, "Substitutes are defined as fruit beverages possessing both natural and synthetic ingredients . . . synthetics do not contain natural fruit solids." In their classification, a fruit drink containing natural fruit solids but also containing synthetic flavor, color, sweeteners, and vitamins would be classed as a substitute.

For the citrus industry the current principal synthetic competitors are Tang, Awake, and Start. All three are synthetic substitutes for orange juice. Tang is in powder form; Awake, a frozen synthetic concentrate; and Start is a synthetic orange powder somewhat similar but less sweet than General Foods' Tang. According to Polopolus and Black (1966), "Awake has attained and apparently will continue to hold approximately 10% of the concentrated orange juice market." The possible market penetration of Awake is shown in the following consumer test: Based upon consumer comparison of Awake and frozen concentrated orange juice at the Florida Pavilion of the New York World's Fair, Awake was preferred by 55% of the respondents, with 34% of the respondents preferring the natural juices. Respondents were unaware that Awake was being tested; they were informed the two products were orange juice. On the basis of comparative ratings of flavor characteristics, Awake was believed by respondents to have a better after-taste, to be thicker, sweeter, more orange in flavor, pulpier, and deeper orange in color than the standard frozen concentrated orange juice (Anon. 1965B). Black and Polopolus indicated that in 1966 the advertising budget for Awake was $5 million; for Start, $3 million; while the advertising budget for Tang was not known. They did suggest that the total advertising budget for synthetic orange products apparently exceeded the combined advertising expenditures of the Florida Citrus Commission and the Florida citrus processors (Black and Polopolus 1966).

In speculating on the substitution of synthetics for fruit there are definitional problems. For example, are synthetically-flavored Jello, Deserta, and other synthetically-flavored dessert gels substitutes for natural fruit? Although sales value of these products is not public, the advertising budgets alone do run into millions of dollars. Is synthetically-flavored orange, grape, or strawberry soda pop a substitute for real juice products? Are the synthetically-sweetened and synthetically-flavored children's drink powders such as Kool-Aid, Funny Face, Keen, etc., classified as substitutes for natural fruit juices? Again, for these latter products total sales figures are not available but advertising budgets are in the millions.

Recently there has been commercial activity to develop fruit analogs. General Foods was recently issued a patent for a process to produce simulated fruits. The structure of a fruit is built using alginates and other ingredients, then synthetic color and synthetic flavor are added. These are probably being designed to be incorporated into breakfast cereals. This may be an economical method of producing simulated fruits. For example, Day (1967) stated that synthetic strawberry flavor was 1/20th as expensive as natural flavors and the cost of synthetic raspberry is 1/28th the price of raspberry juice.

Synthetic Sweeteners

Corkern and Poats (1968) suggested the market loss of sugar due to synthetics in 1967 was around $76 million. My estimate in 1964, with sugar at 10 cents per lb, would have been a market loss of around $94 million (Greig 1968B). These differences are not important; the important aspect is that synthetic sweeteners were increasing and had obtained a significant share of the market. However, the Food and Drug Administration banned the use of one of the major synthetic sweeteners, cyclamates, as of January 1, 1970. This, of course, drastically affected the marketing of many food products, since a mixture of cyclamates with saccharin, the other most prevalent synthetic sweetener, was a common practice. While saccharin has the greatest degree of sweetening ability, to many people it has a bitter after-taste. Cyclamates have less sweetening capacity but not as much of an after-taste. Combined, the two products have a synergistic effect on sweetness and the bitter after-taste of the saccharin is masked.

Many authors suggested that consumer popularity of "no-cal" or "low calorie" food products was due more to alleged cosmetic benefits rather than to health benefits. Principal users were women who wished to "maintain" their current weight. The popularity of the synthetics with food processors was both the advertising appeal and their cost. An equivalent amount of sweetness could be produced much more cheaply from synthetic than from nutritive sweeteners. At 1966 wholesale price levels, the sweetening equivalent of 1 lb of sugar could be purchased in synthetic form (a mixture of 1 part saccharin to 9 parts cyclamates) for 1.22¢. The wholesale price of sugar has been over 9.0¢ per lb. Sugar cannot be produced anywhere in the world at prices approaching the price of synthetics (Greig 1968B).

The principal uses of synthetic sweeteners have been in low calorie carbonated beverages, dry beverage bases, dietetic foods (canned and frozen fruits, jellies, desserts, salad dressings, etc.), and in retail packages of the synthetics (in liquid, tablet, and powder forms).

While projections are dangerous at this point in time because of legal and health restrictions on the cyclamates and possibly other synthetic sweeteners, other products probably will be found to replace the banned cyclamates. Sweeteners derived from licorice roots and grapefruit and orange peels may be practical substitutes for cyclamates. Other products are being tested (Leger 1969).

Whether the true market for low calorie products was a fact which will redevelop or a fad dealt a death blow by the banning of cyclamates by the Food and Drug Administration is difficult to predict.

Other Agricultural Products

Synthetic fiber, leather, soaps, etc., will not be discussed here as they are not directly related to food processing. However, the limited coverage above on milk, meat, fruit, and sugar are not meant to be all-inconclusive. Synthetics and substitutes may, of course, be developed for other types of food products.

A REVIEW OF SOME "NEW" PROCESSING TECHNOLOGIES

Introduction

From an historical perspective, most of the food we eat is processed either by very old processing technologies or very new processing technologies. The origins of drying, brining, smoking, wine making, cheese making, and grain milling and bread baking are lost in antiquity. However, the basic technological processes by which most meat reaches the consumer, except for the addition of some refrigeration, has not changed in centuries.

Some staple foods used for hundreds of years are nearly inedible without processing. The olive is very bitter unless brine-cured. Mandioca (*Manihot utilissima*) sometimes called cassava or yucca may contain toxic quantities of hydrocyanic acid unless processed. This bitter mandioca is ground and heat dried to drive off the hydrocyanic acid. The product is a course flour (farinha de mandioca), still a staple in Brazil. The process of making this flour was evolved by the native Indians, long before Brazil was civilized.

In some cases, very old products have evolved through new technologies into very modern products. For example, evidence suggests that the ancient Incas had commercial trade in dehydrated potatoes whereas instant mashed potatoes have had extremely rapid rate of growth in the United States over the past 10-12 yr, with practically no commercial production prior to World War II.

Historically, canning is a relatively recent innovation; it was developed by Appert during the time of Napoleon. Fast freezing was initiated in the late 1920's and early 1930's but nearly all the commercial development has been since the 1940's. During and subsequent to World War II several new processing technologies have been developed. Concentration of orange juice was developed during World War II; dehydrofreezing in 1946[5] (however, a Greek patent was issued in 1939); vacuum concentration with essence recovery in 1946; commercial application of microwave cooking began in the 1940's, although literature dates back to 1893; vacuum drying in 1954; most applications of freeze drying since 1955 (although a Russian patent on the process was issued in 1921); foam-mat drying in 1959; the explosive puffing process for fruits and vegetables in 1961; foam-spray drying in 1961; and, most recently, commercial irradiation which was cleared for bacon in 1963 but clearance was withdrawn in 1969).

To partially illustrate the rapidly evolving new processing technologies for food 13 "new" processing technologies will be briefly reviewed. The reviews, in many cases, will pertain as much to consumer acceptance, economics, and commercialization as to their basic technologies.

---

[5] The dates indicate the date of the first scientific paper, except for microwave cooking and for irradiation. For microwaves the date is of first commercial applications and for irradiation the date of first clearance. However, this clearance was subsequently withdrawn in the United States by the Food and Drug Administration.

Dehydrofreezing and Dehydrocanning

Dehydrofreezing and dehydrocanning are methods of food preservation which involve drying the commodity to approximately 50% of its fresh weight and volume before freezing or canning (Powers et al. 1958). The main objective of dehydrofreezing is to reduce weight and bulk of the product while maintaining quality. As a result of the reduced weight and bulk, packaging, storage, and shipping costs are reduced (Kaufman and Powers 1957). Other advantages are reduction of drip upon thawing and ease of controlling moisture content. Technical papers have been published dealing with dehydrofreezing of several products including apples (Talburt et al. 1950), peas (Talburt and Legault 1950), and apricots (Powers et al. 1956), as well as for other fruits and vegetables (Talburt and Linquist 1954; Copley 1957).

Quality comparisons (Boggs and Talburt 1952; Greig et al. 1960, 1962) and market tests to develop market potentials (McGrath and Sills 1957; Greig and Stuckman 1960; McGrath and Kerr 1963) have indicated a very high potential for several dehydrofrozen items. Peas have been commercially dehydrofrozen in Oregon, pimientos in California, mashed potatoes in Idaho, and at least eight commercial plants* are currently dehydrofreezing apple slices in New York State. Experimental work has been conducted on apricots, cherries, blueberries, and peaches with promising results.

Vacuum Concentration with Essence Recovery

Vacuum concentration is a standard technique for concentrating fruit juices. This is principally the process used in concentration of citrus and other juice products (Cross and Gemmill 1948; Kelly 1949; Schwartz 1951; Heid and Kelly 1953; Tressler and Joslyn 1961; Walker 1961; U.S. Dept. of Agr. 1962). Part of the water content of the juices is evaporated at relatively low temperatures under vacuum. The advantage of low temperature evaporation is that an uncooked flavor may be maintained.

In some products, such as frozen orange juice concentrate, some quantities of fresh, unpasteurized juices must be added to the concentrated portion if a good flavor and odor are to be obtained. In other juice products, such as apple, grape, and cherry juices, much flavor and aroma may be contained in the volatile constituents that are lost even at the relatively low temperatures of vacuum concentration. The essence recovery process was developed to capture these volatile constituents, concentrate them, and add them back to concentrated juices (Milleville and Eskew 1946; Morris 1949; Homiller and Griffin 1949; Phillips et al. 1951). This process has been effective with apple, grape, and other juices (Griffin et al. 1947; Eskew et al. 1950, 1951) but not in the case of citrus products (Morgan et al. 1953).

Because of essence recovery, many juices can be concentrated to a 7-fold concentration (reconstituted with 6 parts of water to 1 part of concentrate) compared to the normal 4-fold concentration of citrus products. Technical details on superconcentration (Eskew et al. 1951; Homiller and Eisenhardt 1951;

Eskew 1952, 1953; Aceto *et al.* 1953) of apple, grape, cherry, and other juices have been developed as well as engineering cost data (Eskew *et al.* 1952; Aceto *et al.* 1953; Redfield and Eskew 1953; Kaufman *et al.* 1950).

The principal advantages of concentration are reduction in packaging, storing, handling, and distribution costs.

Quality comparisons (Eskew and Phillips 1954; Hunter 1959) of super-concentrated apple juice to the single-strength juice have yielded significant preferences for the concentrated form. Similarly, market tests (Boyton *et al.* 1951; McGrath and Weidenhamer 1963) have shown the product to have an appreciable market potential; also, most of the sales of superconcentrated apple juice were in addition to sales of single-strength apple juice.

Many of the fruit juices superconcentrated by the essence recovery process are used for reprocessing into jellies and jams and in fruit drink blends. At the present time no juice is sold at retail as a seven-fold concentrate. Typically, if sold as a concentrated juice, it is sold as a 4-fold concentrate (reconstituted by adding 3 parts of water to 1 part of juice concentrate). In the manufacturing process, the essence may be concentrated to as high as 150 to 1. The essence is then added to the concentrated juice and the juice is frozen or canned.

In 1963, there were at least 12 facilities within the United States with vacuum concentrating and essence recovery equipment. The principal uses are for grape, apple, and cherry juices. However, the process is adaptable to a wide range of fruit juices.

Vacuum Drying and Vacuum Puff Drying

In vacuum drying, water is removed from fruit and vegetable pieces or juices under high vacuum and relatively low temperatures. Theoretically, the process should work on many fruits and vegetables but the principal application has been on juices or purées. Most of the vacuum drying procedures for juices involve a concentration step before the drying stage.

One of the more recent developments is vacuum puff drying (Sluder *et al* 1947; Strashun 1951; Strashun and Talburt 1953). However, several early developments in citrus juice drying involved vacuum drying (Heyman 1943; Burton 1947; Hayes *et al.* 1946). In the puff drying process, a high vacuum causes the juice product to puff up to 15 to 20 times its original volume into a spongy structure. It is then dried at relatively low temperatures (product temperature under 160°F) and crushed into a powder. Vacuum drying or vacuum puff drying has been reported on oranges (Bonnell *et al.* 1955; Strashun and Talburt 1954; Notter *et al.* 1959), grapefruit (Bonnell *et al.* 1955), lemonade (Notter *et al.* 1955), pineapple (Notter *et al.* 1958), apple (Notter *et al.* 1959), and tomato juice (Kaufman *et al.* 1955; U.S. Dept. of Agr. 1955).

Fruit and vegetable juices may, of course, be dried by drum drying, spray drying, or freeze drying. Drum drying has been judged unsuitable for preparing most fruit and vegetable juice powders because they are too difficult to rehydrate. High production costs and large capital investments in equipment have deterred the commercial exploitation of freeze drying citrus juices into powder form (Campbell *et al.* 1945; Flosdorf 1945A). Although powders prepared experimentally by freeze drying were readily reconstituted, they reportedly showed a tendency to cake and develop off-flavors during storage (Flosdorf 1945B).

The advantages of the vacuum puff drying process are in the quality and reconstitutability of the product (Anon. 1954, 1955) and the relatively low cost since it may be produced as a continuous process (Fixari *et al.* 1957, 1959).

Although adaptable to a wide range of possibilities, commercial application has to date been rather limited. One European firm has used the vacuum drying process to dehydrate vegetable pieces for dehydrated soups. One California firm has used the process on applesauce and a wide range of specialty fruit and vegetable items. The puff drying process is commercially used to produce orange juice powder by one firm in Florida and tomato powder by a firm in California. Reportedly in Argentina a facility is being developed for orange juice powder.

Drum Drying

Initial investigations of drum drying fruit or vegetable products were aimed toward developing an instant dehydrated mashed potato (Cording *et al.* 1954). In the case of potatoes, cooked mashed potatoes were dried on large heated metal drums and the resulting thin sheet of dried product broken up into small flakes.

Although the older granule process (Olson and Harrington 1951, 1955; Hendel 1959) had yielded an acceptable dehydrated mashed potato from western grown potatoes, apparently an acceptable quality product could not be obtained from the eastern grown potatoes which had a lower dry matter content. Thus, one of the purposes of the potato flake process was to enable processors to obtain a high quality product from eastern grown potatoes.

The first technical paper on the potato flake process was published in 1954 (Cording *et al.* 1954), followed by papers on quality control (Cording *et al.* 1955), commercial costs (Eskew *et al.* 1955), consumer preferences (Greig and Larzelere 1957) and marketing potentials (Dwoskin and Jacobs 1957; Greig 1957; Greig *et al.* 1958). By 1960, at least 10 commercial facilities to produce potato flakes had been built in the United States with several million hundredweight of potatoes per year being dehydrated by this process. Subsequent research has increased the quality (Cording *et al.* 1957; Copley *et al.* 1959; U.S. Dept. of Agr. 1959; Eskew *et al.* 1960) and reduced the cost of the process (Claffey *et al.* 1961).

Drum drying may be applicable to a wide range of slurried and puréed products. The process has been used to produce dehydrated sweet potatoes and pumpkin. For sweet potatoes the first technical papers appeared in 1961 (McFarlane 1961; Deobald 1961; Spadaro and Patton 1961) while other technical data on quality and costs were developed in 1962 (Deobald *et al.* 1962; Decossas *et al.* 1962) and data on market potentials in 1963 (Dwoskin 1963). By

1963, at least 2 firms were commercially producing dehydrated mashed sweet potatoes in the United States and 1 firm was commercially producing dehydrated pumpkin.

Several foreign countries including Germany, Ireland, and Scotland commercially dehydrate mashed potatoes by drum drying and the process has been recommended in Brazil for dehydrating mandioca (yucca) (Anon. 1963) to be used as a mashed vegetable.

Freeze Drying

Freeze drying consists of dehydrating frozen foods under vacuum so the moisture content changes directly from a solid form to a gaseous form without having undergone the intermediate liquid stage. In this process the product maintains its original size and shape with a minimum of cell rupture. The products are packaged and stored in dry form at room temperatures (Eskew 1949).

Essentially, vacuum freeze drying involves the same processing as for frozen food, plus the added operation of removing the water to around 2% residual moisture content under vacuum (Nair 1963). Hence, valuable characteristics not found in frozen foods are necessary to justify the added expense of the costly freeze drying process.

Although a Russian patent was issued on freeze drying as early as 1921 (Tchigeon 1960) much of the early pioneering work was done in Denmark (Bird 1963A) and the United States in the 1940's (Eskew 1949). The first attempt at commercialization was in a fish dehydration plant in Norway during 1946-1948, but the facility closed shortly thereafter. During 1951-1961, the British Ministry operated a research station at Aberdeen, Scotland for food dehydration. Their work resulted in many innovations in freeze drying and subsequent reduction in costs of the process (Anon. 1961B). By 1957, the process appeared promising enough that several U.S. and European companies were in small-scale production or had pilot plants. In 1963, at least 10 U.S. companies were in commercial production with an estimated 1962 production of 5 million pounds of dried product, and an estimated 20 European companies were in production (Bird 1963B; Nair 1962).

Extensive literature has been published on freeze drying in recent years (Corridon 1963), and there is no question that the process is applicable to a wide range of food products (Wieser 1954; Meyer and Jokay 1959; MacDougall 1961; Graff 1961; Kolodny 1962; Lee 1962). The major problem concerns the economics of freeze drying compared to canning or freezing, or compared to other concentrating and dehydrating techniques. One report indicated costs from as high as 8¢ per lb of water removed for a plant with a 4-ton capacity per day of raw product to a low of 4.4¢ per lb with a 32-ton capacity (Bird 1963B); another report indicated a cost of as low as 3¢ per lb of water removed for still larger capacity plants.

Costs for drum drying are around 1¢ per lb of water removed and spray drying around 2¢ per lb (Anon. 1952). Because there is little change in size of the products in freeze drying and because the package must be impervious to moisture vapor and oxygen, packaging costs are high.

In freeze drying, as in other dehydration techniques, it's difficult to dehydrate large pieces of a product. As size increases, so do time and cost in dehydration, and quality and reconstitution problems. Typically, dehydrated meat products have been limited to shrimp and meat chunks (normally around 1/4-in. cubes) for dehydrated soups or as ingredients in other prepared dishes. Many of the problem areas have been identified by the Quartermaster Food and Container Institute (Graf 1961).

There have been failures as well as successes with freeze-dried foods. In 1965, General Foods Corp. apparently had 50% of the total freeze drying capacity of the United States at the Post Division in Battle Creek to freeze dry strawberries, blueberries, and peaches for incorporation with breakfast cereals. After a few years these breakfast cereals with the incorporated freeze-dried fruits were withdrawn from the market because of lack of consumer acceptance.

Because of cost-convenience-quality relationships, one of the largest markets for freeze-dried foods is probably the armed forces. The largest consumer market (1969) is in freeze-dried coffee. Another market with some potential is the reprocessing or remanufacturing market. The institutional trade and the market to campers may also take considerable quantities of freeze-dried foods.

Freeze drying appears to be most practical for high-priced products such as coffee, tea, and spices, or for items that cannot be dehydrated satisfactorily by other processes such as meat, asparagus, and some fruits and vegetables.

Foam-mat Drying

The foam-mat drying process involves drying thin layers of stabilized foam material by heated air at atmospheric pressure (Rockwell et al. 1963). The process is adaptable to many liquids or puréed foods. The foam is prepared in a continuous mixer by the addition of gas and, when required, a small amount of edible foam stabilizer. The prepared foam is spread on perforated trays (or a perforated continuous belt); the foam is then cratered by blowing air jets up through the perforations (Morgan et al. 1961).

The foam is dried by hot air, crushed into a powder form, and packaged. If the product is hygroscopic, it is packaged in a low humidity room maintained at 15% RH or less. As most foam-mat-dried foods are very porous in structure, they are capable of nearly instant rehydration even in cold water.

The initial development was first reported in 1959 (Morgan et al. 1959; Morgan and Randall 1960; Ginette et al. 1960). Improved or additional data on the technique was reported in 1960 (Ramage 1960) and in subsequent years (Lawler 1962; Morgan 1962; Bissett et al. 1963; Veldhuis et al. 1962). By 1961, many liquid foods had been successfully foamed and dehydrated experimentally including orange, grapefruit, lemon, lime, tomato, pineapple, apple, and grape juices, mashed potatoes, baby foods, and even honey, molasses, and instant carbohydrate products including starch and flour (Morgan et al. 1961).

The principle advantages of the process are that the products are dried at relatively low temperatures at atmospheric pressure. Compared to ordinary air-dried foods, foam-mat-dried powders are of superior quality, are nearly instantly soluble in water, and processing costs are expected to be less than for vacuum or freeze drying. Foaming with gases has been used as an adjunct to vacuum drying (Aceto et al. 1962; Sinnamon et al. 1957; Eskew 1963), and has been adapted for use in spray drying (Hanrahan and Webb 1961; Hanrahan et al. 1962; Pallansch 1963).

Typically, a concentrate rather than a single strength juice is dehydrated. In some cases, such as orange juice, the resulting powder is reformed into a thin sheet of high density by running the powder through heated metal rollers. The sheet is then broken into flakes having a higher bulk density than the powder (Morgan 1963). To enhance the flavor of reconstituted citrus juices, encapcillated citrus oils may be added to the dried juice powders (Schultz et al. 1956).

The application of the foam-mat drying process to commercial use has been very rapid. By 1963, at least three equipment companies were fabricating foam-mat dryers and several commercial facilities were using the process for a variety of products. Foam-mat drying is used commercially for preparing tomato powder for dry soup mixes and for drying pizza and spaghetti mixes. Lemon powder is being made commercially for export. It is assumed that the instantized flour being marketed in the United States is produced by an adaption of the foam-mat drying process. Coffee and tea are being compared industrially with the same products made in other ways and pilot quantities of pineapple, grape, and banana powders have been made (Morgan 1963). Reportedly, one plant in Peru is to dehydrate lime juice and a plant in Argentina is to prepare a powder of puree of beef stock by the foam-mat process.

Explosive Puffing

In the explosive puffing process, fruit or vegetable pieces are partially dehydrated in a conventional manner and then heated in a closed vessel having a quick-opening lid. When the water contained within the pieces is heated above its atmospheric boiling point and pressure has thereby been developed in the chamber, the pieces are instantly discharged. The flashing of water vapor from within each piece creates a porous structure that permits much faster dehydration and much more rapid rehydration of dried product (Eisenhardt et al. 1964; Eskew et al. 1963).

The rapid final dehydration by conventional means is important from the cost standpoint and the rapid rehydration important from the standpoint of convenience in product use. The process is estimated to increase commercial dehydration costs by 10-15%; however, rehydration time is much less than for conventionally dried products. For example, potato and carrot cubes of 3/8 x 1/2 x 1/2-in. size rehydrate in 5-6 min by simmering in water while conventional cubes require 30 min or more.

This technique is similar to that for producing puffed breakfast cereals which are "shot from guns." The puffing gun for fruits and vegetables (Eskew 1963) and the processing technology have been reported in a series of publications (Cording and Eskew 1962; Sullivan *et al.* 1963).

The puffing technique has several advantages for fruit and vegetable pieces. It is the first low-cost process that will produce relatively large pieces of de-hydrated fruits and vegetables which reconstitute rapidly

The explosive puffing process was first reported in 1961 (Eskew *et al.* 1961; Roberts 1961). Explosive puffing has been applied in pilot operations to sweet potatoes (Sullivan *et al.* 1963), carrots and beets (Copley *et al.* 1963), as well as to apple slices and blueberries (Cording 1963). Research is in progress on other items.

Laboratory panels have indicated potatoes and carrots have no off-taste when prepared by this process (Eisenhardt *et al.* 1962) and consumer panels have indicated blueberry muffins from quick-cooking blueberries were as acceptable as muffins using canned blueberries (Isidro *et al.* 1964). Possible applications in fruit and vegetable processing are numerous. The process is so new that detailed cost data are not available and extensive product testing has not been carried out. However, in early 1964, at least one commercial firm was offering quick-cooking carrots from the explosive puffing process.

Irradiation[6]

Irradiation involves the exposure of foods to certain ionizing radiations, namely either gamma or electrons. After the discovery of X-rays in 1895 and of radioactivity in 1896, there was a flurry of activity in studying the biological effects of these new forms of energy. The bactericidal effect of X-rays was observed as early as 1898. In 1909, a United States patent was obtained on killing beetles in tobacco by X-rays; and in 1930, a French patent was obtained on the preservation of foods by ionizing radiation.

In 1943, the first United States studies on irradiation of food were under-taken under the auspices of the Army Quartermaster Corps. While it has long been known that ionizing radiation can kill microorganisms, nearly all the re-search on food sterilization has been conducted since 1943 when larger sources of ionizing radiations started to become available through the U.S. Atomic Energy Commission. By 1947, it had been determined that the radiation preser-vation of food was theoretically feasible; however, at that time the largest source of Cobalt 60 in the world was capable of sterilizing only a few grams of meat a day.

During the 1950's, research on the irradiation of foods was conducted by nearly 150 different universities or organizations in the United States; many of these studies were under contract to the U.S. Army. Similarly, during the 1950's Canada, France, Germany, the United Kingdom, and Japan had begun to expand

---

[6]Credit for much of this review of irradiation is given to Dr. Walter M. Urbain, Dept. of Food Science, Michigan State University, E. Lansing, Mich.

their activities in this field (U.S. Dept. of Com. 1968A). By 1962, more than 4000 references were available about irradiation and radioactive contamination of foodstuffs (U.S. Dept. of Com. 1968B).

In 1968, work on food irradiation was reported in 76 countries. There are a number of research facilities for studying irradiation of foods in the United States, some in government installations such as the U.S. Army Natick Laboratories at Natick, Mass., and others in universities including a 50,000 curie Co^{60} source in the Food Science Department at Michigan State University.

Except for canning, invented approximately 150 yr ago, irradiation is the first really new food preservation method developed since the dawn of history. Many food products cannot be exposed to the high temperatures and pressures of thermal sterilization without suffering serious quality and nutritional losses. Irradiation is a sterilization without heat and avoids many of the problems encountered with heat. Foods sterilized by irradiation can be stored (if in a suitable package) at room temperature indefinitely.

The basis of the preservative action of radiation, in some cases, is the destruction of spoilage microorganisms such as bacteria, yeasts, and molds. Other organisms, such as insects and parasites, also can be destroyed. Fruits and vegetables are themselves living organisms. Radiation can interfere with the normal life processes of such foods and delay spoilage due to senescence. The delay of the ripening of green bananas and the inhibition of potato sprouting are examples of this radiation effect.

There have been problems with odors, flavors, and colors of irradiated foods. In some cases, ways to solve these problems have been found. For example, by irradiating at subfreezing temperatures good flavored sterilized beef has been produced. Food treated with relatively small amounts of radiation such as with pasteurizing doses, seldom exhibit these undesirable changes in sensory characteristics.

In the United States, the use of radiation on foods is controlled by the Food and Drug Administration and by the Dept. of Agr. These regulatory agencies have required proof of technical effect of the process and proof of the safety of the irradiated foods for human consumption. The extremely cautious attitude of the FDA towards any possible health hazard for consumers has required extensive tests including the feeding of animals. At the present time only two foods – potatoes and wheat – have been approved for irradiation.[7] Investigation of the safety of other foods is being carried out by the U.S. Army and the AEC.

Although there is little practical experience to indicate the cost to irradiate foods on a commercial basis, there are carefully developed estimates. The amount of radiation employed, the scale of the operation, the efficiency of the radiation source are principal cost factors. Figure 7.1 shows the irradiation costs in cents per pound as estimated by the U.S. Dept. of Com.

---

[7]Irradiated bacon was approved by the FDA in 1963 and subsequently withdrawn in 1969

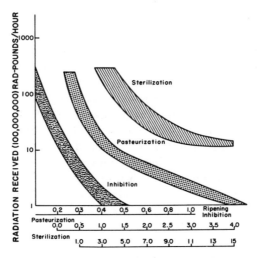

IRRADIATION COSTS, CENTS/ POUNDS

FIG. 7.1. COST OF IRRADIATION VERSUS
SOURCE CAPACITY FOR INHIBITION,
PASTEURIZATION, AND STERILIZATION

Irradiation at this time is not projected as a replacement to current processing techniques but as an additional food processing method. Studies have been conducted on irradiation in conjunction with current processing technologies. While there is no agreement on when irradiation of food might be approved by the FDA and when the process might become commercially and economically feasible in the United States, there is complete agreement that it is possible. Reportedly, at least three commercial-scale food irradiation facilities are in operation in Russia, and irradiated foods are being served on railroad cars and in restaurants in Russia (Josephson 1969).

Microwaves[8]

The use of microwaves represents the first radically different means of cooking or heating foods in centuries. All previous methods generate heat that penetrates a product from the outside. The food is in contact with or surrounded by solids (metal), liquids (water), or gas (air). These environments are at a much higher temperature than the food or its cooking temperature. Microwave cooking is characterized by its rapid, uniform heating throughout the mass, and selective heating of water or other polar molecules, allowing complete freedom from older, more restrictive means. As an example, a food material can now be cooked or heated while it is surrounded by cold air (Olson 1968).

Microwaves are a form of radio frequency energy generated by power tubes called magnetrons. They may be reflected, transmitted, or absorbed. Thus,

[8]Dr. L. E. Dawson, Food Science Dept., Michigan State University, E. Lansing, Mich., prepared this chapter section.

metals reflect; glass, paper, and plastics transmit; and foods absorb the energy and convert it to heat.

Microwaves are not really new, but their application to food heating and equipment development are new. The ability of high frequency electrical fields to heat or affect biological systems has been known since 1893 (Anon. 1965A). Food heating and cooking with microwaves really began in the 1940's following the radar developments of World War II; however, the first feasible microwave oven was not developed until in the early 1950's. Present equipment utilizes microwave frequencies around 915 or 2450 megacycles. These were assigned by the Federal Communications Commission for industry, science, and medical use, and most ovens for cooking, defrosting, or heating foods have been built to operate at these frequencies. Some foods, because of composition or physical size, are cooked more satisfactorily at one frequency than at another, and some applications may utilize both frequencies.

One precaution necessary with the use of microwave ovens is the need for nonmetallic food containers. Glass, pottery, paper, and plastic, including most of the new plastic dinnerware, are suitable for use with microwaves. The food, containing moisture, is thoroughly heated before the container becomes warm. Containers only become warm through conduction of heat from food, not from the microwave energy.

The first microwave ovens manufactured were designed similar in size and appearance to conventional ovens, and were proposed for home or restaurant use for quick preparation of foods. More recently, conveyorized units have been developed which can be tied in with a continuous processing operation, including the packaging and freezing. This allows maximum automation and labor saving, and has contributed much to the increased utilization of microwaves in the food processing industry.

Current microwave applications in the food industry include cooking, baking, heating, blanching, thawing, pasteurizing, puffing, and drying, or combinations of these. Today thousands of ovens are going to restaurants and vending markets, with an increasing number to industrial applications.

Cooking. – The largest single industrial installation (1968) in the world is in the food industry, where 20,000 lb of chickens can be cooked in 8 hr (Anon. 1966A). This installation uses a combination of steam and microwave energy to result in less loss of juice during cooking, and a more juicy and flavorful product. Chicken pieces are breaded after cooking, frozen, and packaged for distribution. This opens the way for different combinations of cooking methods, such as cooking in flexible packages, cooking after breading and browning, or cooking many other meat items.

Dehydration and Cooking. – The largest total volume of food processed by microwave energy is potato chips (Olson 1968). One problem in chip manufacture is the control of the browning reaction. Proper use of microwaves has allowed chips to be dried at a temperature low enough to avoid excessive browning. The trick is to remove chips from the cooking fat as soon as their moisture is down to 6%. Microwaves are then used to flash off excessive moisture to a 2% level. The temperature is kept below 250°F and a desirable light brown color is obtained. This method allows the use of potatoes which would turn dark brown in the conventional fryer.

Uniform, low moisture content of finished bakery foods such as biscuits and crackers can be accomplished with an electronic oven (Heppner *et al.* 1965). This process speeds up the final drying stages, resulting in controlled browning and crispness.

Microwave energy is also being used to reduce the drying time (up to 75%) for freeze-dried foods (Copson 1958; Copson and Decareau 1957). Products successfully freeze-dried with an assist from microwaves are raw and rare beef rib steaks, precooked haddock fillets, chicken breasts, raw shrimp, whole precooked lobster tails, and whole mushrooms (Decareau 1961).

Thawing and Heating. – One of the rapidly developing applications for microwaves in the food industry is in the area of institutional or restaurant use for heating quick-order meals or portions of meals.

The use of a microwave cooker offers special advantages for hotels and restaurants. Meal preparation time is lessened, since food can be precooked and frozen, if desired, and then just warmed before serving. This can be a great help during rush hours, especially where there is a labor shortage. In hospital kitchens, microwave cookers make it possible to provide a more varied menu for patients on low-fat diets, and are gaining acceptance and use for each of these purposes (Schmidt 1961).

Numerous vending machines are used in office buildings and industrial plants for rapid heating of lunch items, including soups, packaged meat sandwiches, and weiners. Soups can be packaged in hermetically-sealed plastic pouches or in cans, and heated in the pouch or in a supplemental container. Wrapped sandwiches, refrigerated until used, can be dispersed, placed in the oven for a specified short time, and thoroughly heated.

Other uses of microwaves in the food field include defrosting of frozen foods (Cathcart and Parker 1946; Pircon *et al.* 1953; Jason and Sanders 1962; Bengtsson 1963; Decareau 1964; Walter 1965), pasteurizing and mold control of foods (Cathcart *et al.* 1947; Bartholomew *et al.* 1948; Olson 1965), and in blanching vegetables (Hard and Ross 1956; Jeppon 1964).

Costs. – The fact that the product being processed is its own source of heat is a significant consideration in cooking efficiency. Removal of fully-cooked food from a cold microwave oven in slightly warm dishes still remains surprising. This lack of heating of the environments leads to cooking efficiencies (Pollack and Foin 1960).

Experience in British bakeries (biscuit and crackers) indicates that overall production costs are less when a dielectric oven is added to a gas-fired oven to boost capacity to lower the final moisture content. Most units have increased production from 15 to 50%. About 1/3 kw are needed to remove a pound of water in the short time the product is in the oven (Anon. 1965A).

In the chicken cooking installation in the United States where 20,000 lb per shift were continuously processed, it has been shown that capitalization of the facility can be amortized over a 3-yr period (Anon. 1966A). Savings in labor costs and increased yields were included in this calculation.

Aseptic Canning and Packaging[9]

Aseptic canning is a process in which the food is commercially sterilized outside the can or package, aseptically placed in previously sterilized containers that are then aseptically sealed. Aseptic canning permits passing the product through an efficient heat exchanger and bringing it to sterilization temperature within seconds as compared to minutes or hours when heated conventionally in the container. After sterilization, the product is rapidly cooled, using the same types of heat exchangers with refrigerants rather than steam (Martin 1948; Lewis and Bee 1967; Anon. 1969).

Initially, aseptic canning was only suitable for liquid foods or foods of thin consistency. However, by changing the heat exchanger and the pumps and lines leading to the aseptic canning line, chunk-type foods, such as chow mein, beef stew, or chicken a la king can be aseptically canned. With chunk-type foods direct steam injection heat exchangers are used to achieve rapid sterilization.

Great quantities of food materials, such as tomato purée or paste or apricot purée, are used in the production of further processed foods such as catsup or bakery products. It is expensive to package these in small containers. Aseptic processing permits these products to be quickly sterilized in efficient heat exchangers and aseptically packaged in 55-gal. drums. This technology has advanced to the point where commercially sterile food can be aseptically filled into previously sterilized tank cars.

Aseptic packaging is also being done in glass containers and in flexible packaging materials.

An aseptic bottling method for ultra high temperature (UHT) sterilized cream was recently put on a commercial basis. There are, however, some engineering problems related to glass breakage from thermal shock to be solved. Coffee cream is being packaged in single service paper packets in a continuous operation. With these less heat resistant packaging materials, chemicals, such as hydrogen peroxide, are combined with heat to make lower temperatures effective in sterilization.

Aseptic processing is being used in an increasingly wide range of commercial operations to provide high quality processed food products.

Osmotic Dehydration[10]

Osmosis is the process involving the movement of water through a semi-

---

[9] Dr. C. L. Bedford, Food Science Dept., Michigan State University, E. Lansing, Mich., prepared this chapter section.

[10] Dr. C. L. Bedford, Food Science Dept., Michigan State University, E. Lansing, Mich., prepared this chapter section.

permeable membrane from a dilute solution to a more concentrated solution until equilibrium is reached. The solute is unable to diffuse through the membrane in the reverse direction, or does so very slowly, so that the major result of this process is the transfer of water to the concentrated solution.

The transfer of water by osmosis is applicable to fruit pieces since they contain sugars and other solutes in dilute solution and their cellular structure acts as an effective semipermeable membrane.

Osmotic dehydration of fruit pieces involves immersing them in a concentrated solution of sugar or by tumbling them in dry sugar. The fruit is reduced to about 50% its initial weight, after which it is drained and either frozen or dried further in an air or vacuum drier (Ponting et al. 1966). It is usually not worthwhile to reduce the fruit weight more than 50% by osmotic dehydration because of the increased time required.

Osmotic dehydration has several advantages: (1) fruit is not subjected to a high temperature over an extended time so heat damage to color and flavor are minimized; (2) use of sugar or sugar syrup reduces loss of fresh fruit flavor; (3) discoloration by enzymatic oxidative browning is prevented by the syrup and eliminates the necessity of using high levels of sulfur dioxide in further drying; and (4) fruit acid content is lowered and this, combined with a slight increase in sugar content, provides a more pleasant dried product to use as a snack item or for incorporation into cereal flakes or pies.

There are some disadvantages. (1) It may not be desirable to reduce acidity. This can be corrected by adding fruit acid to the syrup bath. (2) A thin film of syrup is left on the fruit. If undesirable it may be removed by a quick rinse in water after osmotic dehydration. (3) Fruit dried to a very low moisture content may become rancid after a few weeks' storage at room temperature due to retention of flavor oils. In some fruits it may be necessary to add a fat antioxidant when the dried fruit is packaged. (4) The cost of osmotic drying plus air or vacuum drying is greater than the latter alone. It is, however, less expensive than freeze drying and has more fruit flavor than freeze-dried fruit.

This process is so new that detailed cost data are not available and extensive product testing has not been carried out. However, it appears to provide a means of producing a high quality, low moisture dried fruit.

Filled and Imitation Milk[11]

The substitution of milkfat with other fats and oils in certain dairy products has been done for several years. Notable examples are in frozen desserts, sterile concentrates, and spreads. Laws and regulations have played a role in the extent of manufacture of products of this type; consequently, some products may be purchased by consumers in one state and not in another. More recently the appearance of filled and imitation milks has occurred in retail stores in many

---

[11]A. L. Rippen, Dept. of Food Science, Michigan State University, E. Lansing, Mich., prepared this chapter section.

areas in the United States. The threat these products pose for the huge fluid milk market has caused understandable alarm in the dairy industry and is worthy of further discussion here.

State laws are not uniform in defining and labeling filled or imitation milks. Some states require that filled milk be labeled imitation milk while others require that no mention be made of milk at all in the label. In this discussion, filled milk refers to whole or low fat milk where the milkfat has been replaced with some other fat or oil. The Federal Filled Milk Act of 1923 specifies that the milk-solids-not-fat may be supplied in concentrated or dried form as well as fresh skim milk. Imitation milk contains no milk products as defined in the Filled Milk Act, but is produced in semblance of milk with ingredients from a variety of sources some of which may be derived from milk. Interstate shipment of filled milk is prohibited by federal law; however, no such barrier exists for imitation milk.

The fat used in both filled and imitation milks is usually hydrogenated coconut fat (Brink *et al.* 1969). The property of bland flavor stability during processing and marketing makes coconut fat a good natural fat for these products.

Flavor stability appears to be related, in part, to the extent a fat is saturated. Coconut fat is a highly saturated fat with an iodine number of 8.7 (Severn 1964). This compares with a 32.9 value for milkfat. Several more highly unsaturated fats have been tried, mostly experimentally, but have often resulted in a finished product with an unacceptable flavor. A lightly hydrogenated soybean oil (iodine No. 118) has, however, demonstrated in filled milk formulations to be sufficiently stable in flavor to warrant its consideration for use in filled and imitation milks (Modler 1969).

In the processing of filled and imitation milks homogenization is commonly employed. Emulsification of the fat is usually necessary to obtain a homogeneous product without oil separation. The type of emulsifier used has an influence on the products' flavor stability. More highly saturated emulsifying agents such as certain mono- and diglycerides have shown greater effectiveness in extending product shelf-life with respect to flavor.

Many formulations are possible, particularly with imitation milk where a number of combinations of edible food products are possible. In addition to the basic ingredients which supply the fat, protein, and carbohydrates, several vitamins and minerals may be added to enhance nutritive value. The Food and Drug Administration has proposed that imitation milk meet minimum nutritional standards or clearly show on the label "below standard in quality" and name the deficiency. The FDA proposes that an 8-oz serving of imitation milk contain a minimum of some essential nutrients as follows:

Nutrient	Amount
Protein (biological value equivalent to casein)	8.5 gm
Calcium	290 mg
Phosphorous	220 mg

Vitamin A	375 USP units
Riboflavin	0.40 mg
Optionally, Vitamin D, when added not less than	100 USP units

When whole milk contains so many nutrients and other characteristics, it presents a big challenge for anyone attempting to imitate the product completely. Analyses of several imitation milks marketed in recent years have shown them to be generally inferior nutritionally when compared with whole milk. Some imitation milks, however, contain as much or more of a given nutrient than the quantity found in milk. Analyses of selected samples of commercial imitation milk and filled milk have been compared with whole milk (Natl. Dairy Council 1968) and are shown in Table 7.8.

Imitation milk is quite often fortified by the addition of vitamins A, D, and riboflavin. The common ingredients listed include water, corn syrup solids, vegetable fat, sodium caseinate, potassium, phosphate, salt, carrageenin, polysorbate 60, iron, artificial color, and flavor. Sometimes sorbic acid has been added at a rate not exceeding 1/10 of 1.0%. Occasionally iodine is added. Up to the present time, most commercial imitation milks appear to be deficient in protein and calcium when compared to whole milk, probably their most serious nutritional shortcoming. Improvements in flavor and protein technology will undoubtedly result in the incorporation of larger quantities of calcium and protein in the future.

The economics of filled and imitation milks offer serious consideration for processors and consumers. Moede (1968) has prepared cost figures for filled and imitation milks (Tables 7.9 and 7.10) using selected ingredients and prices.

At present price levels the filled and imitation milk ingredient cost is substantially lower than fluid whole milk in many U.S. markets. Pricing on the basis of class utilization for milk-solids-not-fat can, however, have a significant effect on ingredient cost, especially in filled milk. Pricing at the Class I level raises the cost when compared with the market price for nonfat dry solids.

Some consumers have indicated they will buy products prepared in semblance of whole fluid milk (Hetrick 1969). Price differentials and flavor and nutritional properties remain as important factors, however, in influencing consumer acceptance of the milk substitutes.

Cryogenic Freezing[12]

Cryogenic freezing methods utilize liquified or solidified gases (cryogens) and have boiling points of about $-100°F$ or colder (Rasmussen 1969) to achieve extremely rapid food freezing. Just as there is disagreement on the exact meaning of terms such as "sharp," "quick," "rapid" or "ultrarapid", and "slow" freezing (Fennema and Powrie 1964) so are there some differences of opinion on

---

[12]Dr. T. Wishnetsky, Dept. of Food Science, Michigan State University, E. Lansing, Mich., prepared this chapter section.

TABLE 7.8

ANALYSES OF SELECTED SAMPLES OF WHOLE, FILLED, AND
IMITATION MILKS

Nutrient	Whole Milk	No. 1	Filled Milk No. 2	No. 3	Imitation Milk
Fat (gm/100 gm)	3.420	3.775	3.125	3.365	3.685
Nonfat solids (gm/100 gm)	8.885	10.215	9.130	8.840	8.085
Protein (gm/100 gm)	3.380	4.085	3.365	3.080	0.880
Carbohydrate (gm/100 gm)	4.795	5.265	4.935	5.025	6.700
Calcium (mg/100 gm)	125.500	148.500	143.000	117.000	23.850
Phosphorous (mg/100 gm)	99.500	114.500	102.500	94.500	14.250
Vitamin A (USP units/qt)	447.000	none	1195.000	none	4010.000
Riboflavin (mg/qt)	0.725	0.790	0.860	0.755	none

Source: Natl. Dairy Council (1968).

TABLE 7.9

COST FIGURES FOR FILLED MILK

Ingredient	Percent of Finished Product	Unit Price per Lb ($)	Estimated Ingredient Cost per 1/2 Gal. (¢)
Nonfat dry milk	9.66	0.21	8.72
Vegetable oil	3.00	0.17	2.13
Emulsifier and stabilizer base	0.23	3.00	2.75
Total solids	12.89		13.60
Water	87.11		0.01
Total	100.00		13.61

Source: Moede (1968).

TABLE 7.10

COST FIGURES FOR HYPOTHETICAL IMITATION MILK

Ingredient	Percent of Finished Product	Unit Price per Lb (¢)	Estimated Cost per 100 Lb ($)
Fat (coconut oil)	3.00	21.0	0.630
Protein (soy protein isolate)	3.50	37.0	1.332
Emulsifier (sorbitan monostearate)	1.00	40.5	0.405
Buffer (disodium phosphate)	0.25	9.0	0.0225
Stabilizer (carrageenan)	0.15	165.0	0.248
Body agent (corn syrup solids)	3.50	8.0	0.280
Sweetener (sugar)	1.00	10.8	0.108
Water	87.60		
Total	100.00		3.0255
Approximate ingredient cost per 1/2 gal.			0.13

Source: Moede (1968).

the choice of -100°F as the temperature boundary between cryogenic and noncryogenic processes and materials. For purposes of this discussion, however, the above definition is satisfactory.

Liquid nitrogen (boiling point -320°F) and comminuted Dry Ice or Dry Ice snow (sublimation point -109°F) are the only cryogens currently being used commercially for food freezing. Some of the early experimental work on cryogenic freezing systems involved the use of liquified nitrous oxide (boiling point -127°F). However, the commercialization of nitrous oxide for food freezing applications has not taken place, largely for economic reasons.

Brown (1968) reported that in 1966 there were about 35 cryogenic freezing installations in the United States. Estimates in 1969 indicate that this number has increased to about 100. Most commercially successful cryogenic operations thus far have involved products of animal origin (i.e., beef, fish, seafood, and poultry). To a lesser extent (in terms of quantities frozen), many other products are being successfully processed in cryogenic systems, including bakery products, pizzas, onion rings, and commissary items.

Cryogenic food freezing was in its commercial infancy during the early 1960's. During this period, some erroneous ideas took hold concerning the capabilities of cryogenic systems for freezing "unfreezables," tomatoes being the prime example. Inaccuracies resulted, in part from irresponsible advertising by segments of the industrial gas industry and in part probably from the tendency of the lay press to exaggerate benefits of any new technology. Actually, tomatoes and other fruits susceptible to serious textural damage during freezing and thawing cannot yet be frozen successfully, though future technological developments may make this possible.

Brown (1968) had described the major advantages of cryogenic freezing over mechanical refrigeration systems. He stresses the fact that reduced dehydration during freezing can mean higher production yields for products such as shrimp and that consequent savings may equal or exceed the entire cost of freezing. Also included in his review are descriptions of typical liquid nitrogen freezing tunnels and of the thermodynamic and mechanical principles involved in such systems.

In terms of capital investment, a cryogenic freezing system is substantially cheaper than a mechanical system providing comparable production capacity. However, the unit cost of liquid nitrogen (or other cryogen) and the quantity of cryogen required to freeze the food are, in the long run, the major cost factors to be considered in a cryogenic system. Rasmussen (1967, 1969) has discussed cost factors involved in cryogenic freezing and compared costs of liquid nitrogen and air-blast freezing. His calculations show a substantially higher cost for the liquid nitrogen method.

Some of the factors tending to lower the cost of a cryogenic freezing operation are: (1) Large-scale usage of liquid nitrogen (since unit price of liquid nitrogen drops sharply with increased rate of usage). Hence, a processor having a large scale operation has an inherent price advantage over a processor requiring smaller quantities. Economies in liquid nitrogen storage and utilization also tend to favor the large user. (2) Close proximity to a liquid nitrogen manufacturing facility (since cost of transport and in-transit loss of product contribute significantly to overall product cost). (3) Year-round rather than seasonal operation (since liquid nitrogen for a relatively short, seasonal operation generally costs more than that for a much smaller usage on a year-round basis). (4) Freezing tunnel design that permits efficient heat transfer and maximum utilization of refrigeration capacity of the liquid nitrogen.

Improvements in product quality (e.g., texture, color, flavor, reduced drip loss) directly attributable to the faster freezing capability of cryogenic systems vary considerably from one product to another. Even for those products mentioned earlier as having had the greatest degree of commercial success (beef, fish, etc.), there are still differences of opinion among scientists as to degree of quality improvement and conditions under which such improvements occur. The subject has been explored by Tressler (1968) and by Fennema and Powrie (1964). The latter review is the most comprehensive treatment available of the subject. Among other things, the authors point out that product damage during thawing may, in some cases, wipe out the advantages gained through cryogenic freezing.

Since cryogenic freezing systems have not yet stood the test of time, the best way, usually, for an individual processor to gage their merit for his own product(s) is to: (1) Obtain preliminary cost figures for both equipment and cryogen from several suppliers. (2) Attempt to balance the difference in freezing cost between cryogenic and other available systems against the anticipated benefits (e.g., reduced dehydration. lowered labor costs, space advantages, higher selling price through improved quality, and other miscellaneous processing advantages). (3) If results of (1) and (2) above are favorable, obtain proposals from several suppliers relating to equipment costs, cost of liquid nitrogen, estimated quantity of liquid nitrogen required per pound of product frozen under specified conditions of use and the terms of whatever guarantees they are willing to provide. (4) Arrange for a one-month or several-month lease of equipment to verify the anticipated merits of the system and to obtain a reasonably reliable estimate of processing cost under practical, in-plant, conditions of use. (5) If satisfied with results of (4), negotiate terms of equipment purchase and long-term liquid nitrogen supply contracts.

Immersion freezing methods utilizing brine, propylene glycol, and ethylene glycol have been used commercially for many years. More recently, an immersion freezing system has been developed that utilizes Freon 12, an FDA-approved chlorinated fluorocarbon having a boiling point of $-22°F$. Strictly speaking, this is not a cryogenic process because of the higher-than-cryogenic temperature of the freezant. Nevertheless, it appears to be comparable in terms of product freezing rates and therefore should be able to offer advantages comparable to those of a cryogenic system. Much will probably depend upon processing cost which has been claimed (Lawler and Trauberman 1969) to be less than 1¢ per lb of food frozen in a large-scale operation. Until the system is more fully tested under commercial conditions, the validity of these cost estimates cannot be judged but they are substantially lower than those achieved by existing cryogenic methods.

BIBLIOGRAPHY

ANON. 1952. London freeze dry symposium. Food Eng. Jan., 44-46.
ANON. 1954. Speed-dried heat sensitive liquids. Food Eng. 26, No. 1, 36.
ANON. 1955. Superior dehydrated juices from continuous vacuum process. Food Eng. 27, No. 3, 71.
ANON. 1961A. Food Field Rept., June.
ANON. 1961B. The accelerated freeze drying method of food preservation. Gr. Brit. Min. Agr. Fisheries Food 169. H. M. Stationery Office, London.
ANON. 1963. Marketing facilities for grain and tuberous crops – Brazil. Weitz-Hettelsater Engrs., Kansas City.
ANON. 1965A. High frequency heating grains. Food Eng. 37, No. 11, 62-63.
ANON. 1965B. World's Fair taste tests Awake. CMCR, San Francisco.
ANON. 1966A. Microwave oven with steam atmosphere produces higher quality, more profitable precooked chicken. Food Process.-Marketing 27, No. 4, 92-96, 100.
ANON. 1966B. Studies of organization and competition in grocery manufacturing. Natl. Comm. Food Marketing Tech. Study 6.
ANON. 1967A. Proteins grow on high-purity alkanes. Chem. Eng. News 45, 46-48.
ANON. 1967B. Basic research, applied research and development in industry, 1965. Natl. Sci. Found. NSF 67-12.
ANON. 1968. Vegetable protein item billed as 'New Food' in first test. Marketing Insights, Oct. 28.
ANON. 1969. A Complete Course in Canning. The Canning Trade, Baltimore.
ACETO, N. C., ESKEW, R. K., and PHILLIPS, G. W. M. 1953. High density full flavor cherry juice concentrates. Glass Packer 32, 54.
ACETO, N. S., SINNAMON, H. I., SCHOPPET, E. F., and ESKEW, R. K. 1962. Continuous vacuum drying of whole milk foam. J. Dairy Sci. 45, 501-507.
ACETO, N. E., et al. 1963. Requirements and costs for preserve essence equipment. Glass Packer 32, No. 1, 23-25, 56, 58.
BARTHOLOMEW, J. W., HARRIS, R. G., and SUSSEX, F. 1948. Electronic preservation of Boston Brown Bread. Food Technol. 2, No. 2, 91-94.
BENGTSSON, N. 1963. Electronic defrosting meat and fish at 35 and 2450 MCS – a laboratory comparison. Food Technol. 17, No. 10, 94-100.
BIRD, K. 1963A. A directory of freeze drying: food processors, equipment firms and others. Econ. Res. Serv. Rept. F-D 4, U.S. Dept. Agr., Washington, D.C.
BIRD, K. 1963B. Freeze drying of foods: cost projections. U.S. Dept. Agr. M.R.R. 639, Washington, D.C.
BIRD, K., ARTHUR, H., and GOLDBERG, R. 1968. The technological front in the food and fiber economy. Harvard Business School, June.
BISSETT, O. W., et al. 1963. Foam-mat dried orange juice. I. Time-temperature drying studies. Food Technol. 17, No. 2, 92-95.
BLACK, W. E., and POLOPOLUS, L. 1966. Synthetics and substitutes in the Florida citrus industry. In Synthetics and Substitutes for Agricultural Commodities. Publ. 1, Univ. Florida, Gainesville.
BOGGS, M. M., and TALBURT, W. F. 1952. Comparison of frozen and dehydro-frozen peas with fresh and stored pod peas. Food Technol. 4, 438-442.
BONNELL, J.M., STRASHUN, S. I., and DORSEY, W. R. 1955. Commercial production of orange and grapefruit crystals. Florida State Hort. Soc., 114-116.
BOYTON, J. A., DWOSKIN, P. B., and ROBERT, S. A. 1951. New concentrated apple juice – its appeal to consumers. Bur. Agr. Econ., U.S. Dept. Agr., Washington, D.C.

BRINK, M. F., BALSKY, M., and SPECKMAN, E. W. 1969. Nutritional value of milk compared with filled and imitation milks. Am. J. Clin. Nutr. 22, No. 2, 168-180.

BROWN, D. C. 1968. The application of cryogenic fluids to the freezing of foods, Vol. 13. In Advances in Cryogenic Engineering, K. D. Timmerhaus (Editor). Plenum Press, New York.

BURTON, L. V. 1947. High vacuum technique used for drying orange juice. Food Ind. 19, 617-622, 738, 740, 742, 744.

BUZZELL, R. D., and NOURSE, R. E. M. 1966. Product innovation, the product life cycle and competitive behavior in selected food processing industries, 1947-1964. Rept. to the Natl. Comm. Food Marketing. Arthur D. Little, Acorn Park, Mass., Feb.

CAMPBELL, W. L., PROCTOR, B. E., and SLUDER, J. C. 1945. Research reports on quartermaster contract projects. Food Technol. Lab., Massachusetts Inst. Technol., Cambridge, Mass.

CATHCART, W. H., and PARKER, J. J. 1946. Defrosting frozen foods by high-frequency heat. Food Res. 11, 341-344.

CATHCART, W. H., PARKER, J. J., and BEATTIE, H. G. 1947. The treatment of packaged bread with high-frequency heat. Food Technol. 1, 174-177.

CLAFFEY, J. B., ESKEW, R. K., and DRAZGA, F. H. 1961. Estimated costs and equipment for commercial production of potato flakelets. U.S. Dept. Agr., Agr. Res. Serv., ARS 73-36.

CLEMENT, W. E. 1960. Consumer prices and processed food. Talk at 15th Ann. Food and Nutr. Inst., Tuskegee Inst., Alabama.

COPLEY, M. J. 1957. The outlook for freezing and dehydrofreezing in food preservations. Res. paper Am. Soc. Refrig. Engr., Chicago.

COPLEY, M. J., ESKEW, R. K., SULLIVAN, J. F., and EISENHARDT, N. H. 1963. Quick-cooking dehydrated vegetables – carrots and beets. Food Eng. 35, No. 6, 52-55.

COPSON, D. A. 1958. Microwave sublimation of foods. Food Technol. 12, No. 6, 270-272.

COPSON, D. A., and DECAREAU, R. V. 1957. Microwave energy in freeze-drying procedures. Food Res. 22, 402-403.

CORDING, J., JR. 1963. Explosive puffing dehydration of fruits and vegetables. Eastern Util. Res. Develop. Div., Agr. Res. Serv., U.S. Dept Agr. Proc. Eastern Expt. Sta. Collaborators Conf. Food Process. Tech., Oct.

CORDING, J., JR. and ESKEW, R. K. 1962. Method of control of texture of dehydrated potatoes. U.S. Pat. 3,038,813.

CORDING, J., JR., SULLIVAN, J. F., and ESKEW, R. K. 1959. Potato flakes: a new form of dehydrated mashed potatoes. IV. Effects of cooling after precooking. U.S. Dept. Agr., Agr. Res. Serv. ARS 73-25.

CORDING, J., JR., WILLARD, M. J., ESKEW, R. K., and EDWARDS, P. W. 1954. Potato flakes: a new form of dehydrated mashed potatoes. I. Pilot-plant process using double drum dried. U.S. Dept. Agr., Agr. Res. Serv. ARS 73-2.

CORDING, J., JR., et al. 1955. Potato flakes: a new form of dehydrated mashed potatoes. II. Some factors influencing texture. U.S. Dept. Agr., Agr. Res. Serv. ARS 73-9.

CORDING, J., JR., WILLARD, M. J., ESKEW, R. K., and SULLIVAN, J. F. 1957. Advances in the dehydration of mashed potatoes by the flake process. Food Technol. 9, 236.

CORKERN, R. S., and POATS, F. 1968. Synthetics and agricultural substitutes in food and nonfood markets. Marketing and Transportation Situation, U.S. Dept. Agr., Nov.

CORRIDON, G. A. 1963. Freeze drying of foods, a list of selected references. Natl. Agr. Library, Library List 77, U.S. Dept. Agr., Washington, D.C.

CROSS, J. A., and GEMMILL, A. V. 1948. Revolutionary evaporator raises quality and lowers cost. Food Ind. 20, 1421-1423.

DAY, E. A. 1967. The Impact of Synthetic Flavors on Agriculture. Conf. New Foods, Flavors, and Analogs. Cornell Univ., Ithaca, N.Y., Apr. 24-25.

DECAREAU, R. V. 1961. How microwaves speed freeze-drying. Food Eng. 33, No. 8, 34-36.

DECAREAU, R. V. 1964. Microwave defrosting and heating. Cornell Hotel Restaurant Quart. 5, No. 1, 76-78.

DECOSSAS, L. M., et al. 1962. Today's food plant costs – to build, equip, operate. Good Eng. 34, No. 4, 82-85.

DEOBALD, H. J. 1961. Progress report on U.S.D.A.'s instant sweet potato puree. Food Process. *22*, No. 6, 76-78.

DEOBALD, H. J. *et al.* 1962. Pre-cooked dehydrated sweet potato flakes. U.S. Dept. Agr., Agr. Res. Serv., *ARS 72-23.*

DWOSKIN, P. B. 1963. Market test of instant sweet potatoes in selected institutional outlets. U.S. Dept. Agr., *M.R.R. 580.*

DWOSKIN, P. B., and JACOBS, M. 1957. Potato flakes – a new form of dehydrated mashed potatoes; market position and consumer acceptance. U.S. Dept. Agr., *M.R.R. 186.*

EISENHARDT, N. H., CORDING, J., JR., ESKEW, R. K., and SULLIVAN, J. F. 1962. Quick-cooking dehydrated vegetable pieces. Food Technol. *16*, No. 5, 143-156.

ESKEW, R. K. 1949. Freeze Drying. Reinhold Publishing Corp., New York.

ESKEW, R. K. 1952. 7-fold concentrate. Chemurgic Dig. *II*, 24.

ESKEW, R. K. 1953. Recent development in the recovery of volatile fruit concentrate. Proc. 44th Ann. Meeting Flavoring Extract Mfr. Assoc., May 11-13.

ESKEW, R. K. 1963. Vacuum foam drying. Proc. Conf. Food Processing Techniques, Eastern Util. Res. Develop. Div., A.R.S., U.S. Dept. Agr., Philadelphia, Oct. 22-23.

ESKEW, R. K., and PHILLIPS, G. W. M. 1954. Apple juice from super-concentrate is preferred. Glass Packer, March.

ESKEW, R. K., CORDING, J., JR., and EISENHARDT, N. H. 1961. Dehydrated fruit and vegetable products capable of rapid rehydration. U.S. Dept. Agr., Agr. Res. Serv. Correspondence Aid *C.A.–E-27*, May.

ESKEW, R. K., CORDING, J., JR., and SULLIVAN, J. F. 1963. A gun for the explosive puffing of fruits and vegetables. Food Eng. *35*, No. 4, 91-92.

ESKEW, R. K., HOMILLER, R. P., and PHILLIPS, G. W. M. 1951. Process for making frozen concentrated fruit juices. U.S. Pat. 2,573,699. Nov. 6.

ESKEW, R. K., REDFIELD, C. S., and PHILLIPS, G. W. M. 1951. High density, full flavor apple juice concentrate. U.S. Dept. Agr., *AIC-315*, Aug.

ESKEW, R. K., PHILLIPS, G. W. M., HOMILLER, R. P., and EISENHARDT, N. H. 1950. Superior juice concentrate – yet only a single pass. Food Ind. *22*, 60-61.

ESKEW, R. K. *et al.* 1951. Frozen concentrated apple juice. Ind. Eng. Chem. *43*, 2397.

ESKEW, R. K. *et al.* 1952. High density full flavor grape juice concentrate. U.S. Dept. Agr., *AIC-342*, Sept.

ESKEW, R. K. *et al.* 1955. Potato flakes: a new form of dehydrated mashed potatoes. III. Estimated commercial cost. U.S. Dept. Agr., Agr. Res. Serv. *ARS 73-12.*

ESKEW, R. K. *et al.* 1960. Potato flakes of increased density. U.S. Dept. Agr., Agr. Res. Serv. *ARS 73-30.*

FENNEMA, O., and POWRIE, W. D. 1964. Fundamentals of low temperature food preservation. *In* Advances in Food Research, C. O. Chichester *et al.* (Editors). Academic Press, New York.

FIXARI, F. W., CONLEY, W., and BARD, G. 1959. Continuous high vacuum drying techniques. Food Technol. *3*, 217.

FIXARI, F. W., CONLEY, W., and VIALL, G. K. 1957. Continuous vacuum dehydration reduces costs. Chem. Eng. Progress *53*, No. 3, 110.

FLOSDORF, E. W. 1945A. Desiccation of citrus fruit juices. U.S. Pat. 2,380,036.

FLOSDORF, E. W. 1945B. Drying by sublimation. Food Ind. *17*, No. 1, 22-25, 98, 100, 102, 104, 106, 108.

FOX, S. W. 1963. The outlook for synthetic foods. Food Technol. *17*, No. 4, 22-26, Apr.

FRENCH, B. C. 1958. Some economic aspects of pie consumption. Michigan State Univ. Agr. Expt. Sta. Quart. Bull. *28*, No. 3, 41-53.

GINNETTE, L. F., GRAHAM, R. P., and MORGAN, A. I. 1960. Process of dehydrating foams. Pat. 2,981,629.

GRAF, R. L. 1961. Present status of freeze-dried foods for the military. Res. Develop. Assoc., Food Container Inst. Action Rept. *13*, No. 14, 181-185.

GREIG, W. S. 1957. The restaurant, hotel and institutional market for dehydrated mashed potatoes. Michigan State Univ. Agr. Econ. Mimeo *691.*

GREIG, W. S. 1964. Quality competition and product development. *In* Agricultural Market Analysis, V. L. Sorenson (Editor). Bur. Business Econ. Res., Michigan State Univ., East Lansing, Mich.

GREIG, W. S. 1967. The restaurant, hotel and institutional market for dehydrated mashed potatoes. Michigan State Univ. Agr. Econ. Rept. *691*.

GREIG, W. S. 1968A. Balance sheets, income statements and financial operating ratios for the food processing industry, 1965-1966. Michigan State Univ. Agr. Econ. Rept. *117*.

GREIG, W. S. 1968B. Consumer images of sugar and synthetic sweeteners. Michigan State Univ. Agr. Expt. Sta. Res. Bull. *18*.

GREIG, W. S., BEDFORD, C. L., and LARZELERE, H. E. 1962. Consumer preference among apple varieties in fresh and processed forms. Michigan State Univ. Agr. Expt. Sta. Quart. Bull. *44*, No. 3, 505-526.

GREIG, W. S., GRANT, M. E., and LARZELERE, H. E. 1960. The effects of methods of freezing apple slices on consumer preference for pies. Michigan State Univ. Agr. Expt. Sta. Quart. Bull. *42*, No. 4, 929-935.

GREIG, W. S., and LARZELERE, H. E. 1957. Consumer preferences among dehydrated mashed potato products. Natl. Potato Council News *5*, No. 2.

GREIG, W. S., STRAND, F. O., and LARZELERE, H. E. 1958. Relative retail sales and elasticity of demand for dehydrated mashed potato products. Michigan State Univ. Agr. Econ. Mimeo *723*.

GREIG, W. S., and STUCKMAN, N. W. 1960. Market potentials for dehydrofrozen and dehydrocanned apple slices. Michigan State Univ. Agr. Econ. Mimeo

GRIFFIN, E. L., TOLLEY, F. B., and HELLER, M. E. 1947. Comparison of the essences from nine varieties of apples Fruit Products J. , and Am. Food Manufacturer *27*, 4-5.

HANDY, C. 1968. Unpublished Ph.D. data, Cornell University.

HANRAHAN, F. P., and WEBB, B. H. 1961. U.S.D.A. develops foam-spray drying. Food Eng. *33*, 37-38.

HANRAHAN, F. P., TOMSMA, A., FOX, K. K., and PALLANSCH, M. J. 1962. Production and properties of spray-dried whole milk foam. Dairy Sci. *35*, No. 1, 27-31.

HARD, MARGARET McG., and ROSS, E. 1956. Dielectric scalding of spinach, peas and snap beans for freezing preservation. Food Technol. *10*, No. 6, 241-244.

HARP, H. H., and MILLER, M. E. 1965. Convenience foods: the relationship between sales volume and factors influencing demand. Dept. Agr., Agr. Econ. Rep. *81*, Aug.

HARRIS, R. G., and DWOSKIN, P. B. 1958. Convenience foods and their costs to consumers. The marketing and transportation situation. U.S. Dept. Agr. AMS, Aug.

HARTMAN, W. E. 1967. Meat-like products from plant sources. Presented at Conf. on New Foods, Flavors, and Analogs, Cornell Univ., Ithaca, N. Y. Apr. 24-25.

HAYES, N. V., COTTON, R. H., and ROY, W. R. 1946. Problems in the dehydration of orange juice. Proc. Am. Soc. Hort. Sci. *47*, 123-129.

HEID, J. L., and KELLY, E. J. 1953. The concentration and dehydration of citrus juices. Canner *117*, No. 5, 9-13, 21-22, 24, 26-27, 30, 32; No. 6, 13-15, 18,33.

HENDEL, C. E. 1959. Dehydrated mashed potatoes-potato granules. *In* Potato Processing, 2nd Edition, W. J. Talburt, and Ora Smith (Editors). Avi Publishing Co., Westport, Conn.

HEPPNER, W., RABINSKY, R. THORBURY, T., and ROBE, K. 1965. Crisper crackers without scorching. Food Process. Marketing *26*, No. 10, 186-187.

HETRICK, J. H. 1969. Consumer attitudes toward the use of filled milk. Dairy Marketing Facts *A E 4205*, Coop. Ext. Serv. Univ. Illinois, Urbana.

HEYMAN, W. A. 1943. Porous expanded citrus fruit products. U.S. Pat. 2,328,544.

HIEMSTRA, S. J. 1968. Food consumption, prices and expenditures. U.S. Dept. Agr. ERS Agr. Econ. Rept. *138*, July.

HOFFMAN, A. C. 76th Contress. Large-scale organization in the food industries, TNEC Monogram *35*, 76th Congress, 3rd Session.

HOMILLER, R. P., and EISENHARDT, N. H. 1951. Process for the preparation of full-flavored fruit concentrates. U.S. Pat. 2,572,846.

HOMILLER, R. P., and GRIFFIN, E. L., Jr. 1949. Process for the production of apple esssence. U.S. Pat. 2,479,745.

HOOVER, S. R. 1967. Petroleum and other chemical sources of food. Presented at Conf. on new foods, flavors and analogs. Cornell Univ., Ithaca, N. Y. Apr. 24-25.

HUNTER, J. S. 1959. Consumer preference for a 6 to 1 apple juice concentrate. U.S. Dept. Agr. Marketing Res. Rept. *343*.

ISIDRO, D. S., GREIG, W. S., BEDFORD, C. L., and LARZELERE, H. E. 1964. Consumer preference tests for dehydrofreezing and explosive-puffing of blueberries. Michigan State Univ. Agr. Expt. Sta. Res. Rept. *20*.

IVES, J. R. 1966. Synthetics and substitutes for agricultural commodities – meat and by-products. *In* Synthetics and Substitutes for Agricultural Commodities, Publ. *1*, Univ. Florida, Gainsville.

JASON, A. C., and SANDERS, H. R. 1962. Dielectric thawing of fish. I. Experiments with frozen herrings. Food Technol. *16*, No. 6, 101-112.

JEPPON, M. R. 1964. Techniques of continuous microwave food processing. Cornell Hotel & Restaurant Admin. Quart. *5*, 60-64.

JOHNSON, M. J. 1966. Growth of microbial cells on hydrocarbons. Science *155*, 1515.

JOSEPHSON, E. S. 1969. Food irradiations. U.S. Army Natick Laboratories quoted in Supermarket News, Febr. 10.

KAUFMAN, V. F., and POWERS, M. J. 1957. How dehydrofreezing cuts packaging, shipping costs on processed fruit. Food Eng. *29*, No. 1, 93-96.

KAUFMAN, V. F., MIMO, C. C., and WALKER, L. H. 1950. Frozen apple juice concentrate: application of laboratory data to prospective commercial operations. U.S. Dept. Agr., Agr. Res. Serv. *AIC 293*.

KAUFMAN, V. F., WONG, F. F., TAYLOR, D. H., and TALBURT, W. F. 1955. Problems in the production of tomato juice powder by vacuum. Food Technol. *27*, No. 9, 120.

KELLY, E. J. 1949. New low-temperature evaporator doubles plant production. Food Ind. *21*, No. 10, 76-79.

KOLODNY, R. M. 1962. Freeze drying in Europe today. Food Process. *23*, No. 9L, 38-40.

LAWLER, F. K. 1962. Foam-mat drying goes to work. Food Eng. *34*, No. 2, 68.

LAWLER, F. K., and TRAUBERMAN, L. 1969. What to know about freon freezing. Food Eng. *41*, 67-72.

LEE, F. H. 1962. The new future for dehydrated foods. Res. Develop. Assoc., Food Container Inst. Action Rept. *14*, No. 1, 44-51.

LEGER, R. R. 1969. It's an ill wind . . . ban on cyclamates is boon for other sweeteners. Wall Street J., Nov. 14.

LEWIS, L. D., and BEE, G. R. 1967. New developments in heat processing. Equipment Canning Trade *89*, No. 17. 6-9.

MacDOUGALL, D. B. 1961. The formulation and development of composite precooked dehydrated foods. Food Process. Packaging *30*, No. 352, 3-10.

MAGLE, J. L. 1966. Food companies push new items. New York Times, Jan. 23.

MARTIN, W. M. 1948. Flash process, asceptic fill are used in new canning unit. Food Ind. *20*, 832-834.

McBRIDE, G. 1968. Substitute dairy products. Michigan State Univ. Dept. Agr. Econ., Mimeo Rept.

McFARLANE, V. H. 1961. Products from moist type sweet potatoes with special emphasis on pre-cooked dehydrated sweet potato flakes. Talk given at the first Natl. Sweet Potato Ind. Meeting, Richmond, Va.

McGRATH, E. J., and KERR, H. W., Jr. 1963. Dehydrofrozen apple slices – their potential in selected markets. U.S. Dept. Agr. Market Res. Rept. *578*.

McGRATH, E. J. and SILLS, M. S. 1957. Restaurant acceptance of dehydrofrozen peas. U.S. Dept. Agr. Market Res. Rept. *198*.

McGRATH, E. J., and WEIDENHAMER, M. 1963. The market potentials for superconcentrated apple juice. U.S. Dept. Agr. Market Res. Rept. *582*

MEES, C. E. K., and LEERMAKERS, J. A. 1950. The Organization of Scientific Research. McGraw-Hill Book Co., New York.

MEYER, R. I., and JOKAY, L. 1959. Application of lyophilization to cheese products. J. Dairy Sci. *42*, No. 5, 908.

MILLEVILLE, H. P. and ESKEW, R. K. 1946. Recovery of volatile apple flavors in essence form. Western Canner Packer *38*, 51-54.

MODLER, H. W. 1969. Physical and chemical stability of soybean oil filled milk. M.S. Thesis, Dept. Food Sci., Michigan State Univ., East Lansing, Mich.

MOEDE, H. H. 1968. Costs, sales, and the market for filled and imitation dairy products. Milk Dealer *57*, No. 6, 14-16.

MOORE, E. L. *et al.* 1945. The concentrating and drying of citrus juices, Processing and Institutional Food Tech., 160-168.

MORGAN, A. I., Jr. 1962. Present status of foam-mat drying produces good instant powders from liquid foods cheaply. Food Process. *23*, No. 12, 56-57.

MORGAN, A. I., Jr. 1963. Foam-mat drying of liquid form food. Proceedings Conf. Food Process. Tech., Eastern Util. Res. Develop. Div., Agr. Res. Serv. U.S. Dept. Agr., Philadelphia.

MORGAN, A. I., Jr., and RANDALL, J. M. 1960. Dehydration of lacteal fluids. U.S. Pat. 2,934,411.

MORGAN, A. I., Jr., GINNETTE, L. F., RANDALL, J. M., and GRAHAM, R. P. 1959. Technique for improving instants. Food Eng. 31, No. 9, 86-87.

MORGAN, A. I., Jr., GRAHAM, R. P., GINNETTE, L. F., and WILLIAMS, G. S. 1961. Recent developments in foam-mat drying. Food Technol. 15, No. 1, 37,39.

MORGAN, D. A., VELDHUIS, M. K., ESKEW, R. K., and PHILLIPS, G. W. M. 1953. Studies on the essence from Florida orange juice. Food Technol. 7, 332-336.

MORRIS, R. H., 3rd. 1949. Production and utilization of volatile fruit concentrate. Proceedings 40th Ann. meeting Flavoring Extract Manufacturers Assoc.

NAIR, J. H. 1962. A guide to freeze drying at home and abroad. Food Canada 22, No. 3, 13-15.

NAIR, J. H. 1963. Present status and outlook for freeze drying. Proceedings Conf. Food Process. Tech. Eastern Util. Res. Develop. Div., U.S. Dept. Agr., Philadelphia.

NATL. DAIRY COUNCIL. 1968. Relative nutritional value of filled and imitation milks. Dairy Council Dig. 39, No. 2, 7012, Chicago.

NIELSEN, A. C. 1960. Special report to the Cereal Institute Inc. covering recent trends in breakfast cereals to Aug. 1. A. C. Nielsen Co.

NOTTER, G. K., BREKKE, J. E., and TAYLOR, D. H. 1959. Factors affecting behavior of fruit and vegetable juices during vacuum puff drying. Food Technol. 13, No. 6, 341-345.

NOTTER, G. K., BREKKE, J. E., and WALKER, L. H. 1955. Stabilized lemonade powder. Food Technol. 9, 503.

NOTTER, G. K., TAYLOR, D. H., and BREKKE, J. E. 1958. Pineapple juice powder. Food Technol. 12, 363.

OLSEN, C. M. 1965. Microwaves inhibit bread mold. Food Eng. 37, No. 7, 51-53.

OLSON, C. M. 1968. Promising applications of microwave energy in the food and pharmaceutical industry, Paper presented to 1968 Varian Ind. Microwave Technol. Seminar.

OLSON, R. L., and HARRINGTON, W. O. 1951. Dehydrated mashed potatoes – a review. U.S. Dept. Agr. Bur. Agr. Ind. Chem., Albany, Calif. AIC 297.

OLSON, R. L., and HARRINGTON, W. O. 1955. The technology of potato granule manufacture. Am. Potato J. Mar., 106-111.

PALLANSCH, M. J. 1963. Foam-spray drying – a new technique for dehydrated product improvement. Proceedings Conf. Food Process. Tech., Eastern Util. Res. Develop. Div., Agr. Res. Serv., U.S. Dept. Agr., Philadelphia.

PALM, C. E. 1967. Changing concepts of foods and their sources. Conf. New Foods, Flavors, and Analogs. Cornell Univ. Apr. 24-25.

PENROSE, EDITH T. 1959. The Theory on the Growth of the Firm. John Wiley & Sons, New York.

PHILLIPS, G. W. M. et al. 1951. Experimental unit for recovery of volatile flavors. Ind. Eng. Chem. 43, 12-14.

PIRCON, L. J., LOQUERCIO, P., and DOTY, D. M. 1953. High frequency heating as a unit operation in meat processing. J. Agr. Food Chem. 1, No. 13, 844-847.

POLLACK, G. A., and FOIN, LOUISE C. 1960. Comparative heating efficiencies of a microwave and a conventional electric oven. Food Technol. 14, 454-457.

POLOPOLUS, L., and BLACK, W. E. 1966. Synthetics and substitutes and the Florida citrus industry. Dept. Agr. Econ., Univ. Florida Rept. FCC-ERD-66-4.

PONTING, J. D. et al. 1966. Osmotic dehydration of fruits. Food Technol. 2, 1365-1370.

POWERS, M. J., TALBURT, W. F., JACKSON, R., and LAZAR, M. E. 1958. Dehydrocanned apples. Food Technol. 8, 417-419.

POWERS, M. J., TAYLOR, D. H., TALBURT, W. F., and WALKER, L. H. 1956. Dehydrofrozen apricots: preparation. Food Technol. 10, 489-492.

QUACKENBUSH, G. G. 1966. Dairy industry substitutes, in synthetics and substitutes for agricultural commodities. Publ. 1, Univ. Florida, Inst. Food Agr. Sci., May.

QUACKENBUSH, G. G. 1967. Dairy products – modifications and substitutes. Conf. New Foods, Flavors and Analogs. Cornell Univ., Ithaca, N. Y. Apr. 24-25.

RAMAGE, W. D. 1960. Foam-mat drying – recent developments in freeze-dehydration of foods; a military-industry meeting, Chicago, Ill. Res. Develop. Assoc., Food Container Inst.

RASMUSSEN, C. L. 1967. Economics of present and future freezing methods. Natl. Assoc. Frozen Food Packers Tech. Serv. Bull. 36, Washington, D. C.

RASMUSSEN, C. L. 1969. Use of cryogens for freezing foods – quantities needed. Natl. Assoc. Frozen Food Packers Tech. Serv. Bull. 37. Washington, D. C.

REDFIELD, C. S., and ESKEW, R. K. 1953. Apple essence recovery costs. Glass Packer, Feb.

REDMAN, L. V. 1928. Economic aspects of industrial research and development. Ind. Eng. Chem. 20, 1242.

RICKS, D. et al. 1966. Great Lakes tart cherry industry processor survey. Michigan State Univ. Agr. Econ. Rept. 58.

ROBERTS, N. E. 1961. Process procedures, quick-cook dehydrated foods. Food Eng. 15, 45.

ROCKWELL, W. C. et al. 1962. How foam-mat dryer is made. Food Eng. 34, No. 8, 86-88.

SCHMIDT, W. 1961. The heating of food in a microwave cooker. Philips Tech. Rev. 22, No. 3, 89-102.

SCHMOOKLER, J. 1957. Inventors, past and present. Rev. Econ. Stat. 39, 321-333.

SCHULTZ, T. H., DIMICK, K. P., and MAKOWER, B. 1956. Incorporation of natural fruit flavors into fruit juice powders. I. Locking of citrus oils in sucrose and dextrose. Food Technol. 10, 57-60.

SCHUMPETER, J. A 1947. Capitalism, Socialism and Democracy, 2nd Edition. Harper & Row, New York.

SCHUMPETER, J. A. 1949. The Theory of Economic Development. Harvard Univ. Press, Cambridge, Mass.

SCHWARTZ, H. W. 1951. Comparisons of low-temperature evaporators. Food Technol. 5, 476-479.

SINNAMON, H. I., ACETO, N. C., ESKEW, R. K., and SCHOPPET, E. F. 1957. Dry whole milk. I. A new physical form. J. Dairy Sci. 40, 1036.

SLUDER, J. C., OLSEN, R. W., and KENYON, E. M. 1947. A method for the production of dry powdered orange juice. Food Technol. 1, 85-94.

SOLO, CAROLYN S. 1951. Innovation in the capitalist process: A critique of the Schumpeterian theory. Quart. J. Econ. 65, 417-428.

SPADARO, J. J., and PATTON, E. L. 1961. Precooked dehydrated sweet potato flakes. Food Eng. 33, No. 7, 46-48.

STEWART, J. B. 1959. Functional features in product strategy. Harvard Business Rev. XXXVII, 2.

STRASHUN, S. I. 1951. The drying of fruit and vegetable products. U.S. Pat. 2,557,155.

STRASHUN, S. I., and TALBURT, W. F. 1953. WRRL develops techniques for making puffed powder from juice. Food Eng. 25, No. 3, 59.

STRASHUN, S. I., and TALBURT, W. F. 1954. Stabilized orange powder. I. Preparation and packaging. Food Technol. 8, 40.

SULLIVAN, J. F., CORDING, J., Jr., and ESKEW, R. K. 1963. Quick cooking dehydrated sweet potatoes. Food Eng. 35, No. 11, 59-60.

SWERN, D. (Editor). 1964. Bailey's Industrial Oil and Fat Products, 3rd Edition. Interscience Publishers, New York.

TALBURT, W. F., and LEGAULT, R. R. 1950. Dehydrofrozen peas. Food Technol. 4, 286.

TALBURT, W. F., and LINDQUIST, F. E. 1954. Dehydrofreezing of fruits and vegetables. Food Sci. 26, No. 4, 361, Abstr.

TALBURT, W. F., WALKER, L. H., and POWERS, M. J. 1950. Dehydrofrozen apples. Food Technol. 4, 496.

TCHIGEON, G. B. 1960. Investigation and application of freeze drying foods. Intern. Congr. Refrig. Processors 10, No. 3, 31-35.

TECH. ASSISTANCE INFORM. CLEARING HOUSE. 1968. High protein food supplements. TAICH News 15, Fall.

TRESSLER, D. K. 1968. Cryogenic freezing. In The Freezing Preservation of Foods, 4th Edition, Vol. 1, D. K. Tressler et al. (Editors). Avi Publishing Co., Westport, Conn.

TRESSLER, D. K., and JOSLYN, M. A. 1961. Fruit and Vegetable Juice Processing Technology. Avi Publishing Co., Westport, Conn. Out of print.

TRESSLER, D. K., and JOSLYN, M. A. (Editors). 1971. Fruit and Vegetable Juice Processing Technology, 2nd Edition. Avi Publishing Co., Westport, Conn.

U.S. DEPT. of AGR. WESTERN UTIL. RES. BRANCH. 1955. Continuous process proves successful for puffed tomato powder. Western Canner Packer 47, No. 7, 16.

U.S. DEPT. OF AGR. 1959. Further improvements of texture of reconstituted potato flakes by use of emulsifiers. U.S. Dept. Agr. Agr. Res. Serv. CA-E-17, Washington, D.C.

U.S. DEPT. OF AGR. 1960. Consumption of processed farm foods in the U.S. U.S. Dept. Agr. A.M.S. MRR 409, June, Washington, D.C.

U.S. DEPT. OF AGR. 1962. Chemistry and technology of citrus, citrus products, and by-products. U.S. Dept. Agr., Agr. Handbook 98, Washington, D.C.

U.S. DEPT. of COM. 1968A. Food irradiation activities throughout the world. Washington, D.C.

U.S. DEPT. OF COM. 1968B. The commercial prospects for selected irradiated foods. Washington, D.C., TID-24058.

URBAIN, W. M. 1968. Status of radiation preservation of foods. Natl. Res. Council – Natl. Acad. Sci., Washington, D.C.

VELDHUIS, M. K. et al. 1962. Progress in foam-mat drying of orange juice. Citrus Engineering Conf., Am. Soc. Mech. Engrs. 1, No. 8, 71-79.

WALDORF, W. H. 1964. Demand for manufactured foods, manufacturers' service and farm products in food manufacturing – a statistical analysis. U.S. Dept. Agr. Econ. Res. Serv. Tech. Bull. 1317.

WALKER, L. H. 1961. Volatile flavor recovery. In Fruit and Vegetable Juice Processing Technology, D. K. Tressler, and M. A. Joslyn (Editors). Avi Publishing Co., Westport, Conn.

WALTER, L. 1965. Dielectric thawing for frozen foods. Canner Packer 36-37, Feb.

WEISER, H. 1954. Application of the freeze-drying process in food preservation. Milk Producers J. 45, No. 12, 15-16, 40-42.

WILLIAMS, R. R. 1956. Chemistry as a supplement to agriculture in meeting world food needs. Am. Scientist 44, 317-329.

CHAPTER 8

W. Smith Greig

Locational Changes in Food Processing

THE THEORIES OF LOCATION OF INDUSTRIAL ACTIVITY

The theory of industrial location is relatively simple but the application of the theory can be very complex. Industrial location as a science is relatively new. Von Thunen (1826) developed a theory of land rent based on locational advantages over a century ago. However, one of the first basic theories of industrial location was developed by Alfred Weber in 1909 (Weber 1929). More modern and comprehensive scholars on the location of industrial activity have been Ohlin (1933), Hoover (1937), Losch (1954), and Isard (1956, 1960, 1969).

With the development of the computer and its usefulness in solving complex mathematical problems, many studies have been undertaken in location analysis in the past 20 yr. In 1966, Leuthold and Bawden published an annotated bibliography of spatial studies nearly all in agricultural or related industries. This bibliography contained approximately 150 studies, most of which were completed between 1950 and 1964 (Leuthold and Bawden 1966). Until quite recently the complexity and detail of the models were limited by the capacity or size of the computers.

Location analysis is currently an interdisciplinary science; at most universities some aspects of location analysis are taught in many different fields. In 1969 at Michigan State University alone, aspects of locational analysis were offered in courses taught in the Departments of Economics, Agricultural Economics, Geography, Marketing and Transportation, Resource Development, and Engineering, as well as in the fields of economic development and international trade. The analytical methods used in analysis are taught in specialized courses in statistics and in mathematics. Because the field of location analysis is relatively new, even the terms describing it are not standardized. Terms such as "spatial studies," "spatial equilibrium models," "interregional competition," "transportation models" and "space economy" may all have about the same meaning.

On the simplest possible basis, Hoover (1937) divides factors affecting industrial locations into three parts: procurement costs or costs of obtaining inputs, processing costs, and distribution costs. This is straightforward enough, but let's add some complexities. To do this we will take the case of a fruit and/or vegetable processor.

Procurement Costs. – (1) At a minimum, procurement costs are based on density of production. If the plant is a multiproduct plant the goal would be to minimize total transportation costs for all inputs of raw products. (2) Similarly, the costs of inputs such as packaging materials, cans, cartons, cases, and usable chemicals and supplies will cost more the farther the plant is from a supplier.

Processing Costs. – Processing costs may vary depending on (1) cost of the raw product (and elasticity or supply of the raw products), (2) quality factors,

(3) labor wage rates, (4) length of the processing season, (5) product mix, (6) size or scale of operations, (7) state and local taxes, (8) fuel and electricity costs, (9) cost and availability of water, (10) by-product utilization, and (11) waste disposal costs.

Distribution Costs. — These may vary depending on (1) relative distances to market (this may depend on population densities and per capita consumption — which, in turn, may depend on income and other factors — and on location of competing processors), (2) direction of flow of products, (3) back hauls, (4) scale of shipments, and (5) availability of product mix (for mixed loads).

To determine the optimum location for a specific type of fruit and vegetable processing plant, one needs only to add together all the above cost factors for each possible location and determine the least cost location. True? Not completely. Even if it were possible to assign an economic term to each of the costs listed above and physically handle the data for the costs for every possible location, there are social, political, psychological, and economic values in location that are only subjectively measurable.

Social and psychological factors which may affect the location of a particular processing plant might be: the value of differences in climate; differences in schools, colleges, and universities; availability of hospitals; effectiveness of law enforcement agencies; availability of entertainment and recreational facilities; the general level of living in the area; the ethnic background of the residents; etc. There is a substantial body of literature that suggests manufacturing plants are built where plant managers and plant owners like to live.

Political factors may involve the present and long-range outlook concerning taxes, future labor laws, welfare programs, and other legal and political aspects of doing business in a particular state or county.

Some economic factors not easily measurable are the availability of the relevant infrastructure. This may include financial institutions familiar with the needs of the industry, storage and freight industries, technical service personnel, educational level of the workers (and residents), market news services, protection against risk and uncertainty (contractual arrangements, futures markets, insurance, etc.), availability of industry-wide advertising and promotion, and farmer attitudes toward change — and this may depend on ages of farmers, sizes of farms, alternative opportunities, and general progressiveness of the farm-producer industries.

There are sophisticated analytical techniques to measure the economic advantages of one area over another as far as plant location is concerned. Recently analytical techniques have been developed to determine the minimum number, sizes, and locations of processing plants to serve particular markets (local, national, or international). But even with the best econometric models, the ultimate entrepreneurial decisions may be based on an evaluation of subjective social, political, psychological, and subjective economic factors.

LOCATIONS OF PRODUCTION AND PROCESSING CHANGE

To a large extent many of our current food processing locations are consumer-oriented. There is a strong (but not direct) relationship between the population in a state and the amount of food processing. The greatest amount of value added in food processing is in California, Illinois, New York, Pennsylvania, and Ohio (Table 8.1). Noted exceptions to this general statement are meat packing in Iowa, Illinois, and Minnesota; dairies in Wisconsin and Minnesota; canned and frozen foods in California, Florida, and New Jersey; grain mills in Illinois, Michigan, and Iowa; and confectionery products in Illinois, whiskey in Kentucky, and beer in Wisconsin.

If we place the value added on a per capita basis, then a different relationship appears. Delaware, Maine, Iowa, S. Dakota, and Nebraska have substantially more processing per capita than the other states (Table 8.2). Per capita production of food products by major product class can easily be computed from census data. However, our interest is in why locations change, more than that of specifying current locations.

Locations of much of the food processing in the United States are rapidly changing. A change in location is seldom the closing of a plant in one area and physical movement of its equipment and facilities to another area — rather it is a change brought about by differentials in growth rates. These differentials among areas may be caused by a variety of reasons. Many of these reasons will be mentioned in the description of specific examples which follows.

THE MEAT SLAUGHTERING INDUSTRY

Although the quantities of meat slaughtered in the United States has increased at a rapid rate, the numbers of meat slaughtering plants are decreasing and the locations of slaughter are changing. Meat slaughtering is shifting between areas. Within areas, processing is being decentralized.

There has been a shift of cattle slaughter from the east to the North Central region and to the west, and a shift of hog slaughter to the south. The numbers of hog slaughtering facilities have increased in the south while cattle slaughtering facilities in the west have expanded. The shifts among areas of the United States in numbers of slaughtering plants between 1950 and 1965 are given in Table 8.3.

Decentralization within regions is largely reflected by a growth of slaughtering facilities in production areas and a decline of their importance in our largest cities.

Both the movement between areas and decentralization within areas are because of the development of technologies for storing meat and the economies of transporting meat rather than live animals. In addition, decentralization also occurred because of obsolete plants in the larger cities combined with labor problems, higher wages, and increasing tax loads.[1] The movement of cattle

---

[1] Conversations with officials of CAP (Corporacion Argentina de Productores de Carne, Argentina meat producers association) in 1967 indicated, similar problems in Argentina. Officials of CAP had already visited decentralized slaughter plants in the United States, such as Iowa Beef Packers, with a view toward decentralizing their own slaughtering operations.

TABLE 8.1

TOTAL VALUE ADDED IN FOOD MANUFACTURING, BY MAJOR PRODUCT CLASSES
FOR THE 20 LEADING STATES IN EACH PRODUCT CLASS, 1963

State Rank	All Food and Kindred Products (SIC 20)	Meat Products (SIC 201)		Dairies (SIC 202)		Canned and Frozen Food (SIC 203)		Grain Mills (SIC 204)	
	Value Added ($1000)	State Rank	Value Added ($1000)	State Rank	Value Added ($1000)	State Rank	Value Added ($1000)	State Rank	Value Added ($1000)
1 Calif.	2,412,559	Iowa	281,560	Calif.	262,307	Calif.	626,233	Ill.	365,323
2 Ill.	2,059,037	Ill.	203,655	N.Y.	256,449	N.Y.	211,699	Mich.	182,272
3 N.Y.	1,846,827	Calif.	195,853	Penn.	248,510	Fla.	177,780	Iowa	177,034
4 Penn.	1,355,664	Minn.	173,804	Wisc.	229,700	Ill.	167,930	Calif.	173,513
5 Ohio	1,051,910	Ohio	139,747	Ohio	215,413	Penn.	160,697	Ind.	103,665
6 N.J.	1,034,623	N.Y.	134,769	Ill.	179,369	N.J.	153,080	Ohio	107,997
7 Texas	929,524	Texas	132,252	Mich.	132,803	Ohio	125,874	Texas	107,921
8 Mich.	729,211	Penn.	127,075	Texas	124,688	Wash.	94,356	N.Y.	94,845
9 Wisc.	754,500	Nebr.	115,537	Mass.	110,526	Mich.	91,687	Mo.	88,551
10 Iowa	653,155	Maine	109,239	Minn.	110,103	Ore.	84,298	Tenn.	69,074
11 Ind.	642,850	Wisc.	102,192	N.J.	83,168	Ind.	73,723	Nebr.	65,668
12 Mo.	629,933	Ind.	97,896	Ind.	82,354	Wisc.	71,854	Minn.	62,806
13 Minn.	587,507	Mo.	95,762	Mo.	79,932	Hawaii	63,012	Penn.	62,224
14 Mass.	506,119	Kans.	84,646	Fla.	74,657	Minn.	55,892	Kans.	61,369
15 Fla.	499,694	Mich.	74,370	Iowa	65,676	Md.	46,232	Ga.	36,881
16 Ky.	444,202	Ga.	71,100	Tenn.	57,502	Mass.	44,749	Wisc.	36,227
17 Ga.	441,953	N.J.	61,103	Md.	56,720	Idaho	44,627	Ark.	33,223
18 Md.	419,836	Md.	60,964	Wash.	54,852	Maine	35,467	Ala.	33,047
19 La.	367,891	S. Dak.	59,676	Conn.	49,732	Alaska	33,537	Wash.	26,155
20 Wash.	360,590	Del.	54,634	Ky.	47,371	Ga.	32,905	N.J.	20,575
Subtotal	17,727,963		2,375,834		2,521,832		2,425,632		1,838,688
U.S. Total	21,843,075		2,882,580		3,184,867		2,778,810		2,271,054

TABLE 8.1 (Continued)

State Rank	Bakery Products (SIC 205)		Confectionery Products (SIC 2071)		Beverages (SIC 208)[1]		Miscellaneous Foods (SIC 209)[2]	
	State Rank	Value Added ($1000)	State Rank	Value Added ($1000)	State Rank	Value Added ($1000)	State Rank	Value Added ($1000)
1	N.Y.	342,845	Ill.	159,508	N.Y.	378,561	Ill.	343,620
2	Calif.	303,738	N.Y.	74,478	Calif.	367,587	Calif.	307,105
3	Penn.	288,404	Penn.	71,811	Ill.	308,126	N.J.	287,558
4	Ill.	264,299	Calif.	51,238	Ky.	288,516	Texas	221,482
5	Ohio	192,554	N.J.	47,112	Wisc.	219,316	N.Y.	124,369
6	N.J.	170,774	Mass.	45,761	N.J.	204,370	Ohio	109,670
7	Texas	122,186	Ga.	22,767	Penn.	192,605	La.	67,972
8	Mich.	100,267	Va.	21,409	Mo.	186,109	Ind.	56,764
9	Ga.	91,427	Ind.	14,618	Ind.	149,647	Mo.	55,665
10	Mass.	88,113	Texas	12,578	Texas	144,253	Ga.	49,671
11	Mo.	86,675	Minn.	11,796	Okla.	141,245	Mass.	49,474
12	N. Car.	76,159	Miss.	7,861	Md.	130,528	Tenn.	48,544
13	Ind.	59,183	Wash.	6,281	Mich.	94,240	Minn.	47,564
14	Wisc.	55,469	Wisc.	6,164	Ga.	84,267	Va.	44,765
15	Fla.	53,944	Ore.	3,931	Minn.	75,735	Iowa	40,687
16	Md.	48,818	Utah	3,920	Fla.	65,744	Mich.	38,764
17	Ore.	45,912	Colo.	3,766	Wash.	59,967	Md.	34,049
18	Va.	43,363	Md.	3,718	La.	58,885	Nebr.	27,581
19	Wash.	40,177	Fla.	2,774	Colo.	56,792	Wisc.	26,064
20	Colo.	39,215	N. Car.	2,717	Mass.	54,474	Wash.	21,862
Subtotal		2,513,522		574,209		3,260,967		2,003,230
U.S. Total		3,030,822		635,393		3,724,834		2,423,269

Source: Bur. Census, U.S. Dept. Comm.

[1] Includes malt liquor, wines and brandy, distilled liquor, bottled and canned soft drinks and flavorings.

[2] Includes cottonseed oil mills, soybean oil mills, vegetable oil meals, animal and marine fats and oils, shortening and cooking oils, roasted coffee, manufactured rice, macaroni, and spaghetti, and food preparations not elsewhere classified.

TABLE 8.2

PER CAPITA VALUE
ADDED BY MANUFACTURE OF ALL FOOD AND KINDRED PRODUCTS
(SIC 20) BY STATE, 1954, 1958, AND 1963

	1963	1958	1954		1963	1958	1954
	(Dollars)				(Dollars)		
Hawaii	244.5	—	—	N. Y.	104.3	100.8	86.3
Iowa	236.8	197.7	137.3	Utah	101.9	98.0	65.7
Nebr.	215.7	191.4	148.7	Mass.	95.5	82.5	64.5
Ill.	198.6	168.1	147.2	Tenn.	93.4	75.1	55.6
Wisc.	185.6	161.7	143.0	Mich.	90.7	86.0	73.1
Minn.	167.5	155.5	127.5	Texas	90.6	76.3	63.1
Alaska	161.9	—	—	Fla.	90.3	70.4	61.3
Idaho	161.2	121.0	84.3	Vt.	88.2	90.2	68.5
N. J.	158.2	140.0	123.9	Ark.	81.8	57.0	42.3
Mo.	142.8	132.4	111.2	Va.	76.1	61.7	48.0
Ky.	142.3	117.2	102.8	R. I.	69.8	58.2	49.6
Calif.	137.4	129.3	110.0	Mont.	67.8	58.4	52.0
Ind.	134.5	114.3	91.7	N. Car.	67.4	52.9	37.2
S. Dak.	134.3	121.5	85.7	Conn.	62.2	58.9	43.2
Colo.	131.9	104.1	79.5	Okla.	60.5	58.1	45.6
Ore.	126.7	114.9	85.8	Ala.	60.2	47.1	11.1
Md.	125.3	109.7	93.4	Miss.	57.2	45.9	29.0
Wash.	121.9	106.9	86.5	N. Dak.	57.0	48.9	31.9
Penn.	118.8	98.1	76.5	Ariz.	51.6	48.3	41.2
Del.	113.8	126.5	10.2	Wyo.	51.0	38.8	31.8
Maine	110.9	91.1	67.9	N. H.	48.7	35.5	31.5
La.	107.9	87.6	—	W. Va.	42.3	36.6	26.7
Kans.	107.9	100.8	85.7	S. Car.	39.3	31.3	23.0
Ga.	105.1	89.2	72.3	N. Mex.	34.9	32.3	22.1
Ohio	105.0	91.8	76.9	Nev.	29.0	29.0	34.8

TABLE 8.3

NUMBERS AND LOCATIONS OF MEAT SLAUGHTERING PLANTS, 1950 — 1965

Region	1950 Plants		1955 Plants		1960 Plants		1965 Plants	
	No.	% of Total	No.	% of Total	No.	% of Total	No.	% of Total
North Atlantic	774	23.9	619	19.3	599	19.0	516	17.5
East North Central	800	24.7	774	24.1	722	23.0	657	22.2
West North Central	313	9.7	290	9.0	312	9.9	368	12.4
South Atlantic	370	11.4	445	13.8	418	13.3	383	13.0
South Central	510	15.8	622	19.3	631	20.1	588	19.9
West	471	14.5	467	14.5	462	14.7	445	15.0
Total	3238	100.0	3217	100.0	3144	100.0	2957	100.0

Source: Anon. (1966A, B).

slaughter westward is due, in part, to the movement of our population westward.

Many of the newer plants being built in livestock producing areas in the United States are more highly specialized; many slaughter only one species.

The analysis of Logan and King (1962) on economies of scale in beef slaughtering and that of Huie (1969) on the minimum number, size and location of beef slaughtering plants in Michigan strongly suggest a considerable decrease in the number of slaughtering plants in the United States.

THE CHANGING LOCATION OF THE POULTRY INDUSTRY

Broilers

In 1945, the South Central States of Arkansas, Alabama, Kentucky, Tennessee, Mississippi, Louisiana, Oklahoma, and Texas produced 12.2% of the broilers grown in the United States. By 1965, even though total broiler production had increased over fivefold, these same states produced 43.3% of the broilers. In these states, broiler production went from 48 million birds in 1945 to 655 million in 1965 (Table 8.4). In 1945, the South Central and South Atlantic States commanded 68% of total broiler production; in 1965, nearly 86%.

There have been many reasons why, historically, broiler production moved out of the midwestern and central portions of the United States to the south. Several authors have suggested that integration arrangements were more acceptable in the south, where the financial arrangements were often handled by integrators such as large feed companies. Others suggest that the southern farmers had fewer alternative opportunities and would work for a lesser "management" wage, and that hourly labor wage rates were cheaper.

Other reasons suggested are that housing costs for the birds are less because of climatic conditions and that freight rates for grain from the midwest are favorable.

TABLE 8.4

COMMERCIAL BROILER PRODUCTION IN THE UNITED STATES
BY REGIONS, 1945—1965

| Region | Production in Millions of Birds | | | | | % of Increase |
	1945	1950	1955	1960	1965	1945-1965
North Atlantic	42.9	79.1	139.1	147.1	137.1	303
East North Central	29.7	52.6	76.3	79.1	54.1	73
West North Central	9.8	25.6	38.3	46.7	45.1	360
South Atlantic	204.8	298.1	475.3	777.9	987.1	382
South Central	44.7	123.3	292.8	655.0	1011.3	2162
Western	33.6	52.6	70.0	89.6	99.2	195
United States	365.5	631.5	1091.7	1795.7	2331.3	+537

Source: Anon. (1961, 1965).

Egg Production

Egg production, while increasing rather slowly in the United States, is also undergoing major changes in location (Table 8.5), moving out of the East and North into the South and West. Between 1953 and 1965, the North Atlantic, the East North Central, and the West North Central regions had absolute decreases in egg production ranging from 11 to 29%. As in broilers, the biggest increases in production were in the south. Between 1953 and 1965 egg production increased over 100% in the South Atlantic region and over 64% in the South Central region.

Much of the increase in the West may be attributed to population growth. However, this is certainly not the case in the South. The reasons for increases in egg production in the South are the same as those for increases in broiler production.

CHANGES IN LOCATION IN THE FLOUR MILLING INDUSTRY

For many years the flour milling industry has been located in the wheat-producing regions of the Midwest and North Central regions of the United States. An exception was the Buffalo, New York area, with cheap water transportation rates on wheat from the North Central region and a large dairy feed market in New York state for the by-products from flour milling. Until quite recently, it was as cheap to ship flour by rail as wheat because most of the Midwestern and North Central mills had in-transit shipping privileges. In the last few years, innovations in barge, truck, and rail transportation have reduced freight rates on wheat, but not to the same extent on flour. The rates on flour have not been reduced because it is much more perishable than wheat and cannot utilize some of the same types of transportation, such as barges. This change in rate relationships between wheat and flour has encouraged the construction of flour mills closer to population centers (Goldberg 1968).

TABLE 8.5

COMMERCIAL EGG PRODUCTION IN THE U.S.
BY REGIONS, 1953, 1963, AND 1965

Region	1953	1963	1965	Change 1953-1965	
	Production in Millions of Eggs			Millions	Percent
North Atlantic	10,724	9,528	9,565	−1159	− 11
East North Central	11,243	9,763	9,218	−2025	− 18
West North Central	15,859	12,597	11,274	−4585	− 29
South Atlantic	5,197	9,744	10,588	+5391	+104
South Central	7,730	10,973	12,672	+4942	+ 64
Western	7,138	10,429	11,011	+3873	+ 54
United States	57,891	63,034	64,391	+6500	+11.2

Source: Anon. (1964, 1965).

Special rail rates on wheat — such as the use of the "Big John" hopper cars, the train-load rates and rent-a-train innovations — have considerably reduced the freight rates for wheat. The change in milling-in-transit rates to permit more rail competition with truck and barge shipments has placed the mills with opportunities for only rail shipments of flour at a distinct disadvantage. Previously, the railroad milling-in-transit customer had the same rate as any competitor located in production or consumption centers because he was given a through milling-in-transit rate. When truck and water carriers began to provide cheaper forms of transportation at assembling or distribution points, several railroads reduced rates at these competitive points, but not for their milling-in-transit customers who had only rail as their principal form of transportation. In essence, the railroads considered these mills "captured customers." Many flour mills have been closed in the Kansas City area because of these changes in freight rates and new ones are being built in large population centers such as Pennsylvania and Florida.

THE SHIFT IN ORANGE PRODUCTION AND PROCESSING

Orange production increased at a rapid rate in Florida in the 1930's, but it was not until the mid-1940's that Florida passed California as the major orange producer. The development of frozen concentrated citrus juice during World War II gave a great impetus to Florida production of oranges for processing. The navel and valencia orange produced in California were not as well adapted as the Florida oranges for the production of juice concentrates. During the late 1950's and 1960's Florida produced from 3 to 4 times as many oranges per year as California. Around 85% of the Florida orange crop is processed. Approximately 62-65% of the Florida crop is used for frozen concentrated orange juice, and 8-10% is canned or used in salad sections. The remaining 7-10% is used for chilled orange juice.

In the 1930's, Florida orange processing was only around 11% of the total U.S. orange processing; but by the 1960's, Florida's share of the total was over 90% (Table 8.6).

Most authors cite the development of the technology of frozen concentrate as the major factor in the shift of orange production from California to Florida, although some also suggest urbanization of California as a contributing factor.

THE SHIFT IN ONION PRODUCTION AND PROCESSING

For years until the 1960's, New York and California were almost equal in onion production. New York was the major late summer or fall crop-producing state and California was the major spring-producing state. Michigan, Oregon, and Colorado were also major summer states in onion production and Texas was another major spring producer.

In the late 1950's and in the 1960's, onion dehydration became an important method of utilizing the onion crop. To date (1969) all of the onion dehydration in the United States is in California. Commercial dehydration is done by only

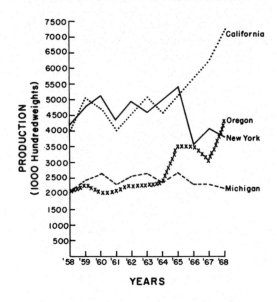

FIG. 8.1. ONION PRODUCTION FOR PRINCIPAL
PRODUCING STATES, 1958-1968

four firms: Basic Vegetable Products Co. with plants in Kingman and Vacaville,
Gilroy Foods (a subsidiary of McCormick & Co.) at Gilroy, Gentry Corp. also at
Gilroy, and Rogers Brothers Co. With the development of onion dehydration in
California there has been a great increase in onion production in California.
Between 1958 and 1968 onion production nearly doubled (Fig. 8.1). Although

TABLE 8.6

PRODUCTION AND PROCESSING OF ORANGES
FOR CALIFORNIA AND FLORIDA, 1935-1936 to 1967-1968

Crop Year	Total Production		Total Processing		% of Production Processed		% of All Processing in Fla.
	Fla.	Calif.	Fla.	Calif.	Fla.	Calif.	
	(1000 boxes)		(1000 boxes)				
1935-1936	15,900	32,809	213	1,728	1.3	5.2	11.0
1940-1941	28,600	50,778	4,008	5,801	14.0	11.4	40.9
1945-1946	49,800	44,010	19,220	7,025	38.6	16.0	73.2
1950-1951	67,300	45,210	41,915	13,304	62.3	29.4	75.9
1955-1956	91,000	38,370	64,884	10,173	71.3	26.5	86.4
1960-1961	86,700	25,000	69,250	5,360	79.9	21.4	92.8
1965-1966	100,400	36,500	82,528	10,660	82.2	29.2	88.6
1966-1967	139,500	37,400	121,624	10,000	87.2	26.7	91.9
1967-1968	100,500	19,600	83,404	7,610	83.0	38.8	91.6

Source: Citrus Fruits, by States, Production, Use, Value. U.S. Dept. Agr. Statist. Rept.
Serv.

no statistical data are available on utilization of the California onion crop, we can suggest that around 70-80% of the total California crop is dehydrated. This, in effect, suggests that up to 5,600,000 cwt were dehydrated in 1968. Thus, utilization for dehydration in California in 1968 was probably greater than total onion production in any other state.

There are several reasons why onion dehydration is centered in California. (1) It started there. (2) Allegedly, a white onion is highly desirable because of consumer and institutional preferences (and white onions are difficult to grow in humid production areas because of thrip damage). (3) Through the years, California has developed onions with high dry matter content – resulting in larger yields of dehydrated onion than would be the case in other production areas. (4) Fresh onions are not stored in current dehydration practices; but California dehydrators have a long season by obtaining onions from Mexico, throughout the length of California, and as far north as Oregon. Thus, a late summer or fall area would operate out of storage or have large procurement costs (Greig and Marine 1962).

Some private estimates place the growth rate of the onion dehydration industry at around 25% per yr. The author suggests that while the growth rate will slow, the total onion dehydration industry will continue to grow for some time.

A second major shift in onion production may occur because of the development of the frozen French fried onion ring industry. While freight is a relatively minor cost of distributing dehydrated onions, it is a major cost in frozen French fried onion rings. Thus, the location of this developing industry may be completely different from the location of the dehydration industry.

PRODUCTION OF GREEN PEAS

Large quantities of green peas were grown 20 yr ago for the fresh market. The peas were shipped fresh in-the-pod. Because of their highly perishable nature, there were many areas that seasonally produced green peas. Florida, California, and Texas produced in the winter and early spring; Mississippi, Georgia, S. Carolina, N. Carolina, and Virginia in the spring and early summer; Maryland, New Jersey, Idaho, Washington, New York, and Colorado were also summer producers. Now, however, very few green peas are grown for fresh market, but a much larger quantity is grown for processing. Nearly all the production of peas for processing is now located in only a few states. Wisconsin leads with 125,000 acres (in 1967) followed by Washington with 90,000, Minnesota with 73,000, Oregon with 55,000, and Illinois with over 20,000 acres.

Most of the peas for processing are in states with relatively cooler climates. Because peas mature too rapidly in the hotter growing climates, the production in cooler termperatures permits a longer harvest season and greater length of time of processing, thereby reducing overhead costs for plant and equipment.

Peas are perhaps typical of several perishable crops that have changed from being a "fresh market" product produced seasonally in many states to a processed product produced in consolidated specialized areas in a few states. Other products that have followed the same consolidation and specialization pattern are corn, green beans, spinach, lima beans, tomatoes, and asparagus.

POTATO PRODUCTION AND PROCESSING

The location of potato processing is affected by many factors. There are many forms of potato processing, but we will only mention three specific types.

Potato Chips

Potato chipping is a principal form of processing, the location of which is primarily market-oriented. Early in the development of this industry quality deterioration problems caused specialized stocking and shelf-rotation problems. Further, because of the high volume-low bulk density of the product, transportation cost of the finished product was high. Typically, plants were built to serve individual cities or metropolitan areas. This tendency has continued even though most of the deterioration problems have been overcome. While some large plants, i.e., in Pennsylvania, service areas from Florida to New York, most plants still serve limited areas. Apparently there are considerable economies of scale in potato chip plants and the industry as a whole would probably have a more efficient operation with a lesser number of plants.

Dehydrated Mashed Potatoes

Attempts to commercially dehydrate mashed potatoes were tried on Eastern grown (New York) potatoes prior to World War II, but because of quality problems (low specific gravity) the industry was relocated in Idaho. After World War II (particularly after 1955) the industry was greatly enlarged — primarily in Idaho. With the development of the potato flake process (see section on New Technologies, Chap. 7) Eastern potatoes yielded a high quality product and dehydration plants were built in Maine, Minnesota, Michigan, Washington, North Dakota, and Oregon. In general, the largest amount of dehydration is still located in Idaho with greatly expanding facilities in Washington and Oregon. In addition to high dry matter content potatoes, there are large areas of irrigated lands suitable for potato production. The Western potato growers apparently are more willing to grow potatoes under contractual arrangements than growers in the East. A simple analysis by the author some years ago indicated that Idaho growers would grow potatoes under contract at prices lower than average grower prices for fresh market potatoes of the previous several years. Apparently the reduction in price risk was worth a small loss in price itself.

Frozen French Fried Potatoes

Quality, whether real or imagined, has some important locational effects in frozen French fried potato production. To the institutional market, length of cut of the slice and a high dry matter content (less oil absorption and crisper fried potato) are important quality considerations. Typically, Western grown potatoes have a higher dry matter content than Eastern grown potatoes (even when the variety is the same). A casual examination of regional FOB plant prices will show a 1-2¢ per lb advantage for Western processed frozen French fries. Even in years when Eastern grown potatoes are superior to Western grown by all known quantitative quality measures, the Western frozen French fries still command a premium. Apparently, part of the price effect is psychological or due to past advertising expenditures — not to real quality difference.

Potato growers under most contracts receive less than $2.00 per cwt for the raw product. When Midwestern or Eastern processors would have up to $0.75-$1.00 per 100 lb freight advantage to market, without a quality differential for Western potatoes, the Midwestern and Eastern processors would apparently have a considerable locational advantage (Greig 1966).

In integrated operations where frozen French fried potatoes and dehydrated mashed potatoes are produced in the same plant, typically the larger potatoes go for frozen French fries, and the smaller ones for dehydrated mashed. In part, the potatoes for dehydrated mashed may be less completely trimmed and peeled than for French fries. In a sense, much dehydration is from the by-products of the frozen French fry line, i.e., smaller potatoes, small cuts of French fry slices, and less completely peeled potatoes. Thus, even though freight rates are widely different (per 100 lb of raw potato) both industries are raw product-oriented and typically are located together.

There is some evidence to suggest, in early stages of development both of the frozen French fries and dehydrated mashed, that quality considerations of the raw product were of extreme importance. However with more sophisticated processing technologies, quality differences of the raw product are becoming less important. However, the psychological or past advertising advantages obtained by the West show no indication of being overcome, particularly at the institutional level which is still the largest market.

With the development of the frozen French fried potato and the dehydrated mashed potato industries the production location moved from areas supplying early spring and summer markets to the late crop areas. Further, there was a great expansion of production in Idaho, Washington, and Oregon.

LOCATION OF MILK PRODUCTION HAS NOT CHANGED

The location of milk production in the United States has changed relatively little in the past 15-20 yr. Specific data by states and regions for milk production in 1953 and 1967 are presented in Table 8.7. The biggest change has been a decrease in the South Central region and an increase in the West. In the West the increase has mostly been in California and this is probably primarily due to population increases.

Snodgrass and French (1958) of Purdue University, suggested that, based on production costs (the cost differentials among states in feed and labor costs), processing costs (based on labor wage differentials among states), and distribution costs (freight costs for milk and dairy products), in 1953 Minnesota and Wisconsin should have had 46.7% of the milk production in the United States.

TABLE 8.7

PRODUCTION OF MILK ON FARMS
BY STATES AND REGIONS
WITH PERCENT CHANGE BY REGION, 1953, 1967

| State | Production | | | | % Change in Production 1953-1957 |
| | 1953 | | 1967 | | |
	Million Lb	% of Total	Million Lb	% of Total	
Maine	675		629		
New Hampshire	372		388		
Vermont	1664		1896		
Massachusetts	817		737		
Rhode Island	146		87		
Connecticut	726		693		
New York	9343		10,401		
New Jersey	1153		871		
Pennsylvania	5971		8856		
Region total	20,867	17.3	22,558	18.9	+8.1
Ohio	5710		4731		
Indiana	3750		2530		
Illinois	5192		3337		
Michigan	5577		4693		
Wisconsin	15,989		18,557		
Region total	36,218	30.0	33,848	28.4	−6.5
Minnesota	8590		10,316		
Iowa	5928		5627		
Missouri	4198		3148		
North Dakota	1781		1249		
South Dakota	1369		1600		
Nebraska	2183		1667		
Kansas	2460		1746		
Region total	26,509	21.9	25,353	21.2	−0.4
Delaware	209		142		
Maryland	1391		1540		
Virginia	2022		1776		
West Virginia	787		446		
North Carolina	1695		1488		
South Carolina	596		521		
Georgia	1218		1040		
Florida	638		1576		
Region total	8556	7.1	8529	7.1	0.0
Kentucky	2469		2500		
Tennessee	2492		2144		
Alabama	1377		812		
Mississippi	1259		1106		
Arkansas	1302		693		
Louisiana	806		1032		
Oklahoma	1880		1315		
Texas	3261		3080		
Region total	14,846	12.2	12,862	10.8	−13.3

TABLE 8.7 (Continued)

PRODUCTION OF MILK ON FARMS
BY STATES AND REGIONS
WITH PERCENT CHANGE BY REGION, 1953, 1967

| State | Production | | | | % Change in Production 1953-1957 |
| | 1953 | | 1967 | | |
	Million Lb	% of Total	Million Lb	% of Total	
Montana	529		358		
Idaho	1352		1443		
Wyoming	215		161		
Colorado	891		829		
New Mexico	218		307		
Arizona	293		539		
Utah	693		745		
Nevada	87		134		
Washington	1765		1958		
Oregon	1230		961		
California	6610		8724		
Region total	13,883	11.5	16,159	13.6	+16.4
U.S. Total	120,883	11.5	119,309	100.0	−1.3

Actual 1953 production, Snodgrass and French's "ideal modified model" for 1953, and 1967 actual milk production are listed in Table 8.8. Minnesota, Wisconsin, New York and California have increased production but not nearly to the extent as was suggested in 1953. The models suggested by Snodgrass and French were not predictive models — their purpose was to show discrepancies in the market from the ideal situation based solely on 1953 data. Assuming that in 1953 the differences between actual locations and ideal locations were real and measurable, this does not in itself suggest that locations would change decidedly through time. First of all, the factors affecting locational costs change; and second, there are many institutional factors that may prevent relocation of industries. But the fact remains that while much milk production was apparently "mislocated" in 1953, by 1967 only relatively minor shifts had been made in the direction suggested by economic studies.

APPARENT MISLOCATION OF SOME INDUSTRIES

Just as the Snodgrass and French study showed milk production to be "mislocated" in 1953, other studies have shown other food processing industries apparently to be mislocated. Greig and Heifner (1968), reported on studies of optimum location of four vegetable freezing industries based on raw product costs, labor wage rates, differentials in processing, length of processing season, and rail freight rates to markets. There were wide differences between their "optimum locations" based on the four cost factors studied, and the current processing locations for freezing green peas, green snap beans, lima beans, and spinach. In explaining why current locations were so different from optimum locations, they suggested that "other factors could outweigh the effects of raw product costs, processing labor costs, length of processing season and its effects on fixed costs, and transportation costs to market. For example, economies of scale and multiproduct possibilities could exert a considerable effect on location." They further suggested that many locations in processing were "man-made" locations — that is, the locations were developed based on entrepreneurial ability rather than pure cost factors alone. Although it is not unusual that some economic studies, such as the ones by Snodgrass and French, and Greig and Heifner, show food processing industries to be mislocated — it is the degree of apparent mislocation that is surprising. The milk production study showed economic advantages in major relocations in milk production and the vegetable freezing study also showed advantages in major changes in location. Fourteen years after the analysis of milk production there had been only a moderate trend toward the optimum as specified in the study. This is not to suggest that the results of the milk production study were wrong, but to indicate again that there are many factors affecting location and the rigidity of established locations that cannot be measured.

The studies by Snodgrass and French and by Greig and Heifner used relatively few inputs compared to the variety of possibilities. Each used only 3 or 4 major costs; perhaps different results would have been obtained with more. The vegetable freezing models are currently being reevaluated using (1) procurement cost

TABLE 8.8

ACTUAL FARM PRODUCTION OF MILK BY STATES,
1953 AND 1967, AND "IDEAL" PRODUCTION MODEL FOR 1953

	Percent of Total Actual Production[1]	Percent of Total Ideal Modified Model[2]	Percent of Total Actual Production[3]
	1953	1953	1967
Minnesota	7.1	27.5	8.6
Wisconsin	13.2	19.2	15.6
New York	7.7	13.5	8.7
Iowa	4.9	9.4	4.7
California	5.5	5.2	7.3
Ohio	4.7	4.7	4.0
Indiana	3.1	3.4	2.1
Illinois	4.3	3.2	2.8
Alabama	1.1	3.1	0.7
Michigan	4.6	2.4	3.9
South Carolina	0.5	2.0	0.4
Pennsylvania	4.9	1.6	5.7
Mississippi	1.0	1.5	0.7
Other States	37.4	3.3	34.8

[1] Anon. (1954).
[2] Snodgrass and French (1958).
[3] Anon. (1968).

data (based on raw product production densities), (2) economies of scale in processing and in storage, (3) a better allocation of overhead costs based on length of season for each particular commodity and for all processing by the plant, (4) more detailed labor wage rates, (5) state and local taxes, (6) fuel and electricity costs, (7) both rail and truck costs to markets, and (8) raw product costs.

The methodology used in locational analysis is improving. Many more relevant cost factors can now be included in the models (with expansion of computer capacity). It is suggested that economic studies of the location of food processing will become a realistic method of measuring locational advantage and a significant aid to entrepreneurs making locational decisions.

A SUMMARY OF FACTORS AFFECTING LOCATION CHANGES

Some of the factors affecting changes in location of some of the food processing industries suggested in the previous examples are as follows:

In meat slaughtering, development of new technologies in meat storage and changes in the relative transportation costs between meat and live animals affected economic locations. Decentralization was caused by obsolete plants (the development of more efficient processing technologies which made the old plants obsolete) and by labor problems, higher wage rates in the large cities, and higher tax loads.

In broiler and egg production, acceptability of vertical integration in the South, less alternative opportunities, lesser hourly wage rates, and apparently the acceptability of lesser "management" wages, resulted in significant increases in production in the South.

In flour milling, relocations are resulting from changing differentials in freight rates between unprocessed wheat and flour.

In oranges, the development of new processing technologies and the adaptability of Florida oranges for frozen orange juice concentrate with some possible effect from urbanization of groves in California resulted in great shifts in location.

In onions, a "new" processing technology (dehydration) with differences in climate, varieties, and length of season had an effect on increasing production in California.

In peas, a shift from fresh to processed forms (with seasonability of production no longer of great importance) resulted in concentration in least cost production areas — with climate largely determining these areas.

In potatoes, with increased processing, the high cost seasonal areas are decreasing and the least cost fall crop areas are increasing. The location of the "new" technologies of frozen French fries and potato dehydration is partly due to quality factors and also to the willingness of growers to contract.

In some vegetable freezing, it was suggested that entrepreneurial ability may be a strong location-determining factor — that many locations of food processing may be "man-made" rather than resulting from "pure" economic factors.

ADDITIONAL FACTORS AFFECTING CHANGES IN LOCATION

There are many general factors which affect locations of food processing industries in addition to the specific ones mentioned for specific industries. Four of these more general factors will be briefly discussed. They are (1) the nationalization of markets, (2) economies of scale in processing, (3) integration of marketing stages, and (4) the tendency toward agglomeration (several firms tending to locate close together in some industries). In addition, several specific factors affecting location of food processing, not previously mentioned, will be discussed briefly.

The Nationalization of Markets

With the development of better transportation systems, communication systems (including national media for advertising), the development of national retail chain food stores, and standardized packages, the markets for many food products changed from local or regional markets to national (or international) markets. Many food product producers now must think in terms of national distribution rather than regional or local distribution, thus the perspective for plant location is greatly enlarged. Processors must now think in terms of the location of a plant or plants to minimize costs for national distribution. The size of the "ball park" in which the "game" is played is much larger. For many products, the selection of a processing plant site is now really an international problem and will probably become more so in the future.

Economies of Scale in Processing

Partially related to the nationalization of markets is the economies of scale in plant and in firm size. Apparently, in most food processing there are significant economies to scale. The economies of scale in physical processing facilities have apparently overcome the diseconomies to scale in raw product procurement costs and in physical distribution costs. This results in few large plants serving regional or national markets rather than in small plants serving local markets. This, of course, varies with the particular processing industry – but the tendency in most food processing is for fewer and larger plants. The phenomenon of fewer and larger plants makes location even more critical as the physical quantities of agricultural inputs for a particular plant may increase greatly.

Integration of Marketing Stages

Vertical integration as a locational factor in broilers and eggs was specifically mentioned earlier. However, the prospects for vertically integrated marketing arrangements is becoming a general factor to be considered in many food processing industries. One of the central issues of Galbraith's *The New Industrial State* is the tendency toward bigness in industry. With bigness, forward planning is essential; and for forward planning, control over prices is necessary (Galbraith 1968). One of the best methods of control over prices in agricultural processing is through vertical integration (Mighell and Jones 1963; Harris and Massey

1968). By "control over prices" it is not suggested that the processor "sets" the price as much as he may eliminate much of the risk and uncertainty of future prices.

Vertical integration or vertical coordination of all stages of production through the processing level may be obtained by many different methods and to all degress of completeness. Complete integration through the processing stage would mean that the processor would own the raw product production enterprise or vice versa. The next degree of completeness might be a long-term contractual relationship, the next an annual contract, etc. While in some enterprises the processor can reduce price risk and uncertainty by hedging on the future market, i.e., in wheat, corn, soy beans, etc., in others, particularly broilers, eggs, potatoes, vegetables, and some fruit, much of the production and processing is under vertically integrated contractual arrangements.

Vertical integration or vertical coordination offers efficiencies other than pricing efficiencies. There are physical efficiencies in management control and in physical handling as well as in the avoidance of price risk. There have been many instances of entrepreneurial decisions on location based on the willingness of raw product producers to accept vertically integrated arrangements with processors.

Vertical integration or vertical coordination, by various methods, will become an increasingly important aspect in much processing. In fact, raw products produced under atomistic market conditions will probably nearly completely disappear in many segments of American agriculture.

Agglomeration of Processing Enterprises

While there has been an apparent trend toward deagglomeration in meat slaughtering (decentralization), in other industries there is a tendency toward centralization. This, as are most factors of location, is interrelated with economies of scale and nationalization of markets. Agricultural processing industries are the instruments through which many specialized farm production areas have been developed. A case in point would be the potato enterprise in Idaho, Washington, and Oregon and the onion enterprise in California.

There are many reasons why many processing industries tend to locate in proximity to others – this largely deals with the infrastructure as well as with procurement, processing, and distribution costs. The advantages of some degree of concentration of processing industries are in availability of financial institutions familiar with the needs of the industry; availability of trained labor, of specialized equipment and repair services for the equipment, and of specialized consulting on technical aspects of production and processing; market news services; government inspection services; trained brokerage services; specialized insurance programs; a back-up supply of raw product because of the large quantities produced in the specialized area; and availability of storage and freight agencies familiar with or designed to handle the problems of the industry. Further, the specialized area, if of any consequence, probably obtains a large amount of services from agricultural experiment stations and the extension services of colleges and universities. This may include variety breeding, cultural experiments, insect and disease control programs, as well as the efforts of food scientists, engineers, etc. In the specialized production areas there may be advertising and promotion programs financed by the growers. Generally, in specialized areas the level of expertise of the producers is higher and more widespread. Further, grower-processor coordination is much easier. Changes in product form and changes in transportation costs, of course, are general factors affecting location (Greig 1956).

Other Factors Affecting Location

There are some other quite specific trends in costs in food processing that may exert a considerable weight on future locations of processing. Specifically,

TABLE 8.9

AN INDEX OF DEFLATED INPUT EXPENDITURES BY FIVE
FOOD PROCESSING INDUSTRIES, 1958 AND 1963
(1947 = 100)

Input Expenditures	Meat Products	Dairy Products	Canning and Preserving Products	Grain Mill Products	Bakery Products
Adjusted cost of goods sold					
1958	133	292	350	158	256
Agricultural	118	221	217	80	161
Nonagricultural	211	509	431	333	258
1963	160	331	420	214	369
Advertising					
1958	159	248	265	204	243
1963	189	260	262	315	220
Depreciation					
1958	199	271	194	289	213
1963	256	288	234	447	264
Production workers' wages					
1958	131	114	123	104	111
1963	116	93	52	108	52
Nonproduction workers' wages					
1958	136	365	227	135	119
1963	163	564	250	63	153
Compensation of officers					
1958	100	175	83	86	93
1963	113	163	76	89	92
Fringe benefits					
1958	113	219	96	133	214
1963	78	158	57	94	532
Taxes					
1958	160	270	194	164	184
1963	225	375	245	269	292

Source: Nelson and Chumley (1968).

both labor costs and agricultural inputs as a percent of total costs have decreased significantly in the past, and these trends are expected to continue (Nelson and Chumley 1968).

The relative increases in costs have been in taxes, advertising and promotion, and in container and packaging costs. Thus, the increases in costs of food processing have not been agricultural in nature.

The relative changes in agricultural and nonagricultural inputs between 1947 and 1958 for five major food processing categories are listed in Table 8.9. Similarly, the relative changes in production workers' wages, nonproduction workers' wages, compensation of officers, advertising, depreciation, taxes, etc., are also listed. The Table is difficult to read; for example, based on the year 1947 = 100, the real wages (wages adjusted for inflation) paid to production workers (not the wage rate per hour, but the total expenditures for production workers) in the canning and freezing industry decreased from 123% (of the 1947 year base) in 1958 to only 52% of the base year in 1963. Between 1958 and 1963 there was a real decrease in wages paid in all the industries listed except the grain mill products industry. Big increases were in taxes, depreciation, and advertising, while there were decreases in production workers' wages and in relative value of agricultural raw products.

Thus, the data suggest an increasing importance of state and local taxes in making location decisions, with state laws governing depreciation also becoming more important. Apparently, in much food processing the locational effects of wages are lessening because this is becoming a smaller input. However, wage rates as well as agricultural input costs — although both are decreasing — are still major factors in location as there are major differences between states and areas in these costs. The variability among areas is probably greater for these two cost factors than for most other inputs. Cost differences among states of many of these inputs will be presented in detail in the following chapter.

BIBLIOGRAPHY

ANON. 1954. Farm production, disposition, and income from milk. Agr. Marketing Serv., U.S. Dept. Agr., Washington, D.C.
ANON. 1961. Poultry and egg situation. Agr. Marketing Serv., U.S. Dept. Agr., Washington, D.C., Sept.
ANON. 1964. Poultry and egg situation. Agr. Marketing Serv., U.S. Dept. Agr., Washington, D.C., May.
ANON. 1965. Chickens and eggs: Production, disposition, cash receipts, and gross income, 1964-1965 by States. Crop Reporting Serv., U.S. Dept. Agr., Washington, D.C., Apr.
ANON. 1966A. The food marketing industries. U.S. Dept. Agr., Washington, D.C.
ANON. 1966B. Marketing and transportation situation. Agr. Marketing Serv., U.S. Dept. Agr., Washington, D.C., May.
ANON. 1968. Dairy situation. Agr. Marketing Serv., U.S. Dept. Agr., Washington, D.C., Nov.
GALBRAITH, J. K. 1968. The New Industrial State. The New American Library. New York.
GREIG, W. S. 1965. Locational effects of new technologies in fruit and vegetable processing. Michigan State Univ. Agr. Expt. Sta. Res. Rept. 35, May.
GREIG, W. S. 1966. Population, transportation, irrigation, and potato economics. 16th Natl. Potato Util. Conf., Fort Collins, Colo., July 27.

GREIG, W. S., and HEIFNER, R. G. 1968. Locational effects of selected economic factors in fruit and vegetable processing. Michigan State Univ. Agr. Expt. Sta. Res. Bull. *19*.

GREIG, W. S., and MARINE, C. L. 1962. Onions and their processing potential. Michigan State Univ. Agr. Econ. Mimeo *852*, Mar.

MARINE, C. L., and GREIG, W. S. 1966. Estimating sales potentials for new food products – new onion products. Michigan State Univ. Agr. Expt. Sta. Res. Rept. *55*, Nov.

GOLDBERG, R. A. 1968. Agribusiness coordination, a systems approach to the wheat, soybean, and Florida orange economies. Div. Res. Graduate School of Business Admin., Harvard Univ., Cambridge, Mass.

HARRIS, M., and MASSEY, D. T. 1968. Vertical coordination via contract farming. U.S. Dept. Agr. Econ. Res. Serv. Misc. Pub. *1073*, Mar.

HOOVER, E. M. 1937. Location Theory and the Shoe and Leather Industries. Harvard Univ. Press, Cambridge, Mass.

HUIE, J. M. 1969. Number, Size, and Location of Beef Slaughtering Plants in Michigan. Ph.D. Thesis, Michigan State Univ., E. Lansing, Mich.

ISARD, W. 1956. Location and Space Economy. Technology Press, MIT, Cambridge, and John Wiley & Sons, New York (published jointly).

ISARD, W. 1960. Methods of Regional Analysis. Technology Press, MIT, Cambridge, and John Wiley & Sons, New York (published jointly).

ISARD, W. 1969. General Theory: Social, Political, Economic and Regional. The MIT Press, Cambridge, Mass.

LEUTHOLD, R. M., and BAWDEN, D. L. 1966. An annotated bibliography of spatial studies. Wisconsin Agr. Expt. Sta. Res. Rept. *25*, Aug.

LOGAN, S. H., and KING, G. A. 1962. Economies of scale in beef slaughter plants. Giannini Found. Res. Rept. *20*, Univ. California, Dec.

LOSCH, A. 1954. The Economies of Location, 2nd Edition revised, translated by W. H. Waglon. Yale Univ. Press, New Haven, Conn.

MIGHELL, R. A., and JONES, L. A. 1963. Vertical coordination in agriculture. U.S. Dept. Agr. Econ. Res. Serv., Agr. Econ. Rept. *19*.

NELSON, P. E., Jr., and CHUMLEY, T. W. 1968. The changing input structure of selected food processing industries: agriculture's declining share. Marketing and Transportation Situation. U.S. Dept. Agr., Agr. Marketing Serv., Feb.

OHLIN, G. 1933. Interregional and International Trade. Harvard Univ. Press, Cambridge, Mass.

SNODGRASS, M. M., and FRENCH, C. E. 1958. Linear programming approach to the study of interregional competition in dairying. Purdue Univ. Agr. Expt. Sta. *S.B. 637*, May.

VON THUNEN, J. H. 1826. *Der Isolierte Staat in Beziehung auf Landwirtschaft und Nationalokonomie*, Hamburg, Germany. (German)

WEBER, A. 1929. Theory of the Location of Industries, translated by C. J. Frederick. Univ. Chicago Press, Chicago.

CHAPTER 9

W. Smith Greig | # Cost Differences Among States in Food Processing

The total cost of delivering a processed food product to a market from any particular location in the United States is the cumulation of a very large matrix of different costs. Many of these costs were mentioned in the previous chapter: (1) raw product costs or procurement costs and costs of other inputs, (2) the costs of processing which are affected by labor wage rates, fuel and electrical costs, taxes, size of operation, length of the processing season, product mix or complementarity of products, quality factors, cost and availability of water, by-product utilization, and waste disposal costs, and (3) transportation costs to market. Many of these cost factors, even for the same product, vary widely among states or among locations within a state. The purpose of this chapter is to identify some of the more important costs and to measure the difference among states. Labor wage rates, taxes, fuel and electrical costs, length of the processing season, and transportation costs to market will be discussed in some detail while raw product costs and raw product procurement costs will only be briefly mentioned.

LABOR COSTS AMONG STATES

The total number of production workers in food processing has been decreasing while total food processed has been increasing. Thus, there has been an increasing substitution of labor by capital, i.e., labor-saving equipment. There also has been a significant increase in labor productivity. Wage rates to labor have increased substantially through time. The combined effect of all these factors is that labor as a percentage of total costs in food processing has decreased materially through time; however, labor remains one of the principal costs in food processing. Since labor costs are still a major input cost, differences among states in labor wage rates naturally affect food processing costs among states. Again, it should be pointed out that proving that labor costs in food processing are 30% greater in 1 state than another does not prove that processing costs are 30% greater; other cost differences may more than offset the premium on labor.

Estimates of the cost for wages as a percentage of total inputs in food processing for five food processing industries are listed in Table 9.1. In the case of meat products, dairy products, canning and freezing, grain mill products, and the baking industry, there have been substantial decreases in wages for labor when measured as a percentage of total input costs. While labor costs have been decreasing as a share of total inputs, advertising, depreciation, taxes, and fringe benefits have been increasing. There is a shift in wages paid as a percentage of total inputs between production workers and nonproduction workers. While wages to production workers, as a percentage of total input costs, decreased rather significantly in each of the industries, wages to nonproduction workers increased in all the industries except the grain mill products industry.

The degree to which the cost of wages to production workers has decreased in some industries is shown by data in the canning and freezing industry. In this industry the cost of production workers as a percentage of total input costs decreased from 39.7% of costs in 1947 to 8.8% in 1963.

Of the five industries for which data have been developed, wages to workers in 1963, both production and nonproduction workers, ranged from 6.4% of total input costs in the grain mill products industry to 19.8% of total costs in the bakery products industry. These calculations have been based on total cost of input, including raw agricultural products and cost of packages, containers, etc. The principal cost in most food processing is probably for the raw product and the next most important cost in the majority of food processing operations probably is for labor.

The absolute costs of production workers' wages have not shown the consistent decrease as those of wages relative to total costs. In fact, in the meat products and grain mill products industries the total absolute costs of production workers increased between 1947 and 1963, while the total absolute costs of production workers in the canning and freezing industry and the bakery products industry decreased by nearly 1/2 (Table 9.2). Nonproduction workers total wage costs increased by a large amount for all industries except the grain mill products industry between 1947 and 1963.

The concepts in the preceding paragraph may be difficult to interpret at first glance. Perhaps a fuller explanation is necessary. If, for example, the total wages

TABLE 9.1

WAGE COSTS AS A PERCENT OF TOTAL INPUT COSTS BY
MAJOR FOOD PROCESSING INDUSTRIES,
1947, 1958, and 1963

Industry	Percent of Total Inputs		
	1947	1958	1963
Meat products			
Production workers' wages	8.3	8.2	6.2
Nonproduction workers' wages	2.6	2.6	2.7
Dairy products			
Production workers' wages	20.2	9.1	6.5
Nonproduction workers' wages	4.2	5.9	8.2
Canning and preserving			
Production workers' wages	39.7	21.2	8.8
Nonproduction workers' wages	3.4	3.4	3.6
Grain mill products			
Production workers' wages	8.9	6.1	4.8
Nonproduction workers' wages	5.1	4.5	1.6
Bakery products			
Production workers' wages	24.3	14.8	5.4
Nonproduction workers' wages	22.0	14.3	14.4

Source: Nelson and Chumley (1968).

paid for production workers in the whole meat products industry ın 1947 are set to equal 100, then the total costs of all production workers in this industry in 1963 would be 116, or 16% greater than in 1947, after discounting the effect of price inflations on the dollar value of each hour of labor.

RANGE IN HOURLY EARNINGS IN
FOOD PROCESSING AMONG STATES

The average hourly earnings of production workers in food processing, by state, for the years 1963 to 1967 are given in Table 9.3. The Table illustrates several points: (1) the increasing costs in nearly all states, and (2) the wide differences in costs among states. Concerning the latter, in 1967 the average hourly earnings of a production worker in Arkansas averaged $1.79 while that of a production worker in Iowa averaged $3.21, or 79% more than in Arkansas. As the data are for hourly wages only and do not include fringe benefits, the absolute differences in total cost to an employer are undoubtedly greater thari those specified. In 1967, 4 of the states, Arkansas, Mississippi, North Carolina, and Virginia, had hourly earnings under $2.00, while 8 of the states had hourly earnings of $3.00 or more. In general, most of the south had relatively low wages, while the west and north had relatively high wages.

Because total food processing is a combination of so many types of activities and is performed in so many locations, i.e., from mostly urban in the case of bakeries to more rural in the case of fruit processing, I will first show some labor costs by industries, then will specify in some detail the costs in hourly wages and fringe benefits to an employer for one specific industry. The example used in

TABLE 9.2

INDEX OF TOTAL COSTS OF WAGES IN FIVE
FOOD PROCESSING INDUSTRIES (1947 = 100)
DEFLATED BY A COST INDEX, 1958 and 1963

Industry	1947 Base	1958	1963
Meat products			
Production workers' wages	100	131	116
Nonproduction workers' wages	100	136	163
Dairy products			
Production workers' wages	100	114	93
Nonproduction workers' wages	100	365	564
Canning and preserving			
Production workers' wages	100	123	52
Nonproduction workers' wages	100	227	250
Grain mill products			
Production workers' wages	100	104	108
Nonproduction workers' wages	100	135	63
Bakery products			
Production workers' wages	100	111	52
Nonproduction workers' wages	100	119	153

Source: Nelson and Chumley (1968).

TABLE 9.3

AVERAGE HOURLY EARNINGS OF PRODUCTION
WORKERS IN ALL FOOD PROCESSING,
1963-1967

State	1963	1964	1965 (Dollars)	1966	1967
Alabama	1.66	1.71	1.79	1.83	2.01
Arizona	2.28	2.32	2.37	2.48	2.58
Arkansas	1.49	1.55	1.62	1.67	1.79
California	2.77	2.85	2.95	3.06	3.19
Colorado	2.61	2.71	2.85	2.92	3.05
Connecticut	2.48	2.58	2.58	2.72	2.81
Delaware	1.72	1.81	1.92	1.97	2.12
Florida	1.72	1.83	1.86	1.95	2.02
Georgia	1.77	1.88	1.97	2.06	2.19
Hawaii	1.93	2.03	2.16	2.30	2.42
Idaho	1.95	2.06	2.17	2.20	2.30
Illinois	2.67	2.73	2.81	2.95	3.03
Indiana	2.44	2.49	2.63	2.74	2.84
Iowa	2.74	2.84	2.90	3.03	3.21
Kansas	2.53	2.61	2.66	2.72	2.81
Kentucky	2.15	2.46	2.53	2.59	2.78
Louisiana	2.04	2.11	2.18	2.24	2.25
Maine	—	—	1.84	1.88	2.00
Maryland	2.04	2.14	2.14	2.25	2.41
Massachusetts	2.25	2.31	2.36	2.46	2.59
Michigan	—	—	—	—	—
Minnesota	2.69	2.76	2.84	2.88	3.00
Mississippi	1.53	1.57	1.61	1.67	1.83
Missouri	2.71	2.74	2.81	2.91	3.03
Montana	2.34	2.49	2.48	2.68	2.80
Nebraska	2.40	2.50	2.55	2.63	2.82
Nevada	—	—	—	—	—
New Hampshire	2.09	2.18	2.29	2.38	2.50
New Jersey	2.71	2.76	2.83	2.90	3.05
New Mexico	—	—	—	—	—
New York	2.55	2.64	2.75	2.83	2.91
North Carolina	1.49	1.57	1.63	1.71	1.83
North Dakota	2.03	2.07	2.16	2.27	2.40
Ohio	2.61	2.66	2.74	2.85	2.96
Oklahoma	1.94	1.99	1.99	2.05	2.22
Oregon	2.46	2.55	2.62	2.68	2.78
Pennsylvania	2.27	2.33	2.44	2.53	2.64
Rhode Island	2.51	2.55	2.63	2.71	2.82
South Carolina	1.63	1.74	1.74	1.86	2.02
South Dakota	2.34	2.45	2.48	2.55	2.72
Tennessee	1.96	2.04	2.10	2.17	2.24
Texas	1.99	2.07	2.11	2.20	2.27
Utah	2.45	2.58	2.66	2.77	2.78
Vermont	1.98	2.05	2.11	2.22	2.36
Virginia	1.64	1.70	1.75	1.86	1.96
Washington	2.71	2.79	2.88	2.93	3.00
West Virginia	1.86	1.90	1.93	1.99	2.06
Wisconsin	2.41	2.55	2.63	2.75	2.91
Wyoming	2.07	2.11	2.19	2.23	2.18

Source: U.S. Dept. Labor (1968B).

this latter case will be the canning and freezing industry.

Average hourly earnings in the meat products, dairy products, and bakery products industries for 1963-1967 for selected states are given in Table 9.4. Data for all states are not available, but again the wide differences among states are readily apparent. In the three industries listed, North Carolina was the only southern state for which data were readily available and in each case North Carolina's wage rate was substantially below each of the other states. Another point which should be made is that for the three industries specified, the wage rates are generally higher than for the average of all food processing in each state. The higher wage rates for these industries compared to other food processing may be due to the location of the industries within the states and perhaps also to the degree of unionization.

A DETAILED EXAMPLE OF LABOR IN THE
CANNING AND FREEZING INDUSTRY

Average Hourly Labor Wage Rates

Production worker costs as a percentage of total inputs in the canning and freezing industry are substantially above those for most other food processing industries, including industries in meat products, dairy products, grain milling, and baking products.

TABLE 9.4

AVERAGE HOURLY EARNINGS OF
PRODUCTION WORKERS IN THREE FOOD
INDUSTRIES FOR SELECTED STATES
1963-1967

	1963	1964	1965 (Dollars)	1966	1967
Meat processing					
California	3.00	3.08	3.19	3.30	3.43
Illinois	2.92	2.98	3.09	3.21	3.30
Iowa	3.09	3.22	3.30	3.47	3.67
Nebraska	2.67	2.92	2.93	3.00	3.21
New York	2.81	2.91	2.96	3.03	3.16
North Carolina	1.53	1.61	1.72	1.79	1.91
Ohio	2.75	2.82	2.93	3.09	3.24
Texas	2.29	2.31	2.30	2.32	2.36
Dairy processing					
California	3.26	3.39	3.55	3.63	3.80
Illinois	3.07	3.21	3.35	3.47	3.13
Kansas	2.06	2.15	2.21	2.29	2.30
Nebraska	2.25	2.32	2.40	2.47	2.55
New York	2.79	2.95	3.03	3.15	3.20
North Carolina	1.58	1.64	1.73	1.83	1.99
Pennsylvania	2.32	2.42	2.53	2.64	2.77
Bakeries					
California	3.28	3.35	3.45	3.57	3.67
Illinois	2.59	2.70	2.79	2.88	3.02
New Jersey	2.45	2.54	2.60	2.69	2.78
North Carolina	1.72	1.78	1.84	1.94	2.04
Ohio	2.47	2.57	2.65	2.75	2.83
Pennsylvania	2.21	2.26	2.34	2.53	2.71

Source: U.S. Dept. Labor (1968B).

Wages of production workers in fruit and vegetable processing have increased substantially on an absolute basis through time but the total costs of production workers have been outrun on a percentage increase basis by such costs as packaging materials, taxes, advertising, depreciation, compensation of officer, and raw products.

For the canning and freezing industry for 10 states for which data are available from 1958-1966 (Table 9.5), the average hourly earnings of production workers have increased on the average at a rate of 4% per yr. For these 10 states the average hourly earnings increased from $1.67 in 1958 to $2.20 in 1966, an increase of 32% in 8 yr. Further, this is not the employer's cost because fringe benefits, unemployment insurance, workman's compensation and federal Social Security (FICA) taxes are not included. These costs are probably increasing more rapidly than the basic hourly earnings of production workers. For example, in 1960 FICA taxes were 3% of the first $4800 of earnings. In 1968, FICA taxes were 4.4% of the first $7800, and by 1975, under current laws (1969), it will be 5.65% of the first $7800.

Not only are labor costs an extremely important input to the canning and freezing industry, but they have a strong influence on interstate location of processing because of wide differences between states in employers' costs of production workers. For example, in Table 9.5, the 1966 hourly earnings of production workers in California were nearly 65% greater than in Oklahoma and 59% greater than Florida.

Because the cost of production workers is important to the employer, both in terms of total input and in terms of its effect in interregional competition or its locational effect between states, hourly earnings and costs to the employer per production worker will be presented in some detail.

First, the hourly earnings for production workers are specifically defined. The definitions for both are given in footnotes 1 and 2 of Table 9.5. Hourly earnings are gross returns to the employee and do not include Social Security benefits, workman's compensation, unemployment insurance, and federal Social Security (FICA taxes) payments by the employer, or other fringe benefits. Production workers include all working foremen and nonsupervisory workers including office and clerical workers as well as production workers, repairmen, etc. The term production workers includes nearly all employees except those in supervisory and administrative positions.

Obviously, to obtain total costs of production workers specific other costs such as workman's compensation, unemployment insurance, and FICA taxes must be added to the average hourly earnings.

Unemployment Insurance

Unemployment insurance is a highly complex system. Each state has its own laws and regulations of payments from employers and benefits to workers. Further, under the Federal Unemployment Tax Act the employer must pay 3.1% taxes on the first $3000 per yr earned by each employee (under certain conditions of employment). However, if a state has its own approved

TABLE 9.5

AVERAGE HOURLY EARNINGS[1] OF PRODUCTION WORKERS[2]
IN THE CANNING AND FREEZING INDUSTRY[3]
BY STATES, 1958 to 1966[4]

State	Average Hourly Earnings (Dollars Per Hour)								
	1958	1959	1960	1961	1962	1963	1964	1965	1966
Arkansas							1.51	1.60	1.69
California	1.94	2.03	2.15	2.26	2.34	2.39	2.48	2.58	2.65
Colorado							1.68	1.68	1.68[5]
Delaware							1.53	1.56	1.67[5]
Florida	1.31	1.32	1.32	1.39	1.48	1.52	1.50	1.56	1.67
Idaho							1.90	2.00	2.00
Illinois	1.83	1.96	2.02	2.03	2.07	2.17	2.17	2.22	2.47
Indiana	1.53	1.54	1.54	1.63	1.72	1.73	1.79	1.80	1.89
Iowa							1.96[5]	2.10[5]	2.00[5]
Kentucky[5]							1.51[5]	1.60[5]	1.69[5]
Louisiana							1.48	1.53	1.61
Maine							1.66	1.70	1.69
Maryland							1.53	1.56	1.67
Michigan	1.54	1.64	1.68	1.80	1.82	1.81	1.80	1.78	1.95
Minnesota							1.74	1.75	1.80
New Jersey	1.98	2.06	2.11	2.24	2.32	2.39	2.45	2.48	2.53
New York	1.61	1.68	1.73	1.72	1.72	1.73	1.80	1.89	2.00
North Carolina							1.50	1.60	1.66
Ohio							1.99	2.09	2.24
Oklahoma							1.50	1.53	1.61
Oregon	1.70	1.76	1.89	1.99	2.04	2.07	2.14	2.19	2.24
Pennsylvania	1.55	1.64	1.68	1.73	1.76	1.91	1.97[5]	2.07[5]	2.17[5]
South Carolina[5]							1.50[5]	1.56[5]	1.67[5]
Texas							1.51	1.59	1.72
Virginia							1.54	1.58	1.66
Washington	1.78	1.54	1.94	2.00	2.08	2.20	2.27	2.36	2.39[5]
West Virginia							1.61	1.64	1.69[5]
Wisconsin							1.59	1.63	1.75

[1] Average hourly earnings are on a gross basis reflecting not only changes in basic hourly and incentive wage rates, but also such variable factors as premium pay for overtime and late-shift work, and changes in output of workers paid on an incentive plan. Averages of hourly earnings differ from wage rates. Earnings are the actual return to the worker, while rates are the amounts stipulated for a given unit of work or time. The earnings do not measure the level of total labor costs to the employer since the following are excluded: irregular bonuses, retroactive items, payments of various welfare benefits, payroll taxes paid by employers, and earnings by employees not covered under the production worker or nonsupervisory employee definition.

[2] Production workers include working foremen and all nonsupervisory workers (including leadmen and trainees) engaged in fabricating, processing, assemblying, inspecting, receiving, storage, handling, packing, warehousing, shipping, maintenance, repair, janitorial and watchmen services, product development, auxilliary production for plant's own use (e.g., power plant) and record keeping and other services closely associated with the above production operations. Nonsupervisory employees included as production workers includes employees (not above the working supervisory level) such as office and clerical workers, repairmen, sales persons, operators, drivers, attendants, service employees, linemen, laborers, janitors, watchmen, and similar occupational levels, and other employees whose services are closely associated with those of the employees listed.

[3] The canning and freezing industry is defined by the U.S. Dept. Com. as Standard Industrial Classification (SIC) 203. Included are SIC 2031 (canned and cured seafoods), SIC 2032 (canned specialties), SIC 2033 (canned fruits and vegetables), SIC 2034 (dehydrated food products), SIC 2035 (pickles, sauces, and salad dressings), SIC 2036 (fresh or frozen packaged fish), SIC 2037 (frozen fruits and vegetables). In many instances SIC 2031 (canned and cured seafoods) and SIC 2036 (fresh or frozen packaged fish) were not included, for example, for California and New York. Thus, the data are predominantly weighted by the processed fruits and vegetable industry.

[4] Data for selected states, 1958-1966 is from U.S. Dept. Labor (1967). Employment and earning statistics for states and areas 1939-1966, from Bur. Labor Statistics. Data for other selected states 1964-1966 from the individual state cooperating agencies' Current Employment Statistics Program, which cooperate with the Bur. of Labor Statistics, U.S. Dept. Labor.

[5] Estimated from incomplete data.

unemployment compensation system, then 90% of the first 3% (or 2.7% on the first $3000 earned) is forgiven in the form of an offset. This leaves only 0.4% of the first $3000 earned by each employee to be paid to the federal government under the Federal Employment Tax Act. Each state in the United States does have an approved unemployment compensation system, thus under the Federal Employment Tax Act each employer would pay 0.4% of the first $3000 earned. Since this is constant throughout the United States this tax will be disregarded in the subsequent analysis of interregional competition.

States can vary widely in total payments (as percentage of total payroll or percentage of taxable payroll) from different industries within the state. This is or should be based on actual statistics or historical data on unemployment rates in each industry. Further, states vary widely both in payments and in benefits. Benefits vary as to total payments per week of unemployment and the number of weeks unemployment can be drawn. Further, in some cases, i.e., Michigan in 1958, the total unemployment compensation system may be overdrawn requiring loans from the federal system, and a general increase in rate structures to employers. Within a specific industry, individual firms have different rate structures based on historical records of each firm's unemployment. For example, in New York in 1967, of the 272 firms in the canning and freezing industry, the unemployment compensation rates were as follows: 76 firms paid 3.3% on taxable payrolls; 18 firms 3.1%, 52 firms 3.0%, 3 firms 2.9%, 19 firms 2.8%, 2 firms 2.7%, 7 firms 2.6%, 3 firms 2.5%, 4 firms 2.4%, 8 firms 2.3%, 5 firms 2.2%, 10 firms 2.0%, 4 firms 1.8%, 9 firms 1.6%, 5 firms 1.4%, 7 firms 1.2%, 6 firms 1.0%, 7 firms 0.9%, and 27 firms 0.8%.

In most cases the cost to the employer for unemployment insurance does not cover the actual benefits charged to the fund by unemployed workers in the canning and freezing industry. Thus, in effect, this industry is subsidized to some degree by other industries having lesser rates of unemployment. For 10 states for which data were available on unemployment compensation, charges and benefits varied from 116 to 260% of the charges to the employers (Table 9.6). Thus, only actual charges to employers are classified as a part of employers' cost of production workers. The actual cost of benefits should not be overlooked, as probably in the long-run, payments or costs in most industries will be nearly equal to benefits received.

Workman's Compensation

Workman's compensation insurance costs also vary widely between states. Although this aspect was not investigated, probably insurance costs vary with size of firms and with each firm's historical accident and death record. Each state may have different laws or legal precedents concerning payments to workers injured or killed on the job. Therefore, commercial insurance companies issuing compensation insurance will have different rate structures in the different states. Some few states such as Ohio, Washington, and West Virginia have monopolistic state workman's compensation funds, rather than insurance handled by private insurance agencies. Workman's compensation insurance costs obtained from the National Council on Compensation Insurance, and from the individual states having monopolistic state funds are listed in column 2 of Table 9.7 for the major states in the canning and freezing industry. These compensation insurance rates are for the most general insurance classification, "Canneries, N.O.C. (not otherwise classified) Code 2111." There are many classifications for insurance purposes, but this single classification probably covers the greatest number of individual firms within the industry.

Both workman's compensation and unemployment insurance, as they affect labor cost to the employer and as they differ among states can affect location of industries.

Federal Social Security Taxes (FICA taxes)

Since FICA taxes are based on a percentage of employee earnings, they also exert a regional effect or compound the effect of wage rates and their resulting locational effects. The 1968 FICA tax on employers was 4.4% of the first $7800 of payroll. Thus, if a production laborer works 8 hr a day, 250 days a year or 2000 hr a year at the average hourly wage rates in California and Florida, he would earn 2000 x $2.92 in California and 2000 x $1.84 in Florida, or $5840 in California and $3600 in Florida. The FICA taxes would be $256.96 in California and only $151.92 in Florida. Thus, the FICA tax differences have increased the difference in cost between California and Florida for a production worker from $2160 to $2265 or an increase in the difference in cost of 4.4%. (This 4.4% increase will be true in all cases where the production workers makes less than $7800 per yr.)

TABLE 9.6
UNEMPLOYMENT INSURANCE COSTS TO EMPLOYERS
AND BENEFITS TO WORKERS
(AS A PERCENT OF TOTAL PAYROLL)
IN THE CANNING AND FREEZING INDUSTRY
FOR SELECTED STATES, 1966

State	Cost to Employers (% of Total Payroll)	Benefits to Workers (% of Total Payroll)	Benefits as a % of Costs to Employer
California	2.5	6.5	260
Florida	2.5	2.9	116
Michigan	2.1	4.3	205
New York	1.4	3.2	228
North Carolina[1]	1.63	2.36	145
North Dakota	2.97	4.07	137
Oregon	2.01	4.3	214
Washington	1.56	2.69	172
West Virginia	2.4	2.7	112
Wisconsin	2.047	2.76	135

Source: Individual state cooperating agencies' Current Employment Statistics Program, which cooperate with the Bur. Labor Statist., U.S. Dept. Labor.
[1] Average for 1964 and 1965; 1966 data not available.

TABLE 9.7

EMPLOYER COSTS OF PRODUCTION WORKERS IN THE CANNING AND
FREEZING INDUSTRY, INCLUDING AVERAGE HOURLY EARNINGS,
WORKMAN'S COMPENSATION, UNEMPLOYMENT INSURANCE, FEDERAL SOCIAL SECURITY
TAXES (FICA), AND TOTAL EMPLOYER COSTS BY STATES, 1966

State	Avg. Hourly Earnings[1] 1966 (Dollars)	Workman's Compensation[2] 1966 (% of Total Payroll)	Unemployment Insurance[3] 1966 (% of Total Payroll)	FICA Taxes[4] 1968 (% of Total Payroll)	Total Fringe Benefits[5] 1966 (% of Total Payroll)	Total Costs to Employer Per Hour 1966[6] (Dollars)
Arkansas	1.69	2.78	1.64	4.4	8.82	1.84
California	2.65	3.45	2.50	4.4	10.35	2.92
Colorado	1.68	2.51	1.50[7]	4.4	8.41	1.82
Delaware	1.67	1.20	2.50[7]	4.4	8.10	1.81
Florida	1.67	2.99	2.50	4.4	9.89	1.84
Idaho	2.00	2.97	2.40	4.4	9.77	2.20
Illinois	2.47	2.45	.55	4.4	7.40	2.65
Indiana	1.89	1.89	1.40	4.4	7.69	2.04
Iowa	2.00[7]	2.47	.39	4.4	7.26	2.15
Kentucky	1.69[7]	.70	1.30	4.4	6.40	1.80
Louisiana	1.61	1.90	2.30	4.4	8.60	1.75
Maine	1.69	1.90	1.87	4.4	8.17	1.83
Maryland	1.67	2.74	2.28	4.4	9.42	1.83
Michigan	1.95	5.22	2.10	4.4	11.72	2.18
Minnesota	1.80	2.56	1.99	4.4	9.05	1.96
New Jersey	2.53	4.69	1.39	4.4	10.48	2.80
New York	2.00	3.70	1.40	4.4	9.50	2.19
North Carolina	1.66	1.32	1.63	4.4	7.35	1.78
Ohio	2.24	1.80	1.50	4.4	7.70	2.41
Oklahoma	1.61	5.06	1.73	4.4	11.19	1.79
Oregon	2.24	3.73	2.01	4.4	10.14	2.47
Pennsylvania	2.17[7]	1.50[7]	3.73	4.4	9.63	2.38
South Carolina	1.67[7]	2.58[7]	2.36	4.4	9.58	1.83
Texas	1.72	2.99	1.06	4.4	8.45	1.87

Virginia	1.66	1.32	1.30	4.4	7.02	1.78
Washington	2.39	3.28	1.56	4.4	9.24	2.61
West Virginia	1.69	2.87[7]	2.40	4.4	9.67	1.85
Wisconsin	1.75	1.68	2.05	4.4	8.13	1.89

[1] Obtained directly from the individual state cooperating agencies' Current Employment Statistics Program which cooperate with the Bur. Labor Statist., U.S. Dept. Labor.

[2] In most cases obtained for the classification Canneries—N.O.C., Code 2111, from the Natl. Counc. on Compensation Insurance, 200 East 42nd St., New York. Some states have monopolistic funds, i.e., N. Dakota, Ohio, Washington, and W. Virginia. These were obtained directly from state agencies.

[3] Same as footnote[1] Does not include 0.4% of the first $3000 income to each production worker paid by the employer to the federal government under the federal Unemployment Tax Act.

[4] In 1968 under FICA, the employer pays 4.4% of the first $7800 income to each worker. In 1966, the employer paid 4-1/8% of the first $4800. Data were insufficient to adjust 1966 FICA taxes as a percent of total payroll. The 1968 FICA taxes as a percent of total payroll are overstated in cases where a production worker makes over $7800 per yr.

[5] Total of columns 2, 3, and 4.

[6] Average hourly wage rate plus workman's compensation, unemployment insurance and FICA taxes.

[7] Estimated from data on food processing.

FICA taxes have increased substantially through time and under present (1967) laws will continue to increase until 1987. For example, in 1960 FICA tax was 3.0% of the first $4800 income, the schedule after 1967 is based on the first $7800 income and at the following rates:

Year	%	Year	%
1968	4.4	1976-79	5.7
1969-70	4.8	1980-86	5.8
1971-72	5.2	1987-after	5.9
1973-75	5.65		

The average hourly earnings in the canning and freezing industry, workman's compensation insurance rates, unemployment compensation rates, and FICA taxes, are listed in Table 9.7 for the major fruit and vegetable processing states in the United States. These data are combined to give employers' costs of production workers (column 6).

Not all employer costs or fringe benefits have been listed. Many employers may have comprehensive health insurance or medical benefit plans, paid holidays and/or vacations, life and/or accident insurance plans (other than workman's compensation), subsidized company cafeterias, recreational facilities, etc. All of these may involve substantial costs to the employer above the basic hourly earnings of the individual employees.

A BRIEF SUMMARY OF LABOR COSTS

Labor costs vary among food processing industries and vary widely among states. Labor costs in food processing are rising substantially and probably at a rate higher than the general rate of inflation in the United States. Of the industries on which data were presented, the canning and freezing industry had the lowest wage rates. This is probably because the industry tends to be more rurally located, is seasonal, and probably more nonunionized than most other food processing enterprises. In some cases absolute labor costs of production workers on a deflated basis have increased, for example, in the meat products industry and in the grain mill industry. In other cases there have been substantial decreases in total production worker labor—in the canning and freezing industry and in the bakery industry. This is largely a reflection of the substitution of machinery for production workers. This trend is expected to continue and labor costs will continue to decrease. The development of synthetics, substitutes, and analogs will further this trend since these products will be more standardized and will permit more mechanization with less production seasonality. Labor costs as a percentage of total costs have consistently decreased through time; this trend will continue as will the shift from production workers to nonproduction workers. Food processing facilities, particularly in the case of synthetics, substitutes, and analogs, can easily be visualized, where the labor requirement in processing is that of an engineer monitoring electronically controlled processing, packaging, and storing of the food products.

TAX DIFFERENCES AMONG STATES

Introduction

It should be recognized that the absolute level of taxes on a firm in any location is only one side of the coin. Other aspects are the services the firm receives for the taxes it pays. While taxation comparisons in different locations can be made arithmetically, many services may only be subjectively evaluated. For example, how does one measure the differences in quality of school systems, hospitals, police departments, fire departments, public libraries, and public recreational facilities? Differences in highway systems, transportation facilities, social welfare programs, and quality of local and state governments may also have a bearing on plant location. Water supply systems, electrical systems, natural gas pipelines, sewage and waste disposal systems may be publicly financed in some locations and not in others. The amount and quality of publicly-supported agricultural research and research in food technology may be much greater in some states than in others. No attempt is made in this study to evaluate the differences in services, only tax levels themselves are considered.

A Review of the Importance of State and Local Taxes

In a study of the changing input structure in food processing, Nelson and Chumley (1968) found that local and state taxes were the most rapidly increasing input costs. For example, between 1947 and 1963 these tax costs increased 125% in meat processing, 275% in dairy products processing, 145% in the canning and freezing industry and 169% in the grain mill products industry. At the same time the cost of production workers (total wages paid for production workers) increased by 16% in meat products, decreased 7% in dairy products, decreased 48% in canning and freezing, and increased 8% in the grain mill products industry. State and local property taxes in 1963 represented 0.6% of the cost of goods sold by the meat products industry, 1.2% in the dairy products industry, 1.9% in the canning and freezing industry, and 0.8% in the grain mill products industry.

Greig (1968) estimated that in 1965-1966 state and local taxes had increased in the dairy products industry to 1.4% of inputs and to 1.1% in the grain mill products industry while canning and freezing remained at 1.9% and the meat products at 0.6% of inputs.

State and local taxes when measured as a percentage of total inputs sound rather small. However, here we will compare state and local taxes to depreciation, and state and local taxes to profits after all taxes, including federal taxes.

In 1965-1966 local and state taxes in the canning and freezing industry were 83% as large as total depreciation charges, 68% of depreciation in the dairy industry, 78% of depreciation in the meat products industry, and 60% of depreciation in the grain mill products industry (Internal Revenue Service 1968).

When calculated as a percentage of net profit after taxes, local and state taxes in the canning and freezing industry were equivalent to 52% of net income, 56% in the dairy industry, 89% in the meat products industry, and equivalent to 37% of net income after all taxes in the grain mill products industry. When compared to total profits, the tax load appears to be a substantial input cost. Profits in the meat products industry in 1965-1966 were relatively low and taxes, when compared to profits, were relatively higher than in other, more profitable food processing industries.

With local and state taxes so high relative to net profits, certainly if there are substantial differences among locations in the tax loads, these differences could easily affect profitability.

In evaluating the effect of local and state taxes on profitability it should be remembered that local and state taxes are deductible expenses in calculating federal income taxes. For example, if 2 firms were both near the federal income tax rate level of 50%, and the difference in state and local taxes were $10,000 per yr, the tax difference effect on profits after all taxes would be only around $5000. The true effect of state and local taxes can only be determined after calculating net profit after all taxes including federal taxes.

Attempts to measure the effect of taxes on economic development or industrial development among locations have yielded variable results (Stenson 1968). Surveys of businessmen to estimate the importance they place on taxes generally show that taxes rank below such other factors as markets, transportation, and availability of labor in their influences on locational decisions. Studies of possible relocations of established firms for possible tax savings generally show that, in most cases, tax savings were a small part of total costs and total geographical variable costs. Studies comparing tax levels to economic growth have had conflicting results. Wrightman (1968) in a recent comprehensive study concluded that "state-local tax differentials between similar communities in the Northeast Region of the United States are sufficiently large to influence industrial location."

It is our opinion that while local and state taxes are not as important an input as raw product, labor, and distances to markets, differences in local and state taxes can have a significant effect on profit levels.

Methodology in Comparing Taxes Among States

The Model Firms. — Each tax may affect each firm in a different way. Sales taxes on building materials and equipment could be important to a low volume, relatively low profit margin, seasonal food processor, but perhaps minor to a high volume, high profit margin electronics manufacturer. Inventory taxes could be substantial costs to a seasonal food processor who must carry inventories throughout the year for his customer, but minor to a fluid milk processor who carries little more than a few days' supply of processed milk. Typically, many tax studies choose model firms with wide ranges in profitability and operating characteristics to show the differences in effect of taxes on the different types of firms. In the study reported here three model firms were chosen, each to represent a particular type of food processing industry. The three industries were (1) the canning and freezing industry (SIC 203),[1] (2) the dairy industry (SIC 202), and (3) the grain mill products industry (SIC 204). State and local taxes for only the canning and freezing industry will be reported here. The details of the taxes on the other two industries may be found in the original report (Greig 1969).

Financial data to develop these model firms were obtained from the 1965-1966 tax year in the *Source Book of Statistics of Income* (Internal Revenue Service 1968). The financial data used were near the weighted average of all firms in each industry reporting corporate federal income tax data to IRS for the tax year 1965-1966.

Analysis of Local and State Property Taxes. — According to the Dept. of Com. there are over 84,000 tax collecting districts in the United States. Apparently there is no centralized collection and tabulation of the effective property tax rates charged in these different districts. While some state agencies, for example, in Oregon, publish assessment ratios and property tax rates for different areas for the state as a whole, few states perform this service. "What we have is a $20 billion tax supplying nearly 1/2 of all combined state-local tax revenues and 7/8 of the tax revenue of some 80,000 local governments, whose administration over large portions of the country is seriously inefficient and inequitable" (Bird 1965). The author's purpose is not to question the efficiency or equity of local-state property taxes, but to indicate the difficulty of obtaining accurate and reliable data.

In nearly all states of the United States, the laws of the state specify that property, for tax purposes, must be assessed at "true," or "real," or "fair" market value. Some exceptions are in Chicago and Cleveland, for example, where "book value" of property may be used for tax purposes. The determination of appropriate local property tax rates was obtained by a survey of the tax assessors in each of the cities of the United States where a commercial fruit and vegetable processing plant was located. This survey yielded over a 50% usable return. These data were supplemented by a regional survey of selected fruit and vegetable processors to check the original returns from the tax assessors. In nearly all cases the check yielded nearly identical rate structures.

Wrightman (1968) in his study discussed the inequity in assessment and the "sub rosa" deals to obtain low local property tax rates. Neither the time nor the tools were available to question how closely the value as assessed by the assessor approximated the true market value. The study specifically assumed that the true market value was fairly assessed by all tax assessors. Or more specifically, the study determined the legal local property tax rate; these tax rates were then applied uniformly to the value of the model firms. The question of assessed

---

[1] (SIC) is the Standard Industrial Classification code used by the Bureau of Census (see Chap. 1 and 2).

value was, in effect, not considered. The assessed value was a fixed value of the model firms to which the local legal tax rate was applied.

Analysis of State Taxes. – The analysis of sales taxes on building materials and equipment, use taxes, incorporation or initial filing fees, licenses, franchise fees, capital stock taxes, state income, gross receipts or gross profits taxes, and other forms of state taxes were made for the model firms in each of 26 states by a national accounting firm.[2]

Appropriate 1968 tax laws in each of the states were used. Because of the complexity of the tax laws, many assumptions or specifications were made concerning the model firm. The firm was a new firm, built and operated in 1968 under 1968 tax laws, it was incorporated in the state in which it is processing, and only does business in that state, etc.

Local, State, and Federal Taxes on a Model Firm Representative of SIC 203 for 1968. – *Description of a Model Firm Representative of SIC 203.* – The balance sheet and income statement to describe Model Firm A came almost completely from the *Source Book of Statistics of Income* for the tax year 1965-1966 as published by IRS. In this publication IRS provides detailed financial data (91 lines of financial data) on 14 asset sizes of firms, for all firms reporting corporate income tax returns. In 1965-1966 there were 1963 firms, primarily canners or freezers (SIC 203) who filed corporate federal income tax returns. Model Firm A approximates the weighted average balance sheet and income statement for these 1963 firms.

For example, the size of the firm used in Firm A in the canning and freezing industry is a firm with $2,000,000 in total assets. This is near the weighted average asset size of $1,921,000 of the 1963 firms reporting federal corporation income taxes in 1965-1966. Similarly, each item in the balance sheet and income statement for Model Firm A is approximately the weighted average for all firms as reported by IRS for the 1965-1966 tax year.

While only 1 size of firm is used to represent the canning and. freezing industry, a common analysis of all of the 14 asset sizes used by IRS shows few major differences in the percentage of total assets subject to local property taxes. That is, land, buildings, equipment, and inventories were a relatively constant percentage of total assets, regardless of the total asset size of the firm (Greig 1968). Thus, while only one asset firm size is used in developing differences among states in property taxes, relative differences would appear to hold on a wide range of size classes.

Similarly, after an asset size class of $1,000,000 was reached, profits as a percentage of total assets, or as a percentage of stockholders' equity were not greatly different. Of the 7 asset size classes from $1,000,000 to $250,000,000 in total assets developed by IRS, profits on equity after taxes ranged from 7.2 to 11.8%. In our model, firm profits as a percentage of equity (after all taxes but

---

[2]Touche, Ross, Bailey and Smart (Chicago offices).

before investment credit) ranged from 7.5 to 9.8% depending on the state in which it was located.

The balance sheet and income statement for Model Firm A, representative of the canning and freezing industry (SIC 203) are listed in Tables 9.8 and 9.9. For Model Firm A, gross income before local, state, and federal taxes was $191,744 for the tax year 1968.

The Method of Determining the Appropriate Property Tax Rate. – To compare property tax rates for the canning and freezing industry, it was considered appropriate to determine tax rates at the industry's current location. We attempted to determine taxes from a sample of the approximately 700 cities which currently have a fruit or vegetable processing plant, rather than attempt to determine taxes from a sample of approximately 80,000 taxing districts in the United States. From a directory of the canning and freezing industry (Anon. 1969C) a questionnaire was mailed to the city tax assessor at each city where a fruit and vegetable plant was located. In many cases, the county was the tax assessing authority and the county assessor returned the completed questionnaire. Thus, in several cases (for example, California) large portions of the state are represented rather than representing specific cities. Over a 50% return of usable tax schedules was obtained from the initial mailing and a second mailing was not considered necessary.

The questionnaire was designed to determine the assessment ratio, that is, the percentage of true market value at which the property was evaluated, and also the rate of taxation per each $1000 of assessed value. From this the rate of taxation per $1000 market value was determined. Rates on land, buildings, equipment, and inventories were determined separately.

Within many states the ranges in property taxes between locations was large. The range in property tax rates for fruit and vegetable processing plant locations and the simple arithemetic average for the total returns obtained from each state are given in Table 9.10. The simple arithmetic average was used in tax computations to compare differences between states.

One county in Maryland, apparently desperately in need of new business, offered no taxes on any new firm with a capital investment of over $100,000. Because of differences in rates on land, buildings, equipment, and inventories, it is difficult to say which states have the highest property taxes unless the rates are applied to the operation of a specific firm. This will be done for each of our three model firms.

The 26 states chosen for the analysis are those relatively important in the fruit and vegetable processing industry. It is suggested that the 26 states listed probably represent from 90-95% of the U.S. canning and freezing industry (SIC 203).

The calculation of average property taxes for the model firm by states, is listed in Table 9.11. This is simply a multiplication of the average property tax rate (Table 9.10) times the value of land, buildings, equipment, and inventories listed in the balance sheet for Model Firm A. Total property taxes range from $7583 in Pennsylvania to $44,716 in Nebraska for Model Firm A.

TABLE 9.8

BALANCE SHEET FOR MODEL FIRM A
REPRESENTATIVE OF THE CANNING AND FREEZING INDUSTRY (SIC 203)
AS OF DECEMBER 31, 1967

Current Assets			**Current liabilities**	
Cash	$ 76,800		Accounts payable	$ 313,200
Accounts receivable	302,000		Mortgage, notes, bonds	
Inventories	594,800		(under 1 Yr)	349,200
Total current assets	973,600		Other current liabilities	127,600
			Total current liabilities	790,000
Property, plant and equipment			**Long-term liabilities**	
Land	29,800		Loans from stockholders	52,800
Buildings and improvements[1]	299,300		Mortgage, notes, bonds	
Machinery, equipment and			(over 1 Yr)	215,400
fixtures[1]	555,700		Other liabilities	41,000
Total fixed assets	884,800		Total long-term liabilities	
			(other than stockholders'	
			equity)	309,200
Other non-current (nondepreciable)			Stockholders' equity	900,800
assets	141,600			
Total assets	$2,000,000		Total liabilities and	
			stockholders' equity	$2,000,000

[1] The IRS data in *Source Book of Statistics of Income* listed all depreciable assets together. It was assumed that buildings and improvements were 35% of depreciable assets and machinery, equipment, and fixtures were 65% of depreciable assets.

Sales Taxes on Building Materials and Equipment and Use Taxes on Equipment Rentals. — Many states have a sales tax on building materials and in some cases a tax against the completed cost of buildings including labor costs in construction. Similarly, there may be a sales tax on equipment purchases for use in manufacturing. Some other states may have a use tax on equipment rentals. In computing the sales taxes on buildings and on equipment, 2/3 of the cost of the building was assumed to be building materials cost ($199,532) and 1/3 of the total was assumed to be labor costs ($99,678). For equipment for tax purposes 4/5 was assumed to be equipment costs ($444,560) and 1/5 assumed to be labor costs of installation ($111,140). Also Model Firm A paid $26,600 per yr as rental for equipment.

The sales taxes and use taxes for each of the 26 states for building and equipment purchases and equipment rentals are given in Table 9.12. While some states allow taxes on equipment rentals to be expensed rather than capitalized, in all cases for the computation for total tax purposes, all sales taxes were capitalized. The use taxes on equipment rentals were expensed.

For buildings the taxes were capitalized based on a 40-yr life, but using an accounting practice of the double-declining balance—therefore, the effective first year tax charge was 5% of the total sales tax on buildings. On equipment the sales taxes were capitalized based on a 15-yr life, also using a double declining

TABLE 9.9

INCOME STATEMENT FOR MODEL FIRM A
REPRESENTATIVE OF THE CANNING AND
FREEZING INDUSTRY (SIC 203) FOR CALENDAR YEAR 1968

Sales and business receipts	$4,396,000
Cost and expenses (exclusive of taxes)	
Direct costs of operations and sales (other than packaging material)	$2,637,900
Containers, packaging materials and supplies[1]	843,800
Compensation of officers	62,400
Repairs	24,100
Bad debts	4,600
Rent on equipment	26,600
Interest expense	43,900
Depreciation	
(a) Buildings $299,300 @ 40 yr by by double declining balance	14,965
(b) Equipment $555,700 @ 15 yr by double declining balance	74,091
Advertising	50,600
Other deductions	421,300
Total costs and expenses (before taxes)	$4,204,256
Income before state, local, and federal taxes	$191,744

[1] Assumed to be 20.0% of total costs.

TABLE 9.10

RANGE AND SIMPLE AVERAGE OF LOCAL AND STATE PROPERTY
TAX RATES FOR LOCATIONS WITH FRUIT OR VEGETABLE
PROCESSING PLANTS FOR 26 STATES, 1968

State	Land	Building	Equipment	Inventories	Usable Returns No.
		(Dollars per $1000 Market Value)			
Arkansas					
Low	11.40	11.40	11.40	11.40	
High	17.30	17.30	17.30	17.30	
Average	14.68	14.68	14.68	14.68	5
California					
Low	18.06	18.06	18.06	18.06	
High	30.03	30.03	30.03	29.97	
Average	24.56	24.56	24.41	24.41	46
Colorado					
Low	21.61	21.61	21.61	21.61	
High	29.10	29.10	29.10	29.10	
Average	25.53	25.53	25.53	25.53	4
Delaware					
Low	6.39	6.39	6.39	0	
High	13.86	13.86	13.86	0	
Average	9.51	9.51	9.51	0	5
Florida					
Low	14.10	14.10	14.10	14.10	
High	36.00	36.00	36.00	31.89	
Average	26.02	26.02	26.02	16.98	10
Idaho					
Low	8.40	8.40	8.40	8.40	
High	21.24	21.24	21.24	21.24	
Average	15.74	15.74	15.74	16.91	8
Illinois					
Low	18.67	18.67	18.67	18.67	
High	29.25	29.82	29.82	28.57	
Average	24.28	24.28	27.33	23.04	8
Indiana					
Low	18.07	18.07	18.07	18.07	
High	39.40	39.40	39.40	39.40	
Average	27.02	27.02	27.02	27.02	19
Iowa					
Low	20.77	20.77	20.77	20.77	
High	27.21	27.21	27.21	27.21	
Average	23.23	23.23	23.23	23.23	3
Louisiana					
Low					
High					
Average	18.11	22.27	22.27	39.37	1
Maine					
Low	24.0	20.40	20.40	0	
High	33.84	33.84	33.84	33.84	
Average	27.40	21.60	21.60	18.57	5
Maryland					
Low	0	0	0	0	
High	28.51	28.51	28.51	28.61	
Average	16.05	16.05	16.05	16.56	10
Massachusetts					
Low	22.15	23.00	23.00	0	
High	41.60	41.60	41.60	41.60	
Average	28.75	28.75	34.95	19.72	5

TABLE 9.10 (Continued)

State	Land	Building	Equipment	Inventories	Usable Returns
		(Dollars per $1000 Market Value)			No.
Michigan					
Low	5.10	7.56	7.56	7.56	
High	42.60	42.60	42.60	42.60	
Average	22.40	22.93	22.93	22.93	41
Minnesota					
Low	28.00	28.00	28.00[1]	28.00[1]	
High	47.08	47.08	47.08[1]	47.08[1]	
Average	38.27	38.27	36.28[1]	36.28[1]	10
Nebraska					
Low	29.56	29.56	29.56	29.56	
High	30.88	30.88	30.88	30.88	
Average	30.22	30.22	30.22	30.22	2
New Jersey					
Low	27.30	27.30	6.50	0	
High	79.00	79.00	6.50	0	
Average	43.32	44.13	6.50	0	8
New York					
Low	10.50	10.50	10.50	0	
High	53.93	53.93	53.93	0	
Average	29.60	29.60	29.60	0	23
N. Carolina					
Low	4.95	4.95	4.95	0	
High	22.00	22.00	22.00	16.50	
Average	12.67	12.67	12.67	6.04	9
Ohio					
Low	12.36	12.36	12.36	14.36	
High	22.04	22.04	22.04	34.71	
Average	17.77	19.05	19.05	20.69	8
Oregon					
Low	19.50	19.50	19.50	19.50	
High	33.63	33.63	33.63	33.63	
Average	27.30	27.30	27.30	26.62	10
Pennsylvania					
Low	16.40	16.40	0	0	
High	35.80	35.80	0	0	
Average	23.04	23.04	0	0	12
Texas					
Low	3.75	3.75	3.75	3.75	
High	36.00	36.00	36.00	36.00	
Average	20.85	20.85	24.87	24.87	18
Virginia					
Low	4.00	4.00	4.00	4.00	
High	15.00	15.00	15.00	15.00	
Average	10.43	10.43	10.33	5.32	10
Washington					
Low	13.84	13.84	13.84	13.84	
High	21.77	21.77	21.77	21.77	
Average	17.14	17.14	17.14	17.14	14
Wisconsin					
Low	21.12	21.12	21.12	9.40	
High	39.85	39.85	39.85	17.49	
Average	28.62	28.62	28.62	12.31	35

[1] Minnesota has a tax either on equipment or inventories.

TABLE 9.11

LOCAL AND STATE PROPERTAXES FOR MODEL FIRM A, REPRESENTATIVE OF THE
CANNING AND FREEZING INDUSTRY (SIC 203) BY STATE, 1968

	Land		Buildings		Equipment		Inventory		Total
	Rate (Dollars Per $1000)	Amount (Dollars)	Rate (Dollars Per $1000)	Amount (Dollars)	Rate (Dollars Per $1000)	Amount (Dollars)	Rate (Dollars Per $1000)	Amount (Dollars)	Amount (Dollars)
Arkansas	14.68	437	14.68	4,394	14.68	8,158	14.68	8,732	21,721
California	24.56	732	24.56	7,351	24.41	13,565	24.41	14,519	36,166
Colorado	25.53	761	25.53	7,641	25.53	14,187	25.53	15,185	37,774
Delaware	9.51	283	9.51	2,846	9.51	5,285	0	0	8,414
Florida	26.02	775	26.02	7,788	26.02	14,459	16.98	10,100	33,253
Idaho	15.74	469	15.74	4,711	15.74	8,747	16.91	10,058	23,985
Illinois	24.28	724	24.28	7,267	27.33	15,187	23.04	13,704	36,882
Indiana	27.02	805	27.02	8,087	27.02	15,015	27.02	16,071	39,989
Iowa	23.23	692	23.23	6,953	23.23	12,909	23.23	13,817	34,371
Louisiana	18.11	540	22.27	6,665	22.27	12,375	39.37	23,417	42,998
Maine	27.40	817	21.60	6,465	21.60	12,003	18.57	11,045	30,330
Maryland	16.05	478	16.05	4,804	16.05	8,919	6.56	3,902	18,103
Massachusetts	28.75	857	28.75	8,605	34.95	19,422	19.72	11,727	40,611
Michigan	22.20	662	22.93	6,863	22.93	12,742	22.93	13,639	33,905
Minnesota[1]	38.27	1140	38.27	11,454	36.28[1]	20,161	36.28[1]	0	32,755
Nebraska	30.22	904	30.22	9,045	30.22	16,793	30.22	17,975	44,716
New Jersey	43.32	1291	44.13	13,208	6.50	3,612	0	0	18,111
New York	29.60	882	29.60	8,859	29.60	16,441	0	0	26,190
North Carolina	12.67	378	12.67	3,792	12.67	7,041	6.04	3,593	14,803
Ohio	17.77	530	19.05	5,702	19.05	10,586	20.69	12,306	29,124
Oregon	27.30	814	27.30	8,171	27.30	15,171	26.62	15,834	39,989
Pennsylvania	23.04	687	23.04	6,896	0	0	0	0	7,583
Texas	20.85	621	20.85	6,240	24.87	13,820	24.87	14,793	35,475
Virginia	10.43	311	10.43	3,122	10.33	5,740	5.32	3,164	12,337
Washington	17.14	511	17.14	5,130	17.14	9,525	17.14	10,195	25,360
Wisconsin[2]	28.62	853	28.62	8,566	28.62	15,904	12.31	7,322	32,645
Average	23.16	691	23.21	6,947	20.60	11,838	16.93	9,658	29,134

NOTE: Some figures may not total because of rounding.

[1] Minnesota has a tax on either equipment or inventories.
[2] The State of Wisconsin gives a rebate on county and city property taxes. The rebate is included; the figures are net taxes.

TABLE 9.12

STATE SALES TAXES ON BUILDING MATERIALS PURCHASES, EQUIPMENT PURCHASES, AND USE TAXES ON EQUIPMENT RENTALS FOR MODEL FIRM A, REPRESENTATIVE OF SIC 203 BY STATES, 1968 TAX YEAR

	Building Materials		Equipment		Equipment Rental		Total Sales or Use Taxes (Dollars)
	Sales Tax Rate (%)	Tax (Dollars)	Sales Tax Rate (%)	Tax (Dollars)	Sales Tax Rate (%)	Tax (Dollars)	
Arkansas	3	5986 (c)[1]	0		0		5,986
California	5	14,965 (c)[2]	5	22,228 (c)[1]	5	1330 (e)[1]	38,523
Colorado	3	5986 (c)	3	13,337 (e)	3	798 (e)	20,121
Delaware	0		0		0		0
Florida	2.1	5986 (c)[2]	2-3[3]	11,114 (e)	3-4[3]	998 (e)	18,098
Idaho	3	5986 (c)	0		0		5,986
Illinois	5	9977 (c)	5	22,228 (e)	0		32,205
Indiana	2	3991 (c)	0		0		3,991
Iowa	3	5986 (c)	3	13,337 (e)	3	798 (e)	20,121
Louisiana	2	3991 (c)	2	8,891 (e)	2	532 (e)	13,414
Maine	4.5	8979 (c)	4.5	20,005 (e)	4.5	1197 (e)	30,181
Maryland	3	5986 (c)	3	13,337 (e)	3	798 (e)	20,121
Massachusetts	3	5986 (c)	0		0		5,986
Michigan	4	7981 (c)	4	17,782 (c)	4	1064 (e)	26,827
Minnesota	3	5986 (c)	3	13,337 (c)	3	798 (e)	20,121
Nebraska	2.5	4988 (c)	2.5	11,114 (e)	2.5	665 (e)	16,767
New Jersey	3	5986 (c)	0		0		5,986
New York	6	11,971 (c)	0		0		11,971
North Carolina	3	5986 (c)	1	4,446 (c)	1	226 (e)	10,698
Ohio	4.5	8979 (c)	0		0		8,979
Oregon[4]	0		0		0		0
Pennsylvania	6	11,972 (c)	0		0		11,972
Texas	3	5986 (c)	3	13,337 (e)	3-4[3]	865 (e)	20,188
Virginia	4	7981 (c)	0		0		7,981
Washington[5]	4.5	13,469 (c)	4.5	20,005 (e)	4.5	1197 (e)	34,671
Wisconsin	3	5986 (c)	3	13,337 (c)	3	798 (e)	20,121

[1] (c) Must be capitalized; (e) may be expensed.
[2] California and Florida tax is on building materials and labor; in some states the tax is only on building materials.
[3] The rate increased during 1968.
[4] Rate will be 3% as of July 1, 1969, if approved.
[5] Washington allows a reduction in state income (actually gross profits) tax equal to sales tax paid on plant expansion.

balance, giving an effective first-year accounting cost for these taxes of 13.33% of the total tax cost. Use taxes for equipment rental were expensed, that is, for tax purposes. The total tax was charged against the first year's operation.

(The effective taxes we are computing are the first year's tax on a new enterprise with the initial sales taxes capitalized.)

The total sales taxes, before capitalization, ranged from zero in Delaware and Oregon to as high as $38,523 in California. (Oregon had a 3% tax under consideration during 1968.)

Initial Filing Fees, Licenses, Franchise, and Income Taxes

The initial filing fees or incorporation fees are listed in Table 9.13; for tax purposes these items are expensed. These fees ranged from $50 in Texas and Louisiana to $2380 in Florida. The details of the costs of incorporation or for initial filing fees vary widely among states and will not be discussed in detail.

Annual licenses and annual franchise or capital stock taxes are also listed in Table 9.13. For states in which these costs were over $1000 per yr a footnote explains the particular tax. These fees ranged from zero to as high as $4954 in Michigan. In the case of Michigan there is a franchise tax of five mills on capital stock and earned surplus.

State income taxes, gross receipts taxes or gross profit taxes for each state are also listed in Table 9.13. These ranged from zero in Florida, Illinois, Maine, Ohio, and Texas to as high as $21,975 in Indiana. (Since there is no state income tax in Ohio, a 1% city income tax was charged.) Again, the methods of taxing, the exemptions, exclusions, etc., vary widely from state to state. Some states compute state income taxes after allowing for federal income taxes (i.e., Iowa, Louisiana, and Minnesota), some states have a gross receipts tax (i.e., Indiana and Washington), other states exempt income up to a certain point (i.e., Arkansas, Iowa, Louisiana, and Wisconsin), while others have a straight percentage of income after allowing for relatively standard deductions. The details of computing each state income tax, gross receipts or gross profits will not be discussed in detail because of the volume of analysis necessary.

Local, State, and Federal Taxes and Net Income

For the Model Firm the gross income before any tax considerations was $191,744 in each state. After calculating state income taxes, the federal income tax and net profit after all taxes was determined. Actually, taxes and net income were calculated by 4 different methods—with and without the 10% federal surtax and with and without the 7% federal investment credit. Only one method is illustrated in Table 9.14, with the federal surtax but without investment credit.

The local property taxes are the same as were previously listed. The state taxes are a combination of filing or incorporation fees, licenses, franchise or capital stock taxes, sales taxes (capitalized), use taxes and income, gross receipts or gross profits taxes that the firm would pay under its first year of operation.

Total taxes, including federal corporation income taxes with the surtax but without investment credit ranged from $103,267 in Delaware to $124,281 in

TABLE 9.13

INCORPORATION OR INITIAL FILING FEES, ANNUAL LICENSES,
ANNUAL FRANCHISE OR CAPITAL STOCK TAX, AND STATE INCOME,
GROSS RECEIPTS OR GROSS PROFITS TAX, CORPORATION A
(REPRESENTATIVE OF CANNING AND FREEZING INDUSTRY)
BY STATES 1968

State	Incorporation or Initial Filing Fee	Annual Licenses	Annual Franchise or Capital Stock Tax	State Income, Gross Receipts or Gross Profits Tax	
	(Dollars)	(Dollars)	(Dollars)	(Dollars)	Description
Arkansas	96	0	991	7,982	5%[8]
California	100	50	0	10,527	7%
Colorado	187	0	100	7,540	5%
Delaware	550	1104[1]	303	9,069	5%
Florida	2380	85	1000	0	0
Idaho	137	10	180	10,028	6%
Illinois	525	0	930	0	0
Indiana	1802	0	5	21,975	1/2 of 1% of gross receipts
Iowa	1001	0	110[2]	6,939	8%[9]
Louisiana	50	0	1815[2]	3,006	4%[10]
Maine	100	0	100	0	0
Maryland	201	0	70	11,869	7%
Massachusetts	450	0	35[3]	11,313	7.5%
Michigan	460	25	4954[3]	6,964	5.6%
Minnesota	926	1	0	9,268	11.33%[11]
Nebraska	451	12	500[4]	2,821	2%
New Jersey	1000	0	1962[4]	7,241	4.25%
New York	500	20	0[5]	11,512	7%
North Carolina	360	0	1472[5]	10,437	6%
Ohio	1751	15	3920[6]	1,564	1% city taxes
Oregon	125	0	125	6,693	6%[12]
Pennsylvania	1842	0	383[7]	11,863	7%
Texas	50	0	3396[7]	0	0
Virginia	180	0	225	8,930	5%
Washington	901	10	456	15,473	0044 gross receipts
Wisconsin	901	50	10	9,463	7%[13]

[1] $5 plus 1/40 of 1% of gross receipts.
[2] $1.50 per $1000 stockholders' equity.
[3] Five mills on capital stock and surplus.
[4] Two mills on net worth and earned surplus.
[5] $1.50 per $1000 capital stock and surplus.
[6] Rate: 4/10 of 1% of capital stock and surplus.
[7] Rate: $2.75 per $1000 on capital stock and surplus.
[8] 5% of Net State Income minus $450.
[9] 8% of Net State Income minus $2500.
[10] 4% of Net State Income, after Federal Taxes, minus $120
[11] After Federal Income Taxes
[12] 6% with credit from State Inventory taxes.
[13] 7% of Net State Income minus $195.

Indiana. Similarly, net profit after taxes ranged from $67,463 (7.5% on equity) in Indiana to $88,477 (9.8% of equity) in Delaware. Indiana (with 1/2% gross receipts tax) had the lowest net income followed by Massachusetts, California, Nebraska, and Michigan. Relative profitability among states may easily be compared. For example, Wisconsin had 2.7% higher profits than Michigan, New York had 7.2%, Ohio 8.5%, and Pennsylvania had profits 17.8% above Michigan for the model fruit and vegetable processing firm.

Net Income by Four Methods of Calculating Federal Taxes

Capitalizing the 7% federal investment credit on the purchases of equipment for Model Firm A based on a 15-yr life of the equipment, but crediting it on a double declining basis (the same method as applied to charges for sales taxes), raises the net income of each firm around $5185 for the first year. The results of the 4 methods of computing net income, i.e., with and without the 10% federal surtax and with and without the 7% investment credit, are listed in Table 9.15. Because of much recent speculation of whether both or either the surtax or the investment credit provision of the federal corporate income tax will be continued, all four methods of computation are listed. Of course a surtax and investment credit was the legal method of computation for the tax year 1968. In each case the greatest difference in net income was between Indiana and Delaware. Comparing Indiana and Delaware by each of the 4 methods gives Delaware a minimum of 29% greater profits than Indiana.

Taxes on Dairy and Grain Mill Processors

Using approximated weighted balance sheets and income statements for the dairy products industry and the grain mill products industry and the same procedures on taxation yielded results similar to that of the canning and freezing industry.

The model firm in the dairy products industry had assets of $1,300,000 and profits before taxes of $152,000. The model firm in the grain mill products industry had assets of $2,000,000 and profits before taxes of $182,000. The results of differences in taxation among states for these two model firms are reported in Tables 9.16 and 9.17. The range in differences in return on equity was a 24% difference in dairy processing and a 31% difference in grain mill products processing, due entirely to differences in taxation among states.

Taxes Not Considered

Unemployment insurance taxes are an important form of taxation. The cost of this tax for analytical purposes may probably be best handled as a labor cost rather than dealt with as a separate tax cost. Unemployment insurance costs for each state are publicly available (U.S. Dept. of Labor 1968). These taxes in the canning and freezing industry were specified in Table 9.7 and were added to labor wage rates to obtain total costs to employers among states.

TABLE 9.14

GROSS INCOME BEFORE TAXES, LOCAL PROPERTY TAXES, STATE TAXES, FEDERAL TAXES, TOTAL TAXES, NET INCOME AFTER TAXES, AND INCOME AS A PERCENT OF STOCKHOLDERS' EQUITY FOR MODEL FIRM A, REPRESENTATIVE OF SIC 203 BY STATES, 1968

State	Gross Income Before Taxes (Dollars)	Local Property Taxes (Dollars)	State Taxes (Dollars)	Federal Taxes[1] (Dollars)	Total Taxes (Dollars)	Net Income After Taxes (Dollars)	Net Income As Percent of Stockholders' Equity
Arkansas	191,744	21,721	9,388	77,675	108,764	82,980	9.2
California	"	36,116	15,769	66,695	118,580	73,164	8.1
Colorado	"	37,744	10,711	68,490	116,975	74,769	8.3
Delaware	"	8,414	11,026	83,827	103,267	88,477	9.8
Florida	"	33,253	5,144	73,274	111,671	80,073	8.9
Idaho	"	23,985	10,649	75,804	110,438	81,306	9.0
Illinois	"	36,882	4,902	72,028	113,812	77,932	8.7
Indiana	"	39,989	23,972	60,320	124,281	67,463	7.5
Iowa	"	34,731	10,995	70,158	115,484	76,260	8.5
Louisiana	"	42,998	5,063	68,762	116,803	74,941	8.3
Maine	"	30,330	4,513	75,693	110,536	81,208	9.0
Maryland	"	18,108	15,053	76,576	109,732	82,012	9.1
Massachusetts	"	40,611	12,097	66,261	118,969	72,775	8.1
Michigan	"	33,905	16,235	67,617	117,757	73,987	8.2
Minnesota	"	32,755	13,429	69,706	115,890	75,854	8.4
Nebraska	"	44,716	6,181	67,218	118,115	73,629	8.2
New Jersey	"	18,111	10,502	78,983	107,596	84,148	9.3
New York	"	26,190	12,611	73,604	112,405	79,339	8.8
North Carolina	"	14,803	13,426[2]	79,186	107,415	84,829	9.4
Ohio	"	29,124	7,749[2]	74,622	111,495	80,249	8.9
Oregon	"	39,989	6,943	69,311	116,243	75,501	8.4
Pennsylvania	"	7,583	14,686	82,333	104,602	87,142	9.7
Texas	"	35,475	6,388	71,986	113,849	77,895	8.6
Virginia	"	12,337	9,734	82,437	104,508	87,236	9.7
Washington	"	25,360	19,872	70,228	115,460	76,284	8.5
Wisconsin	"	32,645	12,679	70,160	115,484	76,260	8.5
Average	191,744	29,150	11,124	72,807	116,083	78,663	8.7

[1] Federal taxes including surtax but without investment credit

[2] Net income with federal surtax and without investment credit-stockholders equity in Corporation A is $900,800.00

SUMMARY OF TAXES

The services a firm receives for the taxes it pays may be as important as tax rates themselves. Unfortunately, services are difficult to measure quantitatively while the taxes themselves may be measured arithmetically. Time series data have shown state and local taxes to be one of the most rapidly increasing input costs in the food processing industry. To meaningfully measure the effect of taxation on profits all taxes must be considered at the same time. That is, a comparison of only property taxes among states, or a comparison of only corporate income taxes would yield inconsistent and incomplete results. One type of taxation may offset another within a state. Similarly, federal corporate income taxes effectively reduce the difference among state in state and local taxation. In a detailed study of the effect of state and local taxes on returns to equity in food processing, differences among states as great as 31% in returns to equity were found based solely on differences in taxes. Differences in return on equity of 10–15% among states based on tax differences were fairly common. While the literature on the effect of taxation on general manufacturing plant

TABLE 9.15

NET PROFITS AFTER TAXES (LOCAL, STATE, AND FEDERAL)
BY FOUR METHODS OF CALCULATING FEDERAL TAXES FOR MODEL
FIRM A, REPRESENTATIVE OF SIC 203

| State | Without Investment Credit | | Wth Investment Credit Capitalized | |
	With Surtax (Dollars)	Without Surtax (Dollars)	With Surtax (Dollars)	Without Surtax (Dollars)
Arkansas	82,980	90,014	88,165	95,199
California	73,164	79,227	78,557	84,620
Colorado	74,769	81,013	80,079	86,323
Delaware	88,477	96,098	93,662	101,408
Florida	80,073	86,734	85,362	52,023
Idaho	81,306	88,197	86,491	93,382
Illinois	77,932	84,480	83,325	89,873
Indiana	67,463	72,947	72,648	78,132
Iowa	76,260	82,359	81,570[1]	87,669[1]
Louisiana	74,941	81,132	80,209[1]	86,400[1]
Maine	81,208	88,089	86,580	93,461
Maryland	82,012	88,975	87,322	94,285
Massachusetts	72,775	78,799	77,960	83,948
Michigan	73,987	80,134	79,302	85,449
Minnesota	75,854	81,796	81,164[1]	87,106[1]
Nebraska	73,629	79,740	78,918	85,029
New Jersey	84,148	91,321	89,333	96,506
New York	79,339	86,030	84,524	91,215
N. Carolina	84,829	91,528	90,056	96,755
Ohio	80,249	87,033	85,434	92,218
Oregon	75,501	81,802	80,686	86,987
Pennsylvania	87,142	94,627	92,327	99,812
Texas	77,895	84,439	83,205	89,749
Virginia	87,236	94,730	92,421	99,915
Washington	76,284	82,668	81,656	88,040
Wisconsin	76,260	82,638	81,570	87,940

[1] Approximations rather than exact profits. In these states, federal taxes are deductible in calculating state taxes. Rather than calculating the complete tax schedules for these states an approximation was made.

TABLE 9.16

GROSS INCOME BEFORE TAXES, LOCAL PROPERTY TAXES, STATE TAXES, FEDERAL TAXES, TOTAL TAXES, NET INCOME AFTER TAXES, AND INCOME AS A PERCENTAGE OF STOCKHOLDERS' EQUITY FOR MODEL FIRM B, REPRESENTATIVE OF SIC 202 (DAIRY INDUSTRY) BY STATES, 1968

State	Gross Income Before Taxes (Dollars)	Local Property Taxes (Dollars)	State Taxes (Dollars)	Federal Taxes[1] (Dollars)	Total Taxes[1] (Dollars)	Net Income After Taxes[1] (Dollars)	Net Income as Percent of Stockholders' Equity[1,2]
Arkansas	152,000	8,683	8,237	64,172	81,097	70,908	9.5
California	"	14,507	28,454	50,423	93,384	58,616	7.9
Colorado	"	15,100	9,647	60,039	84,786	67,214	9.0
Delaware	"	4,426	9,028	66,002	79,456	72,544	9.7
Florida	"	14,251	4,971	62,956	82,178	69,822	9.4
Idaho	"	9,457	9,655	63,015	82,127	69,873	9.4
Illinois	"	15,037	3,831	63,143	82,011	69,989	9.4
Indiana	"	15,982	21,930	53,088	91,000	61,000	8.2
Iowa	"	13,738	9,080	61,058	83,876	68,124	9.1
Louisiana	"	15,140	5,687	62,109	82,936	69,064	9.3
Maine	"	12,658	3,466	63,536	79,660	72,340	9.7
Maryland	"	8,297	12,263	62,227	82,787	69,213	9.3
Massachusetts	"	17,559	10,930	58,063	86,552	65,448	8.8
Michigan	"	13,529	14,256	58,440	86,215	65,785	8.8
Minnesota	"	11,940	11,508	60,725	84,173	67,827	9.1
Nebraska	"	17,875	5,133	60,958	83,966	68,034	9.1
New Jersey	"	10,231	15,505	59,518	85,254	66,746	9.0
New York	"	13,776	11,656	59,150	84,582	67,418	9.0
North Carolina	"	6,666	12,058	63,718	82,442	69,558	9.3
Ohio	"	11,417	7,364	63,228	82,009	69,991	9.4
Oregon	"	16,062	7,697	60,583	84,342	67,658	9.1
Pennsylvania	"	4,434	13,362	63,710	81,506	70,494	9.5
Texas	"	13,937	4,856	63,183	81,976	70,024	9.4
Virginia	"	5,526	8,502	65,700	79,728	72,272	9.7
Washington	"	10,138	20,422	56,970	87,530	64,470	8.7
Wisconsin	"	14,871	11,247	59,315	85,433	66,567	8.9
Average	152,000	12,126	10,798	60,963	83,885	68,113	9.1

[1] With federal surtax but without federal investment credit.
[2] The owners' equity was $744,900.00.

TABLE 9.17

GROSS INCOME BEFORE TAXES, LOCAL PROPERTY TAXES, STATE TAXES, FEDERAL TAXES, TOTAL TAXES, NET INCOME AFTER TAXES, AND INCOME AS A PERCENTAGE OF STOCKHOLDERS' EQUITY FOR MODEL FIRM C, REPRESENTATIVE OF SIC 204 (GRAIN MILL PRODUCTS INDUSTRY) BY STATES, 1968

State	Gross Income Before Taxes (Dollars)	Local Property Taxes (Dollars)	State Taxes (Dollars)	Federal Taxes[1] (Dollars)	Total Taxes[1] (Dollars)	Net Income After Taxes[1] (Dollars)	Net Income As Percent of Stockholders' Equity[2]
Arkansas	182,000	15,062	9,901	75,775	100,738	81,262	7.3
California	"	25,070	15,479	67,536	108,085	73,915	6.6
Colorado	"	26,194	16,304	63,930	106,428	75,572	6.8
Delaware	"	5,916	11,302	79,903	97,121	84,879	7.6
Florida	"	23,044	6,739	73,220	103,003	78,997	7.1
Idaho	"	16,622	11,106	74,306	102,034	79,966	7.2
Illinois	"	25,792	4,550	72,926	103,268	78,732	7.1
Indiana	"	27,723	32,087	57,366	117,176	64,824	5.8
Iowa	"	23,835	11,545	70,265	105,645	76,355	6.8
Louisiana	"	29,524	7,102	69,564	106,190	75,810	6.8
Maine	"	21,261	5,438	74,848	101,547	80,453	7.2
Maryland	"	12,633	14,849	74,436	101,918	80,082	7.2
Massachusetts	"	28,657	12,782	67,066	108,505	73,495	6.6
Michigan	"	23,486	17,632	67,235	108,353	73,647	6.6
Minnesota	"	21,132	13,356	70,736	105,224	76,776	6.9
Nebraska	"	30,996	6,598	69,097	106,691	75,309	6.7
New Jersey	"	10,365	11,301	77,506	99,172	82,828	7.4
New York	"	18,411	13,490	72,103	104,004	77,996	7.0
North Carolina	"	10,321	13,437	76,402	100,160	81,840	7.3
Ohio	"	20,136	9,421	73,340	102,897	79,103	7.1
Oregon	"	27,734	6,985	70,615	105,334	76,666	6.9
Pennsylvania	"	3,898	15,768	78,562	98,228	83,772	7.5
Texas	"	24,836	6,772	72,230	103,838	78,162	7.0
Virginia	"	8,637	10,117	79,044	97,798	84,202	7.5
Washington	"	17,586	12,992	72,801	103,379	78,621	7.0
Wisconsin	"	22,235	14,596	69,499	106,330	75,670	6.8
Average	182,000	20,043	11,988	71,935	103,966	78,034	7.0

[1] With federal surtax but without federal investment Credit.
[2] The owners' equity was $1,116,000.00.

locations yields inconsistent results, it is suggested that in locating most food processing plants, differences in local and state taxation among states are important and significant cost inputs. Differences in local taxation within many states should also significantly affect profitability of the food processing firm.

ELECTRICITY AND FUEL COSTS AMONG STATES

Purchased electricity and fuel costs by processors of food in the United States were slightly over 500 million dollars in 1963. Electricity costs were nearly 250 million and costs of purchased fuels slightly over 250 million dollars (Table 9.18). While in all food processing the combined average cost of purchased electricity and fuel is somewhat less than 1% of total value of FOB sales, in some particular industries these cost items are of much significance. For example, in freezing or dehydration of relatively low valued vegetables, the cost of fuel and electricity can be of prime importance. Even as a weighted average cost for the industry, fuel and electrical costs are in the same range as costs of compensation of officers, or cost of all repairs, or equivalent to about 1/2 the cost of depreciation. Thus, if there are wide regional differences in fuel and electrical costs, these differences (all other factors being equal) could significantly affect locations of food processing industries.

The purpose of this section is to explore the differences among the 48 conterminous states in the United States in fuel and power costs and also to briefly explain rate structures for gas and electricity both within and among states.

Electricity and Gas Rate Structures

Most all states have legal jurisdiction over the electrical rates and gas rates charged by private and corporate electrical and gas companies, but not over public facilities such as municipal or other government-owned facilities.

The control feature generally is a limitation on the return on capital invested. Thus, each gas or electric company may have a monopoly in specific geographical areas, but the prices charged are limited or specifically allocated, based on a return on capital. In Michigan, for example, in 1968, there were 72 private and municipal electric companies. However geographically, Detroit Edison and Consumer Power companies covered most of the state. The other 70 companies are municipal companies or companies serving small pocket areas. So in Michigan there can be as many as 72 different rate structures for electrical service charged by the 72 companies.

In Michigan, the Public Service Commission is delegated the authority to control the rates of the private and corporate electrical and gas companies. Each company must file its rate structures with the Michigan Public Service Commission and the rate structure must be approved. The rates within a state can vary widely, as the rates are based on the return on capital invested. Thus, the rates can vary with differences in cost of fuel or power to generate electricity, age and efficiency of the generating equipment, age of transmission lines, state of

TABLE 9.18
TOTAL COSTS OF PURCHASED FUEL AND ELECTRICAL ENERGY BY FOOD PROCESSING FIRMS, 1963

Type of Processing and SIC Code	Coal coke ($1000)	Purchased Fuel and Electricity				
		Fuel oil ($1000)	Gas ($1000)	Other fuels ($1000)	Electricity ($1000)	Total ($1000)
Meat products (SIC 201)	5,714	7,095	16,332	7,855	19,497	56,473
Dairies (SIC 202)	11,461	16,474	24,100	11,932	59,379	123,346
Canned and frozen foods (SIC 203)	5,500	11,412	16,475	4,329	25,958	63,674
Grain mill products (SIC 204)	11,468	4,409	11,861	3,812	38,301	69,851
Bakery products (SIC 205)	598	7,702	18,713	4,787	23,005	54,805
Sugar and confectionery (SIC 206 and 207)	12,695	7,893	18,397	1,169	12,461	52,615
Beverages (SIC 208)	8,228	7,486	12,985	5,669	25,470	59,838
Fats and oils (SIC 2091—2096)	7,177	4,633	13,481	3,940	23,909	53,140
Miscellaneous foods (SIC 2095—2099)	1,890	3,133	7,266	1,791	20,719	34,799
Total	64,731	70,237	139,610	45,284	248,699	568,561

Source: Census of Manufacturing, U.S. Dept. Com.

technology, efficiency of workers, size of generating equipment relative to service areas, etc., etc. The rates of the gas companies depend on sources of supply, age and efficiency of the pipelines, size of the company, etc.

While the basic rate structure must be approved by the Michigan Public Service Commission, there are many variations in rates to the individual user. In electrical usage the rates may be based on the 'demand' by the user. The demand is a term specifying the size or capacity of the electrical service system. For example, for an industrial user the demand may be a 75 kw, 150 kw, or a 300 kw system or more. This is a sort of peak load system. There generally is a charge for demand as well as for the actual kilowatt hours of electricity actually used.

Generally, there are different rates for residential, commercial, and industrial users of electricity. Each of these rate structures must usually be approved by a state agency, for example in Michigan, the Michigan Public Service Commission. However, for large users of electricity, there may be specific contracts between the user and supplier of electricity. The rates of these specific contracts are determined by negotiation and are outside the jurisdiction of the Public Service Commission; however, the contracts must be filed with the Public Service Commission.

Many factors can go into an electrical bill or electrical cost to a commercial or industrial user whether or not a contract is used. Such things as demand or peak load, high loads, high usage, seasonal usage, interrupted service, time of day usage, etc., are considered. The rates for gas also may have many determinants.

Each state may vary widely in the details of control of rate structures. It is not known whether the Michigan details or characteristics fit most other states. But generally there is state control and generally this control is based on the rate of return on investment.

Cost of Electricity Among States

Most food processing plants would probably qualify for the industrial electric rate service. The larger ones, of course, would probably be under a contract rate. The rate structures for each individual electric company in the United States is published by the Federal Power Commission (FPC). Further, the FPC publishes *Typical Electric Bills* which is a summary of actual billings to users for electricity, classified by the type of user, i.e., residential, commercial, or industrial. To illustrate the difference in costs among states to food processors, the industrial bills for demands of 75 kw, 150 kw, 300 kw, 500 kw, and 1000 kw are presented by states (Table 9.19). The states in Table 9.19 are ranked from lowest cost to highest cost based on a demand of 300 kw and a usage of 120,000 kw-hr per month. For each state the figure given is the simple average of the costs from all the electrical companies in the state.

The range in these average electrical costs by states is from $868 (for a demand of 300 kw and a usage of 120,000 kw-hr) in Tennessee to a high of $2052 in Maine. Thus, for a similar processing plant, electrical costs in Maine could be 2.36 times that of a plant in Tennessee.

TABLE 9.19

TYPICAL INDUSTRIAL ELECTRIC BILLS BY STATES, JAN. 1965 (RANKED FROM LOW TO HIGH BASED ON A DEMAND OF 300 KILOWATTS AND A USAGE OF 120,000 KILOWATT HOURS)

State	75 Kw Demand Usage, Kwh (Dollars)		150 Kw Demand Usage, Kwh (Dollars)		300 Kw Demand Usage, Kwh (Dollars)		500 Kw Demand Usage, Kwh (Dollars)		1000 Kw Demand Usage, Kwh (Dollars)	
	15,000	30,000	30,000	60,000	60,000	120,000	100,000	200,000	200,000	400,000
Tenn.	193	283	358	498	648	868	1008	1308	1808	2408
Ore.	192	279	361	507	661	888	1047	1361	1890	2483
Wash.	202	294	355	516	633	891	976	1390	1972	2597
Mont.	268	398	465	680	840	1220	1340	1940	2590	3740
N. Car.	229	337	435	650	840	1267	1367	2067	2594	3889
Idaho	282	408	546	738	973	1270	1568	2009	3161	4241
Nebr.	269	409	505	705	930	1291	1489	2079	2886	4049
Wyo.	297	427	532	734	916	1336	1472	2139	2850	4097
Calif.	283	413	523	771	902	1338	1433	2146	2708	4111
Ala.	242	360	483	733	943	1371	1519	2173	2858	3888
Utah	281	393	528	730	1002	1407	1607	2283	3091	4442
Ga.	301	472	543	820	977	1430	1492	2216	2736	3925
Va.	308	430	530	770	987	1461	1590	2367	3161	4358
Ky.	314	443	561	803	1006	1477	1691	2380	3087	4544
Texas	323	463	570	829	1027	1490	1582	2284	2787	4110
Okla.	336	467	577	825	1048	1491	1664	2300	3000	4194
Nev.	314	422	575	779	1096	1492	1704	2331	3504	4752
Ark.	321	448	566	797	1010	1493	1690	2354	3134	4380
Miss.	314	443	586	844	1079	1553	1638	2343	2896	4137
Penn.	342	458	625	838	1119	1558	1793	2523	3433	4894
W. Va.	309	460	564	858	1000	1576	1677	2510	3280	4667
S. Car.	320	465	464	844	1060	1580	1501	2113	2676	3808
Vt.	312	445	546	808	1071	1595	1771	2644	3520	5267
N. Mex.	302	451	568	855	1057	1606	1853	2690	3663	5334
Kans.	353	493	621	871	1160	1625	1851	2590	3419	4831
Del.	364	488	646	884	1172	1643	1839	2619	3510	5061

Md.	320	468	591	865	1116	1658	1810	2664	3460	5043
N. J.	381	533	646	930	1090	1679	1665	2529	3140	5114
N. H.	316	447	597	859	1157	1681	1902	2776	3733	5147
Ind.	344	518	620	903	1123	1693	1736	2667	3345	4895
Mo.	355	533	624	902	1178	1710	1927	2762	3714	5374
Ohio	349	502	634	931	1190	1723	1893	2712	3494	5084
Mich.	384	559	738	1088	1256	1734	2011	2764	3851	5327
La.	339	523	606	935	1095	1738	1745	2810	3346	5403
Ariz.	337	497	636	944	1184	1750	1805	2670	3245	4964
S. Dak.	403	590	659	963	1192	1761	1879	2803	3522	5396
Fla.	354	538	661	991	1221	1791	1896	2805	3439	5157
Colo.	335	520	574	936	1091	1794	1758	2899	3341	5470
N. Y.	393	536	675	979	1270	1809	2023	2884	3835	5467
Ill.	385	589	695	992	1252	1817	1956	2792	3551	5172
R. I.	355	512	651	963	1210	1826	1960	2987	3663	5717
Minn.	386	586	738	1061	1273	1847	2028	2941	3502	5282
Iowa	360	570	677	1016	1254	1879	1990	2890	3768	5683
Wisc.	321	561	636	1199	1178	1881	1888	2863	3454	5171
Conn.	375	548	669	1013	1247	1902	1987	3078	3840	5985
Mass.	374	558	688	1026	1264	1932	2042	3086	3888	5913
N. Dak.	417	646	781	1133	1362	1970	2054	3066	3784	5597
Maine	335	542	659	1071	1308	2052	2138	3162	3906	6039

Source: Computed from Anon. (1966).

The range in costs within individual states is quite high (Table 9.20). A 40-50% difference in rates for different areas within an individual state is not uncommon (Table 9.20). For example, within Maine the cost for the same service ranges between $1852 and $2251 (for 300 kw demand and 120,000 kw-hr) depending on which company supplies the service. Similarly, in Washington State this service would range between $658 and $1179. Thus, there is a possibility that a Maine processor could pay $2251 and a Washington processor $658 for the same electric service. The Maine costs would be 3.42 times that of Washington.

Cost of Gas Among States

Data are available on the rates charged by each individual gas company in the United States, and from these data, ranges and averages in each state can be computed. However, a simpler form of state averages is available. *Gas Facts* published by the Statistical Department of the American Gas Association (Anon. 1967) publishes the total quantity of industrial gas used in each state, as well as the total revenue; thus, the weighted average rates can be computed directly for each state.

The weighted average gas rates by states in 1966, ranked from lowest to highest cost, are listed in Table 9.21. The costs in Maine for an equivalent quantity of natural gas are over six times that of Texas.

Costs are based on distances from gas fields, the particular pipelines, and costs and efficiency in moving the gas to the ultimate user. Again, in each state the rates are generally controlled by a state government agency, and, typically, the rate is based on a specific allowed rate of return on capital invested by the private or corporate gas company.

Coal and/or Coke and Fuel Oil

Coal or coke and fuel oils are important sources of fuel to the food processing industry. In 1963, the cost for the use of these fuels by the food processing industries was approximately 135 million dollars. Apparently costs of coal and fuel oils to the average industrial user are not available by states. However, data on these costs to steam-electric generating plants by states are available. *Steam-Electric Plant Factors,* published by the American Coal Association (Anon. 1969B), contains the quantities used and cost of fuel for all publicly- and privately-owned steam-electric utility plants in the United States which file reports with the FPC. In 1967, there were 940 such plants representing 397 companies in 47 states and the District of Columbia. (Idaho had no steam-electric generating plants.) Naturally, fuel is a major cost in these steam-electric generating plants. Since they use substantial quantities of fuel, their costs should be a good indication of the relative costs among types of fuel in different states. The average cost of gas to industrial users and the average cost of gas, coal, and fuel oil to steam-electric generating plants by states are listed in Table 9.22. Several observations concerning the data in Table 9.22 are pertinent. (1) The

TABLE 9.20

RANGE IN TYPICAL INDUSTRIAL ELECTRIC BILLS BY STATES, 1965

(BILLING DEMAND (KILOWATTS) AND MONTHLY CONSUMPTION (KILOWATT HOURS)

State	75 Kw Demand Usage, Kwh (Dollars)		150 Kw Demand Usage, Kwh (Dollars)		300 Kw Demand Usage, Kwh (Dollars)		500 Kw Demand Usage, Kwh (Dollars)		1000 Kw Demand Usage, Kwh (Dollars)	
	15,000	30,000	30,000	60,000	60,000	120,000	100,000	200,000	200,000	400,000
Ala. (avg)	242	360	483	733	943	1371	1519	2173	2858	3888
High	263	396	513	779	1000	1453	1610	2298	3035	4078
Low	174	249	413	450	820	820	960	1260	1760	2360
Ak. (avg)	457	760	899	1487	1770	2934	3266	5400	6500	10766
High	735	1185	1470	2370	2940	4740	4900	7900	9800	15800
Low	385	647	750	1253	1467	2457	2450	4150	4850	8250
Ariz. (avg)	337	497	636	944	1184	1750	1805	2670	3245	4964
High	380	536	714	1027	1310	1845	1979	2870	3423	5650
Low	308	425	581	809	1058	1515	1606	2367	2858	4380
Ark. (avg)	321	448	566	797	1010	1493	1690	2354	3134	4380
High	338	511	622	929	1150	1663	1783	2428	3331	4777
Low	303	394	499	686	956	1328	1567	2187	3029	3942
Calif. (avg)	283	413	523	771	902	1338	1433	2146	2708	4111
High	316	497	622	929	1150	1663	1783	2600	3246	5200
Low	187	289	332	536	633	1041	1030	1630	2060	3153
Colo. (avg)	335	520	574	936	1091	1794	1758	2899	3341	5478
High	413	612	749	1127	1392	2201	2217	3668	3952	6074
Low	249	399	456	726	838	1318	1308	2108	2483	4083
Conn. (avg)	375	548	669	1013	1247	1902	1987	3078	3840	5985
High	420	720	752	1395	1395	2212	2295	4545	4545	9045
Low	321	510	553	879	1080	1668	1740	2720	3390	5070

(Continued)

Table 9.20 (Continued)

Del. (avg)	364	488	646	884	1172	1643	1839	2619	3510	5061
High	397	539	743	1024	1380	1941	2213	3146	4296	6160
Low	348	463	598	815	1068	1494	1653	2356	3117	4512
D.C. (avg)	302	431	546	793	1016	1495	1643	2394	3138	4630
High	311	458	583	855	1092	1608	1770	2535	3323	4853
Low	294	405	510	731	941	1383	1516	2253	2953	4407
Fla. (avg)	354	538	661	991	1221	1791	1896	2805	3439	5157
High	454	715	809	1271	1458	2183	2269	3509	4395	6229
Low	274	417	546	834	981	1630	1515	2336	2849	4478
Ga. (avg)	301	472	543	820	977	1430	1492	2216	2736	3925
High	315	490	558	833	993	1459	1529	2177	2783	3973
Low	269	434	509	779	929	1348	1408	2107	2607	3806
Hi. (avg)	447	696	749	1187	1408	2285	2358	3771	4480	6310
High	561	940	940	1699	1699	3217	2711	5241	5241	8045
Low	365	598	657	911	1247	1755	2033	2880	3748	5443
Idaho (avg)	282	408	546	738	973	1270	1568	2009	3161	4241
High	285	426	556	764	991	1315	1611	2151	one co. only	one co. only
Low	276	374	526	688	965	1248	1547	1938		
Ill. (avg)	385	589	695	992	1252	1817	1956	2792	3551	5172
High	428	713	751	1040	1290	1931	2137	3084	3947	5805
Low	295	474	577	854	1105	1662	1882	2615	3398	4895
Ind. (avg)	344	518	620	903	1123	1693	1736	2667	3345	4895
High	415	666	722	1041	1408	2040	1933	3379	3825	6014
Low	239	438	464	770	914	1482	1514	2320	3014	4396
Iowa (avg)	360	570	677	1016	1254	1879	1990	2890	3768	5683
High	414	737	761	1059	1394	2020	2279	3693	4558	7093
Low	302	467	552	841	988	1567	1555	2475	2927	4678
Kans. (avg)	353	493	621	871	1160	1625	1851	2590	3419	4831
High	381	532	705	972	1284	1464	2012	2722	3702	5086
Low	308	451	544	758	1036	1777	1692	2405	3164	4544
Ky. (avg)	314	443	561	803	1006	1477	1619	2380	3087	4544
High	322	463	581	865	1067	1647	1737	2637	3312	5112
Low	307	432	537	756	975	1372	1560	2216	2928	4326

La. (avg)	339	523	606	935	1095	1738	1745	2810	3346	5403
High	390	666	750	1266	1500	2466	2500	4066	5000	8066
Low	302	433	516	719	884	1267	1376	2014	2604	3880
Maine (avg)	335	542	659	1071	1308	2052	2138	3162	3906	6039
High	359	562	688	1125	1351	2251	2252	3495	4445	6985
Low	285	486	570	971	1140	1852	1900	2792	3422	4876
Md. (avg)	320	468	591	865	1116	1658	1810	2664	3460	5043
High	372	579	723	1080	1368	2052	2228	3268	4168	5936
Low	294	405	510	731	941	1383	1516	2253	2953	4407
Mass. (avg)	374	558	688	1026	1264	1932	2042	3086	3888	5913
High	477	679	844	1208	1478	2207	2325	3616	4516	7148
Low	315	463	552	823	927	1607	1515	2633	2894	5199
Mich. (avg)	384	559	738	1088	1256	1734	2011	2764	3851	5327
High	476	647	883	1244	1267	2011	2181	3052	4257	5984
Low	329	434	647	867	1236	1684	1909	2703	3553	5057
Minn. (avg)	386	586	738	1061	1273	1847	2028	2941	3502	5282
High	413	609	821	1146	1463	2081	2427	3411	4382	6026
Low	365	570	671	999	1126	1704	1731	2624	3138	4924
Miss. (avg)	314	443	586	844	1079	1553	1638	2343	2896	4137
High	321	453	589	846	1099	1607	1760	2607	2935	4284
Low	311	438	582	843	1039	1445	1540	2117	2870	4023
Mo. (avg)	355	533	624	902	1178	1710	1927	2762	3714	5374
High	436	610	785	1109	1483	2086	2397	3388	4509	6469
Low	207	392	392	762	762	1446	1375	1950	2700	3800
Mont. (avg)	268	398	465	680	840	1220	1340	1940	2590	3740
High	268	398	465	680	840	1220	1340	1940	2590	3740
Low	268	398	465	680	840	1220	1340	1940	2590	3740
Neb. (avg)	269	409	505	705	930	1291	1489	2079	2886	4049
High	297	501	549	751	1003	1442	1575	2363	3065	4667
Low	253	339	467	616	808	1097	1282	1764	2468	3432
Nev. (avg)	314	422	575	779	1096	1492	1704	2331	3504	4752
High	354	471	639	873	1218	1677	2018	2729	4018	5389
Low	293	398	522	732	980	1400	1536	2173	2923	4195

(Continued)

Table 9.20 (Continued)

N. H. (avg)	316	447	597	859	1157	1681	1902	2776	3733	5147
High	327	455	618	874	1189	1702	1951	2806	3806	5409
Low	296	432	557	830	1093	1639	1806	2716	3589	5016
N. J. (avg)	381	533	646	930	1090	1679	1665	2529	3140	5114
High	399	561	671	984	1208	1855	1869	2980	3649	5870
Low	366	502	612	974	1019	1506	1592	2380	2990	4565
N. Mex. (avg)	302	451	568	855	1057	1606	1853	2690	3663	5334
High	340	475	571	877	1135	1755	2117	2924	4233	5849
Low	284	439	567	813	956	1426	1516	2105	2916	4068
N. Y. (avg)	393	536	675	979	1270	1809	2023	2884	3835	5467
High	530	733	987	1393	1838	2586	2909	4049	5481	7549
Low	215	283	406	541	777	1047	1252	1721	2396	3351
N. Car. (avg)	229	337	435	650	840	1267	1367	2067	2594	3889
High	270	405	490	760	958	1465	1578	2405	3128	4755
Low	215	320	414	620	804	1190	1307	1950	2381	3571
N. Dak. (avg)	417	646	781	1133	1362	1970	2054	3066	3784	5597
High	432	659	790	1143	1376	1986	2074	3091	3818	5640
Low	404	635	774	1121	1349	1948	2033	3031	3743	5529
Ohio (avg)	349	502	634	931	1190	1723	1893	2712	3494	5084
High	367	601	707	1094	1306	1939	2053	2929	3861	5566
Low	278	406	468	641	937	1282	1511	2087	2921	4099
Okla. (avg)	336	467	577	825	1048	1491	1664	2300	3000	4194
High	345	511	622	929	1150	1663	1783	2426	3186	4335
Low	319	394	499	686	956	1328	1567	2187	2917	3942
Ore. (avg)	192	279	361	507	661	888	1047	1361	1890	2483
High	222	327	405	573	742	1012	1164	1519	2083	2789
Low	142	205	283	407	521	671	812	1050	1494	1969
Penn. (avg)	342	458	625	838	1119	1558	1793	2523	3433	4894
High	380	505	713	949	1310	1783	2080	2868	4005	5580
Low	284	412	526	721	976	1386	1573	2269	2916	4335
R. I. (avg)	355	512	651	963	1210	1826	1960	2987	3663	5717
High	358	515	657	970	1217	1840	1973	3011	3706	5782
Low	355	511	650	961	1191	1787	1924	2917	3536	5522

S. Car. (avg)	320	465	464	844	1060	1580	1501	2113	2676	3808
High	369	531	663	951	1329	1851	1551	2167	2750	3985
Low	215	320	414	624	804	1224	1307	2007	2381	3571
S. Dak. (avg)	403	590	659	963	1192	1761	1879	2803	3522	5396
High	465	687	694	999	1250	1802	1985	2945	3820	5740
Low	375	513	613	901	1126	1704	1731	2624	3138	4924
Tenn. (avg)	193	283	358	498	648	868	1008	1308	1808	2408
High	195	285	360	500	650	870	1010	1310	1810	2410
Low	190	280	355	495	645	865	1005	1305	1805	2405
Texas (avg)	323	463	570	829	1027	1490	1582	2284	2787	4110
High	378	544	656	988	1213	1875	1900	2670	3374	4928
Low	231	368	388	647	658	1178	1018	1886	1918	3718
Utah (avg)	281	393	528	730	1002	1407	1607	2283	3091	4442
High	303	437	570	778	1067	1452	1730	2372	3312	4596
Low	255	351	486	676	956	1342	1497	2176	2849	4261
Vt. (avg)	312	445	546	808	1071	1595	1771	2644	3520	5267
High	369	502	604	826	1208	1613	2013	2688	4025	5375
Low	268	410	493	800	942	1579	1542	2618	3041	5215
Va. (avg)	308	430	530	770	987	1461	1590	2367	3161	4358
High	317	490	590	911	1092	1638	1770	2551	4110	4853
Low	302	405	510	719	920	1383	1393	2286	2536	4052
Wash. (avg)	202	294	355	516	633	891	976	1390	1972	2597
High	268	404	484	732	861	1179	1265	1795	2500	3334
Low	166	238	277	380	466	658	709	1029	1317	1957
W. Va. (avg)	309	460	564	858	1000	1576	1677	2510	3280	4667
High	317	490	590	911	1067	1638	1726	2551	4110	4825
Low	302	427	535	797	920	1482	1393	2418	2536	4553
Wisc. (avg)	321	561	636	1199	1178	1881	1888	2863	3454	5171
High	354	608	695	1024	1261	2390	2021	3162	3702	5842
Low	247	367	442	682	794	1274	1264	2064	2439	4039
Wyo. (avg)	297	427	532	734	916	1336	1472	2139	2850	4097
High	349	496	606	804	984	1425	1558	2252	2991	4320
Low	253	371	463	684	865	1269	1401	2049	2740	3974

Source: Anon. (1966).

steam-electric generating plants obtain gas fuel substantially below the rates to the average industrial users. (2) As the state's average cost to industrial users goes up, the differential between cost to the average industrial user and the steam-electric generating plant greatly increases. (3) Michigan has the highest cost of gas to steam-electric generating plants of any state. (4) Obviously for some states, the most economical fuel for these large-scale users is coke or fuel oil. For the United States as a whole, of the total energy supplied to steam-electric generating plants in 1967, 64% was supplied by coal, 9% by fuel oil, and 27% was supplied by gas.

Under the previous heading (Cost of Gas Between States) it was reported that the cost of gas to Maine industrial users was 6 times the cost of gas in Texas; however, using the cost of fuel to steam-electric generating plants, the cost of oil as fuel in Maine is only 65% more than gas in Texas. While exact break-even points for shifts between gas, oil, and coal or coke cannot be determined for food processors in each state from the data available, the relative costs within and between states for very large users (steam-electric generating plants) can be determined with some degree of accuracy. These relative costs probably apply also to industrial users in food processing.

TABLE 9.21

NATURAL GAS COSTS TO INDUSTRIAL USERS RANKED BY STATE
FROM LOWEST TO HIGHEST COST, 1967

State	($ per 1000 Therms[1])	State	($ per 1000 Therms[1])
Texas	21	Indiana	40
New Mexico	22	Oregon	40
Louisiana	22	Nevada	41
Wyoming	24	Idaho	41
Oklahoma	24	Kentucky	42
Colorado	25	Illinois	42
Kansas	26	West Virginia	44
Arkansas	27	North Carolina	49
Mississippi	27	Virginia	50
Utah	27	Michigan	51
Nebraska	30	Pennsylvania	51
Missouri	31	Ohio	52
Alabama	31	Delaware	52
Montana	32	New Jersey	68
South Dakota	32	Maryland	72
Iowa	33	New York	75
Florida	33	Rhode Island	78
Arizona	34	Massachusetts	85
North Dakota	34	Connecticut	89
California	36	New Hampshire	105
Tennessee	36	Maine	128
Georgia	36	Vermont	—
Washington	37		
Minnesota	37		
South Carolina	39		

Source: Computed from data in Anon. (1967)
[1] A therm is 100,000 BTu's

TABLE 9.22

GAS COST TO INDUSTRIAL USERS AND FUEL COST TO
STEAM-ELECTRIC GENERATING PLANTS, 1967

State	Industrial[1] Gas	Generating Plant[2] Gas	Coal	Oil	State	Industrial[1] Gas	Generating Plant[2] Gas	Coal	Oil
Texas	21.00	19.80	NA	47.90	Ind.	40.00	24.90	21.80	69.80
N. Mex.	22.00	22.30	14.50	31.90	Ore.	40.00	35.30	NA	37.90
La.	22.00	19.90	NA	56.40	Nev.	41.00	19.70	21.10	18.00
Wyo.	24.00	NA	19.40	78.40	Idaho	41.00	NA	NA	NA
Okla.	24.00	18.40	NA	42.30	Ky.	42.00	21.50	17.20	81.10
Colo.	25.00	21.60	22.10	38.90	Ill.	42.00	25.70	23.70	51.90
Kans.	26.00	22.70	25.30	43.90	W. Va.	44.00	40.90	18.70	73.30
Ark.	27.00	25.60	NA	39.20	N.Car.	49.00	32.70	28.20	79.50
Miss.	27.00	24.60	NA	49.30	Va.	50.00	NA	27.10	79.40
Utah	27.00	27.00	22.10	24.90	Mich.	51.00	49.80	29.30	71.70
Nebr.	30.00	26.10	30.90	53.00	Penn.	51.00	31.10	21.80	76.20
Mo.	31.00	22.90	21.90	54.60	Ohio	52.00	33.80	22.50	73.20
Ala.	31.00	22.90	22.80	NA	Del.	52.00	30.80	30.20	56.00
Mont.	32.00	19.70	18.00	21.10	N.J	68.00	31.20	31.90	33.50
S. Dak.	32.00	28.50	29.40	NA	Md.	72.00	48.80	29.90	37.90
Iowa	33.00	25.90	27.60	69.50	N.Y.	75.00	36.50	32.70	36.50
Fla.	33.00	32.50	26.70	32.30	R.I.	78.00	33.40	38.10	31.00
Ariz.	34.00	28.80	24.00	58.70	Mass.	85.00	32.20	35.80	30.30
N.Dak.	34.00	28.50	29.40	NA	Conn.	89.00	32.00	32.60	30.60
Calif.	36.00	30.80	NA	31.40	N.H.	105.00	NA	34.50	30.60
Tenn.	36.00	20.50	19.70	NA	Maine	128.00	NA	NA	29.90
Ga.	36.00	27.10	28.70	43.10	Vt.	—	NA	36.10	NA
Wash.	37.00	NA	NA	35.90					
Minn.	37.00	24.90	31.20	53.20					
S.Car.	39.00	29.10	30.40	37.20					

[1]Source: Computed from data in Anon. (1967).
[2]Source: Anon. (1969B).
[3]A therm is 100,000 Btu's.

TRANSPORTATION COSTS AMONG STATES

Introduction

That some states are located much farther than others from the large centers of population and, therefore, have higher freight rates to market for their products, is readily apparent. From a casual point of view the comparison of freight advantages appears to be fairly simple. However, determination of freight costs and use of them to obtain minimum cost distribution systems and comparative advantages among regions can become a large-scale and complicated problem, often only solvable by computer programming. The maze of Interstate Commerce Commission (ICC) regulations of both rail and truck freight rates is compounded by the exemption of unprocessed agricultural commodities, by contract carriers, continuously changing rate structures, and changing technologies. The advantages of one location over another depends not only on the type of product processed and its appropriate freight costs, but also on where each processing plant is located relative to the total market.

The complexity of rate structures was recently illustrated by an article in the *Wall Street Journal:* "New international air fares go into effect Saturday, and here's how to calculate the new price of a New York-to-London ticket: Take the square root of your zip code, multiply it by the number of Joe Namath's girl friends, subtract the earned run average of Tom Seaver and add 42 cents.

"That of course, only produces the fare if you fly BOAC. You need other formulas for other lines.

"This example is fanciful, to be sure, but travel agents say it is no more confusing—and might even be more accurate—than trying to use the complicated instructions that airlines have drawn up for figuring out new fares. . ." (Anon. 1969A).

Because there are so many classes of products with different rate structures and so many possible point-to-point or zone-to-zone rates, freight costs are almost impossible to summarize or to generalize. In fact there appears to be a growing sentiment that the whole U.S. system of freight regulation by the ICC should be reevaluated, possibly completely discarded; but at a minimum, the costs and charges should be revised based on a more scientific method of cost and service determination.

Certainly it would be an almost impossible task to show the freight cost advantages of all major regions of the United States on a product-by-product basis. Therefore the material on transportation costs will deal more with methods of analyzing a region's comparative advantage in freight costs rather than in specific rate structures—although examples of the latter will be given. A brief review of a method to calculate the optimum numbers of processing facilities in an area or region will be illustrated as a trade-off between size of plant and raw product transfer costs. Another brief review will be given of linear programming and marginal costs of freight among states or regions to determine a minimum cost distribution system. This will be followed by examples of the effects of changing technologies on regional advantages.

Importance of Freight in the Marketing Bill

In 1968, U.S. consumer expenditures of domestically produced farm food products was around $90 billion. Of this amount around $29 billion was the farm value of the food and approximately $61 billion was the cost of the marketing bill (U.S. Dept. of Agr. 1969A). Shipping costs by rail or truck amounted to $4.6 billion dollars in 1968, or around 8% of the total marketing bill (Table 9.23). Air and water freight charges and intracity truck transportation charges are not included in these figures.

In general, railroad freight rate indices for farm food products trended downward from 1957-1959 to 1967, then turned up in 1968. The ICC granted the railroads a general freight rate increase of 3% in late 1967, and selective increases ranging from 3-10% in 1968. Rail and truck costs were around 10% of the total food marketing bill in 1957-1959 compared to only 8% in 1968.

Relative Costs of Rail and Truck Transportation

In general for freight, water transportation is the least costly followed by rail, truck, and air. However, absolute costs or freight charges may be more than offset by the services which may accompany the different kinds of freight. Time in transit, demurrage charges, processing in transit privileges, storage at point of shipment and point of delivery, rerouting possibilities, back hauls, and number of points of partial unloadings all may be very important aspects in distributing food products.

Typically, truck transportation is cheaper for short hauls and rail transportation for longer distances. The break-even distances between rail and truck depends upon the assumptions made and the type of product. In a study of frozen vegetable shipments in 1966, Haidacher (1966) found the break-even distance to be around 1100 miles. Below 1100 miles truck transportation was cheaper, about 1100 miles rail was cheaper. Supalla (1969) in a study of canned fruit found the break-even point to be nearer 500 miles.

Neither rail nor truck rates as regulated by the ICC are based on a ton/mile basis. Typically, rail rates are cheaper going from west to east than from east to west. Many rates are apparently set somewhere between competitive costs of other forms of transportation and what the traffic will bear.

Rate changes are not always as difficult to obtain as it might seem with ICC regulation. In many cases a specific rate can be changed by a railroad or a truck line by proposing the rate change and publishing the proposed rate change, waiting a reasonable length of time to see if there are no objections to the proposed change, and then putting the rate into effect. In most cases for a general rate increase or general rate decrease, a hearing must be held and the ICC accepts or rejects the change in rates based on evidence presented.

In one case, reportedly, a railroad studied the costs of truck transportation of grain from a producing region to a major port and then set rail rates for grain just below the truck operating costs—not total truck costs, but just below direct

TABLE 9.23

COST COMPONENTS OF THE MARKETING BILL FOR DOMESTIC FARM FOODS BOUGHT BY U.S. CIVILIAN CONSUMERS, 1957-1968

Year	Labor[1]	Rail and Truck Transportation[2]	Corporate Profits		Depreciation	Business Taxes[3]	Advertising	Rent (Net)	Interest (Net)	Repairs Bad Debts, Contributions	Other[4]	Total
			Before Taxes	After Taxes								
					Billion $							
1957	16.8	4.0	1.9	.9	—	—	—	—	—	—	—	37.9
1958	17.1	4.1	1.9	.9	—	—	—	—	—	—	—	39.5
1959	17.8	4.0	2.1	1.0	1.4	1.2	1.2	1.1	.2	.7	12.5	42.2
1960	18.7	4.1	2.1	.9	1.5	1.3	1.3	1.1	.2	.7	13.2	44.2
1961	18.9	4.2	2.2	1.0	1.5	1.3	1.3	1.1	.3	.8	13.5	45.1
1962	19.7	4.1	2.2	1.0	1.7	1.5	1.5	1.3	.3	.8	13.8	46.9
1963	20.3	4.2	2.4	1.1	1.7	1.6	1.5	1.3	.3	.9	14.7	48.9
1964	21.1	4.3	2.8	1.4	1.8	1.7	1.6	1.4	.3	.9	15.3	51.2
1965	22.4	4.2	3.0	1.6	1.8	1.9	1.7	1.5	.4	1.0	14.2	52.1
1966	23.7	4.3	3.4	1.8	2.0	2.0	1.8	1.6	.4	1.0	14.5	54.7
1967	25.1	4.4	3.1	1.6	2.1	2.1	1.9	1.6	.4	1.1	15.7	57.5
1968[5]	27.3	4.6	3.6	1.8	2.2	2.3	2.0	1.7	.5	1.1	15.3	60.6

Source: U.S. Dept. Agr. (1969A).

[1] Includes supplements to wages and salaries such as Social Security and unemployment insurance taxes and health insurance premiums; also includes imputed earnings of proprietors, partners, and family workers not receiving stated remuneration.

[2] Includes charges for heating and refrigeration; does not include local hauling; estimates for 1960-1967 have been revised.

[3] Includes property, Social Security, unemployment insurance, state income, and franchise taxes, license fees, etc., but does not include federal income tax. Social Security and unemployment insurance taxes also are included in the labor cost component.

[4] Residual components include other costs approximately distributed as follows in 1968: containers, packaging, and labeling, $7 billion; cost incurred in establishments like schools, colleges, hospitals, recreation centers and airlines, $4 billion; other costs include utilities, fuel, promotion, local for-hire transportation, water transportation, insurance, etc.

[5] Preliminary figures. Beginning with 1960, estimates are for 50 states. Data for 1947-1956 are published in MTS, Aug. 1968.

operating costs.

The regulations affecting contract trucking make studies of freight costs more difficult as the contract trucker may operate under nonpublished rates. The following procedures may apply to a contract trucker. A manufacturer may contract for a truck line to distribute his products. Under ICC regulations the freight rates of the contract must be published. However, after the first year the contract can be renewed and the rates no longer must be made publicly available, although they must be filed with the ICC. The contract rates then become privately negotiated rates between the processor or manufacturer and the truck line. In a study of transportation costs of canned fruit, Supalla (1969) found a large portion of truck shipments were made by contract truckers with no published rates.

The for-hire transportation of unmanufactured agricultural commodities by truck in interstate commerce is exempt from ICC regulation. This is known as the "agricultural exemption," and the for-hire carriers hauling exempt commodities exclusively are known as "exempt carriers."

Miklius and DeLoach (1965) found that "in 1960, an estimated 20,000 exempt carriers were operating in the United States. They hauled around 123 million tons of agricultural commodites, operated some 69,000 motor vehicles and accounted for about 14% of the total transportation of property by all motor carriers." These exempt truckers essentially operate in a "free market." The rates are usually negotiable and many of the truckers operate through truck brokers.

The costs of hauling exempt agricultural commodities is important to most food processors in the procurement of their unprocessed agricultural commodities. However, some food products, for example, dehydrated onions, are considered exempt commodities because the processing is simply that of dehydration, adding no chemicals.

Methods of Measuring Freight Advantages or Disadvantages Among States

To measure the freight advantage of one region or state over another, the appropriate rates for the particular product must be known, as well as the quantities of product produced in the immediate and in competing areas, and the quantities consumed in each consuming area.

On a simplified basis, as an example, suppose 2 processing plants, 1 in Los Angeles and 1 in New York City supply the national market with a unique food product. The break-even point in transportation costs might be a north to south line somewhat west of a Chicago-New Orleans line. However, since more than half the population is on or near the eastern part of the United States (assuming a uniform per capita consumption of the product), the New York City plant would have a significant freight advantage. To complicate the example, assume there are 20 processing plants in 15 different states, each producing a different quantity of the product, with a heavy per capita consumption in southern states, a moderate consumption in the east and light per capita consumption in the

FIG. 9.1. FROZEN CHERRIES: MINIMUM COST (PER 100 POUNDS SHIPPED)
DISTRIBUTION SYSTEM FOR THE UNITED STATES BASED ON
WEIGHTED PER CAPITA CONSUMPTION, 1961

west. How does one measure the relative freight costs among processing
locations? We will illustrate, in general, the method of solution for this type of
problem using a technique called linear programming.

To determine a minimum cost distribution system and to determine marginal
costs of transportation among areas, the following sets of data are necessary: (1)
the total quantity of products produced in each shipping region, (2) a list of
freight rates from each producing region to all consuming regions, and (3) the
quantities of products consumed in each consuming region. For simplicity we
will assume a state is the unit of measure for both producing regions and for
consuming regions (Snodgrass and French 1958).

For example, to determine the relative freight advantages among Michigan,
Wisconsin, Montana, New York, Colorado, Utah, Oregon and Idaho in the
distribution of frozen cherries, we need production of frozen cherries in each
state, consumption, and a matrix of freight rates from each of the producing
states to each of the consuming states (Greig 1963). The production and
weighted consumption of frozen cherries by states are listed in Table 9.24. A
partial matrix of rail rates for frozen fruits and vegetables are listed in Table
9.25. With the computer we can determine the minimum cost distribution
system for all of the frozen cherries produced in the United States. That is, we
can determine the part of the total market each state should supply to minimize
the total cost of transportation for all frozen cherries. The minimum cost
distribution system is shown graphically in Fig. 9.1. In the Figure the arrows

TABLE 9.24

FROZEN CHERRIES: ESTIMATED TOTAL PRODUCTION AND WEIGHTED SURPLUS
AND DEFICIT BY STATES, 1961

State	Population (1000's)	Production (Cwt)	Consumption (Cwt)	Surplus (Cwt)	Deficit (Cwt)
Maine	999		13,071		13,071
N. H.	632		8,274		8,274
Vt.	390		5,101		5,101
Mass.	5,161		67,485		67,485
R. I.	865		11,319		11,319
Conn.	2,597		33,958		33,958
N. Y.	17,402	613,942	227,582	386,360	
N. J.	6,245		81,673		81,673
Penn.	11,376	82,637	148,778		48,628
Ohio	10,097	21,421	132,052		110,631
Ind.	4,715		61,673		61,673
Ill.	10,146		132,687		132,687
Mich.	7,991	1,266,462	104,515	1,161,947	
Wisc.	4,092	264,967	53,526	211,441	
Minn.	3,475		45,456		45,456
Iowa	2,777		36,319		36,319
Mo.	4,346		56,826		56,826
N. Dak.	642		8,401		8,401
S. Dak.	721		9,441		9,441
Nebr.	1,484		19,416		19,416
Kans.	2,219		29,009		29,009
Del.	469		6,142		6,142
Md. + 1/2 D.C.	3,583		46,851		46,851
Va. + 1/2 D.C.	4,569		59,745		59,745
W. Va.	1,773		23,197		23,197
N. Car.	4,731		61,876		61,876
S. Car.	2,436		31,852		31,852
Ga.	4,100		53,628		53,628
Fla.	5,459		71,394		71,394
Ky.	3,082		40,303		40,303
Tenn.	3,634		47,511		47,511
Ala.	3,358		43,907		43,907
Miss.	2,248		29,390		29,390
Ark.	1,823		23,832		23,832
La.	3,330		43,552		43,552
Okla.	2,448		32,004		32,004
Texas	10,116		132,306		132,306
Mont.	709	7,132	9,264		2,132
Idaho	698	13,934	9,137	4,797	
Wyo.	365		4,771		4,771
Colo.	1,907	29,695	24,949	4,746	
N. Mex.	1,020		13,350		13,350
Ariz.	1,509		19,746		19,746
Utah	967	29,314	12,639	16,675	
Nev.	335		4,391		4,391
Wash.	3,006	4,518	39,314		34,796
Ore.	1.864	66,419	24,390	42,029	
Calif.	16,970		221,948		221,948
Total	184,881	2,417,953	2,417,953	1,827,995	1,827,995

Source: Greig (1965).

TABLE 9.25

PARTIAL MATRIX OF COST OF REFRIGERATED RAIL SHIPMENTS OF FROZEN FRUITS AND VEGETABLES (COST IN CENTS PER 100 POUNDS WITH MAXIMUM LOADINGS), 1969

Destination	Augusta, Me.	Lockport, N.Y.	Erie, Pa.	Indianapolis, Ind.	DeKalb, Ill.	Benton Harbor, Mich.	Madison, Wisc.	Boise, Idaho
Augusta, Me.	0	113	121	151	157	148	157	187
Manchester, N.H.	62	98	108	151	148	139	148	187
Montpelier, Vt.	71	96	105	139	146	137	146	187
Boston, Mass.	68	98	108	141	148	139	148	187
Providence, R.I.	71	98	109	141	148	139	148	187
Hartford, Conn.	78	93	102	135	142	134	142	187
New York, N.Y.	93	88	101	129	140	133	141	187
Newark, N.J.	93	91	101	129	140	133	141	187
Philadelphia, Pa.	102	93	95	123	135	127	141	187
Cleveland, Ohio	128	68	55	81	91	80	99	182
Indianapolis, Ind.	151	98	89	0	70	68	79	176
Peoria, Ill.	162	113	105	69	55	70	66	164
Detroit, Mich.	134	73	77	76	81	68	85	176
Milwaukee, Wisc.	154	103	103	78	56	66	49	164
Minneapolis, Minn.	177	131	133	109	88	102	76	151
Des Moines, Iowa	181	135	127	97	76	95	77	158
Jefferson City, Mo.	181	135	127	90	87	97	94	158
Fargo, N. Dak.	196	148	150	132	110	124	100	164
Sioux Falls, S. Dak.	190	143	142	119	99	114	93	158
Lincoln, Nebr.	193	148	142	114	97	113	97	151
Wichita, Kans.	202	155	149	120	108	122	114	151
Dover, Del.	109	93	99	125	36	129	141	187
Baltimore, Md.	112	94	93	116	131	122	116	187
Richmond, Va.	126	109	109	119	137	132	141	187
Charleston, W. Va.	144	97	88	83	101	93	109	182

TABLE 9.25 (Continued)

PARTIAL MATRIX OF COST OF REFRIGERATED RAIL SHIPMENTS OF FROZEN FRUITS AND VEGETABLES (COST IN CENTS PER 100 POUNDS WITH MAXIMUM LOADINGS), 1969

Destination	Augusta, Me.	Lockport, N.Y.	Erie, Pa.	Indianapolis, Ind.	DeKalb, Ill.	Benton Harbor, Mich.	Madison, Wisc.	Boise, Idaho
Raleigh, N. Car.	138	124	123	123	137	134	145	187
Charleston, S. Car.	158	143	142	131	147	143	155	187
Atlanta, Ga.	168	140	134	110	126	125	136	182
Tampa, Fla.	190	178	169	151	166	165	171	198
Louisville, Ky.	157	106	97	57	73	81	93	176
Nashville, Tenn.	171	125	116	81	98	100	107	176
Birmingham, Ala.	177	140	134	104	105	118	127	176
Jackson, Miss.	195	155	148	115	123	129	132	164
Little Rock, Ark.	192	168	141	106	111	120	118	164
Baton Rouge, La.	209	148	160	131	137	144	142	158
Oklahoma City, Okla.	210	165	159	130	123	137	129	158
Houston, Texas	225	182	174	145	149	155	155	164
Helena, Mont.	250	221	215	194	177	187	167	138
Boise, Idaho	187	182	176	176	164	176	164	0
Cheyenne, Wyo.	230	182	177	153	138	154	138	147
Denver, Colo.	234	189	180	157	141	155	142	137
Santa Fe, N. Mex.	247	200	202	171	164	175	167	164
Phoenix, Ariz.	262	206	233	202	197	209	199	114
Salt Lake City, Utah	249	220	212	187	173	182	173	110
Reno, Nev.	273	244	249	229	213	227	213	60
Seattle, Wash.	187	182	176	176	164	176	164	55
Portland, Ore.	187	182	176	176	164	176	164	103
Bakersfield, Calif.	187	182	176	176	164	176	164	68

TABLE 9.25 (Continued)

PARTIAL MATRIX OF COST OF REFRIGERATED RAIL SHIPMENTS OF FROZEN FRUITS AND
VEGETABLES (COST IN CENTS PER 100 POUNDS WITH MAXIMUM LOADINGS), 1969

Destination	Denver, Colo.	Seattle, Wash.	Raleigh, N. Car.	Tampa, Fla.	Minneapolis, Minn.	Fargo, N. Dak.	Dover, Del.
Augusta, Me.	222	187	135	186	175	191	107
Manchester, N.H.	217	187	98	175	166	182	92
Montpelier, Vt.	216	187	132	178	164	180	112
Boston, Mass.	217	187	124	171	166	180	91
Providence, R. I.	220	187	121	169	166	180	89
Hartford, Conn.	214	187	113	162	160	177	80
New York, N.Y.	211	187	101	153	159	176	66
Newark, N.J.	211	187	101	153	159	176	66
Philadelphia, Pa.	206	187	92	147	159	178	53
Cleveland, Ohio	169	182	122	160	121	141	105
Indianapolis, Ind.	152	176	121	149	107	130	128
Peoria, Ill.	136	164	136	158	91	112	141
Detroit, Mich.	163	176	98	162	108	132	121
Milwaukee, Wisc.	145	164	140	167	82	107	141
Minneapolis, Minn.	133	151	169	187	0	71	166
Des Moines, Iowa	117	158	162	174	76	100	161
Jefferson City, Mo.	125	158	155	158	100	123	158
Fargo, N. Dak.	137	164	186	207	71*	0	185
Sioux Falls, S. Dak.	118	158	179	192	71	81	179
Lincoln, Nebr.	100	151	174	181	89	100	174
Wichita, Kans.	100	151	174	172	113	125	182
Dover, Del.	207	187	86	140	161	179	0
Baltimore, Md.	200	187	83	140	157	174	57
Richmond, Va.	204	187	62	128	161	179	77
Charleston, W. Va.	189	182	94	142	134	151	104

TABLE 9.25 (Continued)

PARTIAL MATRIX OF COST OF REFRIGERATED RAIL SHIPMENTS OF FROZEN FRUITS AND VEGETABLES (COST IN CENTS PER 100 POUNDS WITH MAXIMUM LOADINGS), 1969

Destination	Denver, Colo.	Seattle, Wash.	Raleigh, N. Car.	Tampa, Fla.	Minneapolis, Minn.	Fargo, N. Dak.	Dover, Del.
Raleigh, N. Car.	204	187	0	115	165	179	89
Charleston, S. Car.	200	187	76	90	173	191	110
Atlanta, Ga.	179	182	94	97	153	171	102
Tampa, Fla.	205	198	120	0	186	205	148
Louisville, Ky.	157	176	121	138	118	137	102
Nashville, Tenn.	159	176	121	124	129	147	142
Birmingham, Ala.	162	176	110	107	144	163	140
Jackson, Miss.	159	164	136	122	148	163	162
Little Rock, Ark.	139	164	145	140	133	152	165
Baton Rouge, La.	159	158	146	127	159	176	174
Oklahoma City, Okla.	117	158	174	167	127	139	190
Houston, Texas	146	164	171	150	159	174	196
Helena, Mont.	127	138	234	247	144	129	229
Boise, Idaho	131	103	187	198	151	164	173
Cheyenne, Wyo.	56	147	211	214	129	133	211
Denver, Colo.	0	137	210	207	134	137	213
Santa Fe, N. Mex.	90	164	223	214	163	169	233
Phoenix, Ariz.	127	114	240	229	192	195	249
Salt Lake City, Utah	99	110	238	243	160	152	238
Reno, Nev.	144	60	252	255	200	188	253
Seattle, Wash.	170	0	187	198	151	164	187
Portland, Ore.	162	103	187	198	151	164	187
Bakersfield, Calif.	154	68	187	198	151	164	187

Source: Industrial Transportation Services, Detroit, Michigan.

originate at the producing state and end in the state of consumption. The figures are the number of hundredweight of cherries consumed in each state.

With the computer system we can also determine marginal transportation costs among states. The marginal cost of transportation is the cost of transporting one additional unit, in this case an additional 100 lb of frozen cherries. The marginal cost of transportation of frozen cherries by each surplus producing state is listed in Table 9.26.

If Michigan were to process an additional 100 lb of cherries, in all probability this 100 lb would be shipped a long distance—probably to California—and the cost of transportation for this last additional 100 lb would be $2.21. However if Idaho were to process an additional 100 lb they would be shipped a relatively short distance, for example to Nevada, and the cost would be only $0.83. Thus, if 100 lb of frozen cherry production were shifted from Michigan to Idaho, the savings in freight would be $2.21 minus $0.83 or $1.38. Comparisons among states in marginal costs can easily be made directly from Table 9.26. Michigan effectively provides an "umbrella" of freight costs for the other states in the case of frozen cherry products. The average costs of freight can also easily be computed from the computer programs.

The minimum cost transportation models are probably quite different from the actual systems of transportation in our competitive economic systems. There are many cross-overs or cross-hauls in actual practice. For example, New York cherry processors probably have customers in Detroit, and Michigan processors probably have customers in New York City. This would not happen in a minimum cost system. One way of viewing the linear programming models is to assume that if one individual owned all the frozen cherries how would he distribute them to minimize his total freight costs.

Another example could be frozen French fried potatoes (Greig 1966). Using the estimated production of frozen French fried potatoes in 1965 (Table 9.27) and assuming a uniform per capita consumption by states, and the rail rates that were in effect in 1965, a minimum cost transportation system can be developed for the frozen potatoes (Fig. 9.2). The relative marginal costs for rail transportation of frozen potatoes is listed in Table 9.28. Michigan would have a $0.15 per cwt advantage over Maine, $0.18 over the Red River Valley, $0.78 over Washington, and $0.87 over Idaho. However, the model assumes a homogeneous commodity with no price differentials—this is not the case in the real world. There are quality differences with premiums usually obtained by Western potatoes. Similarly there is much cross-hauling. In any case, the West does provide a freight "umbrella" for the Midwest and the East. The size of the umbrella is relative to the proportional amount processed in each region. If Maine, Michigan, or the Red River Valley disproportionately increase the amount they process, their relative freight advantage decreases. It is important to remember that these relationships are not static; changes in any of the three inputs (1) amount produced by regions, (2) freight rates, and (3) quantities consumed by regions, will change the relative freight relationship between areas of production.

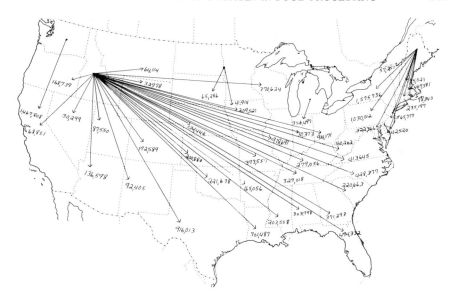

FIG. 9.2. FROZEN POTATO PRODUCTS: MINIMUM COST (PER 100 POUNDS SHIPPED) DISTRIBUTION SYSTEM FOR THE UNITED STATES, 1965

TABLE 9.26

FROZEN CHERRIES: MARGINAL TRANSPORTATION COSTS OF SURPLUS-PRODUCING CHERRY STATES, PURELY COMPETITIVE MODEL, 1961[1]

State	Dollars per Cwt
Idaho	0.83
Oregon	1.12
Utah	1.70
Colorado	1.72
New York	1.74
Montana	1.81
Wisconsin	2.04
Michigan	2.21

Source: Greig (1965).

[1] The difference between any two of these marginal costs is based on the deviation from the optimum solutions and is absolute in nature. They show the reduction in aggregate costs that could be made by shifting 1 unit of production (100 lb) from the state of higher value to the 1 of lower value.

Another relationship to consider in the case of cherries is that if Michigan's marginal freight cost is $1.38 more per hundred-weight of frozen cherries than Idaho, then Michigan must have a $1.38 per 100 lb advantage in production and processing over Idaho, otherwise the industry is mislocated. Similarly if Idaho's marginal freight disadvantage in frozen potatoes, when compared to Michigan, is $0.87, then Idaho must have an $0.87 advantage in production, processing, or quality than does Michigan.

These linear programming freight relationships can be worked out for any product, and it is not always necessary to use computer programming to compare freight advantages or disadvantages. A processor considering a new area may simply compare freight rates from the new area to several major markets with those from major competing areas. However, in all probability the products compete in a national market rather than in isolation in a few markets.

The freight rates listed in Table 9.25 do need some explanation. Any given railroad, serving the routings listed, may have several different rates for frozen fruits and vegetables based on the quantities shipped in each car. Rates may be listed separately from loadings of 40,000–100,000 lb. In nearly all cases the rates decrease significantly from a loading of 40,000 lb to a minimum loading of 100,000 lb. The rates given are for the maximum quantities than can be loaded in a single car. In most but not all cases, the loadings are for at least a 70,000-lb minimum. And in most, but not all cases, there is a charge for refrigeration in addition to the basic rail rate. Typically, this is a flat rate dollar charge per car. These additional charges are included in the rates listed.

Even this type of tabulation of rail rates between areas may not give a true picture of the cost of transportation. Several railroads may have million-pound rates. Under this system, six or more carloads must be loaded the same day, shipped to the same redistribution point, and must have a limited common carrier freight charge from the point of redistribution to final destination. The

TABLE 9.27

QUANTITIES OF FROZEN POTATOES PROCESSED BY STATES, 1965 CROP YEAR

State	Potatoes Utilized in Frozen Form in 1965	
	Raw Product Equivalent (Cwt)	(60% Yield)
Idaho	14,900,000	8,940,000
Maine	7,500,000	4,500,000
Washington	2,900,000	1,740,000
Michigan	1,800,000	1,080,000
Red River Valley	800,000	480,000
Total	27,900,000	16,740,000

Source: Industry Estimates (1966).

million pound rates may be substantially below those of cars shipped individually. Further in some cases, there are train-load rates even lower than the million-pound rates. The million-pound rates and train-load rates are not included in the listing of the rates in Table 9.25.

Methods to Minimize Procurement Freight Costs

If there is a given amount of agricultural production of a crop or commodity in a specific geographical area, how many processing plants should be located there to minimize the total costs of procurement and processing? The answer to this question is a trade-off between the size of plants and procurement freight costs. As a processing plant becomes larger it usually is more efficient, but as it gets larger it must go farther and farther from the plant to obtain its raw product for processing. Using a "systems approach" how can we determine the number, size, and location of processing plants in an area to minimize the total costs of procurement and processing? Obviously, production density of the particular agricultural commodity becomes important in answering this question. Of course, there are wide differences among states in production densities of agricultural crops or commodities and these differences can become important in regional advantages or disadvantages.

There are computer techniques available to analyze the minimum number, size, and location of processing plants to minimize the total costs of procurement and processing for a region, or a state, or for the whole United States for that matter (Stollsteimer 1958). While we will not explore the computational aspects, we will discuss the data needed and the type of results one might expect from using this type of model.

TABLE 9.28

FROZEN POTATO PRODUCTS:
RELATIVE MARGINAL TRANSPORTATION
COSTS PER 100 POUNDS
RAW PRODUCT EQUIVALENT, 1966[1]

State of Origin	Marginal Freight Cost[2] (dollars per Cwt)
Michigan	0.00
Maine	0.15
Red River Valley	0.18
Washington	0.78
Idaho	0.87

Source: Greig (1966).

[1] Assumes a 60% product weight yield.
[2] The difference between any of these relative marginal costs is based on the deviation from optimum solutions and is absolute in nature. They show the reduction in aggregate costs that could be made by shifting 100 lb raw product from the state of higher cost to the one of lower cost.

For example, Wisconsin is a major producer of green peas for processing. We wish to know what would be the minimum number of pea freezing plants, their sizes, and their locations (by counties) to minimize the costs of procurement and processing (Heifner and Greig 1970). The required data are (1) total pea production by counties, (2) a matrix of raw product freight costs (from the center of each county to the center of every other county in Wisconsin—or any specified area), and (3) a measure of the economies of scale in pea freezing operations.

Perhaps each of these three items needs a brief explanation. (1) The production of peas in each county can be obtained in census years from the Census of Agriculture. (2) The matrix of freight costs can be determined by a linear equation developed from industry cost data. (3) The economies of scale data can be developed from economic-engineering studies or engineering estimates. Essentially what is needed is the cost of freezing peas in plants of different sizes.

The production of green peas by counties for Wisconsin is listed in Table 9.29. Estimated raw product freight costs are listed in Table 9.30. Simple linear equations representing these freight costs are: For under 50 miles the cost is 12.5¢ per cwt + 0.147¢ per cwt/mile. For over 50 miles the cost is 12.5¢ per cwt + 0.35¢ per cwt/mile.

The estimated cost function for freezing and the frozen storage of green peas is represented by the linear equation:

Total processing costs = $70,066 + $8785 per cwt processed

This latter cost is based on building and equipment costs, labor wage rates, taxes, insurance, depreciation, repairs, interest on investment, etc., and was obtained by detailed economic-engineering studies of different sizes of plants. The linear equation is a representation of the differences in costs of different sized freezing operations in Wisconsin.

By examination of a map of Wisconsin with county production data, possible locations are picked by "eyeball" estimates. In this case we chose 11 counties as possible sites for processing plants. These counties were Dodge, Fon du Lac, Columbia, Rock, Sheboygan, Oconto, Calumet, Marathon, Trempealeau, Dane, and St. Croix.

With the above types of data, computers can be programmed to obtain an optimum solution of numbers, locations, and sizes of plants. The optimum computer solution was for three pea freezing plants in Wisconsin. These plants would be located in Columbia, Calumet, and St. Croix counties. The total cost of pea freezing would be a hauling cost of $579,688, a processing cost of $22,548,173 and a total hauling and processing cost of $23,127,861. However, and this is important, there are 10 combinations of 3 counties where the hauling costs would be within 5% of the least cost solution. These counties are listed in Table 9.31.

The total hauling and processing costs in Wisconsin:

For 1 plant	$23,299,748
For 2 plants	23,190,571

TABLE 9.29

GREEN PEA PRODUCTION IN WISCONSIN
BY COUNTIES, 1964[1]

County	Green Pea Production (100 Lb Shelled Basis)
Adams	17,568
Barron	35,016
Brown	32,782
Calumet	88,200
Clark	14,448
Columbia	273,840
Dane	169,608
Dodge	345,792
Door	15,168
Dunn	2,808
Eau Claire	12,120
Fon Du Lac	369,048
Grant	12,912
Green Lake	68,880
Iowa	39,456
Jackson	2,904
Jefferson	18,360
Juneau	30,624
Kewaunee	43,032
La Crosse	3,792
Longlade	21,264
Lincoln	2,712
Manitowoc	87,312
Marathon	41,112
Marinette	14,688
Marquette	3,720
Oconto	38,760
Outagamie	67,800
Ozaukee	31,800
Pepin	3,864
Pierce	17,304
Polk	12,648
Portage	7,776
Richland	5,064
Rock	83,208
St. Croix	70,656
Sauk	60,384
Shawano	9,816
Sheboygan	115,512
Trempealeau	31,080
Walworth	60,480
Washington	49,872
Waukesha	7,680
Waupaca	7,728
Waushara	16,368
Winnebago	62,904
Wood	14,856

Source: 1964 Census of Agriculture.

[1] For counties with 100 acres or more.

For 3 plants	23,127,861
For 4 plants	23,154,534
For 5 plants	23,190,148
For 6 plants	23,228,802
For 7 plants	23,276,210

Thus, from 2 to 5 plants would have total cost differences of less than $100,000 per yr. Within a limited range the numbers of plants are not too important. Similarly the 2 plants could be in several different locations with little differences in cost as could the 3, 4, or 5 plant locations.

Essentially, in this particular case there was a broad range in locations and a fairly broad range in numbers of plants that could serve the Wisconsin green pea freezing industry without appreciable cost differences. In other industries with different economies of scale in processing and different procurement costs, the results could, of course, be different. The example shows that there is a methodology available to handle this specific type of problem. In our study of green pea locations (Heifner and Greig 1970) it was found that differences between states in costs greatly over-weighed the possible differences of costs within the states by minimizing the number and sizes of plants. However, from a systems approach the most efficient number of pea processing plants in each area of the United States would be significantly below the number actually in existence.

EFFECT ON LOCATION OF CHANGES IN TECHNOLOGY

Technological changes in product as well as new developments in transportation systems affect the comparative advantages between states or regions. A product innovation which reduces freight is just as effective as a freight rate change itself in changing costs between regions. To be specific and continue the example using cherries, Michigan apparently has around a $1.38 per

TABLE 9.30

ESTIMATED RAW PRODUCT TRANSPORTATION COSTS FOR GREEN PEAS, 1967

Miles From Plant	Cost Per Ton ($)	Tons	How Hauled	Gross Receipts ($)	Cents Per Mile Traveled	Cents Per Cwt
25	2.50	16	semi-trailer	40.00	80.00	12.5
50	4.125	16	semi-trailer	66.00	66.00	20.6
75	7.50	10	semi-trailer in ice water	75.00	50.00	37.5
100	9.00	20	two-tank trailer	180.00	90.00	45.0
150	11.50	20	two-tank trailer	230.00	76.67	57.5
200	14.00	20	two-tank trailer	280.00	70.00	70.0
300	19.50	20	two-tank trailer	390.00	65.00	97.5
500	30.00	20	two-tank trailer	600.00	60.00	150.0

Source: Michigan Processors.

cwt disadvantage when compared to Idaho in marginal costs of freight for frozen cherries. Michigan must also, then, have a $1.38 per cwt advantage in production and processing over Idaho, assuming the cherry industry is efficiently located. Assume a new processing technology is developed whereby the frozen cherries are replaced by a dehydrated cherry product. The cost of freight is much lower per 100 lb raw product equivalent than for frozen. In this case Michigan would be the sole producer of the dehydrated product. Michigan's advantages in production and processing would not be offset by a similar disadvantage in freight costs and Michigan would have an economic advantage in distributing dehydrated cherries to the whole U.S. market. Thus, the change in product technology (resulting in freight changes) completely changes the comparative advantages among regions.

Even a quality change in technology can greatly affect locational economics. For example, much potato processing in the West was originally due to quality differences in the product—and the resulting price premiums for frozen French fried potatoes over those produced in the Midwest and East. There is some evidence to suggest that more sophisticated processing technologies are reducing the quality differences in the product among areas. This suggests a possible increase of production in the Midwest and East as the Western price differentials may no longer cover the freight disadvantages. (See the example previously given in this chapter on marginal cost of freight on frozen French fried potatoes among regions.)

Technological changes in transportation methods or equipment with resulting, cost differences may cause appreciable shifts in comparative advantage. The piggy back shipments, "Big John" bulk railroad cars, tandem trailers, superjet air shipments, containerized ships, etc., all affect interregional competition. In general, rate increase tends to favor those areas located close to markets and a rate decrease tends to favor those areas long distances from market.

TABLE 9.31

OPTIMUM AND NEAR OPTIMUM LOCATIONS FOR THREE GREEN PEA
FREEZING PLANTS IN WISCONSIN, 1968

Percent Hauling Costs Are Above Optimum Location	Locations by Counties		
0.00 (Optimum location)	Columbia	Calumet	St. Croix
0.27	Calumet	Dane	St. Croix
1.49	Fon du Lac	Dane	St. Croix
2.03	Fon du Lac	Columbia	St. Croix
2.72	Calumet	Trempealeau	Dane
3.18	Columbia	Calumet	Trempealeau
3.76	Fon du Lac	Trempealeau	Dane
3.94	Columbia	Sheboygan	St. Croix
4.30	Calumet	Marathon	Dane
4.53	Fon du Lac	Marathon	Dane

Source: Heifner and Greig (1970).

This is a little different from the theory of land rent developed by Von Thunen over a century ago. Von Thunen (1826) noticed that areas near markets could produce products with high weight or volume relative to price, while areas farther from market had to produce more concentrated products—products valuable enough to cover additional freight costs.

SEASONAL AVAILABILITY (OR RAW PRODUCT AVAILABILITY)

Production seasonality of processing crops or commodities must be faced by most food processors. Processing of meat, eggs, milk, and fruit and vegetables, etc., are all affected by seasonal differences in availability of the raw products. With some products, grain for example, the raw products can be stored to maintain full processing plant capacity throughout the year. With others, milk, meat, eggs, poultry, fruit and vegetables, processing plant capacity may be partially or completely unutilized during parts of the year. With most all farm commodities there is a seasonality of supply while demand is relatively stable throughout the year. This is reflected in seasonal price differences. Prices and production levels tend to move in opposite directions. When production is high prices are low, when production is low prices tend to be high. Because of biological differences in the processes of production, each crop or livestock product usually has a distinct seasonal pattern in output and price.

Certainly there are differences among states or regions in the seasonality of products to be processed. This naturally affects the cost of processing and therefore affects interregional competition among areas.

To show seasonality of prices, indices of monthly prices are given for barrows and gilts and potatoes (Fig. 9.3 and 9.4). These types of seasonal indices can be developed for most all agricultural products (Heifner and Ferguson 1968). In Fig. 9.3 and 9.4 the center line is the average and the upper and lower lines contain 2/3 of all the variations in 10 yr of price data. Nearly all states may show somewhat similar price variability as state prices are, to a certain extent, a reflection of national prices. Some areas of the United States probably have less difficulty in scheduling higher utilization of productive capacity of processing facilities than do others.

Perhaps in no area of food processing is production seasonality as important as it is in fruit and vegetable processing. Typically, many of the crops to be processed may be stored for only a very short length of time. The length of the harvest season becomes very important if the physical facilities are to be used over a long period of time each year to reduce overhead costs. Since the climate and soils vary widely throughout the United States, fruit and vegetable production is usually in specialized areas favorable to individual crops or combinations of crops that tend toward complementarity in processing opportunities. Even so, there may be wide differences in length of the processing season for processing plants located in different regions of the country.

Recently, for example, we conducted a national survey of all processing plants which processed green peas, lima beans, spinach, or green beans to

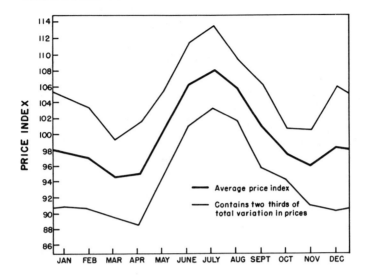

FIG. 9.3. AVERAGE SEASONAL VARIATION IN MICHIGAN FARM
PRICES OF POTATOES, 1958-1967, BASED ON AN INDEX
OF PRICES (AVERAGE PRICE=100)

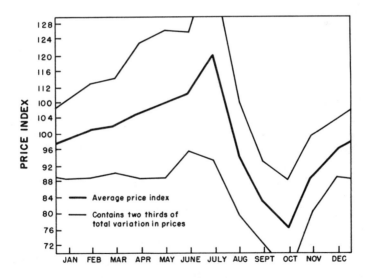

FIG. 9.4. AVERAGE SEASONAL VARIATION IN CHICAGO PRICES
OF BARROWS AND GILTS (U.S. NO. 1, 2, and 3, 200-220 LB) BASED
ON AN INDEX OF PRICES (AVERAGE PRICE=100), 1958-1967

determine the length of season of each of these crops and on "all processing" by these particular processing plants. Seventy-eight returns were obtained from processing plants that processed green peas. The actual hours of processing peas ranged from 328 hr in Maryland to 1160 hr in Oregon. The total length of processing ranged from 1322 hr per yr in Maryland to 3025 hr in California (Table 9.32). In practice some plants operated more hours each day than others; but even assuming a standard 16-hr day, there were still wide differences in the total length of time a processing plant would have operated in different states. Two of the major green pea processing states are Wisconsin and Washington. It is interesting to note that the Wisconsin plants operated 12.6 hr per day while Washington operated 17 hr per day. Similarly, these two states compete with Wisconsin processors operating 1443 hr per yr while Washington processors operated 2463 hr per yr.

Usual planting and harvest dates for both vegetables and fruits are published by the U.S. Dept. of Agr. (1964, 1969B) for most commercial areas of production. These provide useful guides to production areas and to possible product complementarity for processing. However, the commercial practices of processors in each area is probably the best key to processing opportunities.

RAW PRODUCT PRICES AMONG STATES

Raw product costs are probably the greatest single input cost in much food processing. Because price differences among states are so difficult to generalize and because we will not analyze specific commodities, less time will be spent discussing this topic than for many of the other input costs. At the same time it is recognized that price differences among areas are extremely important in processing plant locations. As in the case with other inputs, raw product prices should be viewed as one input in a matrix of many cost factors. Transportation costs to market, labor wage rates, taxes, fuel and electrical costs, length of processing season, economies of scale, etc., can offset differences in raw product costs.

Raw product price comparisons among states are often compounded by differences in quality or grade, seasonality of production, terms of trade or specifications of contract, and differences in points of delivery. Further, there are usually daily, seasonal, and annual fluctuations in prices. Weighted average price differentials among areas are difficult to obtain.

In much vegetable processing, for example, most sales of raw products are under annual contracts. Differences in the terms of the contracts can greatly affect real prices received. Contractual conditions such as the following can affect the real or true price received for the raw product: who furnishes the seed, the fertilizer, the chemicals for insect and disease control, who does the harvesting, what are the price differentials between grades, is a hauling allowance specified, who controls the schedules of delivery, who furnishes the field containers, is a variety or varieties specified, who does the grading, is the contract based on acreages or on quantities to be delivered, what are the terms

TABLE 9.32

AVERAGE LENGTH OF GREEN PEA AND TOTAL PROCESSING SEASON
BY STATES, 1969

| State | No. of Plants[1] | Pea Processing | | | | Total Hr Total Processing All Products |
		Avg. Days Processing	Hr Per Day	Total Hr		
Michigan	7	25.7	13.8	354.7		2219
Maryland	6	26.3	13.1	328.0		1322
Delaware	6	28.1	14.3	430.5		2474
California	6	21.0	13.2	283.8		3025
New York	2	28.0	16.1	450.0		2398
Minnesota	6	30.2	17.0	516.0		1514
Pennsylvania	4	35.0	16.8	653.0		2767
Wisconsin	28	32.0	12.6	407.0		1443
Washington	11	44.0	17.0	748.0		2463
Oregon	2	58.5	21.0	1160.0		2744
Illinois	0	40[2]	14[2]	560.0		1600[2]
Idaho	0	40[2]	16[2]	640.0		2000[2]
Total	78					

Source: Survey of commercial pea processors, 1969.

[1] Number of plants responding to a national questionnaire.
[2] Estimates — data not available.

or conditions under which deliveries may be rejected, etc.

If individual processors in different areas of production have contracts with substantially different terms, then real price differences between states or areas may be difficult, if not impossible, to compare without detailed research.

The most authoritative source for farm prices of agricultural products is the U.S. Dept. of Agr. Prices of nearly all agricultural products are reported for each state in which the crop or commodity is relatively important. Each state has a cooperative federal-state crop reporting service which typically publishes production and price information on each of the state's principal agricultural commodities. The individual state reports are then summarized into national reports by the U.S. Dept. of Agr. Further, many areas have federal-state market news reporters who publish daily farm prices of agricultural commodities as well as wholesale or central market prices in most of the larger cities of the United States.

In addition to the federal-state market news reports and those of the Crop Reporting Service of the U.S. Dept. of Agr., grower organizations or trade groups may keep price series. For example, the American Farm Bureau may have more detailed price series than the U.S. Dept. of Agr. on certain commodities. While the U.S. Dept. of Agr. Crop Reporting Service publishes prices of apples for processing under the headings "Canning and Freezing," "Drying," and "Other Processing," the Michigan Farm Bureau keeps records of prices paid for apples by individual processors, by grade, size, variety, and utilization method. Hauling allowances and who furnishes bulk boxes, if needed, are specified in the Michigan Farm Bureau reports.

Perhaps closely related to prices are estimates of production costs. Many land grant colleges or universities and often the Cooperative Federal State Extension Service publishes cost of production estimates for different agricultural commodities. These reports are not published on a regular basis as are the price reports of the U.S. Dept. of Agr., but cost studies are often available on many of the principal commodities in many states. These studies vary in depth and in approach. New York State (Cornell University), Michigan (Michigan State University), and some other states have substantial numbers of farmers enrolled in cost accounting programs. From the cost account records of these farmers, enterprise cost data are developed. These studies can be analyzed by size of farm, but the data are not state averages, as, typically, only the better farmers are enrolled in the cost accounting programs. The California Extension Service often interviews a small group of "best" farmers and computes costs of production on a recall basis rather than from a detailed analysis of records. Often, colleges and universities conduct in-depth special studies of the cost of production particular commodities.

Processors considering new crops, commodities, or new areas of production on which they do not have estimates of cost of production, might be well served by contacting the appropriate college, university, or the Cooperative Federal State Extension Service in the state.

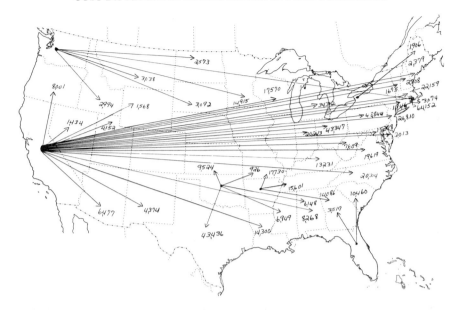

FIG. 9.5. FROZEN SPINACH: MINIMUM COST (PER 100 LB OF PROCESSED PRODUCT)
DISTRIBUTION SYSTEM FOR THE UNITED STATES BASED ON
QUANTITIES PRODUCED, 1961

Over the years the U.S. Dept. of Agr. has developed much industry
cooperation in price reporting. The U.S. Dept. of Agr. and other governmental
agencies, such as the U.S. Bureau of Census, have taken the position that they
will not reveal the operations of individual firms. In many cases where there are
only a few processing plants in a state for a particular product, the U.S. Dept. of
Agr. does not report prices for the raw product because they might reveal the
prices paid by individual firms. This is true of minor processing crops in some
areas—and, in a few cases, true of a substantial processing industry. For example,
Illinois probably processes nearly 20,000 acres of green peas, but because there
are only 2 or 3 major processors of green peas in Illinois the U.S. Dept. of Agr.
has discontinued publishing statistical data on green peas in that state.

To illustrate a case in which there is a considerable price differential among
areas, but also where nonraw product costs offset the price differential, let us
compare freezing of spinach in Arkansas and California. California is by far the
major producer of frozen spinach in the United States (Fig. 9.5). The cost of the
raw product in California for the years 1957-1961 was around $1.21 per cwt.
During this same period, the price for spinach for processing in Arkansas was
$2.50 per cwt, or more than double the California price. However, an analysis of
processing costs and transportation costs to market showed that Arkansas should
have captured a substantial proportion of California's market (Fig. 9.6). The
processing costs and transportation costs to market from California more than

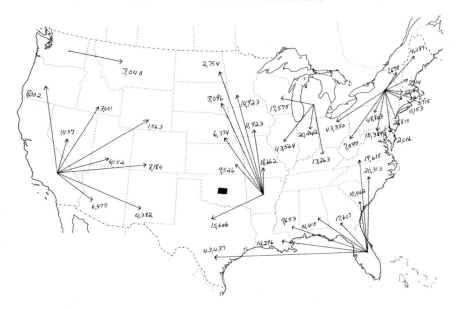

FIG. 9.6. FROZEN SPINACH: MINIMUM COST (PER 100 LB OF PROCESSED PRODUCT)
DISTRIBUTION SYSTEM FOR THE UNITED STATES BASED ON OPTIMUM SYSTEM TO
MINIMIZE AGGREGATE COSTS OF RAW PRODUCT, LABOR, LENGTH OF SEASON,
AND RAIL TRANSPORTATION CHARGES, 1961

offset Arkansas' raw product costs, at least to a large part of the midwest (Greig 1963). It should be noticed that while we stated that Arkansas' raw product price was double that of California, the absolute difference was around $1.25 per 100 lb of raw product.

The degree to which raw product prices affect location is conditioned by both relative and absolute differences in price. In any case price differences must, in most cases, be considered as one of many cost inputs in the analysis of total costs.

BIBLIOGRAPHY

ANON. 1966. Typical electric bills. Federal Power Comm., Washington, D.C.

ANON. 1967. Gas facts. Statis. Dept., Am. Gas Assoc.

ANON. 1969A. New air fares. Wall Street J. Oct. 12, p. 1.

ANON. 1969B. Steam-electric plant factors, 1968. Am. Coal Assoc.

ANON. 1969C. The Directory of the Canning, Freezing, Preserving Industries, 1968-1969. E. E. Judge and Sons, Westminister, Md.

BIRD, F. L. 1965. Advisory Commission on Intergovernmental Relations report on property tax administration. *In* State and Local Taxes on Businesses. Tax Institute of America, Princeton, N. J.

GREIG, W.S. 1965. Locational effects of new technologies in fruit and vegetable processing. Michigan State Univ. Agr. Expt. Sta. Res. Rept. *35*.

GREIG, W.S. 1966. Population, transportation, irrigation and potato economics. 16th Natl. Potato Util. Conf., Fort Collins, Colo.

GREIG, W.S. 1968. Balance sheets, income statements and financial operating ratios for the food processing industry 1965-1966. Agr. Econ. Rept. *117*, Michigan State Univ., East Lansing, Mich.

GREIG, W.S. 1969. The effect of state and local taxes on profits in food processing. Michigan State Univ. Agr. Econ. Rept. *145*.

HAIDACHER, R. C. 1966. Estimation of transportation charge relationships for frozen vegetables. Giannini Found. Res. Rept. *287*, Calif. Agr. Expt. Sta., Berkeley, Calif.

HEIFNER, R. G., and FERGUSON, R. P. 1968. Seasonality in Michigan agricultural prices, 1958-1967. Michigan State Univ. Agr. Econ. Rept. *118*.

HEIFNER, R. G., and GREIG, W. S. 1970. Locating green pea freezing plants to serve the U.S. market. Michigan State Univ. Res. Bull., In Press.

INTERNAL REVENUE SERVICE. 1968. Source book of statistics of income 1965-1966. U.S. Dept. Treasury, Washington, D. C.

MIKLIUS, W., and DeLOACH, D. B. 1965. A further case for unregulated truck transportation. J. Farm Econ. *47*, No. 4, 933-947.

NELSON, P. E., Jr., and CHUMLEY, T. W. 1968. The changing input structure of selected food processing industries: Agriculture's declining share. Marketing and Transportation Situation, U.S. Dept. Agr., Washington, D.C.

SNODGRASS, M. M., and FRENCH, C. E. 1958. Linear programming approach to the study of interregional competition in dairying. Purdue Univ. Agr. Expt. Sta. *S.B. 637*.

STENSON, T. F. 1968. The effects of taxes and public financing programs on local industrial development. U.S. Dept. Agr., Agr. Econ. Res. *133*, Washington, D.C.

STOLLSTEIMER, J. F. 1963. A working model for plant numbers and locations. J. Farm Econ. *45*, No. 3, 631-645.

SUPALLA, R. J. 1969. Unpublished data. Michigan State Univ.

U.S. DEPT. OF AGR. 1964. Fruits and tree nuts: Bloom, harvesting and marketing dates, and principal producing counties, by States. U.S. Dept. Agr., Agr. Handbook *186*, Washington, D.C.

U.S. DEPT. OF AGR. 1969A. The bill for marketing farm food products. Marketing and Transportation Situation, Econ. Res. Serv. U.S. Dept. Agr., Washington, D.C.

U.S. DEPT. OF AGR. 1969B. Usual planting and harvest dates commercial vegetables. . . in principal producing areas. U.S. Dept. Agr., Agr. Handbook *251*, Washington, D.C.

U.S. DEPT. OF LABOR. 1968A. Unemployment insurance tax rates by industry. Manpower Administration. U.S. Dept. Labor, Washington, D.C.

U.S. DEPT. OF LABOR. 1968B. Employment and earnings statistics for states and areas, 1939-1967. Bur. Labor Statis., U.S. Dept. Labor Bull. *1370-5*.

VON THUNEN, J. H. 1826. Der Isolierte Staat in Beziehung Auf Landwirtschaft und Nationalokonomine. Hamburg, Germany (German).

WRIGHTMAN, J. W. 1968. The impact of state and local fiscal policies on redevelopment areas in the Northeast. Res. Rept. to the Federal Reserve Bank of Boston, *40*.

CHAPTER 10

The Purchasing Function in the Food Industry

William A. Cromarty[1]

THE ROLES OF PURCHASING

The purchasing function in food processing and retailing involves multidisciplinary talents. While price or cost is usually considered by buyers as the central problem confronting them, there are accompanying areas also requiring detailed knowledge.

One useful way of looking at the purchasing function is to begin with the end product and work back to the raw materials used in its production. This implies, with sufficiently good grounds, that consumer decisions primarily determine the character of the product in terms of ingredients, form, and packaging. While this is not completely true, it indicates that the purchasing function is not autonomous. Rather, the buyer must buy against product specifications which may be explicitly formulated or generally implied. These specifications may vary in their comprehensiveness but are derived from decisions made by management on the end product to be sold, its form, and its ingredients. This leads us to consider purchasing and quality control.

PURCHASING AND QUALITY CONTROL

Purchasing departments are compelled to work closely with quality control personnel and/or research laboratories. Only by testing the raw materials used in manufacturing end products can a satisfactory set of ingredient specifications be initially developed. The specifications should ensure that the desired product quality is obtained and to permit production without undue disruption. However, the raw material specifications should not be restrictive to the point that they increase product cost relative to adequate substitutes. Or stated another way, the ingredient specifications should give the buyer maximum purchasing flexibility commensurate with maintaining end product characteristics. characteristics.

The quality control laboratory in a potato or corn chipping operation that specifies 100% cottonseed oil may be weighting too heavily the flavor factor of a chip at times when cottonseed oil is high priced relative to a substitute product, such as blended soybean oil. In such instances, the quality control laboratory should determine various satisfactory oil blends. It is important that the personnel of the chipping firm determine the blend since it permits the buyer to control the pricing, to some extent, rather than the supplier of edible oils.

Buyers can assist quality control or product research departments by suggest-

---

[1] Dr. William A. Cromarty is Vice President, Connell Rice and Sugar Company, Inc., Westfield, N. J.

ing alternative raw materials for testing. The rapid shifts in agricultural production make it necessary for product research departments to maintain an open mind on new raw material ingredients and sources. Buyers should constantly update their knowledge on supply sources and production shifts. For example, the buyer who suggests to the quality control laboratory or production departments that high quality strawberries from Poland be blended with lower grade domestic strawberries to make good quality preserves may be making a much greater contribution to his company than the buyer who negotiated the last 1/8th of a cent in price from several domestic suppliers. Or, the buyer who foresees a shortage of white corn for a chipping operation and suggests that the research laboratory develop a product with yellow corn as a substitute is making a major contribution to his company in an indirect, and often unrecognized, manner.

It is important to note that the buyer is not determining initial product specifications. Once these are set in terms of quality desired for end products, or in terms of compatibility with production facilities, the buyer can suggest alternative ingredients that meet these specifications and allow production to continue. The key is to develop specifications which permit flexibility in selection of raw materials.

In food processing firms too small to have adequate research or quality control laboratories, the buyer can often work with suppliers in setting up specifications.

Many major suppliers have research departments which concentrate on supplying products for a general clientele. In most cases, they will change product specifications to meet more specific requirements of individual users; they can often suggest to the buyer how to establish initial specifications.

The food processor is at some disadvantage to the seller in such cases and should be careful not to get "locked in" to particular suppliers because of overly restrictive specifications.

PURCHASING AND PRODUCTION OR MERCHANDISING

In the food processing industry, the raw materials buyer should have some knowledge of the production process in which the raw materials are to be used. It is the buyer's responsibility to see that raw material suppliers are able to meet specifications. However, if the buyer knows the production process and has established good supplier relationships, he is often in a position to suggest substitute raw materials for production, or sale in the case of retail stores. Such suggestions should aim to secure adequate and stable sources of materials since production or sales departments lay great emphasis on uninterrupted material flows. Buyers may also improve the end product in terms of quality or change the product form to improve its handling in the production process.

If a production manager specifies that only flour of southwest origin may be used in a bread baking plant, he may be setting too restrictive a specification. A buyer who is familiar with bread baking can suggest testing other flours which meet the major specifications of protein, ash, and fiber. In those years when the protein premiums for hard red winter wheat are abnormally high, a considerable saving may result by blending it with spring wheat. Or, conversely, a production manager who specifies that hard spring wheats be used when hard winter wheats are lower in cost and equally satisfactory in bread production is not letting the buyer perform his job.

The buyer should work with the production department to plan plant facilities. Plants have been built without rail sidings only because production personnel were not informed on the cost differences between delivery by truck and rail. In other instances, correct decisions on the installation of production equipment can be made only after all forms of product delivery have been evaluated. Competent buyers can supply such information. Perhaps batch production processes can be best supplied from raw materials purchased in bags or other similar small units. However, in other cases the optimum form may be a liquid form with tank wagon or a bulk form with rail car delivery. Buyers who are aware of changes taking place in the supplier industry can predict whether shifts from "bag to bulk" or "solid to liquid" form are likely to occur. The buyer should be management's "ear to the ground" in such cases.

Knowledgeable buyers can also be helpful to production departments when problems in manufacturing arise. A buyer who knows the characteristics of the raw material often understands why problems arise. If the whipping quality of egg whites is below acceptable standards, a buyer who has had experience with other egg whites may suggest changes. Sometimes it is difficult to trace the source of a manufacturing problem in terms of the ingredient involved. Sometimes a restrictive and costly flour specification has been imposed to solve a problem actually caused by the sugar. Buyers who understand sugar characteristics, or who seek technical advice from suppliers, can help production departments solve such problems.

For buyers in the retail food industry, there may be no processing or production departments involved. The counterpart is the merchandising department. A buyer should evaluate new products available from suppliers, do an initial screening of them and be able to present them to the management group deciding upon their addition or exclusion.

The retail food buyer, in many instances, is not physically capable of properly evaluating new products. The demands on his time are great because he may be purchasing hundreds or even thousands of products. Also, the necessary conversion to computerized inventory control increases the reluctance of buyers to add new products. Mastering an ordering system on old products, developing inventory and customer service levels, getting stores to order new items, closing out old inventories or finding space for substitute items in inventory—all are obstacles to the buyer faced with new product lines. In such situations, a person separate from the buyer may be able to make better decisions on the addition or deletion of products.

THE BUYER AND THE SUPPLIER

The purchasing function requires an ability to deal with people in a businesslike manner. Buyers must be able to meet with salesmen and evaluate their presentations. A buyer must learn to allocate his limited time between meeting salesmen, merchandisers, production personnel, management executives, and carrying out his physical responsibilities in acquiring products.

Buyers normally schedule appointments with salesmen or hold certain days open for them to call. This is not a major problem for buyers in the food processing industry. However, it creates demands on the time of buyers for retail food chains. Salesmen usually call on buyers for retail food chains on buying days. This archaic and inefficient practice causes millions of man hours to be lost by vendor representatives. Such costs must obviously be reflected in food prices to consumers. As ordering becomes more mechanized, it is possible that a different system can be developed in which personal calls are made only to service complaints or present new products.

Buyer-supplier relationships should be developed to the advantage of the respective corporations which each represents. Buyers have a function to perform for their corporation—the acquisition of products meeting quality specifications at competitive prices without delivery delays. The supplier should strive to provide such products and service. When each respects the other's integrity and honesty, an atmosphere is created for establishing business advantageous to both parties. Terms of pricing, freight savings, delivery "follow-ups," technical services, pricing outlook, ingredient specifications, packaging changes, price protection and promotional activities are all areas where buyers can benefit from developing good supplier relations and which may never be reflected in purchasing prices.

Buyers should be aware of various pricing techniques. Vendors may offer different pricing methods to different clients and still not be in conflict with Robinson-Patman Act trade restrictions. One of these is the establishment of formula pricing. This cannot be specifically defined; basically, it involves the buildup of product prices from raw material cost to the vendor. For instance, an edible vegetable salad oil may be priced by a supplier according to the price of crude soybean oil futures at Chicago plus a refining and delivery charge which varies with crude soybean oil futures prices. A certain level of sophistication is required by buyers before such arrangements are advantageous. Also, a certain degree of rapport must be established before both parties can reach agreement on such pricing techniques.

THE PURCHASING AGENT AS A TRAFFIC MANAGER

While separate purchasing and traffic departments are desirable, they are not always possible. In smaller companies, such specialization is too costly. The buyer may have to handle many of the traffic or freight problems.

One of the time-consuming tasks is arranging the transportation of purchased commodities. Decisions must be made on the most economical mode of transportation commensurate with timely delivery. Buyers may require information on truck and rail freight rates from all major supplier points. These can normally be obtained from the supplier. For some commodities using a basing point system, there may be "prepays" or special rates established which are lower than the published freight rates. Buyers must be aware of such freight savings. They should follow up purchase orders to see that shipment is made or unloading finished within the free time permitted by the railroads or port facilities, if items are being imported. Demurrage charges for tardiness can be costly.

Often transit privileges are involved. These are special rates established to move commodities in the same general direction even though stopovers for manufacturing or temporary storage are made. Again suppliers or warehousemen may be a source of information for buyers or they may develop such rates from the ICC published tariffs.

Buyers may work closely with traffic departments if back-hauls are possible. When trucks, owned or leased, are delivering products, it may be economical to transport raw materials on return loads. The geographical location of the suppliers chosen by the buyers can have some effect on such economies. It may take careful planning along with some detailed cost analysis to determine the most profitable routing for trucks on both delivery trips and return hauls. The problem may be too small to warrant computer solutions to a linear programming model, but a more simple mathematical analysis may still be used in truck scheduling. Careful analysis may indicate to buyers that back-hauls do not pay when the extra haul time, mileage, and loading and unloading costs are all considered.

Buyers may also be responsible for combining incoming loads in order to take advantage of discounts for various load weights. If a supplier can supply several products, the buyer may realize savings by combining several products on an order to get a freight "break." This practice must be weighed against an increased inventory held. This problem is one commonly called "joint replenishment." Fortunately, computerized techniques can objectively reach least-cost solutions to such buyer problems when many products are involved.

The foregoing sections deal with some of the problems faced by buyers in the food industry. The discussion only highlights the problems and suggests general solutions. Each area could be studied in depth to provide buyer guidelines on action to take.

PURCHASING AND PRICES

Price is paramount with buyers. Whether products are bought for resale or as ingredients in manufacturing processes, the profitability of an operation depends to a great extent on the buyer's ability to buy as well as, or better than, his competitors. The cost of raw materials in the food processing industry often amounts to 2/3 of the total end-product cost. Obviously, significant savings made in purchasing raw materials can result in corresponding significant increases in profits.

BUDGETING

Buyers are normally asked by management to prepare quarterly budgets up to 1 yr in advance. This primarily involves estimating purchase prices for raw materials. Such budgets should be prepared with extreme care without inflating estimated prices to be on the safe side or estimating prices too low expecting to "buy at the bottom." Management uses such budget estimates in planning capital requirements and in allocating capital. An overestimate on budget prices may result in too little capital being devoted to alternative uses such as advertising, equipment expenditures, or new product research. Conversely, underestimating budget prices may result in a squeeze on corporate capital when least expected.

Purchasing departments in some corporations must give ranges on budget prices. Management may then adopt a particular plan using the budget prices for capital acquisition and in planning production and sales volume. This plan holds until budget prices exceed the given range. At that point, new plans for capital acquisition and production and sales volumes may be initiated.

INFORMAL TECHNIQUES OF PRICE FORECASTING

Many buyers, when asked, express confidence in their ability to buy at the low of the market or at least better than their competitors. Few buyers, however, give evidence of such abilities. Successful buyers recognize the immense difficulties of correctly forecasting price movements for raw materials and keep an open mind on accepting new techniques for improving their skills. The vertical and horizontal growth in the food processing industry has increased the complexity of buyers' jobs; at the same time, it has increased the degree of sophistication required in price forecasting.

A buyer's most useful tool in his job is experience. This is a nebulous term but one that should not be overlooked. The experience of successful buyers is something that one would like to capture in formal statistical price models. This is difficult to do. Experience is a conglomerate of many factors. The many interactions of factors make it difficult to specify any one factor. Some buyers are able to single out 1 or 2 factors which they believe are important price determinants for a particular commodity. Price analysts should investigate such factors thoroughly when constructing statistical models. The difficulty with relying too heavily on experience is that it requires a good deal of subjectivity; one does not know how to properly weight each factor determining price. From this standpoint, one should attempt to provide objectivity in price forecasting. This can be done by providing some systematic linkage between the commodity price being forecast and those sets of factors causing the commodity price to fluctuate. For instance, if experience shows that prices are low at particular times of the year, then some seasonal pattern to prices may be present. If prices change because of government action, then government programs must be investigated. If other products are ready substitutes, then they cannot be ignored. A successful buyer's experience can provide the background necessary to decide on such factors affecting prices.

Buyers may make buying decisions on the basis of no information. This is not a completely negative way of purchasing since it at least precludes acting on the wrong information. Such a system merely requires purchasing ingredients as required. The resulting purchase prices would equal the average costs over a long period of time. Such average prices become a sort of norm that buyers attempt to improve upon.

Some buyers make buying decisions based on budget prices; that is, purchases are made whenever ingredient costs are below budget prices. This is a safe way of buying since it always permits corporate management to at least operate within a raw materials budget. However, too much success following this buying policy should cause a reevaluation as to the budget prices relative to actual market prices. If budget prices are consistently set too high, it may permit the buyer to always be under the budget but perhaps still be over the average. Consequently, he would be significantly over the level at which purchases should have been made.

There is a strong tendency for buyers to look backwards when purchasing. In such cases the most recent purchase price becomes the norm to beat. Last year's prices may be such a target. Buyers are tempted to add to coverage as long as each succeeding purchase is lower than the last one. This is sometimes called "averaging down." Conversely, buyers are tempted to refrain from buying when prices are rising. Both policies may be wrong.

Obviously, when prices are declining, the optimum buying policy is to buy only current requirements until prices reach a low point. In a rising price market, buyers should refrain from buying only if they are assured that prices will fall in the near future.

Often buyers rely on vendor information in making purchasing decisions. This may be very valid reasoning. For many products, especially for those with strong franchises, buyers are informed by vendors of pending price increases. They are given the opportunity to purchase prior to the date the price rise becomes effective. In some instances, vendors have more realistic information on future price trends and, as a part of their service, advise the buyers. Reputable vendors do not mislead buyers with such information in order to make sales. Vendors are interested in establishing a mutually beneficial buyer-seller relationship over a long period of time and do not jeopardize it with misinformation.

MORE FORMAL TECHNIQUES OF PRICE FORECASTING

Objective Price Studies

Buyers have specific buying problems with certain commodities. Generalized techniques of price analysis cannot provide adequate answers to buyers' problems. Specific price analyses can be tools for the buyer to use when pricing problems arise. To give an example of this, a bakery flour buyer may be required to purchase 100 cars of flour of 11.5% protein and other specified quality factors each year. This is a specific and real problem to him. A savings of 10¢ per cwt means approximately $10,000 in increased profit for his company. To such a buyer a price analysis which accurately forecasts the average annual wheat price received by U.S. farmers is not helpful. He requires a price forecast for bread flour, which limits the relevant wheats; he requires it for such time periods as permit him to cover his forward flour requirements.

The price being forecast must be the price of the commodity being purchased or one must be able to directly relate the forecast price and the price of the commodity being purchased. Moreover, the forecast prices must apply to time periods that specifically relate to the buyer's ability to make purchases for forward delivery.

The first step in successful price forecasting is to know the buyers problems.

Once the problem has been specified, the next step is to understand the commodity market involved. During the past 20 yr, universities and government agencies have emphasized the development of statistically unbiased and efficient estimators in price analyses. The years of research have resulted in the emergence of several useful techniques. Research is still underway to distinguish the best techniques. Unfortunately, the differences between techniques are much smaller than the differences between commodites where applications are made. This fact not only limits the usefulness of comparative results between techniques, but it has resulted in too little emphasis on commodity analyses per se as against analyses by statistical techniques. Knowing a commodity market means, first of all, understanding its production, harvesting, storing, and marketing processes. It also requires the same knowledge for close substitutes or complements. And if government controls any of these functions, one must understand the government's role as well as be able to anticipate likely government actions.

With sufficient understanding of the commodity market, one can start concentrating on which variables have a consistent and continuous effect on price. Specifying such variables may be quite easy; determining the net impact of each may be extremely difficult. Herein lies the secret of successful price forecasting—knowing the commodity market, specifying the relevant variables influencing its price, and selecting and applying statistical techniques to measure the relative influence of each. This should result in statistical price forecasts. Once the forecast is reached, the only remaining gap to bridge is the development of a set ,of "decision rules" which relate directly to the buyer's coverage problems. In order to indicate how statistical price forecasts are made, several examples are presented. The examples are shown to emphasize various statistical techniques as well as show the variations in required techniques between commodities. Obviously a thorough evaluation of all useful techniques and for all major commodities would require a separate text book.

Balance Sheets

Many buyers develop elaborate information systems on commodities. Much of this information is summarized in what is called a supply-demand balance sheet. Subjective evaluations are made regarding future price movements as a

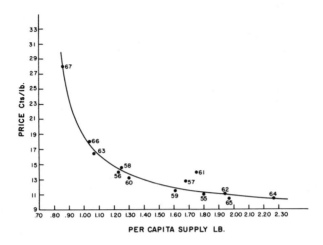

FIG. 10.1. PER CAPITA SUPPLY OF FROZEN RED TART
CHERRIES VERSUS PRICE DURING
PACK SEASON, 1955-1967

result of data changes or expected data changes within the balance sheet.

As an example of a balance sheet, the data on RSP cherries are presented in
Table 10.1.

Scatter Diagrams

If one can get satisfactory price forecasts by evaluating data in a balance
sheet, the job is done. This is unlikely to be the case. An easy step beyond the
balance sheet is to construct a scatter diagram relating price on one axis to
important price determining factors on the other axis. Again, RSP cherries are
used as an example. A specific price series must be used. In this case, it is the
lowest average monthly price for June, July or August of frozen RSP cherries in
30-lb pails, FOB Michigan processors. This is a price that buyers understand and
is selected during a time period when they are usually interested in buying for
future delivery.

The price-determining factors represent some simple manipulations with the
data. Beginning stocks of frozen and canned cherries are added to the quantity
of new crop cherries sold for canning and freezing and the total divided by the
population in the United States on July 1. This approximates the per capita
supply of cherries for the coming year. As seen from the scatter diagram (Fig.
10.1), the lowest monthly price for each year (vertical axis) is plotted against the
per capita supply (horizontal axis) for each year. Except for 1961 (a good
reminder that no technique is perfect), the plotted points form a fairly smooth
curve for the years 1955 to 1967. Also as supplies are large, the price seems to
level off at about 10¢ per lb. This is economically logical since the variable costs

of the processor for picking and delivering fruit along with the processing costs for freezing approximates 10¢ per lb. On the other hand, prices rise very rapidly as per capita supply diminishes. This is an example of an inelastic demand. Certain processors require cherries in franchised products and bid prices up to assure themselves of supplies when crops are small. From a grower's standpoint, there is probably a certain range of prices and production for the industry that maximizes gross income and even net income.

Not many commodities can be dealt with as easily as cherries have in this scatter diagram. The human mind is quite capable of evaluating two-dimensional diagrams such as a scatter diagram. However, if a third factor, e.g., something in addition to per capita supply, is an important price determinant, then a three-dimensional diagram is required. Rather than plot it geometrically, it is easier to turn to statistical analysis.

TABLE 10.1

FROZEN RED TART CHERRIES: U.S. STOCKS, PACK,
SUPPLY AND MOVEMENT, SEASONS 1945–1946 to 1968–1969

Season (July–June)	Beginning Stocks[1] (July 1)	Pack	Total Supply (Million Pounds)	Ending Stocks (June 30)	Disappearance	Season Average Price FOB Michigan/Processors (¢/Lb)
1945–1946	9.6	16.1	25.7	12.6	13.1	18.3
1946–1947	12.6	88.1	100.7	26.0	74.7	21.0
1947–1948	26.0	67.0	93.0	12.9	80.1	16.0
1948–1949	12.9	87.8	100.7	18.0	82.7	15.4
1949–1950	18.0	71.0	89.0	14.0	75.0	15.0
1950–1951	14.0	104.5	118.5	23.5	95.0	13.1
1951–1952	23.5	99.3	112.8	23.2	99.6	12.7
1952–1953	23.2	61.9	85.1	6.1	79.0	13.6
1953–1954	6.1	115.2	121.3	19.6	101.7	15.3
1954–1955	19.6	87.7	106.3	18.1	88.2	15.4
1955–1956	18.1	114.5	132.6	18.4	114.2	12.1
1956–1957	18.4	88.7	107.1	11.8	95.3	14.1
1957–1958	11.8	130.6	142.4	28.0	114.4	11.7
1958–1959	28.0	86.2	114.2	22.5	91.7	14.5
1959–1960	22.5	107.4	129.9	10.0	119.9	14.7
1960–1961	10.0	129.0	139.0	8.8	130.2	15.9
1961–1962	8.8	186.4	195.2	50.5	144.7	13.4
1962–1963	50.5	137.3	187.8	40.8	147.0	10.6
1963–1964	40.8	81.6	122.4	12.1	110.3	18.0
1964–1965	12.1	202.5	214.6	66.1	148.5	10.4
1965–1966	66.1	146.3	212.4	46.1	166.4	11.9
1966–1967	46.1	87.4	133.5	14.2	119.3	23.2
1967–1968	14.2	97.8	112.0	12.8	99.2	31.2

Source: Ricks, D. J. and Bixby, D., 1969. Economic Relationships in Red Tart Cherry Marketing, 1955-68. Michigan State Univ. Agri. Econ. Rept. *142.*

[1]May include some stocks of sweet cherries. However, such stocks, if any, are believed to be small.

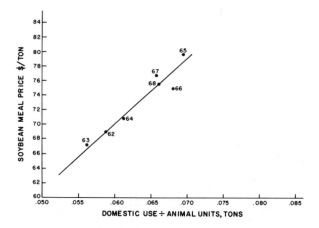

FIG. 10.2. PRICE OF SOYBEAN MEAL VERSUS U.S.
DOMESTIC USE DIVIDED BY ANIMAL UNITS, 1962-1968

As another example in the use of a scatter diagram, data are presented on soybean meal prices and demand (Fig. 10.2). On the vertical axis the scale represents the average price of soybean meal, 44% protein, unrestricted delivery, Decatur basis, for the April-June quarter. On the horizontal axis the scale represents the demand for soybean meal. This demand is the quantity of soybean meal used for livestock feed for the April-June quarter divided by the number of animal units to be fed, i.e., meal fed per animal unit.

As for cherries, the data for recent years are plotted. The dots fall in a fairly straight line pattern and in a fairly narrow range indicating that since 1962, meal prices have been rising as demand per animal unit increased. The line drawn "through" these dots has a specific equation which relates meal prices to the demand per animal unit. This is:

Price of soybean meal in dollars per ton = 18.9 + 857.3 X (Soybean meal fed per animal unit in tons).

If one has sufficient faith in this relationship (i.e., that events of the past 8 yr will continue this year) and if one can estimate the demand per animal unit, then a price forecast for soybean meal can be obtained. To do this, insert the estimated demand per animal unit, e.g., 0.065 tons, into the equation and solve it:

Price of soybean meal = 18.9 + 857.3 X (0.065) = $74.62 per ton.

The price forecast might be considered as the most "likely" price to evolve; at the same time, one recognizes that the eventual prevailing price will be higher or lower than the $74.62 per ton. Knowing that the price will be close to the forecast, requires that some policy be adopted to purchase soybean meal. That is, if current prices for April-June delivery are $3.00 per ton under the forecast, then one might purchase. Or one might merely postpone purchases until the price for April-June delivery is equal to or below the forecast price. Or, if meal was currently owned and prices for April-June delivery were substantially above the forecast, the buyer might recommend "hedging" current inventory by selling soybean meal futures to protect inventory against a potential price decline. Such policies must be developed in conjunction with corporate management.

The above example leads to the development of statistical price forecasts when more than one important price determinant exists. The price-forecasting equation for soybean meal represents a straight line fitted to a two-dimensional plane. If 2 factors determined price, the price-forecasting equation would represent a 2-dimensional plane fitted to a 3-dimensional surface. The form of the equation using x and z as the price determinants, a and b as the weights given to each, and c as a constant factor would have the form:

$$\text{Price} = a \cdot x + b \cdot z + c$$

This leads to the development of formal price models.

Formal Statistical Price Models

It is beyond the scope and purpose of this chapter to develop the theory of econometric models and their development. It is hoped that a brief exposure to one or two examples will whet buyers' interests to seek help for particular price problems.

Before showing the examples, some general observations can be made which may help guide future research by buyers. (1) Know your commodity. There is a great tendency to substitute statistical complexity for knowledge of the commodity. The results are usually disastrous. (2) For most major food commodities, the supply of the commodity has a much greater impact on price than does the demand. (3) Try to construct price-forecasting models based on what you know today. Update the model as new information becomes available. (4) Be aware of the factors not included in your model which can change. These could cause your price forecasts to be quite wrong; they could be weather, war, errors in supposedly known data, and changes in government policies.

The first example is for coconut oil. Practically all coconut oil in the United States comes from the Philippines either as coconut oil or as copra. Copra is crushed in the United States and the oil extracted. The other major producers of coconut oil are Malaysia, Indonesia, and Ceylon. The first factor to influence price is the supply available for export from these four areas for a calendar year. In this analysis an estimate made in April is used.

The second factor determining price is the level of stocks of coconut oil in the United States in early spring. Such data are reported monthly by the U.S. Dept. of Com.

The third factor determining price is the sales of coconut oil made by the U.S. government out of its stockpile. Such stocks have been depleted but were

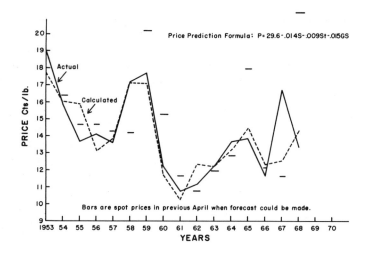

FIG. 10.3. ACTUAL AND CALCULATED PRICES OF CRUDE
COCONUT OIL (PACIFIC COAST), 1953-1968

important during the time period used to develop the price-forecasting equation.

The price being forecast is the average September-February price for crude coconut oil in tank cars, FOB Pacific Coast. By use of a least squares analysis, a forecasting equation was developed having the form:

Calculated price = 29.59¢ per lb - .0142 (export of four countries)- .0093 stocks in the United States)- .0149 (government sales)

In Figure 10.3, the calculated price for each year is plotted as a dashed line le while the actual price is plotted as a solid line.

If the one line were completely superimposed on the other, the three factors included would have completely explained all price variation. Such is not the case, although for most years the deviations between actual and calculated prices are small.

The major exception is 1967. There was good reason for deviation. The war in the Middle East, which closed the Suez Canal, disrupted supplies. Some boats attempting to go around South Africa were sunk. In addition, the Philippine crop suffered from serious typhoon damage. Finally, the first large-scale sale of filled milk products began in the United States. Using coconut oil as the source of fat increased the demand for this oil when supplies were scarce.

Also on the same chart are some horizontal bars. These represent the price level in April when the forecasts were made. A simple yet profitable rule to follow has been to purchase oil whenever the calculated price is above the April price and conversely not to buy in April if the current price is above the calculated price. Fortunately, in 1967 coverage was made prior to the large price increase. This is a good example of making correct decisions based on statistical price forecasts even though the calculated price and the actual price differ greatly.

The final example of statistical price forecasts involves what is usually called a "recursive model." Simply stated, this means that a series of forecasts are made, each one depending upon a previous one, before a price forecast can be made. We use as an example, without showing the computed numbers, a recursive model for shell eggs.

The objective is to forecast the price of shell eggs during the spring period. One would like to do this as far in advance as is practical. Each month, data are published on: (1) the number of egg-type chicks hatched, (2) the number of eggs in incubators to hatch egg-type chicks relative to a year ago, (3) the number of layers on hand at the beginning of the month, (4) the monthly rate of lay, and (5) the monthly egg production. In addition, data are published on prices paid for poultry ration and prices received by farmers for eggs. At particular times of the year, breakdowns on the composition of the laying flock are given, i.e., pullets of laying age, hens of laying age, pullets 3 months and older not laying, and pullets under 3 months.

It is possible to take these data and arrange them in such a form as to permit forecasts of shell egg prices several months in advance. This is called an economic or econometric forecasting model. In the following outline, the relationships have been listed in a "recursive" fashion, i.e., the solution for each step may depend upon a solution for the preceding step.

(1) Egg-type chick hatch is forecast for several months in advance based upon current flock size, its makeup, current egg prices, and expected poultry ration prices.

(2) Current monthly hatch and data on eggs in incubators along with forecast hatch from (1) are projected to give numbers and timing of birds entering the laying flock.

(3) Cull of hens is projected based on flock size, new birds entering, current egg prices, and expected feed prices.

(4) From (2) and (3) additions and subtractions are made to the current laying flock to estimate flock size for future time periods.

(5) The rate of lay is forecast based on trend and the makeup of the laying flock.

(6) The product of (4) and (5) gives egg production for a future time period.

(7) Shell egg prices are forecast using as the primary price determinant the egg production forecast from (6).

(8) Egg product prices, e.g., frozen whole eggs, frozen yolk, and frozen albumen prices can be forecast using, as an important price determinant, the egg price forecast from (7).

At each step, a statistical equation is derived based on historical relationships. The price forecasts become useful targets when buying policies are being developed.

In addition, the buyer can supplement the price forecasts with relevant information as it develops and which is not included in the statistical forecasts. These may include weather as it affects rate of lay, export demand (especially for albumen), or government purchase prices for whole egg mix.

The previous examples are chosen for simplicity and only to indicate to buyers that statistical price forecasts can be developed and can become a useful tool for the buyer. The examples do not begin to indicate the various types of models or techniques which are available. The use of "simultaneous equations," whereby several factors are determined simultaneously, has been omitted. No mention has been made of the various types of statistical fitting techniques which may be employed to develop forecasting equations. The important thing is to master a knowledge of the commodity. In most cases, simple statistical techniques can be used if one knows how to correctly apply them.[2]

BUYING AND THE FUTURES MARKETS

Again in a survey type of analysis, as given in this book, it is not possible to give a comprehensive analysis of the role futures prices can play in purchasing raw materials.

Rather than describe the functions of futures markets and how they operate, it is more helpful to show how they may be used by purchasing personnel. Simply regard "futures" as a legal contract to buy and sell a certain quantity of a commodity for delivery during some future time period. In our case, let us use a contract of soybean oil totalling 60,000 lb.

For instance, when a buyer buys a hydrogenated shortening he is buying crude soybean oil plus a refining process and freight. In fact, one can set up a formula approximately as follows:

Price crude soybean oil, basis Decatur
Add 2.70 ¢ per lb for refining and freight
Gives delivered price, shortening, user's plant

One step more should be added. The price of crude soybean oil, Decatur, is based on the price level at which a futures contract is trading plus a basis. Since futures prices are quoted for time periods in the future, then a price of crude soybean oil, Decatur basis, can be determined for future time periods. For instance, the futures prices for delivery in March, May and July might be as follows on a particular day:

Futures Contract	Futures Price
March	9.50
May	9.25
July	9.15

On the same day, processors of crude oil might be asking the following "bases" or costs above futures prices to get equivalent cash prices at Decatur.

---

[2]For the adventuresome student who wishes exposition to statistical models see A. S. Goldberger, *Econometric Theory,* John Wiley & Sons, New York, 1964.

Futures Contract	Futures Price	Basis	Cash Prices
March	9.50	20	9.70
May	9.25	20	9.45
July	9.15	15	9.30

Adding the futures price plus the basis will give the cash prices of soybean oil for delivery in March, May and July. For April and June delivery futures contracts are not normally traded. Processors, as a rule, use the average of the preceding and subsequent months. One therefore can determine cash prices for forward delivery as follows: to each of the cash prices, a conversion cost is added to get hydrogenated shortening delivered at a user's plant.

Delivery in	Futures Price	Basis	Cash Price	Conversion	Delivered Price for shortening
March	9.50	20	9.70	2.70	12.40
April	9.375	20	9.575	2.70	12.275
May	9.25	20	9.45	2.70	12.15
June	9.20	20	9.40	2.70	12.10
July	9.15	15	9.30	2.70	12.00

It now becomes obvious how futures prices can be used by a shortening buyer. On a particular day he can call an edible oil refiner and get a quote on futures prices, bases, cash prices, and price of shortening for future delivery periods. The buyer, in this case, does not normally buy or sell futures contracts; he merely uses them as a pricing basis. The refiner may or may not take a position in the futures market. He may "cover" by buying the crude oil for future delivery. This may mean that the soybean processor will decide whether to take a position in futures by buying them until he produces the oil or just stay "open" and sell oil at a fixed price although he has not yet produced it.

This is a common type of purchasing operation. Buyers' knowledge of how futures markets operate need not be comprehensive. He must know whether futures prices are going to rise or fall (i.e., timing of purchase) and what kind of conversion costs over futures prices are realistic. In addition to shortening, edible salad oils, margarine, flour, chocolate coatings, corn syrup, sugar, soybean meal, frozen whole eggs, orange juice, and many other items purchased by food processors or food retailers can be purchased based on futures market prices.

There are instances when the buyer may wish to make outright purchases of futures contracts. This might occur for flour. The buyer for a bakery may require flour using a hard red winter wheat of 13% protein. The "spot" or immediate shipment price for such wheat is quoted at some premium over the nearest wheat futures option trading on the Kansas City Board of Trade. The protein premium is determined primarily by the availability of wheat of such protein. This is often determined by weather conditions. Millers buying such wheat and selling flour price the flour according to the futures price for wheat, the premium to be paid for 13% protein wheat, a milling conversion charge, and some subjective or specified allowance for millfeed by-products.

A situation may exist, however, in early spring where a high protein premium exists, e.g., 35¢ per bu, current millfeed prices are low, e.g., $29.00 per ton, and a buyer wishes to cover flour requirements for July-December because he expects wheat prices to rise. Because new crop wheat will be available in July for which the protein premium may be much lower and because millers will want a relatively high milling conversion charge due to the low price of millfeeds, it is not advantageous for the buyer to price his flour. A good alternative when wheat prices are expected to rise is to buy wheat futures. When the protein level of new crop wheat is established and when wheat futures prices have risen, the flour buyer may then sell his wheat futures and price his flour.

Buyers may at times wish to sell futures contracts. Suppose in the fall of the year a decision is made to cover nine months' requirements of soybean meal. This may be done on a fixed price basis with a soybean processor at, let us say, $65.00 per ton. The level of soybean meal futures subsequently rises to $75.00 per ton.

If a price forecast is made at the time when futures prices are going to decline to $67.00 per ton, the company may decide to sell soybean meal futures in a quantity equivalent to their current inventory. To this company the transaction is considered as protecting inventory against a potential price decline. To other companies it might be considered speculation. In either case the success of the transaction depends upon the buyer's ability to forecast prices.

PRICE FORECASTS AND BUYING PROCEDURES

An area of vast importance, but quite undeveloped, is the practical application of statistical price forecasts to actual purchasing decisions. While great sums of money have been spent on the development of analytical techniques for price forecasting, little has been done to develop specific buying practices to be adopted when price forecasts are made. Buyers in different companies may be faced with different corporate restraints on buying practices, but it is still possible to develop certain rules that he can follow when price forecasts are made.

In simple terms, a buyer is faced with three sets of information which he must analyze.

The first relates to a knowledge of the specific commodities he must purchase. This includes the quantities involved and how their utilization is distributed over time. Are they storable or perishable? If storable, what storage capacity is available? A particular problem of large-scale importance exists here for retail food chains.

The second involves decisions on the buying functions discussed earlier. These are quality specifications, transit, freight rates, buying terms, substitute products, knowledge of potential suppliers, etc. Buyers should have completed their knowledge on these functions so that when an actual purchase is made, no delay in action is necessary.

The third body of information covers when to buy and how much or for what period to buy. Deciding when to buy is deciding what price to pay. Corporate policy may impose some limitations on when and how much to buy; but aggressive, intelligent buyers will help to determine the effectiveness of such corporate policy. Examples of corporate restrictions which may or may not be desirable are: (1) Minimum stocks of 30 days must be maintained and maximum coverage cannot exceed 90 days. (2) No special pricing arrangements are to be developed but list prices are to be the buying prices. This precludes the development of buying prices on a toll basis. (3) The use of futures markets as a pricing mechanism is prohibited. (4) Currently held inventory cannot be "hedged" in the futures market. (5) All forward sales must be covered by a purchase and no purchases can be made without an offsetting sale. This is often termed "back-to-back" buying. There are many such rules established and buyers over time can help determine efficiency. In fact, it should be the responsibility of a competent price analyst, be he the buyer or an outside individual, to work with management in developing overall buying policies. This same price analyst should also be able to aid in the timing of purchasing and the quantities to be purchased.

Forecasting techniques are not exact. It would be abnormal for prices to reach and stay at forecast levels. Price forecasting should be designed to help an individual at any point in time decide whether or not to buy and if so, how much.

To do this, forecasting models must be flexible. The flexibility is required by new knowledge becoming available on the factors determining prices. Good forecasting models are designed to incorporate new information as it becomes available. (They may even help to predict what new information will become available.) The attribute of updating price forecasts as new information becomes available gives rise to conditional price forecasts. For instance, one can forecast the "lowest daily futures close for the December corn option at Chicago between September 1 and December 1" based on the U.S. Dept. of Agr. estimate of corn production made on July 10.

This gives a price forecast conditional upon a certain production level for corn. Because the weather acts on potential yields, the potential production will change. Consequently, a new "forecast low for the December option" can be made when the August 10 crop report is issued. If other price determining factors are involved and new information is available on them, then they too may be updated on August 10. This is one of the real values of the statistical price forecast—it provides an objective, scientific way of analyzing those factors which affect price. Often the buyer is aware of these same factors but cannot evaluate them except in a subjective way which does not result in specific price forecasts.

The conditional price forecasts are compared to current buying prices and a decision made on whether or not to make coverage. Experience in working with price forecasting models and in buying are used in developing buying rules. For instance, if the price forecast for the December corn option is 8¢ below the current quote for the December option, a buying rule may simply say, "Don't buy." If, in successive months, the difference between the current and forecast values narrows to 1 or 2¢, then it becomes more difficult to develop decision rules which always result in the correct action. The price analyst knows the magnitude of error associated with his forecasts in the past, and this serves as a guide. In addition, the buyer and/or price analyst can evaluate subjective factors which may affect price in this particular year but which were not specifically included in the statistical analysis. Or, quantitative ranges may be given to production in the coming months to determine the absolute ranges for future conditional price forecasts and thus determine in some sense the likelihood of further price declines.

Very often prices are influenced by data that become available at specific points in time. For instance, price forecasting models have been developed which relate the average monthly price of soybean oil to monthly production, monthly stocks, monthly exports, monthly disappearance, and monthly stocks of soybeans held by the Commodity Credit Corporation. Each month as the data become available, a price forecast is given for the next month. These are not conditional forecasts in the sense that data on stocks, production, etc., will change. These data are known and published. The price forecasts will have certain errors associated with them but buying rules can be developed which are useful tools.

An infinite number of decision rules is possible. It is best to concentrate on those possibilities which fall within corporate working policy, and which maximize profits (i.e., which lower soybean oil net procurement costs).

We have assumed that: (1) Management does not wish numerous reversals of coverage position in the market. (2) Net long positions are permissible by management but net short positions are not. (3) Positions taken in the cash market may be hedged in the futures market.

Various sets of rules can be tested by varying the length of time for which forward coverage is made and the "buffer" level between the forecast prices and the futures price. One example of a set of rules are given below:

(1)   Starting with no coverage—during first 10 days of the month cover 5 months if (a) the forecast change is positive and (b) the forecast change plus last month's actual average price is 20 points greater than the nearest futures quotation on that day.

(2)   With some forward coverage—extend coverage to 5 months if the forecast change is positive, unless on first of month the forecast change plus last month's average price is 30 points less than the nearest futures. If this is so, then don't extend coverage but use inventories for a month.

(3)   If forecast is negative, hedge inventories and stay hedged until forward coverage is again recommended.

Over time the buyer can devise and revise rules which specifically apply to the commodities he buys. They may or may not involve the use of futures prices, hedging inventory, extended or short-term coverage, tolling contracts, price protection, or other relationships. The challenge for improvement is constant, and conscientious, intelligent buyers can make a major contribution to every food processing or retailing firm.

CHAPTER 11

Edward Willoughby[1] | Food Processing and Pollution

INTRODUCTION

The current emphasis on water and air pollution abatement in the United States is bringing greater pressure than ever on the food processing industry to play its full share in the battle. Whereas, a few years ago many food processing plants could be located in remote locations in which no harm was done by the wasting of process effluent to streams and fields, the population density has increased to a point where it is nearly impossible to locate a food processing plant so that its waste products will not be offensive, if not harmful, to the environment. In addition, the costs for waste water treatment from an industrial plant have become a significant part of the total food processing cost.

Particular care must, therefore, be taken with respect to the location of food processing plants and to the effects the plants will have on streams or existing sewage facilities. Once, waste water regulations varied between states and it was possible to find a state, with low population density, whose less restrictive criteria might permit inexpensive solutions to water pollution. This assumes, of course, that this same location was acceptable relative to markets, labor costs, source of foods to be processed, etc. However, the entry of the federal government into this matter has now made all states virtually uniform in their waste water criteria. It is now generally impossible to find a state or city which will accept anything other than substantial treatment of the waste water effluents from food processing plants. Nearly all receiving waters for liquid wastes have been classified with respect to the amount of pollutants that can be loaded into the stream's natural waste assimilation capacity. It is, therefore, now generally necessary to remove 60–90% of the pollutant matter from waste water before it is discharged.

Most food processing plants produce a waste water which is amenable to biological waste water treatment. This can be accomplished by a municipal sewage treatment plant or separate facilities. While such processes can be complicated by the use of chemicals in food processing that inhibit biological treatment, generally these matters may be corrected by the addition of neutralizing agents which will permit the waste waters to be treated by biological as opposed to chemical methods. The following description of possible treatment methods is intended as a cursory review of waste water treatment technology. It is intended that this material shall be considered as a guide to solutions that may be used by food processors. Specific problems can be solved

---

[1]Edward Willoughby, P. E. is Director of Civil Engineering, Giffels Associates, Inc., Detroit, Mich.

only through discussion with waste water regulatory agencies. Final designs for waste water abatement devices, facilities, and systems in connection with a food processing plant should be prepared by qualified engineers since the cost generally warrants expert consultation.

LAGOONS

All clean waters are relatively free of suspended solids, color and toxins and contain dissolved oxygen in a stable condition. These conditions are required to support aquatic life. Pollutants poison streams and lakes, or make them turbid, or rob them temporarily of their dissolved oxygen. This oxygen deficiency is known as a BOD (biochemical oxygen demand) and biological waste treatment processes attempt to satisfy this demand.

One of the greatest problems facing most food processing industries is the development of a waste water treatment system capable of coping with high seasonal and hourly hydraulic and biological loadings, at a cost that does not represent a considerable capital investment which may stand idle during several months of the year when many food plants are not in operation. Because of this, most food processing plant wastes are treated least expensively in lagoons. Lagoons, with very long detention times, permit time for slow changes in their biological and hydraulic capacities to adequately adjust to process surges. These lagoons can be properly designed holding ponds permitting both anaerobic and aerobic biological waste treatment. Anaerobic biological activity involves utilizing those bacteria which thrive in an oxygen free environment. Aerobic bacteria utilizes oxygen demanding bacteria. Both forms of bacteria are often required for a highly effective form of waste water treatment. Lagoons can be used most effectively in rural areas where parcels of flat land are available. In many states, however, their use is restricted by possible ground water contamination considerations which require a water tight lining. Further restriction is also encountered because, while lagoons are relatively inexpensive, they generally provide a lower degree of pollutant removal than any other waste treatment system. Generally, a well operated waste water lagoon can only remove up to 75% of the pollutants encountered in the waste water. A further objection to lagoons often arises in the fact that they are sometimes the source of considerable odor, particularly when operated in an anaerobic condition, which brings objections from adjoining property owners. Lagoons are generally sized for a minimum of approximately 30 days detention of the screened waste waters during which time the algae and bacteria react with the polluted waste waters.

The most simple form of lagoon is an aerobic oxidation pond. This pond is generally not over 4 ft deep permitting sunlight and oxygen to penetrate its full depth. It is usually several acres in size depending on the area requirements determined by volumes to be stored for a 30-day period. In cold weather, however, all lagoons are subject to a reduction in waste removal activity. With water temperatures near freezing all waste water treatment capabilities practically cease. During these periods of time, the effluents from such lagoons may be relatively untreated unless lagoon sizes are ample. Since the process is relatively uncontrollable, such conditions may put the food processing plant operator in difficulties with regulatory agencies. However, during warm weather the action of sunlight, promoting the growth of algae, and wind, promoting needed oxygen transfer at open air water interfaces, may permit lagoons to operate at 3, 4, or even 5 times the capacity normally credited to them by local waste water treatment design codes. These codes vary with the general climate of each state and usually relate permissible loading to BOD. They permit larger loadings in warmer climates and lower in colder climates. The values set by regulatory agencies are based on the average rates of treatment occurring during the entire year. If a lagoon is only going to be used during the warm weather, it is quite possible to prove to a regulatory agency that since no flow will be occurring during cold weather, waste water pollutant loadings can be increased.

Lagoons generally must be fenced to meet state regulatory agency codes. Sometimes this fencing can be quite expensive due to the large area usually required. In addition, they must be constructed so that their banks and sidewalls are structurally stable so that burrowing rodents and small animals will not inadvertently destory a dike and spill the entire contents of the lagoon onto adjoining property.

A sophisticated form of lagoon waste treatment consists of successive anaerobic and aerobic ponds. In such a system the waste water from the food processing plant is screened (with approximately 30 mesh screens depending on solids sizes) and then introduced into a large, deep lagoon in which small solid particulate matter settles to the bottom and is decomposed by anaerobic digestion. The time of detention in such a lagoon may be anywhere from 2–10 hr. During this detention time, the waste water is subjected to biological degradation by anaerobic bacteria. After such treatment the effluent is usually odorous and must be then subjected to subsequent treatment in an aerobic lagoon where the aerobic bacteria further biologically oxidize the waste water. This satisfies the BOD requirements which may be even higher after preliminary anaerobic treatment than found in the untreated waste waters. Maximum lagoon waste treatment efficiencies measured by the degree of pollutants removed generally occur in such a two-stage lagoon system. Ultimately, all lagoons must be cleaned and the accumulation of solid material arising from precipitation of waste water matter, dead algae and dead microorganisms must be removed and carried away to burial in earth pits.

Even moderately sized food processing plants may discharge a waste water having properties similar to that discharged by a small city, in both volume and contaminant properties. Lagoons are, therefore, often generally frowned upon by regulatory agencies where there is any possibility of discharge to an existing relatively unpolluted stream or lake. Since pollutant removal efficiencies are relatively low (60–70%) compared to other methods (90–95%), it can be seen that a great deal of BOD may be impressed on any receiving waters. Also, lagoons generally cannot be used as pretreatment facilities prior to discharge to any available sanitary sewer. Although this would make additional waste treatment possible, the large areas allow considerable storm water to find its way into sanitary sewer systems.

Lagoons are nevertheless popular and do offer the least expensive means of solving pollution problems. Many times the capacity of lagoons can be substantially improved by the addition of oxygen either through mechanical surface aerators or pipes and air diffusion devices located on the bottom of the pond. Such improvements can, however, bring a lagoon into an operating cost approaching that of a conventional waste treatment system.

IRRIGATION SYSTEMS

Another waste water treatment device sometimes considered with lagoons consists of a spray irrigation system. In such a system the waste from the food processing plant is again rough screened to rid it of sizable particles that would interfere with pumping and the entire waste water disposal system is constructed merely of irrigation pipes laid on the ground and equipped with spray nozzles. This system normally covers several acres of ground and basically does nothing but irrigate the surrounding growth, e.g. trees, shrubs, grasses, etc. disposing of the waste water as an enriched or fertilized rainfall on the area. The spray irrigation system is limited by the ability of the soil and vegetation to absorb waste waters without hindering plant growth. Excessive water kills vegetation or reduces its ability to hold and dispose of the waste water absorbed by the ground through transpiration. Spray irrigation requires many acres of relatively level ground and is commonly used where no receiving waters are available and where high annual evaporation rates and high ground percolation rates are favorable to this form of waste water treatment.

Spray irrigation can generally be used only for wastes containing little or no grease or fats. Greases and fats are subject to slow degradation and their accumulation on plants and trees quickly destroys vegetation. Grease may also present severe odor or fly problems in the area.

Both lagoon and spray irrigation systems may be subject to disfavor with regulatory agencies if the systems must also treat the sanitary sewage emanating from a food processing plant. Since system efficiencies are basically at the mercy of nature (sunlight, evaporation, wind, transpiration, etc.), they are not always assuredly successful in degrading or removing pathological biological organisms. While sterilization with chlorine is possible, the system demands required to maintain an assured chlorine residual are quite high, almost precluding the use of chlorine for such purposes.

OTHER TREATMENT METHODS

If the less expensive waste treatment options of lagooning waste waters or spray irrigation are unacceptable for any reason, most food processors will be forced to go to other more expensive and conventional waste water treatment methods. These methods permit a nearly complete waste water treatment system: however, when municipal sanitary sewers are available, it is quite possible that the treatment process can be foreshortened by eliminating succeeding stages so waste waters will be prepared suitably to meet sewer codes. Sewer codes generally set limits on acceptable waste waters so their introduction into a city sewer system will not be detrimental to the sewers or to subsequent waste treatment processes usually operated by the city.

The first step in waste water treatment from a food processing plant is basically a simple operation of mechanically removing the suspended particles in the waste water stream. The screening process offers the greatest possibility for reclaiming material from the waste water stream for reuse, either within the processing plant itself or as a valuable by-product such as fertilizer or animal food.

Most food processors effectively screen their waste water streams with mechanical vibrating screens. These screens are usually relatively fine, retaining such things as peelings, seeds, vegetable skins, meat particles, etc. The material that passes these relatively fine screens contains, however, a great deal of additional suspended matter so small that it does not settle quickly. To remove this fine material it is customary for the screened processing waste waters to be introduced into large primary waste treatment settling tanks where the divided and suspended material is permitted to settle to the bottom of the tank while floating material and grease rise to the surface. Each is collected by a very slowly moving scraper mechanism leading to discharge ports in the tank. The thickened and settled material, containing much particulate matter, is commonly referred to as sludge and will still contain between 96 and 98% water. Though this sludge is still a valuable by-product, the cost of removing the excess water can make its reuse uneconomical.

The clarified effluent from the settling tank is then permitted to overflow or is pumped to succeeding treatment processes. The sludge, relatively rich in food processing waste material, if not reclaimed, is disposed of by dewatering and incineration or digestion processes by which the volume of the waste material is still further reduced. Very often sludge handling and disposal facilities consist of a combination of these systems.

The effluent from the waste water primary treatment system is then sent to additional treatment steps in which the dissolved pollutants or those not large enough to be physically settled from the waste water stream are oxidized and rendered relatively innocuous by biological or chemical methods. This resulting oxidation reduces the BOD and renders the water suitable for discharge to streams. The oxygen demands of the waste water have been thereby satisfied in the process and the waste water will no longer rob dissolved oxygen from receiving streams. Most biological oxidation processes, however, are incapable of completely satisfying the oxygen needs of the food processing waste waters since it is impractical to retain the water long enough for complete oxidation of the polluting material. Hence, the final oxidation processes still take place in the receiving waters. However, this minimum demand on the stream's own water treatment capacity may not be detrimental. In actuality, these waste treatment processes consist of nothing more than speeding up nature's own waste treatment systems found normally in streams. The degree of waste water treatment required is, therefore, a function of the stream's waste assimilation capacity and the ultimate intended use of that water resource. Somepollutants require up to 30 days to biologically degrade in waste waters. It is obviously impractical to maintain those materials in an oxygen enriched environment such as found in secondary waste treatment facilities for that length of time. Even though the process can be accelerated by hastening the normal biological degradation cycle, holding the waste water for 6–7 days is economically impractical.

Although not usual to food processing wastes, some other pollutants such as oils, dissolved metals, chemicals, etc., may be significant in waste waters. These must be removed or rendered inoffensive by chemical treatment methods.

Normal secondary waste treatment processes are usually encountered in two forms in connection with the biological treatment of food processing industry waste waters. The first and most simple to operate consists of a biological oxidation system known as a trickling filter. The name filter is actually a misnomer as no filtration actually is accomplished. The settled primary system waste water effluent, relatively free of suspended solid pollutants but still containing up to 2/3 of the polluting or oxygen demanding wastes, is trickled over a large bed of rocks. This is usually done by means of a rotary distributor which doses the polluted waters on top of a bed of crushed rock anywhere from 4–6 ft deep. The waste water trickles down through the rock over the surface of 3–4 in. stones and is collected in collection troughs constructed beneath the filter. The filter stones, after several days of operation, acquire a slimy film, rich in bacteria, over a great portion of the filter depth. This film contains the bacteria which biologically oxidize or consume the pollutant material dissolved in the waste water. Its appearance and characteristics might be considered similar to the slippery rocks often found in the bed of a stream. Within this slimy film are many varieties of aerobic bacteria which survive by feeding on the pollutants in the waste water thereby removing the oxygen-demanding pollutants.

Many modifications of trickling filter design have been evolved, commonly referred to as rapid rate filters. In a conventional trickling filter, the filter is made large enough so that the water need be applied only once to the filter. Sufficient contact time is furnished for the biological oxidation to take place prior to collection underneath the filter and further treatment. In a high rate trickling filter the waste water is recirculated over the filter 1, 2, or 3 more times with each succeeding cycle providing further biological oxidation. A substantial space saving and construction cost saving can be often accomplished through the use of a high rate trickling filter. As the filter stone bacteria feed upon the pollutants dissolved in the waste water, they grow and multiply. In a conventional filter this continues with the thickness of the film on the stone increasing with each passing day. After several weeks or months, and usually in concurrence with a temperature change or weather change, the film will slip from the stones in large clumps or sheets and find its way into the collecting trough underneath the trickling filter. This produces a turbid and ofttimes offensive effluent. This process, known as sloughing of the zoogleal film, provides an undue load on streams or further waste treatment facilities if required or provided.

In the high rate filter, however, the rapid flow of water over the filter stones causes a constant sloughing at a much lower rate. As a result, the succeeding waste treatment facilities or receiving waters, which may be provided downstream, are loaded more uniformly but at a lesser rate with the wasted bacteria which is more easily oxidized and assimilated.

Following biological oxidation in trickling filters, clarifiers are usually provided to settle the sloughed turbid material which tends to conglomerate into particles known as floc. This substance resembles a fine pulp dispersed in the clear waste water. Very large clarifiers must be provided to collect this material since it has extremely slow settling properties. It must be collected very gently by slow moving scraping and collection mechanisms to prevent agitation and remixing with the waste water. Very often the light sludge collected in such final clarifiers or settling devices will contain as little as 1% solid material, a fact which complicates ultimate disposal.

The second commonly encountered form of secondary treatment processes for food processing waste waters is the activated sludge process and modifications thereof. This process consists of collecting the effluent from the primary waste treatment facilities and introducing it into large tanks into which air is mixed and dissolved in quantities substantial enough to support the rapid growth of the aerobic bacteria to assimilate the substrate or pollutant contained in the waste waters. Air is introduced into these tanks by any one of several methods including mechanical agitation, diffusion by means of dispersion devices on pipes in the bottom of the tanks, or a combination.

The use of activated sludge processes had gained favor since it requires less space for the treatment of large quantities of waste waters and with careful process control, a very complete degree of waste water treatment (pollutant oxidation) can be achieved.

There are many modifications of the activated sludge system. Basically, all these modifications relate to aeration and detention time, methods of adding the primary effluent to the aeration tanks and methods of reusing and wasting the activated (biologically active) sludge collected in succeeding clarifiers.

The return of sludge from the clarifiers to the upstream end of the aeration tanks or to other points of introduction into the tanks is usually necessary to seed the incoming waste water with biologically active aerobic bacteria to accelerate the absorption and absorption of the pollutant material by the aerobic bacteria. The maintenance of a dissolved oxygen content in the aeration tanks coupled with a relatively large amount of biodegradable material available in the polluted waste water also permits a very rapid growth of the bacteria required to remove the pollutant from the waste water.

The activated sludge process has often been compared as similar to pigs in a barnyard. Garbage and refuse is thrown to the pigs and the pigs proceed to consume the waste. The process efficiency is optimized by maintaining the correct relationship between the number of pigs and the amount of garbage. In other words, the efficiency of the activated sludge process is maintained through an optimum number of bacteria within the aeration tanks, an optimum amount of food (biologically oxidizable pollutants) in relation to their number, plus an optimum environment. This environment requires ample dissolved oxygen in the waste water plus an optimum acid-alkali (pH) condition.

Unlike trickling filters, maximum effectiveness of an activated sludge system is dependent on daily and at times even hourly testing to maintain a condition of optimum efficiency. For this reason trickling filters, although frequently less efficient at pollutant removal, are often preferred by food processing industries since their operation does not require the exact control for maximum efficiency required by the activated sludge process.

One form of the activated sludge process, however, is susceptible to efficient operation without the high degree of control required by other activated sludge methods. This process modification is known as extended aeration. In this system, waste waters are aerated for up to 6 times that normally required by the activated sludge process (24 hr). During this time, the aerobic bacteria utilized to consume the pollutants in the waste water are permitted to undergo a full life cycle in the tank, their numbers increasing until they have consumed nearly all the pollutants within the waste water. When the supply of food (pollutants) is exhausted they die until the residue consists principally of what is known as inorganic ash, actually the minute carcasses of the aerobic bacteria.

Chief objections to the extended aeration system are that it requires large tankage and more air per gallon of waste water treated regardless of whether the air is introduced by mechanical agitators or through air diffusion devices.

Following the activated sludge processes, the effluent is conveyed to large settling tanks or clarifiers. At this point, the sludge collected on the bottom of the tank is sent to digesters or returned to the head end of the secondary waste treatment system as required to enhance the biological processes taking place. The design or operation of the final settling tanks or clarifiers requires extreme care since their operation is easily upset. If the sludge is retained too long in the bottom of the tanks, it can turn septic. Anaerobic rather than aerobic conditions will develop and the sludge may float to the top of the tanks, preventing its easy removal. In addition, the physical characteristics of sludge discharged by the trickling filters or activated sludge process may be such that it is not readily amenable to settling. It may not agglomerate into the larger particles necessary to settle or it may be such light, fluffy material that its settling properties are very poor. In any event, the operation of final settling tanks or clarifiers requires great care to assure their optimum performance.

Effluent from the final clarifier, assuming normal operation, can usually be discharged to nearby streams and water courses. It may even be discharged to city sanitary sewers. However, since at this stage 90–95% of the pollutant material has been removed, it is not customary for treated secondary waste waters to be discharged to a sewer. If a sewer is available, waste water treatment provided by the food processing industry usually terminates with primary treatment.

Subsequent to discharge of treated waste water from the final clarifier, it is customary to heavily chlorinate any effluent that may contain pathological organisms. Chlorination is usually not required, however, if the food processing waste waters have not been subject to contamination by bacteria harmful to plants, animals, or human beings.

TERTIARY TREATMENT

In spite of the fact that by this time over 95% of the pollutants customarily contained in the waste water have been removed (usually about 1/3 of the pollutants are removed in the primary treatment and the remainder removed in the secondary treatment) current emphasis on pollution abatement is bringing further requirements on the so-called clean effluents discharged by secondary waste treatment facilities.

Remaining in the effluent are large quantities of phosphates. These phosphates when discharged to streams and rivers, in effect, fertilize the receiving waters. The resulting plant growth in the form of algae are sufficient to pollute the streams with excessive or dead plant matter to the ecclusion of aquatic life. This change in the environment within the stream normally occurs in all waters, due to eutrophication, and is the first step in the conversion of a lake or stream to a swamp and its later conversion, very often, to dry land. Such changes usually take place over thousands of years in bodies of fresh water but the sudden introduction of substantial phosphates has greatly hastened the process. As a result, we are ruining many receiving waters with extensive algae and weed growths.

Consequently, the current waste water abatement emphasis is pointing more and more towards what has been customarily referred to as tertiary treatment. This treatment removes phosphates from the effluent before it is discharged to the receiving lake or stream. To date, however, no truly satisfactory methods have been found that seem economically justified.

One system consists of liming the effluent stream with the resulting precipitation of calcium phosphate which can be used as a crude fertilizer. A second system consists of holding the waste waters in a lagoon for anywhere from 2—4 weeks permitting the algae to bloom in the lagoon. The algae can then be removed by filtration of microstraining and the phosphorous removed from the water along with the billions of tiny plants.

In some states, however, it has been permissible to discharge these algae-bearing waste waters. It is felt that when added to the river the algae will be carried to the sea and their presence in the water may be less detrimental than the presence of phosphates. It is also hoped that future means for removing the algae will be discovered that may prove to be economically feasible. Generally, if the algae are removed from the final effluent of a tertiary waste water treatment process, the remaining BOD (the normal accepted measurement criteria for pollution in waters) is so low that it cannot be measured. Results often indicate that only trace amounts of oxygen demand are remaining in the effluent.

TABLE 11.1

WASTE WATER TREATMENT COSTS IN
FOOD PROCESSING INDUSTRIES, 1968

Industry	Unit of cost measurement	Cost per unit (cents)
Meat packing	Cwt of live weight killed	5-19
Poultry processing	Cwt of live weight killed	5-5
Dairies	Cwt of fluid milk	7.5 - 26
Canned fruits and vegetables	Per case of products	1.3 - 2.8
Frozen fruits and vegetables	Cwt of product	0.1±

Source: The Cost of Clean Water, U. S. Federal Water Pollution Control Admin. U. S. Govt. Printing Office, Washington, D.C. Industrial Waste Profiles 6, 8, and 9, 1968.

SUMMARY

The foregoing discussion is not intended to be a complete dissertation on food processing waste water treatment, but merely a guide to those faced with the problem of waste water treatment in food processing plants. It cannot be overemphasized that when such problems arise it is essential that food processors stay in close contact with the regulatory agencies. They must be knowledgeable of agency standards and retain qualified professional consulting engineers to assist in the design and preparation of their waste water treatment facilities.

Waste water treatment is becoming a major part of food processing costs. It is possible that if primary, secondary, and tertiary treatment were required, up to 5% of future food processing costs might be spent on waste water treatment requirements.

Current probable waste water treatment costs per pound of finished product in certain food processing industries are presented in Table 11.1. These are only guides and should not be considered exact since inflation, technological breakthrough, and volume of food processed will all have a major effect on waste water treatment costs.

BIBLIOGRAPHY

BESSELIEVRE B., 1969. The Treatment of Industrial Wastes. McGraw-Hill Book Co., New York.

CAMP, W. J. and WILLOUGHBY, E. 1968. Extended aeration purifies effluent. Food Eng. 40, 72-74, Aug.

COOLEY, A. M., WAHL, E. D., and FOSSUM, G. O. 1964. Characteristics and amounts of potato wastes from various processing streams. Proc. 19th Ind. Waste Conf., Purdue Univ.

GLIDE, L. C. et al. 1969. An evaluation of cannery waste disposal by spray irrigation. Proc. 42nd ann. Conf. Water Pollution Control Federation.

GRIFFITH, C. C. 1968. Poultry processing waste treatment experience in aerated ponds. Proc. 23rd Ind. Waste Conf., Purdue Univ.

GURHAM, C. F. 1965. Industrial Wastewater Control. Academic Press, New York.

HORASAWA, I. 1968. Stabilization pond treatment of slaughterhouse wastes. Proc. 23rd Ind. Waste Conf., Purdue Univ.

KALINSKE, A. A. 1968. Economics of aeration in waste treatment. Proc. 23rd Ind. Waste Conf., Purdue Univ.

McCABE, BRO. J. and ECKENFELDER, W. W. Jr. 1955. Biological Treatment of Sewage and Industrial Wastes, Reinhold Publishing Co., New York

MANCINI, J. L. and BARNHARD, E. L. 1967. Aerated systems for industrial wastes. Water Pollution Control Federation 39, 978-986, June.

NEMERON, N. L. 1963. Theories and Practices of Industrial Waste Treatment. Addison-Wesley Publishing Co., Reading, Mass.

PATTON, V. D. and WILLOUGHBY, E. 1968. Design of a modern packing waste treatment plant. J. Water Pollution Control Federation 41, 74-78. Jan.

RALLS, J. W., MERCER, W. A., ROSE, W. W. and LAMB, F. C. 1968. Research on waste production in food canning operations. Proc. 23rd Ind. Waste Conf., Purdue Univ.

WILLOUGHBY, E. 1969. Select the 'right' waste treatment system. Food Eng. Aug.

CHAPTER 12

W. Smith Greig

Vertical Integration and/or Systems Coordination

INTRODUCTION

The process of transferring food from its initial production on the farm to its ultimate consumption is often studied by breaking its system down into component parts. Often the system is studied or described by levels in the stages of nroduction—farming, processing, wholesaling, and retailing. At other times it is discussed in terms of specific functions such as assembly, processing, transporting, financing or risk bearing, packaging, storing, title exchange, etc. We shall view vertical integration as one method of coordinating the different levels or different functions in the marketing system.

Mighell (1959) defined vertical integration as follows: "Vertical integration embraces a broad range of interfirm relationships between successive stages in production. Elements in vertical integration exist in almost all interfirm arrangements that affect production other than those arrived at in the open competitive markets." (The term production should be used in the broadest context to include all stages in the marketing and distribution system.) I will include in the definition both integration by ownership and integration by contractual arrangements.[1]

Much of the literature on vertical integration has been written by individuals with agricultural interests. Most deal only with the first stage of integration, that is, between processors and farmers as in the case of poultry and eggs, feed dealers and producers. A fairly common attitude on business integration into agriculture is the concern that agriculture may be owned or controlled by large business firms.

While we are interested in integration between processors and farm producers, we are also concerned with the complete food distribution system. Processor-retailer integration is substantial and is increasing, both between processors and retail food stores and between processors and the food service industry.

INTEGRATION BY BUSINESS INTO AGRICULTURAL PRODUCTION

In this section I will discuss some of the reasons for the extent of integration into agricultural production, as well as some concerns by agricultural interests (Mighell and Jones 1963). The two parameters of control over stages of marketing are integration through ownership and the open competitive market. Since one of the reasons for vertical integration is the state of imperfections in

---

[1] Mighell later excluded contracts from his definition of vertical integration, but for simplicity I will not use his later refinement. See Mighell and Jones (1963).

the open competitive market, I will discuss means to improve atomistic[2] markets, and some possible changes in rules (laws) that may supplement or replace some of the atomistic markets for farm products. Finally, I will speculate on future business integration into agriculture through ownership.

Reasons for Business Integration with Agriculture

A list of incentives for vertical integration or contracts might include: reducing risk, reducing costs, improving management, gaining bargaining power, improving market position, assuring adequate inputs, investing surplus revenues, developing new technology, and obtaining additional capital.

Risk and Uncertainty. — Protection against risk and uncertainty is one of the prime reasons many food processors contract for supplies of raw product. Processors of specialized, perishable products want to be sure of the quantity of the product produced and that its flow to the plant will keep operating costs at a minimum. Further, uncertainties of both price and quantities which might be produced require contracting to stabilize prices. The farmers' operations also include many risks and uncertainties. Price fluctuations on seasonally-produced perishable crops are often extreme. Price insurance has not been deemed feasible, but hedging against the futures market has sometimes been practicable. Maine potato growers often sell futures contracts and the contracts are used as collateral for bank loans for seed, fertilizer, operating expenses, etc., as well as a hedge against price fluctuations. Diversification is also often practiced to reduce risk.

The more uncertain the prices and the amounts which may be produced for processing, the greater the degree of contracting. Most vegetables for processing, including onions for dehydration, potatoes for freezing or for potato chips, most broilers, sugar beets, castor beans, safflower, mustard seed, vegetable seeds, hybrid seed corn, and baby chicks are produced under integrated or contractual arrangements. However, storable commodities or ones for which there are well established markets are not usually contracted for, as in the case of wheat, corn, rice, cotton, hogs, and beef cattle.

Cost Reduction or Economic Efficiency. — Economies of scale in food processing have been discussed in Chap. 3. Economies of scale exist in nearly all stages of production. For example, in the broiler industry the stages in production include: laying flocks for hatchery eggs, hatchery operations, broiler production, feed production, broiler processing, and even the pharmaceutical industry. The most efficient scale of any given stage may not match the most efficient scale of the next stage. For example, the most efficient sized hatchery may serve more than one broiler-producing farm. And 1 processing plant may need to process broilers from more than 1 farm. Integration through ownership

---

[2] Atomistic refers to those markets having large numbers of both buyers and sellers, with none of the buyers or sellers being large enough to affect price.

or contracts is a method of coordinating the system so that the most efficient scale may be used in each stage to result in the least cost production function. Thus, one stage may require several units to best service the next stage.

Also, there may be significant sales or transaction costs if each stage depends on the open competitive market to connect each of the succeeding stages.

It should be noted that in most cases the integrator is the owner of the stage requiring the largest scale of production and the largest amount of capital. In perishable crops the integrator is the processor, in poultry and eggs he is the feed manufacturer or processor. Seldom is the integrator the farm unit, as typically this stage requires smaller amounts of capital for an efficient sized unit.

Management Improvement. – Vertical integration is the extension of some administrative control over more stages of production. Through ownership it gives complete management control. Integration through contracts may also give extensive management control. In crop production, the variety and time of planting may be controlled by the integrator. On some crops, insect and disease spraying schedules may be under the processor's control; in others, time of harvest and actual harvesting operations may also be controlled. In poultry production, the chicks, feed formulations or specifications, and much of the equipment may be supplied or controlled by the integrator.

An early agriculturally-based argument against integration was that much of agriculture was an art rather than a science. "The eye of the master fattens the cattle." The argument suggested that farm management by farm owners would be better than farm management by business management experts. However, most experts would now probably argue that much agricultural production is a science and that the application of science is subject to managerial control by management experts who need not necessarily have extensive farm background.

Bargaining Power and Market Position. – From the standpoint of bargaining power and market position, there is usually a stronger influence for a processor to integrate forward into retailing, than to integrate backward into farming. Compared with many business enterprises it is easier to enter a farming enterprise because of relatively smaller amounts of capital and technology needed. But it would be very difficult for a processor-distributor to acquire control over enough farm production facilities to have much influence on prices or markets for most major commodities.

Under current market rules, i.e., the atomistic market for many farm products, there is little advantage to integrate backward from the standpoint of market structure. However, if the laws are changed, i.e., market orders, or marketing boards, the farmers may be able to control production and price, making it more desirable to integrate backward from the standpoint of market power.

Typically, forward integration (integration closer to the consumer) has a stronger pull than backward integration (integration toward the farmer). In forward integration the firm is getting closer and closer to the consumer where his advertising and promotion and market influence are ultimately aimed. This is true even in the case of the poultry industry where the feed dealer is the integrator. He is trying to assure a market for his product—feed.

Bargaining power and market position considerations are probably more important in other industries than in the food industry. Vertical integration in the aluminum industry, shoe manufacturers who develop retail chain stores, and movie producers who have a chain of theatres are examples of vertical integration for market control.

Whether the tendency is toward forward integration or backward integration is arguable. The point being made here is that backward integration into agriculture is for reasons other than for bargaining power or market position. Both forward and backward integration are apparently increasing.

Assuring Adequate Inputs. — Assuring adequate inputs has been partially discussed as a method of reducing risk. One of the oldest, most widely used types of integration is the contracting of seasonal perishable commodities, for example, vegetables for canning or freezing. In many areas a series of crops harvested as the season progresses are necessary to provide a processing plant with a long operating season. For efficient plant operations certain quantities of products are desirable at rather specific periods of the year. The possibility of over or under supplies if the production decisions were left entirely to the open market are great. Therefore the processor, i.e., the integrator, contracts for production of specific quantities or acreages of specific crops. The integrator may also own farm production facilities so that he may produce some products to reduce total costs. This processor-farm production may be used as a leverage. Typically, all the growers in an area receive the same contract price. The processor may want 20,000 acres of commodity X. He may find that he can get 10,000 acres produced at $1.00 per cwt, 15,000 acres at $1.08, and 20,000 at $1.20. Thus he might contract for 15,000 acres and then grow 5000 acres himself, reducing his marginal cost for a contracted product by 12¢ per cwt. Whether the processor will grow will depend upon the elasticity of supply as well as absolute costs of production.

An excellent example of assuring an adequate input supply is an integrated beef slaughtering operation where the slaughter plant has daily inputs of cattle scheduled for 2 yr in advance. Producers are under contract to supply cattle on a daily basis and the complete capacity of the plant is fully scheduled for every working day a full 2 yr in advance.

Investing Surplus Reserves and Obtaining New Capital. — Most profitable firms hope to expand. The greatest source of capital for business growth in the United States is from surplus reserves. Therefore, most firms are continually searching for new outlets to use these undistributed profits. Furnishing capital to agricultural production may be one of the many possible choices for using excess reserves. From a generic viewpoint, each firm must consider all total possible investments, rank these possibilities according to returns on capital, and select the one or ones with the greatest return. Thus, when control of supplies to a processor is crucial, capital investments to assure this production may be one of the best uses of capital. A feed manufacturer may furnish capital to poultry and egg producers to assure a captured market for his product. Processors of perishable crops may finance specialized production equipment and harvesting equipment. This frees capital requirements of farmers, increasing production and better guaranteeing adequate supplies to the processing plant. The integrator invests his surplus reserves and the integratee obtains new capital. It has been suggested that broiler integration in the South could not have developed in the corn belt states because farmers in the corn belt have a better capital position. Similarly, it is suggested that integrated beef and pork operations will have their initial strength in areas other than the corn belt.

Developing New Technology. − This is related both to cost and efficiencies and also to better management. Technology is probably the determinant of optimum scale of any particular stage in the production process. A change in technology may change scale efficiencies. With a new technology the optimum size unit for a given stage may increase. With increased size comes greater risk. Herein lies the need for integrated operations to assure supply and to avoid risks in price fluctuations.

Another aspect is that many technological uncertainties can be avoided through better management of integrated operations. The contractor often provides inputs of high-quality seeds, feeds, animals, and medicines. In many instances the contractor closely supervises farm production. Under contracts, the mortality rates in producing broilers and turkeys are substantially reduced and conversion of feed to meat increased. Some of the reasons advanced for hog contracts are that under them the mortality rate of baby pigs is reduced, a meat-type hog is produced, and more efficient feeding is promoted. In contracts for production of sugar beets, processing vegetables, seeds, and specialty crops the main objective is reducing uncertainties of type, quality, and delivery time. Contract arrangements are especially valuable in increasing production certainties when new technology, improved products, or inexperienced producers are involved.

Other Reasons. − One of the central issues of Galbraith's *The New Industrial State* (1967) is that forward planning for large industrial firms is essential and that control over prices is necessary in the planning process. To control sources of critical supply and to reduce price risk, the firms integrate and then both supply and price are controlled internally to the firm. This of course may be done by purchase or by contracts. Thus, vertical integration may be necessary to accomplish the long-range planning function of the firm.

Legal reasons may also encourage integration by large firms. Let us suppose, for example, that a large distributor of eggs (a major chain store) claims he should obtain a quantity discount from an egg processor. This might be justified on the reductions in costs in supplying large volumes. However, the processor claims that under FTC regulations he may be charged with unfair trade practices if he supplies the chain with eggs at a lesser price than to his other customers. To avoid possible legal action the chain decides it must purchase the egg processing operation if it is to obtain the efficiencies of large-scale egg procurement.

BARRIERS TO VERTICAL INTEGRATION IN AGRICULTURE

Much of the farming has developed in the United States around rather definite attitudes concerning the sanctity of the family farm. The idea of complete entrepreneurial freedom, including all management decisions, noninterference from government, hard work as a virtue and debt as being close to sin were all ideas associated with the family farm. The idea that a farm background produced a different and better set of moral values was not unusual. Thus, very strong emotional and social ties are associated with the concept of the family farm. As one farm leader put it "political leaders will resist vertical integration in agriculture in their oratory, in their congressional hearings, and in their legislation. The philosophy of the small, owner-operator, family farm is deeply ingrained in our sociological and political mores. . .Political pressure will continue to be on the side of maintaining small family farms, even though modern technology dictates strongly that family farms become larger" (Butz 1958).

There may be much resistance to integration by many farmers unless significantly large incentives are given. Changes in tradition and individual habits are difficult to overcome. If a rapid increase in integration threatens the family farm, perhaps restrictive legislation could be developed. Possible legislation might include market orders and agreements and/or marketing boards as well as legal action to prevent corporate ownership of farm production facilities.

EXTENT OF VERTICAL INTEGRATION INTO FARMING

The extent of vertical integration into farming varies widely among crops. Typically, there has been more integration of crops than livestock. In 1968-1969 probably over 95% of the broilers, fluid milk, and vegetable seeds were produced under integrated arrangements. Most of the fluid milk is marketed under complex contracts dealing more with marketing rather than production control per se. Milk production decisions are decidedly affected through marketing contracts, state and federal orders, health regulations, seasonal pricing, and in some instances producer quotas.

Over 90% of the sugar crops, process vegetables, and hybrid seed corn were produced under integrated arrangements in 1968-1969. Data on integration by ownership are limited; however, it is well known that many processors own part of the acreages they process. For example H. J. Heinz Co. in 1968-1969 produced 10,000 acres of potatoes in 1 block for their processing plant in Idaho. Probably 75% of all citrus, and 75% of all turkeys (up from 50% only 7 yr ago) are integrated. From 40 to 50% of fresh vegetables and potatoes are being produced under contract arrangements. Grower-packer-shipper arrangements are common. An interesting development is that both United Fruit (Anon, 1969A) and Purex (Anon. 1969B) companies plan to nationally merchandise branded fresh vegetables on a year-round basis. Each have acquired substantial acreages of land to produce at least a part of their requirements.

Deciduous fruits have not had the integrated arrangements as have the citrus products. Cooperatives may market up to 20% of the tonnage produced. In Pennsylvania, processors own substantial acreages of apple orchards (Pet, Inc. for example). Similarly, other companies also own orchards in Virginia. As a greater proportion of deciduous fruit, especially apples, are processed, long-term integrated arrangements between processors and producers will develop.[3]

Probably less than 15% of cattle on feed and less than 10% of the hogs are produced under integrated arrangements. It is interesting that the integrated feed-lot operations have been in the west and southwest and that contract hog production has been on the fringes of the corn belt and in the south. Apparently the good capital structure of farms in the corn belt has been a deterrent to contract production.

The beef operations are typically large commercial feeding operations. Feeder cattle may or may not be procured under contract and the feed lot may or may not have contractual or integrated arrangements with a beef packer. While many of the large feeding lots are vertically integrated, others are just examples of commercialization of agriculture. Typically, the commercial beef feeding operation may have 30,000 or more cattle on feed at one time. Apparently feed lot expansion and the corollary slaughter capacity is increasing in Texas. *Feedstuffs* magazine reported that 21 new feed lots were under construction in west Texas, which will add another 500,000 head to feeding capacity. In addition, 31 existing lots have been expanding, adding another 350,000 head to capacity. The article predicted that by 1974-1975, Texas will feed about 5 million head a year and then level off. New slaughter plants are also increasing in Texas. Present capacity is 1.5 million head but new plants under construction will bring slaughter capacity to 2.5 million head per year (Anon. 1969C).

Commercial feed lots are increasing rather rapidly in other parts of the west with not as rapid an increase in the corn belt. An example, and perhaps a new trend, is in the integrated arrangement of Great Markwestern of Hillsdale, Michigan. This is the first example of a major feed lot and slaughter plant under the same management at one location. Initially 30,000 head of cattle will be fed and an initial slaughter capacity will be 300,000 head per year in a 1-shift operation. There are some contracts for feeder cattle and also contracts for corn silage production for feed use.

Although there has been continued interest in contract pig and hog production there is apparently relatively little action in hog integration as compared

---

[3]Duffy Mott's arrangements with Cherry Growers, Inc., Traverse City, Mich., might be an example of this. Duffy Mott acquired the facilities of Cherry Growers, Inc. (a cooperative) and has a contractual arrangement to process and market the products of Cherry Growers, Inc. members.

to beef at the present time (1970).

TRENDS IN INTEGRATION IN FARMING

The trend in agriculture is toward greater and greater specialization. This is because of and also results in improved technology. To take advantage of technological improvements, often much additional capital is needed and the integrator is often one who is willing and able to furnish the capital.

Technology has developed more rapidly in crops than in livestock and integrated arrangements in many crops have been common for a long period of time. The rapid and nearly complete integration of the broiler industry and rapid increase in integration in turkeys and eggs have lent much speculation as to what might happen in beef and pork. Many people think we are approaching some technological breakthrough in livestock production and that there will be large infusions of capital in this sector to capitalize on the new technologies. Apparently in Texas, much of the new capital for the large commercial feed lots is coming from oil and gas interests. This particular trend is one of conglomeration rather than vertical integration per se. But the same interest will probably insist that the feeding operation be a vertically integrated business.

Vertically integrated arrangements in all aspects of agriculture probably will continue to increase and, particularly, beef integration will accelerate.

Many of the current beef processing facilities are outmoded and there are, by far, too many processing facilities. As new facilities are built they will be, at least in part, based on integrated arrangements.

METHODS OF IMPROVING ATOMISTIC MARKETS

It is often stated that the atomistic markets often do not do a good job. Open competitive markets do not always reflect consumer desires or consumer preferences back to the producer. Further, the market allows for wide fluctuations in prices. Forward planning is risky or uncertain. Certainly the open competitive market may be a costly mechanism. Assembling products, shipping them to a central market, from the central market to a processor, then to wholesalers, and finally to retailers can be inefficient and costly compared to direct shipments from processors to retailers. But so much product can bypass central markets that the pricing mechanism may nearly break down. Much egg pricing, even under contract, is based on the New York wholesale price; yet the movement of eggs on the wholesale market of New York is so light that many people are questioning this pricing procedure.

Rather than completely bypassing the open competitive market, can we find ways to make this market more useful? The answer is yes. Among the ways the atomistic markets may be improved are (1) better market news reports, (2) electronic price determination, (3) better price predictions, and (4) additional futures markets.

Better Market News Reports

While the Market News Service of the Dept. of Agr. certainly does a creditable job in price reporting, services can always be improved or expanded. For example, the price quotations are generally on products. Is it feasible to have price quotations on services? Much of the transportation of unprocessed agricultural products is by exempt truckers, with few or no published rates. The U. S. Dept. of Agr. could develop a system of price reporting for transportation services, providing both truckers and shippers much useful information and perhaps improving the efficiency by which exempt commodities are transported. Price reporting of contracts that bypass the central markets would improve efficiency of pricing noncontracted products. Similarly, as more products are processed, daily price reports of products for the food processors might be issued. Some standard methodology of pricing should be developed in processor prices. Is the price a delivered price? Who furnishes the containers? What is the grading system? Better methods need to be developed to determine the net price the farmer receives for his product for processing compared to the net fresh market prices.

Electronic Price Determination

Perhaps the open competitive markets could be greatly improved through the use of electronic computers. The auction of the Ontario (Canada) Hog Producers Marketing Board is an example. The auction is Dutch style; that is, the price is started high and declines until a buyer stops it with a bid and a teletype system is used to broadcast offerings and to transmit bids. Quality variation of the product does not present a problem because all hogs are sold on a carcass grade and yield basis with fixed grade differentials established by law. Grading is under federal inspection. This system has also been tried in the United States on feeder cattle with some success.

A completely electronic system as a theoretical alternative to current practices in trading shell eggs has been developed (Schrader et al. 1968). In this system all bids to purchase or sell shell eggs would go by telephone or teletype directly to a computer. The computer would match bids to sell and offers to purchase. Freight costs could be included. The calculations, with freight included, would minimize marketing costs as well as provide a regional or national trading system.

The advantages of such a system are many: (1) Buyers and sellers could make bids and offers without revealing their identities until the sale is confirmed. (2) A continuous printout of prices could be obtained. (3) Prices could be quantified and a weighted average price determined. (4) The process of trading could be nearly instantaneous and perishability places a premium on speed. (5) Much cross hauling could be eliminated, reducing total marketing costs. This system of electronic egg trading has been tested on a theoretical experimental basis with excellent results in the computer program. The same methodology could be used for a large number of products—both fresh products for processing and processed products.

Futures Market

The electronic egg trading system could be programmed for price determination for deliveries 1 day, 2 days, 3 weeks, or a month later. Thus, the cash market could be tied directly to the futures market. The futures markets are examples of open competitive markets and at the same time are contracts for future delivery. They may represent the closest to the perfect market to any system we have. In the futures markets there are (or can be) large numbers of buyers and sellers, all at the same place, doing business at 1 time, with no 1 large enough to affect prices. (There are, in some cases, legal limits on how much trading one firm can do.) While, certainly, all parties do not have perfect knowledge, much information is available on the commodities that are traded.

Additional futures markets on commodities not now traded might aid in improving the atomistic markets. This could also be a source of credit and could permit hedging by producers and processors.

Price Predictions

The U. S. Dept. of Agr., as a part of its services, might provide a price prediction service which could work in several ways. For annual crops prior to planting, the Department could obtain "intentions to plant." Then, based on average yields, a price for the quantity to be produced would be determined. This would be "fed back" to producers, a "revised intentions to plant" would be determined, and then a new price calculated. This sort of iteration could be continued until intended production and prices which might be received reach equilibrium. Also, as the crops near or reach maturity the expected prices could be computed again. On perennial crops, such as cherries and apples for sauce manufacture, Ricks and Bixby (1969) and Ricks (1969) have come very close in predicting prices for processed products. An expansion of these types of systems would provide much market intelligence to both processors and farmers, and would aid in the firm's forward planning. The use of the electronic computer, with its capability of handling large quantities of data and nearly instantaneous computations, could completely revise current procedures of "intentions to plant," and provide price predictions for many products as well as greatly improve the Market News Service. Certainly, one can foresee actual trading in both unprocessed and processed agricultural products, with the computer as the central facilitating part of the market system. This does not mean that many crops will move farther away from the open market system, but that the open market will be considerably improved.

EFFECTS OF RULES (LAWS) CHANGES AWAY
FROM THE OPEN MARKET SYSTEM

We have discussed vertical integration and the open market system under laws currently in effect (1970). Most of the laws affecting the system have been in effect for several years. If we changed a few rules the effects might be interesting. I am not suggesting, however, that the rules should be changed, merely speculating on some possible different outcomes.

Most nations have a stated or unstated policy of low prices for food. This is a political necessity, as in most developed countries there are more consumers than farmers, and in most underdeveloped countries even with a disproportionately large number of farmers, the impetus for development is in industrial development and the funds for development may come largely from agricultural exports. Agriculture may be taxed (i.e., export taxes) to finance industrial development. Exceptions to this are France, and some other EEC countries which have stringent import controls to protect an inefficient agriculture. On the whole, from a political point of view, the U. S. Congress will probably not permit laws giving farmers or processors the power to significantly raise food prices. Stated realistically, the political power of agricultural interests has greatly decreased. If farmers continue to leave agriculture as indicated by past trends the last farmer will quit farming in 1984. This, of course, will not be the case but it does point up a rapid decline. While government may not give agriculture laws permitting significant increases in price, it may give agriculture additional rules to prevent unduly low prices. These laws or rules might be for expanded usage of Federal Marketing Orders, Marketing Boards, price supports, and a National Farmers Relations Board similar to the National Labor Relations Board.

Federal Marketing Orders and Agreements

Federal Marketing Orders and Agreements for many agricultural commodities are permitted under the Federal Agricultural Marketing Agreement Act of 1937 (with ammendments). Most of the milk in the United States and large quantities of many types of fruits and vegetables are marketed under Federal Marketing Orders and Agreements. Many details on Federal Marketing Orders and Agreements for fruits and vegetables are contained in a 1966 report by the Natl. Comm. on Food Marketing (1966). Federal Market Orders and Agreements are industry programs which must be approved by 2/3 of the producers and at least 50% of the handlers. They control grades, standards, flow to market, and finance research and development. In a Federal Marketing Order the capacity of a producer to produce is not affected; however, controls may be exerted over quantities marketed and time of marketing. In some State Marketing Orders the capacity of a producer to produce is affected. Production quotas for Class I milk are legal in 15 or 16 states. In some states, if a new producer wants to produce Class I milk, he essentially must purchase a quota from someone else. Similarly in vegetables for processing and for fresh market, production of some crops can be and is controlled under certain state orders, notably in California and Florida. Thus both State and Federal Market Orders and Agreements certainly affect the open competitive markets as supply may be controlled. One of the principal problems with Federal Marketing Orders and Agreements is supply response. If an order is effective in the short-run, and as the capacity of the producer to produce cannot be controlled, will this merely increase production and compound the problem?

Rule changes might include: (1) controlling production in Federal Marketing

Orders, (2) removing the limitation of a handler or processor vote, (3) expanding permissible orders to a much wider range of products, and (4) using Federal Marketing Orders and Agreements for a commodity with total United States coverage (most Federal Marketing Orders are now limited to a state or region).

Marketing Boards

Marketing Boards have been widely used in England, Canada, Europe, Australia, Africa, and some South American countries (Sorenson 1968). Essentially all the product is sold through a "Marketing Board." The Board may control acreages, flow to market, handlers of the product, prices, and services rendered. The Marketing Board is, in effect, a monopoly in marketing the particular product. The Board may have dual pricing policies (Australian wheat for local consumption is priced differently from that for export), or it may divert part of the crop to secondary or other uses.

While with Federal Marketing Orders and Agreements the products are sold either on the open market or under contractual arrangements, with the Marketing Board procedure the products are sold through that Board.

The disadvantage of Marketing Boards from the farmer's point of view is that the Board has a large amount of administrative control over his operations. Similarly, there are problems of supply response, new entry, record keeping. shifting among crops, and permanent locations for industries where they were when the Board was legalized. Many agricultural industries in the United States undergo considerable shifts in location with new technological developments.

Marketing Boards would tend to stabilize production where it currently is and would prevent much competition among areas. Apart from the political problem surrounding higher prices, there is the economic problem that substitutes or synthetics may cause. While the recent Natl. Comm. on Food Marketing recommended the use of Marketing Boards in the United States, apparently there has been little or no Congressional support to date. However, a rule change permitting or establishing National Marketing Boards for agricultural products would appreciably change the operations of both farmers and food processors. If the Boards were successful, the value of the land or farm which had a quota would be appreciably increased. (This has been the case in tobacco production under acreage control in the United States.)

A possible benefit to both growers and processors under either Federal Marketing Orders and Agreements or under Marketing Boards is that utilization controls might be applied. Many raw agricultural products yield processed products with different elasticities of demand. And, in theory, to maximize returns the production of products with low demand elasticities should be controlled and those products with higher demand elasticities should be expanded. Typically processed products have higher demand elasticities than their unprocessed counterparts. Thus, fluid market milk production is controlled and the surplus milk is made into cheese or products with a higher elasticity of demand. Similarly, it would probably be wise to control the amounts of potatoes and apples (Greig

1962) going to fresh market and to utilize the rest in products such as potato chips or applesauce which have higher demand elasticities. Returns would be maximized under a system of allocating products based on their elasticity of demand. This would, in most cases, restrict fresh movement and increase processed movement. A dual price system might or should develop for different product uses. An effective dual price system could only be developed in a situation utilizing market controls. Without controls, prices of unprocessed products must be the same for equivalent quality no matter whether the product was for fresh marketing or processing, or no matter the kind or degree of processing.

A National Farmers' Relations Board

Just as labor bargains or negotiates with an industrial firm under the protection of the National Labor Relations Board there has been some speculation that farmers need the authority to bargain with processors under the conditions that an agreement reached through 50% or more of the farmers is binding for all the rest. Similarly, there appears to be some sentiment that some farmer-oriented business firms, such as groups of fresh produce packing houses or small food processors, could act as one in bargaining for price with large accounts such as major chain stores. Rules change to permit more effective bargaining by farm groups could certainly affect processors operations.

Unionization of Farmers and Farm Laborers

It has been suggested that some large agribusiness firms do not desire to integrate by ownership into farming because of the low wages paid to laborers. The public relations interests of the firm would be damaged if factory workers tried to exploit the firm's position in low wages paid to farm labor. If farm labor unionization rapidly develops and farm labor wages rise appreciably, location of crop production may change. Similarly, grower-processor contractual relations may be appreciably different and more business firms might enter into agricultural production.

BUSINESS INTEGRATION INTO FARMING BY OWNERSHIP

On a national basis farm ownership by large business corporations is quite small. In a recent analysis conducted by the U. S. Dept. of Agr., it was concluded that "the total number of corporations directly engaged in farming and ranching is probably about 1% of all commercial farms. These firms operated about 7% of the land in farms and accounted for possibly 8–9% of gross sales of all farm products. More than 2/3 of all corporations were incorporated family businesses and another 12% were 1–man corporations. So called 'outside' or nonfamily corporations represented about 0.2% of all commercial farms and about 2% of gross sales." Nearly 1/2 of the nonfamily or business corporations had gross sales under $40,000. "However, 14% of the business corporation farms had sales over $500,000. Many of these largest operations involve specialized livestock and crop production associated with firms producing one or more farm inputs, or having processing and marketing facilities. Relatively little integration exists with respect to feed grains, wheat, and cotton" (Scofield 1969). While business integration into farming by ownership is currently not large, there are several factors that suggest it will substantially increase. These include: (1) improved technologies of production with increased economies of scale, (2) the obvious relationship between return on investment in agricultural production compared to other business enterprises including the value of land appreciation, (3) agricultural tax breaks, (4) reduction in ideological barriers, and (5) the coordination effects of integration.

Increasing technologies or increasing industrialization of agriculture production increases the scale or size of the farms. This calls for increased capital to operate an efficiently sized farm and may push both the capital requirements and management requirements above the levels of many independent farm operators. Unfortunately we know little about the real economies of scale in farming. Perhaps the upper limits in efficiencies with large size have not even begun to have been tested. Many more farm inputs are now purchased than ever before—machinery, fertilizer, seeds, herbicides, pesticides, fungicides, feed—and there should be significant economies of scale in purchases of these inputs. For example: allegedly, 1 large-scale farmer is able to buy farm machinery directly from the manufacturer at 15% below local dealer costs. Another grows 60,000 acres of soybeans and 30,000 acres of corn. Cattle feed lots with 30,000–60,000 head are not unusual. Cost curves for extremely large operations have not been available. The U.S. Dept. of Agr. currently has studies underway to develop more economic information on very large farming operations. To a large extent capital will probably not be available to the individual farm operator for these larger operations and in most likelihood will be supplied by outside interests.

Few national data are available on earnings on investment in agriculture. The *Farm Income Situation* (U. S. Dept. of Agr. 1969A) does provide data on total farm income, and the *Balance Sheet of Agriculture* (U. S. Dept. of Agr. 1969B) provides national data on returns on capital invested for all farms. However, these latter data are based on current values for land rather than original or purchase price of the land. National average returns on owner's equity in farming was calculated to be only 3.5% for the 1960-1964 period and returns since then range from 4.9% in 1966 to 3.3% in 1967. Details are not available by size of farm and by type of enterprise on a national basis. *Farm Real Estate Market Developments* (U. S. Dept. of Agr. 1968) indicates that annual increases in value of farmland may be greater than the net cash flow generated from the farming operation itself. "U. S. farmland values rose 70% in the last decade. March 1, 1968, state average values ranged from 41% to 132% above the 1957-1959 base. Strongest advances were in the south, where farm real estate values more than doubled in several states. Smaller increases occurred in the Mountain States, Lake States, and Corn Belt." Capital appreciation in farmland has been large. The above figures on return to owner's equity do not include capital appreciation.

Data on returns by enterprise type are available from states where colleges or universities have farm accounting systems. For example, the average returns to owners' investment in Michigan, for 1964-1968, ranged from 4.7% on cash grain farms to 11.3% on potato farms (the 1964 very high price year on potatoes is included in the potato farm calculations) (Hepp 1969). Again, these data do not reveal the potential long-run value of the farm to its owners, as capital appreciation is not included. In the years under study the value of the farmland probably increased 3-4% per yr.

Essentially, we are dealing with three different factors: (1) future economies of scale (which will probably be great), (2) current earnings on equity (and these are from average or slightly above average farms), and (3) land value appreciation. The current earnings reported here are probably substantially under those that would be expected from large, technologically efficient, well-run integrated farms. A large efficient, integrated farm probably has potentials for earnings at least equally as great as for other industrial corporations. And, there probably will be the profit incentive for business firms to integrate into agriculture through ownership. However, on the other side of the coin is the long-run potential for agricultural production to outrun increases in consumer demand for most major U.S. crops. This may, in fact, be a world-wide phenomenon. Land retirement programs, other production restrictions, and price support programs in the United States have only been partially successful in maintaining profitable production of many major U. S. crops. Many economists speculate that without these government programs, prices of many of our agricultural products would be disastrously low. Economists feel that profitable prices can only be maintained through direct government actions, and many are predicting long-run, world-wide gluts of major agricultural commodities—thus food processors may be able to purchase inputs at less cost than by owning agricultural production facilities themselves.

Tax breaks may be one of the principal factors in corporations investing in farms or rural areas. Conger (1969) lists the following reasons for corporate investment in farm land or rural areas: (1) inflationary capital-gains potential (2) tax-free cash flow income, (3) use of tax savings to acquire equities, (4) equity buildup from tax-free organizations, and (5) a reduction of taxes on other income. In a sense, high level federal income taxpayers, i.e., 48% corporate income taxes plus a 10% surtax (1969), and tax rates up to 70% on personal income, are converted into a 25% capital-gains tax through certain types of investments in land, cattle, farming, and real estate. Although specific examples of differentials in tax rates which encourage investment in agriculture will not be listed, Axelrod (1968) provides examples in citrus groves and in cattle breeding and Conger (1969) gives examples in developing apartments or housing in rural fringe areas. Carman (1968) gives a detailed analysis on cattle operations as do the more popular books by Oppenheimer, *Cowboy Economics* and *Cowboy Arithmetic*. Nearly all are based on the income taxes of individuals or firms near or above the 50% level who convert this into a capital-gains tax of only 25%.

Ideological barriers toward farmers contracting with large business firms have decreased through time, which suggests that sociological and political barriers against business ownership of production facilities may also decrease. Some states have laws restricting ownership of farm land by corporations. Oklahoma, Minnesota, North Dakota, and Kansas have legal restrictions and legislation has also been introduced in several other states. However, as the sizes of farms owned by private individuals increase, the barriers to business ownership may decrease.

VERTICAL INTEGRATION INTO RETAILING
AND FOOD SERVICE INDUSTRIES

Perhaps an unsophisticated summary of Galbraith's *New Industrial State,* (1967) is that the modern business enterprise consists of nearly completely integrated systems. The successful large business firm controls all stages of the production and marketing system including having much influence on consumer acceptance and even on the consumer's ability to buy. The firms singled out for FTC or government scrutiny are the same ones which are shown to visiting foreign dignitaries to impress them with the U. S. genius for technological and organizational skills. Following Galbraith's argument then, the idealized firm in the food marketing system should control the food products from their farm production to their ultimate consumption, i.e., either purchase through a retail grocery store, or through a restaurant or public eating place.

By far the most predominant method of obtaining retail grocery store outlets by most large nonretailer-owned food manufacturers is by advertising branded merchandise to build consumer demand for a product. The retail store then carries the product because of consumer demand and potential profits from the item. The same method works for a few products through the away-from-home food market—but not for many others. The restaurant or institutional market seldom carries the brand name on to the consumer. Competition for products in this market is on quality and price—not on brands based on advertising and promotional skills.

In this chapter I have documented farm-processor integration and in a previous chapter I partially documented the extent of food processing by retail food chains. It is much more difficult to establish existing contractual arrangements between nonretailer-owned processors and retailers. The vertical coordination methods between nonretailer-owned processors and retail chain stores have received little or no serious study. We know these integrated arrangements exist but we do not know to what extent. Similarly, the degree of integration between restaurant chains and processors is also difficult to measure. Many restaurant chains do own their own central commissaries for preparing food and often own many types of food processing operations. We can also document the fact that many major food processors are owners or sponsors of restaurant chains. However, the ownership of restaurant chains by processors or retailers may be as much pure conglomeration as it is vertical coordination. That is, many processors may merely be "getting a piece of the action" in the rapidly expanding away-from-home food market rather than using it as a means of coordinating sales of their processed products to the consumer.

Call (1966) in a special study for the Comm. on Food Marketing determined the usage and importance of private labels (distributor's labels) in several classes of food products. Private label merchandise is defined as merchandise packaged mainly to a distributor's specifications either by a distributor or a manufacturer for resale only by a distributor, under a brand name owned by the distributor. Call suggested the following percentages of the following commodites were sold under private label: canned vegetables 24.5%, canned fruit 27.6%, frozen vegetables 46.8%, frozen fruit juice 48.2%, bakery products 52.5%, dairy products 47.9%, coffee 32.9%, bacon 42.1% and wieners 31.8%.

Private labels can have three sources: (1) distributors may own processing plants, (2) through contractual processing and packaging, and (3) by labeling after open market purchases. The distribution among these three sources was not determined. Many private processors maintain a large stock of labels; the product may be bought on the open market and labeled just before shipment. For example, a green bean canner in Arkansas may have a warehouse full of unlabeled cans of green beans just after the processing season. He will label after purchase. The label might be a nationally advertised brand, a chain store brand, or even his own company label.

As private label includes the distributor's own processing, we simply cannot add together the food processing by retail chains and the quantity of private label merchandise to obtain the total quantities of food at retail sold under integrated arrangements.

Brunk (1968) suggests there is much coordination between processors and retailers. "For many years the retailer of food products has been increasing his control over channels of supply. While at any one time this extension of authority has not been spectacular it has been consistent to the point that buying in open markets is confined to fill-in orders. . .to rounding out supply requirements. In lieu of open markets, the retailer has turned to standing orders based on tacit agreements with known suppliers, contractual arrangements for private label, and dual ownership of manufacturing facilities."

While he suggests that coordination is increasing, he gave no quantitative data to suggest the extent of present coordination.

Apparently there are no data available by which one can weigh the importance of contractual arrangements between nonretailer-owned processors and retail grocery stores. I suggest that contractual arrangements or tacit agreements are normal, represent significant quantities of food, and are increasing.

Vertical integration by food processors into the food service industry (away-from-home eating or the hotel and restaurant industry) has not been developed on a quantitative basis, but many examples of processors-restaurant chains integration can be cited.

Kentucky Fried Chicken was contracting for chicken supplies as far as 1 yr. in advance (Anon. 1969D) before this fast service restaurant chain purchased a broiler processing plant. One article suggests that Kentucky Fried Chicken purchased up to 8% of the total U. S. broiler supply in 1969. The initial year-ahead contracts for broilers were equivalent of 13¢ per lb. live weight at the farm.

Holiday Inns has formed a subsidiary which will process meats and frozen entrees. It is also reported that pancake mixes and chicken dips would also be processed (Anon. 1969E). Pillsbury Co. is market testing ready-to-serve fried chicken through grocery stores. The product is delivered to the stores 95% cooked and frozen, and will be finish cooked in the store (Anon. 1969F).

Safeway Stores, in partnership with Holly Farms Poultry Industries, began an initial market test of take-home chicken units sold in Safeway parking lots in Washington, D. C. (Anon. 1969G).

Acme Markets, a Philadelphia-based supermarket chain (821 units) is entering the fast food restaurant franchising field through an agreement with Hardees' Food Systems, a North Carolina-based hamburger shop chain (Anon. 1969H).

General Mills, Inc. has signed an agreement with Minnie Pearl Chicken Systems (now Performance Systems, Inc. of Nashville, Tennessee) for exclusive rights to develop the chicken and roast beef franchises in Europe, the United Kingdom, and Mexico (Anon. 1969I). In addition, General Mills has opened a pilot restaurant in Minneapolis with a take-out pie department and is building a Betty Crocker Tree House Restaurant in Dallas. There are also Union Jack Fish and Chips Shops operated by a Gorton's subsidiary, and Jesse Jones Sausage Restaurant run by its Jesse Jones subsidiary, a specialty meat packer in Raleigh, North Carolina (Anon. 1969J). Armour & Co. has tentatively approved plans to enter the food franchise field with, initially two franchised restaurant chains and a franchised retail food shop chain (Anon. 1969K).

The Ralston Purina Company, a St. Louis-based food processor, will open five restaurants in the St. Louis area by April 1970. The restaurants will be operated by Foodmaker, Inc., a wholly-owned subsidiary of Ralston Purina (Anon. 1969L).

Hunt-Wesson Foods, Inc., a division of Norton Simon, is joint-venturing a franchised fish-and-chip chain called the Whaler. According to a May 3, 1969 report, 2 units had opened and 6 more were planned in 1969, all in California. Shrimp will probably have a prominent place on the menu as Hunt-Wesson owns Southern Shell Fish Company, Inc. of Harvey, Louisiana (Anon. 1969M).

As more frozen foods are served on airlines, United Airlines may build a frozen food processing facility (Anon. 1969N).

Green Giant Company has entered the restaurant business under the name of Jolly Green Giant Restaurants, Inc. (Anon. 1969O).

The H. J. Heinz Co. now has 10 "Sorry Charlie's" take-out fast food outlets in the Los Angeles area (Anon. 1969P). The stores, operated by the Star-Kist Foods subsidiary, feature fish sandwiches, French fries, and soft drinks. (Heinz is a major processor of frozen French fried potatoes as well as being a sea foods processor).

Other well known processors who have gone into the restaurant business include General Foods with their Burger Chef Systems, Inc., Pillsbury with Burger King, Consolidated Foods with Chicken Delight, and United Fruit Company with A & W International (A & W Rootbeer).

In addition to processors entering the fast-food take-out restaurant field, retail grocery store chains are also rapidly entering this field—but mostly on an internal basis. "The most exciting new supermarket development in the 1970's will be a full-scale move to take-out prepared foods. Until now, food retailers have stood idly by while a whole new group of entrepreneurs have created a vast new industry under names such as Kentucky Fried, McDonald's, Wetson's, and hundreds more. While no precise data are available as yet, it is evident that this new industry has already diverted some $5 billion from conventional food stores. Furthermore, sales are increasing at a rate of 15-20% per yr. Present plans call for 50% of the supermarkets in the mid 1970's to have luncheonettes and 84% of the supers are expected to offer take-out service. Today some 5% operate luncheonettes, and only a handful of supermarkets are seriously or systematically offering a good selection of prepared, take-out foods" (Mueller 1969). To a large extent, the prepared take-out foods will probably be prepared in company-owned commissaries.

SUMMARY

Systems coordination, vertical integration, vertical coordination—call it what you will, it is here to stay and probably will increase in both degree and amount. The open market system can be improved and may at some point in time operate under different laws than we have today. However, in the foreseeable future the body politic will not deem it wise to change the rules to an extent that farmers, or producers, or food processors can substantially increase the price of food to consumers. The open competitive market has many disadvantages and to a greater and greater extent the open market will be bypassed. Theoretically, we will end up with a food system completely controlled by ownership or contractual arrangements from farm production to direct consumer consumption. Corporate administrative control over farm operations will increase as new technologies require larger and larger amounts of capital investment in efficiently sized farm operations. The economies of scale in agricultural production have probably not yet begun to have been tested. The very nature of agricultural production will probably change greatly over the next several years both in a physical sense as well as in its administrative control. The economics of integrated systems will probably be too powerful a force to be stalled by the historical social and political image of the concept of the family farm.

BIBLIOGRAPHY

ANON. 1969A. United Fruit Sales Co. acquires Peter Stolick Co. and Monterey Co. The Packer p. 4, Mar. 1.
ANON. 1969B. Purex says it plans to market vegetables under a national brand. Wall Street J. p. 36, Sept. 11.
ANON. 1969C. Feedstuffs, Aug. 30.
ANON. 1969D. Broiler Ind., Sept.

ANON. 1969E. Restaurant News, Mar. 31.

ANON. 1969F. Ready-to-serve chicken Pillsbury trial balloon. Supermarket News *18.* No. 15, 33.

ANON. 1969G. Chain Store Age, Mar.

ANON. 1969H. Acme goes fast-food as Hardee franchiser. Supermarket News *18,* No. 9, 39.

ANON. 1969I. Northwestern Miller, Mar.

ANON. 1969J. Another move by General Mills in eating out field. Weekly Dig. *76,* No. 20, 1.

ANON. 1969K. Nation's Restaurant News, Feb. 3.

ANON. 1969L. Ralston Purina to open drive-ins in St. Louis area. Supermarket News *18,* No. 2, 42.

ANON. 1969M. Hunt enters franchised seafood business. Weekly Dig. *75,* No. 43, 2.

ANON. 1969N. United Airlines may build frozen food plant. Weekly Dig. *75,* No. 44, 1.

ANON. 1969O. Green Giant expanding into sandwich shops. Weekly Dig. *75,* No. 50, 1.

ANON. 1969P. H. J. Heinz discloses formation of chain of fast-food outlets. Wall Street J. p. 15, Aug. 28.

AXELROD, I. I. 1968. Farming as a tax shelter: citrus groves and breeding herds. Taxes-The Tax Magazine. Dec.

BRUNK, M. 1968. The food retailer as manufacturer. Talk given at the Natl. Acad. Sci. Agr. Res. Inst., Washington, D.C.

BUTZ, E. L. 1958. The social and political implications of integration. Eighth Natl. Inst. Animal Agr. Proc., (Purdue Univ.)

CALL, D. L. 1966. Private label products in food retailing. Tech. Study *10,* Natl. Comm. Food Marketing. June.

CARMAN, H. F. 1968. Tax shelters in agriculture: an example for beef breeding herds. Am. J. Agr. Econ. *50,* No. 5, 1591-1595.

CONGER, J. S. 1969. Conglomerate land acquisitions: reasons and use. In Economies of Conglomerate Growth, L. Garoian (Editor). Agr. Res. Found. Oregon State Univ., Corvallis, Ore.

GALBRAITH, J. K. 1967. The New Industrial State. Houghton Mifflin Co., Boston.

GREIG, W. S. 1962. Maximizing total dollar sales of apples and apple products by a utilization model. Michigan State Univ. Agr. Econ. Rept. *889*

HEPP, R. E. 1969. Michigan farm business analysis summary-1968 data. Michigan State Univ. Agr. Expt. Sta. Res. Rept. *95.*

MIGHELL, R. L. 1959. The extent and forms of vertical integration. *In* Vertical Integration in Agriculture, proc. Western Agr. Econ. Res. Council, Reno, Nev., Nov.

MIGHELL, R. L., and JONES, L. A. 1963. Vertical Integration in Agriculture U.S. Dept. Agr., Agr. Econ. Rept. *19.*

MUELLER, R. W. 1969. Talk at the 61st Ann. Meeting Grocery Manufacturers Am. Natl. Comm. on Food Marketing. 1966. Organization and competition in the fruit and vegetable industry. Tech. Study *4,* June.

RICKS, D. J. 1969. Applesauce price relationships 1955-68. Michigan State Univ. Agr. Econ. Rept. *148* Aug.

RICKS, D. J. and BIXBY, D. 1969. Economic relationships in red tart cherry marketing, 1955-68. Michigan State Univ. Agr. Econ. Rept. *142,* June.

SCHRADER, L. F., HEIFNER, R. G., and LARZELERE, H. E. 1968. The electronic egg exchange–an alternative system for trading shell eggs. Michigan State Univ. Agr. Econ. Rept. *119,* Dec.

SCOFIELD, W. H. 1969. Corporate farm ownership and operations. *In* Economics of Conglomerate Growth, L. Garoian (Editor), Agr. Res. Found., Oregon State Univ., Corvallis.

SORENSON, V. L. 1968. Producer marketing organizations: some aspects of the European experience. *In* Agricultural Organization in the Modern Industrial Economy. Dept. Agr. Econ., Ohio State Univ., Apr.

U.S. Dept. of Agr. 1968. Farm real estate market developments. Published three times a year. U.S. Dept. Agr. Econ. Res. Serv. Dec.

U.S. Dept. of Agr. 1969A. Farm income situation. Published quart. U.S. Dept. Agr. Econ. Res. Serv.

U.S. Dept. of Agr. 1969B. The balance sheet of agriculture. Published yearly. U.S. Dept. Agr. Econ. Res. Serv.

CHAPTER 13

W. Smith Greig | A Summary and Speculations
On the Future

SUMMARY

Food processing has been the largest manufacturing industry in the United States and still is the most important when measured in value of shipments. Other industries—transportation equipment and electrical equipment—have bypassed food processing in capital expenditures, value added, and numbers of employees. Food processing will continue to grow (in absolute terms), but will decline in relative importance when compared to other manufacturing industries.

Measured in terms of value added, economic activity in food processing has greatly surpassed that in agricultural production in the United States. While value added continues to increase in food processing, it has substantially decreased in agricultural production. These trends are expected to continue.

Food processing firms are among the largest industrial corporations in the world. In fact about 1 out of 10 of the world's largest industrial corporations are primarily engaged in the manufacture of food or alcoholic beverages. Perhaps as many as 80–90 U.S. food firms had sales of over $100 million each in 1968.

There is a considerable concentration of assets in the U.S. food manufacturing industry. However, it is not nearly as concentrated as other manufacturing industries—transportation equipment, electrical equipment, electronic computing machine companies, etc. In 1966-1967, the 58 largest food manufacturing industries (measured by asset size) in the United States obtained approximately 55% of the total profits after taxes. Each of these firms had over $100 million in assets. Concentration in food processing has been increasing slowly. In fact, in light of the theoretically large economies to scale, it is the relative slowness of the increase in concentration that is surprising, not the rapidity of increasing concentration.

Food processing has not been particularly profitable over the past two decades. Profits in all manufacturing have been greater than those in food processing. Profits have, of course, varied widely among food processing industries and among firms. During the 1950's and 1960's, the meat processing industry generally had low profits while profits in nonalcoholic beverages were relatively high.

Greatly aggregated data indicate a tendency for large firms (those with over $100 million in assets) to be more profitable than smaller firms (firms with less than $100 million in assets). However, because of the wide variability in profits by individual firms and wide variability if segregated by many size classes, statistical tests do not confirm a significant correlation between size of firm and profitability. Similarly, recent tests of market concentration and degree of profitability have yielded nonsignificant results.

An interesting phenomenon in financial analysis is the finding that large firms

346

typically operate with much less leverage than smaller firms. This has a decided effect on profitability when profits are determined as a return on owner's equity. It is not known whether this is merely a conservative position, a lack of capability to expand rapidly enough to use up undistributed profits, or a position forced by legal restrictions on mergers or acquisitions.

Diversification and/or conglomeration (depending upon the definition used) is typical and increasing in the food processing industries. Most large firms operate in several food processing industries and also manufacture products in several nonfood processing industries. Statistical tests have not shown a greater profitability of diversified firms over those less diversified, but they do confirm that diversified firms have a greater stability of profits.

Among the reasons listed for the increasing diversification and conglomeration are (1) to spread risks, (2) to gain economies of scale, (3) because relative rates of growth among industries change, (4) because of legal restrictions on horizontal mergers or horizontal expansion, (5) to gain economic and political power, and (6) growth through tax breaks and/or financial legerdemain. Some leaders in food and business economics suggest legal restraints to prevent conglomeration, per se, of all firms above a certain size class. Others feel that the act of conglomerizing, especially for the last reasons listed above, is worse than being a conglomerate particularly if the firm has arrived at its conglomerate position through internal expansion.

A two-layer system of food processing appears to be developing. One layer is nearly the direct extension of farm production. This is the processing of relatively standard agricultural commodities. In this level of activity the products are relatively standard; there is little distinction between the same commodity manufactured by different firms; cost of entry is not high; advertising and promotion costs are relatively low; and there is, typically, considerable seasonal and annual price variability in the products (unless the raw product price is determined through government programs). Typically, net operating margins are relatively low. Competition among processing firms is in the efficiency of production and the efficiency of distribution.

The second layer or level of food processing is the manufacture of packaged consumer products or convenience food products. In this case, each firm aims at distinctly different, readily identifiable food products. Cost of entry (in terms of R&D costs, advertising and promotion) is high, and profit margins (on successful products) relatively high. Prices of the packaged food products are relatively stable. Competition among firms is in advertising and promotion and in new product development.

The packaged or convenience food product is the layer of processing that is increasing most rapidly. The real power in these firms is in the technocracy or technical competencies of the staff and its ability to create new products or to adapt acquisitions of new products produced by others into the marketing strategy of the firm. Products that the firms produce or market are unique or nonstandard and the concept of a product is of a transient and continually evolving nature. The economic and legal concepts of oligopoly and monopoly, as related to standard definitions of a product, may be becoming irrelevant for the real competition is not among standard and definable products but in the ability of firms to produce and/or market new products. Some economists think that the area needing legislation in the food industry is not in controls on diversification and conglomeration but in assuring better or more rational choice—areas such as advertising and promotion, packaging standards, and unit pricing. These are needed because the consumer is deluged with an ever-increasing array of new products and massive advertising and promotion campaigns concerning them.

The tendency toward larger firms in the food industries has been observed by economists for many years. In looking at some of the theoretical advantages which large firms, or large physical facilities, have over smaller firms or smaller facilities, economies of scale were discussed in: (1) research and development, (2) advertising and promotion, (3) management costs, (4) physical efficiencies in processing and warehousing, (5) transportation, (6) state and local property taxes, (7) financing, and (8) other economies to scale. However, despite the large economies to scale theoretically available to the large food processing firms, they are unable to use them effectively or, apparently, they are counter-balanced by diseconomies to scale. It was shown that the more than 5000 firms in 1965-1966 which had total assets under $100,000, on the average, lost money. However, once a minimum-size level is reached, profitability, apparently, does not increase consistently with increasing size of firm. Most statistical analyses have not shown a significant correlation between profitability and size of firm. If this is an overstatement, then at least the differences in profitability by size classes (asset size) are much less than one would expect, based on theoretical economies to scale, particularly after a relatively low level of capital assets is reached. The dilemma between theoretical economies of scale and apparent lack of significant correlations between size and profitability may partially be accounted for as follows: (1) Perhaps facilities with modest capital investments can capture much of the total economies to scale. (2) Bigness and economies of scale are not synonymous—bigness may be a combination of many inefficient units. (3) Perhaps the large firms compete among themselves in new product development and in advertising and promotion while the smaller firms compete among themselves in efficient production of commodities—perhaps the competition is equally severe in each case. (4) The more conservative financial position of large firms affects their profitability (measured in returns to net worth). (5) There are undoubtedly diseconomies to scale. Perhaps in large bureaucracies there is an unwieldliness and a slow reaction time to new opportunities.

The crucial question concerning structure is how the industry performs from a societal point of view. Performance is an elusive concept to measure. Apparently the food processing industry has performed well. There have not been undue profits; the industry has been technologically progressive; certainly a wide spectrum of processed food products is available at prices consumers are willing and able to pay. Food costs as a proportion of income are consistently falling. Food cost as a proportion of total income is undoubtedly smaller in the United States than in any other country. Criticism of industry performance by the FTC and the Natl. Comm. on Food Marketing was largely concerned with concentration or market shares and apparently these groups nearly equated this one structural characteristic to market performance. Certainly there are many industries in the United States with higher concentration ratios. Further, recent statistical tests have yielded no significant correlation between degree of concentration and profitability.

In any case, many of the economies to scale are real and substantial and there are apparently many plants below a minimum efficient size. This has resulted in fewer but larger processing plants. In fact, between 1958 and 1967 the total numbers of food processing plants decreased by 22.1%. Undoubtedly many of the plants that were closed were the very small inefficient plants with relatively low capital investment.

Combining the statistical trends in decreasing numbers of plants with data on average plant sizes compared to minimum efficient sizes and, also, with studies of optimum numbers of plants for an industry, we can generalize concerning future numbers of processing plants. Combining the statistical data, along with detailed analytical models for soybean crushing, beef slaughtering, and green pea freezing, it is suggested that even at current levels of technology, the optimum number of food processing plants should be from 50–75% less than current numbers.

The statutory regulation of business competition is intended to control (1) structure, (2) conduct, and (3) performance in the food processing industries. Four laws directly regulate structure of the food industry markets. They are the monopolization prohibitions of the Sherman Act, Section 2; merger and acquisition limitations of the Clayton Act, Section 7, the interlocking directorate prohibitions of the Clayton Act, Section 8; and the Packers and Stockyard Act. The main antitrust statutes which regulate conduct of food firms include the Sherman Act, Section 1; the Clayton Act, Section 3, and the Federal Trade Commission Act, Section 5.

Section 1 of the Sherman Act prohibits contracts, combination, or conspiracies in restraint of trade. The term, restraint of trade, covers market conduct including price fixing, market sharing, territorial allocation, boycotts and reciprocal dealing. Section 5 of the Federal Trade Commission Act prohibits "unfair methods of competition in commerce, and unfair or deceptive acts or practices in commerce..." "Unfair methods or competition" has been interpreted to mean all practices prohibited by the Sherman Act, Section 1. This interpretation has, in effect, given the FTC the power to issue cease and desist orders against firms engaging in practices which would otherwise violate the Sherman Act. Regulation of performance is primarily based on two premises: First is the public case of "natural monopolies" where control is necessary to have efficient production of services such as transportation, telephone, electricity, gas, and sometimes water or sewer. In the second case, the primary fear is that without regulation, competition will become so chaotic and price fluctuation so erratic that the supply of the product involved might either be jeopardized or producers might be injured to an extent not in the public interest. Most of the regulation of performance is of the latter kind. It is primarily in the form of price supports to producers of raw agricultural commodites; the regulation is at the farm level not the processing level. An important exception is regulation of the performance of the milk industry. Interpretations and recent landmark cases or court rulings affecting structure, conduct, and performance of the food processing industries were presented in Chap. 4.

Future legislation will probably be enacted to curb conglomeration. Undoubtedly, curbs will be placed on large, nonfood firms acquiring leading food processors, and vice versa. From the author's point of view, it is possible that legislative bodies may over-react in preventing structural changes. Conglomeration to spread risks, to gain economies of scale, and to shift resources to more productive areas should remain legitimate business endeavors. To arbitrarily restrict any business firm to a few specified types of activities could be a real threat to capitalistic free enterprise. A basic foundation of the capitalistic free enterprise system is that capital can freely flow to those enterprises yielding the greatest returns on investment. On the other hand, conglomeration to gain economic power and conglomeration through financial legerdemain and tax breaks should be controlled.

Concerning economic power, apparently the 100 largest U.S. industrial corporations had the same percentage of assets in 1967 as in 1947. Thus one can ask whether conglomeration is really increasing the concentration of assets in the U.S. Certainly, some of the accounting methods in acquisitions and mergers are suspect and should be controlled. Similarly, tax breaks should certainly be continually reviewed.

A dilemma exists in our system. Many of our laws are geared to enforce smallness while our economic system inevitably requires largeness. Would our society benefit more by enforcing smallness to maintain more competition, or by relaxing controls to gain economics of scale? From the author's point of view, some of the legal restraints on structure may have increased the consumer's costs of food.

By most measures of economic activity, food processing is a growing industry. Between 1958 and 1967, value added increased at a simple average rate of 5% per yr; value of shipments increased by 4%; capital expenditures on new plant and equipment increased 8% per yr. (These are undeflated figures.) Total employment has decreased slightly since 1958 but appears to have nearly leveled off since 1962. Trends in employment, value added, value of shipments, and capital expenditures for 44 food processing industries were presented for 1958-1967. Value of shipment trends were also listed for 94 subdivisions in food processing. The 10 most rapidly growing industries (of 94 5-digit SIC codes) increased value of shipments by a simple average rate of nearly 15% per yr. between 1958 and 1967, while the 10 slowest growing industries had absolute decreases in value of shipments.

Increasing capital expenditures and slightly decreasing employment, combined with increased value added and increased value of shipments, indicate a substitution of capital for labor. Similarly, as the rate of capital expenditures exceeds both value added and value of shipments it suggests increasing technological progressiveness. It can also suggest the continuation of over-capacity in food processing. This latter facet has long been a problem in food processing.

Six of the 44 major food processing industries (4-digit SIC codes) account for over 50% of the total employees and around 40% of the value added, value of sales, and capital expenditures in all food processing. These six are: meat packing, canned fruits and vegetables, bread and related products, confectionery products, fluid milk, and canned and bottled soft drinks.

Historically, our food marketing systems have been geared to the concept of scarcity and efficiency. Now, our economy may be approaching that of abundance and affluence. Thus, the distribution system in our "postindustrial" U.S. economy may be forced to make adjustments. One adjustment is the relative growth rates of the away-from-home food market compared to retail grocery store food sales. Between 1958 and 1967, food sales of retail grocery stores increased at a deflated annual rate of 2.5% per yr while sales of public eating places increased at a deflated rate of 5.6% per yr. Some speculate that the retail grocery supermarket may be becoming obsolete, but apparently there is no concensus as to what might replace it. One fairly definite trend is for new supermarkets to have take-out service for prepared foods.

Both chain stores and affiliated independents have continued to expand and now account for over 90% of total retail grocery store sales. Unaffiliated independents are becoming more and more a minor segment of the industry. The growth in chain stores has not been by the top 4 major chains but by the 5th to 20th largest chains. Similarly, the proportion of food sold that has been processed by the four major chains has decreased while that processed by the smaller chains has increased. Chain store processing was around 2.43% of all food processing in 1958 and around 2.63% in 1963. While food processors have long feared the possibility of substantial processing by retailers, recent statistical data do not suggest an accelerating trend toward more food processing by retailers.

One economist has suggested that the chain stores exert a downward influence on prices to processors which results in lower than optimal prices and profits to food processors. This suggests that consumers are, to some extent, subsidized by the processing industries and, ultimately, by the farmer.

In recent years profits in retailing have not been high. Competition has been severe. With the recent slower rate of increase in total retail sales, future competition will probably increase. The relatively unlevered financial position of large retailers is very similar to that of large food processors. Statistical data indicate that large retail grocery store chains make greater returns on assets but lesser returns on equity than do smaller chains.

The away-from-home food market is becoming increasingly important. It accounted for about $28 billion in sales in 1966, this represents around 33% of the total food dollar sales to consumers. Based on recent growth rates, this industry could have total sales of 44—46 billion dollars in 1975. This would represent as much as 40% of the total retail food sales in the United States. The factors contributing to the increasing away-from-home food market are: (1) increasing population, (2) increasing incomes, (3) increasing numbers of women working, and (4) increasing urbanization. Increasing incomes is by far the most important of these.

While independent enterpreneurs operating a single outlet still dominate the restaurant field, chains are rapidly increasing. In 1966 it was estimated that chains had 25% of the outlets and accounted for 1/3 of all away-from-home food sales.

The development of away-from-home food markets, particularly the chains, can easily cause a loss of effective market power of food processors. The ultimate consumer will probably never see the brand name of suppliers to the restaurant chains This may, in effect, place the processor-supplier in the position of a "commodity" processor, competing on cost and efficiency rather than a packaged goods processor competing on brand names, advertising and promotion. The advertising of the restaurant chains will undoubtedly sponsor their own names rather than that of suppliers.

If no new food products were processed, the rate of growth in food processing would closely approximate population growth. In recent years population growth has been at a rate of increase of less than 1.5% per yr (in 1968 and 1969 only around 1.1% per yr). Therefore, the technological base from which new food products are developed becomes very important as few firms consider a 1.5% per yr growth as a satisfactory level. In this perspective, new product development as an instrument of firm growth and the theory of the firm in product competition become central issues.

Most new food products are not processed solely for preservation but for convenience, quality control, and cost reduction as well. Many of the products in the most rapidly growing segments of food processing are available the year round in fresh form. Preservation per se is not a primary reason for their being processed.

Despite the importance of new product development, relatively little R&D is done in food processing compared to most other industries; most commercial research done is by a few large firms. In 1965, 87% of the commercial research expenditures in food processing was done by firms with over 5000 employees; an estimated 68% of all expenditures was by the largest 20 firms. Further, of those food processing firms who did have R&D expenditures the costs were equivalent to only 0.4% of sales, compared to 4.3% of sales for all manufacturing industries. Considering all food processing firms, total R&D expenditures are probably around 0.2% of sales.

In addition to R&D done by business, many colleges and universities have active programs in food processing. Similarly, at least four separate agencies of the U.S. government do research and development work. These are the Dept. of Agr., the Dept. of Interior (Bureau of Commercial Fisheries), the Dept. of Defense, and the Atomic Energy Comm.

New product innovation is costly and risky. This is one of the reasons so few firms have active new product developments. The development of a substantially different new food product may involve a time horizon of from 36 to 55 months. The net negative contribution to profits after the first year of regular introduction may be well over $1 million.

The Natl. Comm. on Food Marketing indicated that actual new product development has been relatively low. "Products which could be considered newly developed or which achieved their initial sales growth in the postwar (World War II) period accounted for between 5 and 7% of grocery store sales in 1964. Few of these 'new products' are the result of even moderately complex technologies and essentially, all the more complex technologies were developed with public funds."

New product development probably has been significantly greater than suggested by the Natl. Comm. on Food Marketing. However, it is substantially less than that often indicated in the popular trade reports.

An area of new product development by commercial firms which involves a more than moderately complex technology is that of analogs, substitutes, and synthetics. In synthetics, most vitamins and certain amino acids, including lysine, tryptophan and methionine, can be produced at fairly reasonable cost. However, at the current limits of knowledge, farm products would still be the cheapest sources of carbohydrates, proteins, and fats even if farm prices were doubled. Nevertheless, some scientists consider synthetic production of all food nutrients an almost inevitable development.

Perhaps 25% of the market for dairy products is now being supplied by products containing 1 or more substitute ingredients. Meat analogs have sales of around $10 million (1969) and are rapidly increasing. Substantial new investments are being made in this field. Synthetic fruit products have captured a substantial share of the fruit juice market. The loss of the sugar market to saccharin and cyclamates was approaching $100 million per year before the U.S. Food and Drug Administration banned the use of cyclamates. Non-naturally occurring food products will play an increasingly wider role in the U.S. food economy.

Because a food product is characterized by the technology that produces it, a series of new processing technologies were reviewed in a technical sense and from the standpoint of economic and commercial possibilities. These new technologies were dehydrofreezing or dehydrocanning, vacuum puff drying, drum drying, freeze drying, foam-mat drying, explosive puffing, irradiation, microwaves, aseptic canning and packaging, osmotic dehydration, filled and imitation milk, and cryogenic freezing. The production of meat analogs was also briefly reviewed.

Locations of food processing in the United States change substantially through time. Changes in a particular industry may come about for a variety of reasons. The location of the meat slaughtering industry is changing both between and within areas. This change is due primarily to the development of technologies for storing meat and the economies of transporting meat rather than live animals. Decentralization is occurring within regions. The cause is obsolete plants in large cities combined with labor problems, higher wages, and increasing tax loads. Broiler and egg production moved to the south and southeast because the capital needs of producers were furnished by integrators such as large feed companies. Other reasons may be that the southern farmers have less alternative opportunities and would work for a lesser management wage. With a developing freight differential between wheat and flour, milling is moving out of the midwest and into the centers of population. Orange production shifted to Florida from California because Florida varieties were much better suited to the production of frozen orange juice concentrate. Onion production in California has increased very rapidly with the development of onion dehydration. Michigan and New York production has remained stable or declined. Green peas (and other seasonal vegetables) relocated in highly specialized production areas when demand changed from fresh to processed products. Potato processing increased in the west because of quality differences in the raw product and willingness of growers to contract. However, with more sophisticated processing methods, processing may tend to move to the North Central and Eastern Regions, particularly if these growers increase their willingness to contract. Even though early studies indicated milk production should increase in Minnesota and Wisconsin, 15 yr later the actual relocation has been minimal. Apparently, some processing locations are man-made and are not due to the pure economic advantages of the region.

The location of the food processing industries is constantly changing. Seldom is a change in industry location abrupt and seldom is the change a physical relocation of plant and equipment. The changes are rather long-run differentials in growth rates among areas. Because of the continuing changes in location, a significant section was included on processing cost differentials among the major food processing states.

Labor costs are a major cost input in food processing. Labor wage rates vary widely among states and by type of food processing. The meat slaughtering industry has one of the highest labor wage rates while the canning and preserving industry has among the lowest. Up to a 50% difference in labor wage rates between states is not uncommon. In addition to the basic labor wage rate, there are substantial differences among states in unemployment insurance and workman's compensation.

State and local taxes are one of the most rapidly increasing input costs. An analysis of all state, local and federal taxes on three model firms, a canner or freezer, a dairy, and a grain mill, were presented for 26 states. Tax differences between the highest tax state and lowest tax state resulted in differences in return on equity as much as 30%. That is, based on tax differences alone, a firm located in one state could have a 30% greater return on equity than the same firm in another state. Thus, it is suggested that state and local taxes have a significant locational effect in much food processing.

Electrical costs are often a significant input, particularly in freezing of relatively low cost and low profit items. Industrial electricity costs vary widely among areas. Electrical costs in Maine, for example, may average twice that for a processing plant in Tennessee. Similarly, there is often a wide range in costs within a state depending upon the individual utility serving the region. A large processor would typically obtain a contract rate from the utility company. Often this is a reduced rate and usually is outside the jurisdiction of state regulatory agencies.

The cost of fuel also varies widely among states. Gas costs are lowest in the south and southwest and highest in the northeast. Because of limited data on the cost of fuel oil and coal, crossover points in these costs among states were not obtained. The cost of industrial gas in Maine is five times that of Texas.

Transportation costs are difficult to analyze in a generalized manner. Everyone knows some areas have greater freight costs to market than other areas. A linear programming system to determine marginal freight costs among areas was discussed. Similarly a procurement cost model was presented to compare procurement costs to size of processing plant. Combining these two models, it is possible to determine the optimum number, size, and locations of processing plants to serve a market. The market may be a state, a region, the nation, or, of course, an international system.

In addition to labor costs, taxes, fuel and electrical costs, and transportation costs to market, many other factors materially affect location advantages among states. Most important are raw product costs, length of the processing season, complementarity of products, and an adequate infra-structure.

From the standpoint of management, the purchasing function in a food processing operation is of crucial importance. Purchased raw product ingredient and packaging material are a major part of the total costs of the final products. Purchasing cannot be viewed in isolation but must be integrated with quality control, merchandising, supplier relations, traffic management, and the budgeting aspects of the firm. Forecasting prices of major ingredients becomes basic to the operation of the firm. Price forecasts range from very informal estimates to detailed, computerized, statistical models from which systematic purchase rules are developed. For major ingredients, the futures market may be used to minimize risk in price changes.

Purchasing of raw material is based more and more on statistical analyses of the commodities and systems involved. These are used to develop formal or informal purchase rules to assist or guide the experienced purchasing agent. Because of the complexity and cost in building and interpreting formal statistical models, many processors use the services of price consultants. As is the case in many other aspects of food processing, the scientific systems approach will probably prevail. The development of formal purchase rules based on statistical probabilities of future prices will become a normal operating procedure in most progressive food processing firms.

Pollution control is becoming an important cost factor in food processing. Most all states have developed or are developing strict requirements concerning the quality of the effluent from food processing plants. Thus the locational effects of pollution control are not only state-to-state but significantly affect site location within a state or region. Possible waste treatment methods were discussed in a technological sense and, also, in general economic terms. In many cases, the final selection of a plant site may depend upon the cost of waste disposal. Certainly in the early stages of planning for a new plant, state and local regulatory agencies should be consulted to determine waste disposal regulations.

Vertical integration or vertical coordination is apparently increasing at all levels of marketing in food distribution systems. By vertical integration or vertical coordination we mean some form of interfirm arrangements other than those arrived at in the open competitive markets. The arrangements may range from tacit agreements to contracts to outright ownership of successive stages in the marketing and distribution system.

In the successful large business firm, planning is essential; in forward planning, control over price is necessary. Modern large businesses consist of almost completely integrated systems. Not only does the successful large business firm control all stages of production and marketing but it also influences consumer acceptance. Often it influences the consumer's ability to buy.

Most of the early literature on vertical integration was written by agricultural interests and dealt primarily with producer-processor arrangements or producer-feed deal arrangements. Theoretically, food distribution systems would be improved with coordinated systems from the producer to the ultimate consumer. Among the reasons for vertical integration are reducing risk, reducing costs, improving management, gaining bargaining power, improving marketing position, assuring adequate inputs, investing surplus reserves, developing new technology, and obtaining additional capital.

The traditional social, political, and emotional concept of "the family farm" has been a strong barrier to integrated marketing systems in many sections of the country. However, these barriers are continually being broken.

In 1968-1969, over 95% of the broilers, fluid milk, and vegetable seeds were produced under integrated arrangements, as well as 90% of the sugar crops, vegetables for processing, and hybrid seed corn. Perhaps 75% of the citrus fruit and 75% of the turkeys are produced under integrated arrangements. Few of the major grain crops, i.e., corn, wheat, and rice are produced under integrated arrangements. Probably less than 15% of cattle on feed and less than 10% of the hogs are under integrated systems. Deciduous fruit production has not had the degree of integration that citrus fruit or processing vegetables have had; but in deciduous fruits, some long-term contracts are developing. The rapid and nearly complete integration in broiler production and the rapidly increasing integration of eggs and turkeys have lent much speculation as to what might happen in pork and beef. Some experts feel that a technological breakthrough in production requiring large infusions of capital would greatly accelerate integration in pork and beef production.

Integration has increased because of imperfections in the open competitive market. Perhaps rather than completely bypassing the open market, we should find ways of improving the open market. Among ways of improving the open market are (1) better market news reports, (2) electronic price determination, (3) better price predictions, and (4) additional futures markets.

Looking at marketing systems, often the rules (laws) of the system are viewed as being static. However, modifications could greatly alter the system. Some possible changes might be (1) Marketing Boards, (2) expanded power of Federal Marketing Orders and Agreements, (3) a National Farmers' Relations Board, and (4) unionization of farmers and farm laborers.

Business integration into farming by ownership has not been large; currently less than 2% of gross farm sales are from "outside" or nonfarmer-owned corporate farms. Integration of business into agriculture will depend upon relative rates of return on investment in agriculture and in other investment areas. Several factors suggest that some types of large agricultural investments might be quite profitable. (1) The real economies in many types of large scale agriculture have not really been tested. (2) Investment in land has, historically, appreciated significantly while investment in plant and equipment depreciates. (3) In many cases there may be substantial tax breaks in agriculture. Corporate or individual tax rates under certain types of agricultural investments may be changed to substantially lower capital-gains taxes. (4) There is the possible substantial savings through the coordination effect of ownership of more than one stage in production. (5) There appears to be a continual reduction in ideological barriers to business investing in agriculture. Good data on profitability in farming, including appreciation in land values through time, have not been available. But the author would suggest that large, well-managed, integrated farms (when land appreciation is included) may be equally as profitable as many other types of business enterprises. This would suggest an acceleration of business investment into farming.

Data on the amount of retailer-owned food processing done by retail grocery chains were presented. Another segment of the industry is the amount of nonretailer owned processing that is done under contractual or integrated arrangements. Limited data are available on the quantities of private-label merchandise sold by retailers. While some private label merchandise is purchased on the open market it is suggested that substantial quantities, if not produced under actual contracts, are produced under at least tacit agreements. Again, even though data are limited, nonretailer-owned food processors may be increasing their integrated arrangements with retail grocery stores.

Processor-restaurant chain integration is another area in which definitive data are lacking. Although many large food processors are sponsoring restaurant chains, in many cases this is more conglomeration rather than vertical integration. That is, the restaurant chain is often a separate business entity with the food processor seldom viewing the chain as a primary integrated market for the products it produces. There are, of course, some highly vertically integrated restaurant chains (Kentucky Fried Chicken would be a good example).

Again, in theory, the optimal system of integration would be completely integrated units from the producer to the ultimate consumer. This then could result in business control or business ownership of farm production units. The economics of integrated systems will probably be too powerful a force to be stalled by the composite historical, social, and political image of the family farm.

SPECULATIONS ON THE FUTURE

Processor-grower Relations to Improve

The relationship between growers and processors, particularly on seasonal perishable crops, has most often been one of conflict, particularly in the area of price negotiations both for contracted or open-market products. The American Farm Bureau marketing branch actively assists farm groups in bargaining with processors. Meanwhile, the National Canners Association apparently has had a policy of actively lobbying against any legislation that might increase the effectiveness of Federal Marketing Orders and Agreements on crops for processing—i.e., any legislation that might assist growers in possible supply control of crops for processing. Further, there appears to be a great deal of regionalism in pricing and contracting so that one production area is pitted against another. While, of course, processors should attempt to get raw products at the lowest possible cost and the growers should try to obtain the highest possible price, both groups would undoubtedly be better off through efforts of collaboration rather than concentrating on areas of conflict. Over-contracting or over-planting produces disastrous results both for the processors and the growers. Growers and processors working together for a common goal of increasing returns to both groups could greatly reduce erratic price swings and assist in stabilizing returns to both groups.

Management is becoming more sophisticated; producer and processor numbers are declining; combining these factors with shifts to less risky production areas and better communications and computer systems, there is no reason why supply control cannot be practiced on a national basis to yield the greatest return to both producers and processors. By supply control, I do not mean control in a legalistic manner that might develop under some variations in Federal Market Orders and Agreements or through Marketing Boards; but rather, a supply control through an information system. The system could work somewhat as follows. For example, let us use green beans for canning and freezing, which are produced in many regions of the United States. First, develop historical price prediction models based on total quantities produced, consumer income, carry over, consumption trends, population growth, etc. Then, through this model make future price predictions (primarily based on size of the crop).

Before each crop year, prior to planting, each grower and/or processor would send his intentions to plant to a centralized computer bank. The computer would total possible national production and feed back to the producers and processors the expected prices (on a statistical probability basis). Both national and regional price data could be developed. Based on this new information each grower and/or processor would send in a revised estimate to plant and the computer would again calculate prices. This system could be repeated (iterated) until intentions to plant and prices reach or at least approach, equilibrium. Through time the system could be refined so that gluts or shortages are greatly ameliorated and production is more nearly equal to demand.

Supply control practiced through information systems would be greatly superior to supply control through a legalistic system. In the latter systems, allocations of production based on historical production tends to decrease competition among areas and to stabilize production in its current locations. Without these systems, competition among areas is severe. Through competition, efficiency and cost reduction remain prime motivating forces. This is good from a societal point of view as it assures that production will be concentrated in the least cost areas. If areas of least cost change, production location will change. However, with "licenses to produce" based on legal systems, production areas become stabilized and the "license" becomes capitalized into the land values (as exhibited in tobacco allotment systems) and inefficiency results.

If both growers and processors wish to increase market power, the objectives of both will be more easily reached through possible systems of collaboration rather than through systems of conflict.

Sensitiveness of Location to Continue

In most all cases, the geographical dispersion of most crops and livestock production, as well as the geographical dispersion of the population dictate a wide variety of optimal locations for most types of food processing rather than a single optimum location. That is, we hardly expect all beef to be slaughtered at one single location in the United States or all fluid milk to be processed at one location. Again, referring to specific studies, the optimal system to serve the United States and export markets at minimum costs might be for 30 or 40 rather widely dispersed soybean crushing plants and 7 to 10 green pea freezing plants. In most studies of location or interregional competition, the products showed severe competition between regions. Further, the competitive balance may be so delicate that relatively minor changes in only a few cost factors could easily affect the competitive structure and thus tend to shift locations. In other words, location of much food processing is very sensitive to a wide variety of different costs. In green pea freezing, for example, we found that optimum location was significantly influenced by relatively small changes in any of the following costs: raw product, freight to market, size of processing plant, state and local taxes (in many but not all cases), length of the pea processing season, length of the total processing season, and regional consumption patterns.

Thus, if changes occur among areas in raw product production costs, in transport methods, in labor wage rates, in technology, and in any of the myriad cost differences among regions, the optimal locations for food processing plants may change. Certainly, the regional changes in locations are sticky and do not typically occur by the shift of physical equipment from one location to another. But, locations change gradually by a differential in growth rates. There is no reason to suggest that the locations of much food processing in the United States has been stabilized; on the contrary, much evidence suggests that locations are continually changing. Further, with better analytical tools available to management, adjustments to cost differentials among regions may be more rapid than in the past. There appears to be little or no evidence to support the thesis that sensitivity to differences in locational advantages will be any less severe in the future.

While data on location are based primarily on the United States, the theory, and the methodologies discussed apply equally well to the problems of international locations.

THE CHANGING MARKETS FOR FOOD

Rate Changes Will Decrease

Projections of certain trends may be enlightening and serve as a basis for management decisions; but projections of other trends can range from meaningless to the absurd. Suppose, for example, the average adult male gains 150 lb in weight from the time he is born until he is 20 yr of age. Everyone knows that the average adult male 80 yr of age will not weigh 600 lb. Or, take the case of automobile occupancy. A motor vehicle survey has revealed that, in 1940, each car on the road contained 3.2 persons. In 1950, occupancy declined to an average of 2.1 persons per car. By 1960, it was down to 1.4 persons per car. If these trends are projected to 1980, every third car traveling by will have nobody in it. If the rate of decrease in farm work continues, the last hour of labor on a Michigan farm will be in November 1984. If the relative rates of national expenditures on R&D and GNP continue, total R&D expenditures in the United States will soon be greater than the GNP. If the rate of growth in numbers of teachers continues and the rate of growth in hours spent in formal education continues, soon 1/2 the population of the United States will be teachers and the other 1/2 students. If the rate of growth in cemeteries continues the United States will be covered with cemeteries in 500 yr. If the rate of population growth continues, the world population will more than double by the year 2000. If trends continue in the decreasing number of hours worked per week, the work week by the year 2000 would be only around 32 hr; and if the trend in family income continues, the average family income in the United States in the year 2000 would be around $20,000 (at the 1965 real value of the dollar). Which of these trend lines are suitable for the basis of management decisions and which are absurd? Or, are they all in the same class? Let's explore population and income trends, as these have a greater effect on the future demand for food than any other factors.

POPULATION GROWTH

U.S. Dept. of Com. data on U.S. population projections for the year 2000 range from as low as 285 million to as high as 375 million people. The upper limit is nearly 33% greater than the lower estimate. Similarly, in 1963 the United Nations projected the world population to be between 5.4 billion and 6.9 billion people in the year 2000, up from around 3.6 billion in 1963. Changes in the rate of net population increases through time can be quite large. Just after World War II, the net increase in population in the United States reached a high of 1.7% per yr. However, in recent years (1968 and 1969), the net annual increase was only around 1.1% per yr, not too much higher than the depression years of the

1930's. Population increases are affected by social and economic conditions as well as by death rates and numbers of women of child bearing age. Just as the net birth rates have fallen in the United States, they have fallen in some other countries. Hungary, for example, has had a negative population growth rate. Some writers suggest that the Hungarians, if given a choice between a child and a car, would take the car. In effect, they chose a higher standard of living rather than more children. With better education, greater urbanization, better birth control methods, and better social security programs, world birth rates could decrease significantly. Projections that the world population will double every 30 yr may be no more meaningful than projections that the last hour of farm work in Michigan will be done in 1984. Certainly, a processor of commodities whose markets may largely depend on population growth is not going to be very excited about the prospect of business expansion in the United States at a rate of only 1.1% per yr. By and large, the rapid rates of population growth are not expected in the developed countries, currently the largest market for processed food, but in the underdeveloped countries of the world. Thus, while increasing population growth is significant, it is not as spectacular as is sometimes projected in popular publications. The points to be made are these: (1) population increases in the United States are expected to be from low to moderate; (2) the current markets for many types of processed foods are those areas of the world where population growth rates are relatively low; (3) many factors can affect net rates of population increases and long-range projections are subject to wide inaccuracies.

INCREASING INCOMES AND LEISURE TIME[1]

Family incomes in the United States have increased dramatically in recent years. Between 1950 and 1964 the medium income of families doubled, from $3300 to $6600. Based on a full employment economy, U.S. Dept. of Com. projections in 1966 were that incomes would rise by more dollars in the future than in the past. Kahn and Wiener in their book, *The Year 2000,* project U.S. family incomes near $20,000 per yr by the year 2000. However, if real incomes are to increase greatly, real productivity also has to increase greatly. Let's explore in more detail the potentials for increasing productivity and also for increasing leisure time.

For an analysis of future productivity it is convenient to break the U.S. economy into three sections: (1) the primary industries-production of goods, mining, farming, manufacturing, and construction, (2) the secondary industries—transportation, communications, and utilities, and (3) the service industries—government, trade, finance, and personal services, i.e., doctors, lawyers, beauticians, barbers, etc. Within the government services are the military, the police, the postal workers, and the state and local government employees including school teachers.

---

[1]For a more detailed analysis see Gilbert Burck, "There'll be Less Leisure Than You Think" *Fortune,* March 1970.

Productivity gains in the primary and secondary industries have been real, large, and relatively consistent. Up to a point, we can expect continued gain in productivity in these two sections. During the past 20 yr the production of goods more than doubled but the number of workers rose only from 28 to 29 million people. Similarly, production of the transportation, communications, and utility industries more than doubled but employment increased from only around 4.4 to 4.6 million people.

The problem area is in the service industries where employment is growing most rapidly and where productivity gains are apparently small. Between 1948 and 1968 the number of employees in the service industries increased from 28 million to nearly 48 million, or a 70% increase. By 1980 there will be around 65 million people employed in the service industries—or around 2/3 of all jobs in the United States. Productivity of service workers is difficult to measure. While the quality of services offered by the medical professions may have increased, the number of patients one doctor can treat has not increased greatly. Similarly, the number of students per teacher has decreased decidedly over the past 20 yr. Has the productivity of a mail carrier increased? How do you measure the productivity of the military or of police departments?

The question is, "Will the real increases in productivity of the primary and secondary industries be strongly ameliorated by the lack of productivity gains or only small gains in productivity of the future largest employer, the service industries?" Stated in another way, "Can we really trust simplistic, straight-line projections of future real incomes for the average U.S. family?" The answer is that we really can put less faith in long-run projections of future real incomes than in long-run projections of population.

Perhaps the negative aspects have been emphasized too much. The point to be made is that while real incomes probably will increase in the future it is doubtful if future increases will be as great as the rate of increases between 1948 and 1968.

Burck has suggested that neither future gains in productivity nor gains in leisure time will be as great as is often popularly predicted. His lack of increases in leisure time was predicated on the fact that service industries are a time-consuming industry.

Predictions of population and imcomes are normally considered in many management decisions in food processing. The purpose of this section was to question some of the underlying assumptions in projections of both of these factors. Many simplistic straight-line projections of either population growth or real income growth are thought to be subject to substantial errors. As both population growth and income are the factors primarily responsible for increased demand for processed foods, projections of each should be reviewed on a continuous basis.

I suggest the trends of both population growth and increasing real incomes will continue but probably at decreasing rates. There will, therefore, be a continually increasing demand for more food (total demand will increase at about the rate of population growth), and probably a much stronger increase in demand for more services attached to the sale of food (this latter is largely a reflection of increasing real incomes).

The strong demand for services attached to the sale of food is shown in statistical series of the growth rates of convenience or packaged food products and, also, in the relative growth rates of the away-from-home food market compared to retail grocery store sales. The emphasis on convenience of nearly completely prepared foods will continue as this is the principal method by which the food processing industry may increase sales dollars. The rate of increase in sales of commodities is relatively slow, particularly as some U.S. foreign markets appear to be drying up. Who will do the ultimate selling of the convenience of prepared foods to the consumer has not yet been determined. The retail grocery store will certainly strive for a larger share of the prepared take-out food market. If food processors wish to gain some market power in the prepared food business they have two apparent options available to them: either integrate vertically with a restaurant or fast food take-out chain or develop branded unique prepared foods to be sold through retail grocery stores. Most other paths will lead to a loss of market power. Sales to nonvertically integrated restaurants or take-out food chains will be on a basis of cost and quality; the brand identification to the consumer will undoubtedly be that of the restaurant chain rather than the processor's. brand. Through this method the processor has no market power with the ultimate consumer. Similarly, in prepared take-out foods sold through retail stores, sales will be on efficiency and quality unless the processor has a branded, unique, readily identifiable product. There is a real possibility that in a shift to prepared take-out food service and the increasing away-from-home food market, many national food processors may lose their national brand identity to the ultimate consumer of the products. In effect, loss of brand identity to the consumer may change the position of the food processor from a convenience or packaged goods processor to that of a commodity processor as far as the economics of marketing are concerned.

As of 1969 and 1970 the rapid rate of growth in the away-from-home food market had apparently slowed down and some franchise restaurant chains were in financial troubles. Over-expansion of the restaurants and a general slowing of the U.S. economy were responsible. There may be severe future competition between grocery store chains and restaurant and take-out food service operations; the sure winner will be the increased conveniences or services attached to the sale of food. Who will make the ultimate sale to the consumer is the question. The question is not whether more convenient food products will be sold.

DO FOREIGN OPERATIONS OFFER BETTER POTENTIALS?

If we combine the present over-capacity in much U.S. food processing with the relatively low population growth rate, i.e., if we assume that total domestic demand for many commodities will increase only at a rate of 1.2–1.5% per yr, then long-run domestic competition will be severe. An obvious question then is why not locate where there is an under-capacity in food processing facilities and the total demand for commodities is increasing at over 5% per yr. This argument is based on commodities or nonunique food products, i.e., sugar, vegetable oil, meat, canned and frozen fruits and vegetables, grain, etc.

Although international sales are currently important to many U.S. food processing firms and many underdeveloped countries show a 3% annual population increase, the commercial marketing of food products is increasing at over 5% per yr. The cause is the rapid rate of urbanization. Many people who once lived on subsistance farms were not part of the commercial market for food products. However, once they move to an urban area they become a part of the commercial market. Thus, in many countries the effective commercial demand for quantities of food may be increasing at rates well above population growth rates.

In this connection, once the investment in research, development, and commercialization of a unique packaged or convenience food has been made for U.S. markets, this scientific industrialization process could be readily shifted to other markets. More and more operations will be based on world markets and world trade rather than depending primarily on the U.S. market.

OWNERSHIP AND MANAGEMENT OF FIRMS WILL CHANGE

Many firms who manage and operate food processing industries will be losing their identity as food processors. From a management and ownership viewpoint, business has changed appreciably through time. At one time, most businesses were small and operated with an owner-manager. Later, as more complex technologies were developed requiring more capital, public ownership tended to increase. The manager may still have been a larger stockholder. Still later, most large corporations shifted to professional, hired management. In many cases those who owned the company had a decreasing influence on the operations of the firms. With rapid technological progress and increasing complexities, the power of one man to comprehend and direct the wide range of competencies required in most large firms was surpassed; a staff of specialists was hired to assist management. Thus in many firms, the power structure shifted to a staff of specialists or to the technocracy. Owners or stockholders became even further divorced from management. As the firm grew in size and complexity, many new product lines were developed. The firm integrated horizontally and vertically. As rates of industrial growth changed through time, the firm diversified further or became a conglomerate. In effect, two layers of management developed. Central corporate management handled financial matters and general policy while the subparts of the conglomerate had nearly autonomous operating managers. There was no longer allegiance to a product line or separate manufacturing unit. Each part of the conglomerate was viewed as to its present and future contribution to profits. The power shifted from general operating business management to the financial management specialists.

As these trends developed in business in general, the corollary in food processing is seen in the owner-operator of a small food processing firm which specialized in a single commodity, for example, pickles. Initially, processing required little capital and only modest technical competencies. Through time, the owner-operator added other commodity lines. Eventually he publicly sold stock to raise capital to expand with more costly technologies. Eventually stock ownership became more widely dispersed and at retirement the owner-operator was replaced with professional management. Through time, with addition of commodity lines, the concept changed from a pickle processor to a fruit and vegetable processor. As ownership became more dispersed, the real owners or stockholders relied more and more on professional management until the actual control of the firm was effectively held by salaried professional managers who may have owned little, if any, stock in the company. As the firm grew, a larger technical staff was hired. Before making any major decision the manager relied more and more on a strong staff of specialists. Other food and nonfood manufacturing firms were acquired; the R&D laboratory was started; packaged food products were developed; mammoth advertising and promotion campaigns were launched to create sales and establish a brand name. The firm changed from a fruit and vegetable processor to a food processor. The next step is obvious. For a variety of reasons the food processor merged with or was acquired by a nonfood manufacturing corporation. The identity as a food processor was lost; the firm had become a business firm. As part of a conglomerate, its financing and central policies are determined by central management. Central management consists primarily of individuals with competencies in financial management who have no technical background nor allegiance to food processing. Central corporate management decides on the allocation of funds among the subparts of the conglomerate, including food processing.

In this fictional example, the natural history of management started with the owner-operator, then changed to professional management under direction of large stockholders, and from there to professional management who gained effective control without ownership, and moving from that to a staff of specialists directed by the manager (the technocracy). This latter phrase could properly be called "scientific industrialization." Finally, management of operating parts of the conglomerate are directed or controlled by a centralized core of financial managers. At the same time, the image of the firm and its sphere of operations changed from pickle processor to fruit and vegetable processor to food processor to business firm. The effective area of operations, or possible sphere of influence of this last stage is greatly enlarged. Any business venture of potential profitability can now be considered by the company.

There are many advantages to diversification and conglomeration. Modern communications and computer capabilities have extended management control (particularly financial management control) over much wider spheres of business influence. Dangers of social ills with increasing conglomeration are potentially offset by social good. While many people apparently "view with alarm" the recent waves of mergers and conglomeration, perhaps there would be a greater danger if business firms were arbitrarily restricted from entering any legitimate business activity. Thus these speculations for the future suggest a great deal more conglomeration of food processing and nonfood processing firms. Along with this development the current food processing identity of many firms will be masked and possibly lost.

TECHNOLOGICAL PROJECTIONS

The technological base of food processing is continually widening and deepening. It is often stated that there are more food scientists living today than have lived in all past history. By and large however, the greatest number of food scientists are not engaged in research projects to develop new and revolutionary food processing technologies. To a large extent they are engaged in more modest activities to improve quality or convenience or to reduce costs of more standard technologies. Progress in much food processing will be made by a constant chipping away of old norms and standards rather than through startling new advances in processing methods—a new machine here, a cost reduction there, added convenience here, a new package there, a better variety or breed, improvement in quality, a better source of supply, a better form of business organization, etc. These efforts, continually compounded, result in cheaper, more convenient processed food products, with wider and wider selections for the world's consumers at prices they are willing to pay.

The new basic technologies of irradiation preservation and microwave cooking should not be overlooked. The future of irradiation in the United States is clouded since the Food and Drug Administration revoked its commercial use pending further investigation. The health aspects are still at issue. Perhaps many bona fide uses for commercial irradiation of food will be developed. Microwave cooking, perhaps, will gain widespread acceptance. Some microwave ovens have been in use in restaurants for over 20 yr, pointing out the relatively slow acceptance of new technologies.

From the realm of possible technological approaches two areas show promise of appreciable progress. The first is in a continuous development of prepared or convenience food products; the second, and partially related to the first, is the development of synthetics, substitutes, and analogs. The first will primarily take advantage of adaptations of processing technologies as we know them now, the second will depend upon more basic technological and scientific discoveries. Vitamins and certain amino acids can be produced at quite reasonable prices at present; perhaps in the future, the proteins, fats, and carbohydrates can be economically produced synthetically and combined into many forms of new foods. Apparently much progress is being made in the conversion of petroleum into palatable proteins through the use of microorganisms. The possibilities for synthetics, substitutes, and analogs appear almost unlimited. The average American consumer is long divorced from the farm and is becoming indifferent as to whether a food product is "natural" or synthetic as long as the quality, convenience, and price are comparable.

The slow but steady erosion of the butter market illustrates the profound effect a substitute can have on a natural food product. However people do not change dietary habits easily. In South America new, cheap, high protein substitutes have met decided resistance even in cases of extreme poverty and protein deficiencies. Perhaps the keys to acceptance of new substitutes and analogs in the United States will be quality and the degree of difference between the new products and the old. The more effectively the synthetic product imitates the familiar food and the more improvement it offers, the more readily it will be accepted. Because of seasonality, cost, nonuniformity of maturity and quality of natural foods, there will be an almost inexorable development of synthetic, substitute, and analog food products. However, progress will probably be slow.

The successful food processing firms will be those who early recognize and interpret social, economic, political, and technological changes. These changing conditions profoundly affect both the products which can be developed and those which will be accepted. These conditions will be the constraints within which the firm sets its goals so that the chipping and nicking away of old standards, old methods, and old traditions will form a new and useful pattern for long-range development.

Index